OECD Environmental Performance Reviews: New Zealand 2017

OECD
BETTER POLICIES FOR BETTER LIVES

Please cite this publication as:
OECD (2017), *OECD Environmental Performance Reviews: New Zealand 2017*, OECD Publishing, Paris.
http://dx.doi.org/10.1787/9789264268203-en

ISBN 978-92-64-26802-9 (print)
ISBN 978-92-64-26820-3 (PDF)
ISBN 978-92-64-26829-6 (epub)

Series: OECD Environmental Performance Reviews
ISSN 1990-0104 (print)
ISSN 1990-0090 (PDF)

Photo credits: © Kyrien/Shutterstock.com.

Corrigenda to OECD publications may be found on line at: *www.oecd.org/about/publishing/corrigenda.htm*.

Preface

People of New Zealand enjoy a very good environmental quality of life, with low air pollution and easy access to nature. The natural environment is a key economic asset. The country's land, freshwater and seas provide the basis for internationally competitive agriculture, forestry and fishery sectors. Despite its remoteness, millions of tourists visit the country every year, attracted by its pristine wilderness and spectacular landscapes.

This third *OECD Environmental Performance Review of New Zealand* acknowledges that New Zealand has strengthened policy co-ordination and environmental management and leads the international research effort to reduce greenhouse gas (GHG) emissions and water pollution from agriculture. It has made greater use of market-based instruments to put a price on environmental "bads" such as GHG emissions and landfilled waste, although the use of energy and road vehicles is taxed at relatively low levels.

New Zealand's growth model, however, has started to show its environmental limits, with increased GHG emissions, freshwater contamination and threats to biodiversity. Addressing GHG emissions from agriculture, and especially from dairy farming, should remain a priority if the country is to achieve its 2030 climate mitigation target under the Paris Agreement. The *Review* identifies the need to further explore the economic opportunities that more sustainable resources use could yield. Developing a long-term vision for a transition towards a low-carbon, greener economy would help New Zealand defend the "green" reputation it has acquired at international level.

The *Review* pays special attention to water resources management and sustainable urban development. New Zealand has reformed its national freshwater policy and the *Review* welcomes this fundamental step towards safeguarding water quality and availability. However, the management of diffuse nutrient pollution from pastoral agriculture remains a significant environmental challenge, as it is with most countries. Speeding up the implementation of the freshwater policy would help reduce investment uncertainty and the risk of further pressure on freshwater resources and ecosystems. New Zealand has pioneered the use of a water quality cap-and-trade market in one catchment. This can provide useful lessons to other countries. But it remains an exception and the *Review* suggests broadening the use of economic instruments to encourage water-use efficiency and pollution reduction.

While New Zealand cities are green and environmental quality is good, population growth and urban expansion are posing increasing pressures on housing, transport, waste and water infrastructure. Private cars are by far the dominant mode of transport and congestion levels are high. The challenge for Auckland – which is home to a third of the country's population – and other fast-growing cities is to accommodate a larger population while avoiding unsustainable urban expansion. According to the *Review*, this will require addressing the current institutional fragmentation, a complex urban planning system and misalignment of land-use, transport and infrastructure decisions. Using pricing instruments such as road tolls, congestion charges and water tariffs will help local governments finance investment in much-needed infrastructure and services, while encouraging more efficient use of resources and land, and containing urban sprawl.

This *Review* is the result of a constructive policy dialogue between New Zealand and the other members of the OECD Working Party on Environmental Performance. It provides 50 recommendations to help New Zealand green its economy and improve its environmental governance and management. I am confident that this collaborative effort will also provide other OECD Members and Partner countries with insights on how to deliver solid economic growth in a way that protects their environmental asset base.

Angel Gurría
Secretary-General of the OECD

Foreword

The principal aim of the OECD Environmental Performance Review programme is to help member and selected partner countries improve their individual and collective performance in environmental management by:

- *helping individual governments assess progress in achieving their environmental goals*
- *promoting continuous policy dialogue and peer learning*
- *stimulating greater accountability from governments towards each other and public opinion.*

This report reviews New Zealand's environmental performance since the second review in 2007. Progress in achieving domestic objectives and international commitments provides the basis for assessing the country's environmental performance. Such objectives and commitments may be broad aims, qualitative goals or quantitative targets. A distinction is made between intentions, actions and results. Assessment of environmental performance is also placed within the context of New Zealand's historical environmental record, present state of the environment, physical endowment in natural resources, economic conditions and demographic trends.

The OECD is indebted to the government of New Zealand, the Auckland Council and Environment Canterbury for their co-operation in providing information, for the organisation of the review mission to Auckland, Christchurch and Wellington on 9-13 May 2016, and for facilitating contacts both inside and outside government institutions.

Thanks are also due to the representatives of the two examining countries, Miranda Lello (Australia) and Pete Fox (United Kingdom).

The authors of this report were Carla Bertuzzi, Ivana Capozza, Britta Labuhn, Hannah Leckie and Eugene Mazur from the OECD Environment Directorate. Nathalie Girouard and Ivana Capozza provided oversight and guidance. Carla Bertuzzi provided statistical support; Annette Hardcastle provided editorial and administrative support; and Mark Foss copy-edited the report. Preparation of this report also benefited from the co-operation of Sylvia Beyer of the International Energy Agency, as well as from inputs and comments from several members of the OECD Secretariat, including Christophe Andre, Johanna Arlinghaus, Andrew Barker, David Carey, Delphine Clavreul, Guillaume Cohen, Anthony Cox, Kwame Frimpong, Michelle Harding, Elisa Lanzi, Xavier Leflaive, Alexander Mackie, Walid Oueslati, Aleksandra Paciorek, Jehan Sauvage, Clara Tomasini, William Tompson, Elena Tosetto, Ioannis Tikoudis, Simon Upton and Kurt Van Dender.

The OECD Working Party on Environmental Performance discussed the draft Environmental Performance Review of New Zealand at its meeting on 9 November 2016 in Paris, and approved the Assessment and Recommendations.

Table of contents

Part II

Progress towards selected environmental objectives

Tables

Figures

Reader's guide

Signs

The following signs are used in Figures and Tables:

. . : not available

– : nil or negligible

. : decimal point

Country Aggregates

OECD Europe: This zone includes all European member countries of the OECD, i.e. Austria, Belgium, the Czech Republic, Denmark, Estonia, Finland, France, Germany, Greece, Hungary, Iceland, Ireland, Italy, Latvia, Luxembourg, the Netherlands, Norway, Poland, Portugal, the Slovak Republic, Slovenia, Spain, Sweden, Switzerland, Turkey and the United Kingdom.

OECD: This zone includes all member countries of the OECD, *i.e.* the countries of OECD Europe plus Australia, Canada, Chile, Israel, Japan, Korea, Mexico, New Zealand and the United States.

Country aggregates may include Secretariat estimates.

Currency

Monetary unit: NZD

In 2016, USD 1.00 = NZD 1.433

In 2015, USD 1.00 = NZD 1.434

In 2014, USD 1.00 = NZD 1.205

Cut-off date

This report is based on data available up to September 2016 and on some updated information available up to November 2016.

Disclaimer

The statistical data for Israel are supplied by and under the responsibility of the relevant Israeli authorities. The use of such data by the OECD is without prejudice to the status of the Golan Heights, East Jerusalem and Israeli settlements in the West Bank under the terms of international law.

This document and any map included herein are without prejudice to the status of or sovereignty over any territory, to the delimitation of international frontiers and boundaries and to the name of any territory, city or area.

Abbreviations and acronyms

AEE	Assessment of Environment Effects
ANZECC	Australia and New Zealand Environment Conservation Council
AUP	Auckland Unitary Plan
BGA	Business Growth Agenda
CWMS	Canterbury Water Management Strategy
CCO	Council-controlled commercial organisations
CER	Certified emission reduction unit
CH_4	Methane
CIIL	Crown Irrigation Investments Limited
CO_2	Carbon dioxide
DMC	Domestic material consumption
DOC	Department of Conservation
E. coli	*Escherichia coli*
EEZ	Exclusive Economic Zone
EGS	Environmental goods and services
EPA	Environmental Protection Authority
ERU	Emission reduction unit
ETS	Emissions trading system
EV	Electric vehicle
FMU	Freshwater management unit
FTA	Free Trade Agreement
GBP	British pound
GDP	Gross domestic product
GHG	Greenhouse gas
HSNO Act	Hazardous Substances and New Organisms Act
IAF	Irrigation Acceleration Fund
LAWA	Land, Air, Water Aotearoa
LAWF	Land and Water Forum
LGA	Local Government Act
LTMA	Land Transport Management Act
LULUCF	Land use, land-use change and forestry
MfE	Ministry for the Environment
MPI	Ministry for Primary Industries
MUL	Metropolitan Urban Limit
MSW	Municipal solid waste
N_2O	Nitrous oxides
NES	National Environmental Standard
NGO	Non-governmental organisation
NLTF	National Land Transport Fund
NMVC	Non-methane volatile organic compound
NOF	National Objectives Framework
NO_x	Nitrogen oxides
NPS	National Policy Statement
NPS-FM	National Policy Statement for Freshwater Management
NRS	Natural Resources Sector
NZ ETS	New Zealand Emissions Trading Scheme

NZD	New Zealand dollar
NZUs	New Zealand Units
ODA	Official development assistance
PCE	Parliamentary Commissioner for the Environment
PM	Particulate matter
PPP	Public-private partnership
PPP	Purchasing power parity
R&D	Research and development
RMA	Resource Management Act
RUC	Road user charge
SDGs	Sustainable Development Goals
SHA	Special Housing Area
SO_x	Sulphur oxides
TPES	Total primary energy supply
WFD	Water Framework Directive
WHO	World Health Organization

BASIC STATISTICS OF NEW ZEALAND (2015 or latest available year)*

(OECD values in parentheses)[a]

PEOPLE AND SOCIETY

Population (million)	4.6	(1 274)	Population density per km^2	17	(35)
Share of population by type of region:			Population compound annual growth rate, latest 5 years	1.1	(0.56)
Predominantly urban (%)	45	(49)	Income inequality (Gini coefficient)	0.33	(0.32)
Intermediate (%)	55	(26)	Poverty rate (% of population with less than 50% med. income)	10	(11)
Rural (%)	-	(25)	Life expectancy	82	(81)

ECONOMY AND EXTERNAL ACCOUNTS

Total GDP (GDP, billion NZD)	241		Imports of goods and services (% of GDP)	27	(29)
Total GDP (GDP, billion USD, current PPPs)	170	(51 165)	Main exports (% of total merchandise exports)		
GDP, latest 5-year average real growth (Compound annual growth rate)	2.7	(1.9)	Dairy produce; birds' eggs; natural honey; edible products of animal origin, not elsewhere specified or included	24	
GDP per capita (1 000 USD, current PPPs)	37	(40)	Meat and edible meat offal	14	
Value added shares (%)			Wood and articles of wood; wood charcoal	7	
Agriculture	7	(1.7)	Main imports (% of total merchandise imports)		
Industry including construction	22	(23)	Vehicles other than railway or tramway rolling-stock; parts and accessories thereof	13	
Services	71	(75)	Nuclear reactors, boilers, machinery and mechanical appliances; parts thereof	13	
Exports of goods and services (% of GDP)	28	(29)	Mineral fuels, mineral oils/products of their distillation; bituminous subst.; mineral waxes	10	

GENERAL GOVERNMENT

Percentage of GDP

Expenditure	40	(44)	Education expenditure	6.3	(5.4)
Revenue	40	(42)	Health expenditure	7.0	(6.5)
Gross financial debt	41	(86)	Environment protection expenditure	0.3	(0.8)
Net lending/net borrowing	-0.1	-(2.0)	Environmental taxes (% of GDP)	1.3	(1.6)
			Environmental taxes (% of total revenue)	4.2	(5.1)

LABOUR MARKET, SKILLS AND INNOVATION

Unemployment rate (% of civilian labour force)	5.8	7.9	Patent applications in environment-related technologies (% of all technologies)[b]	12	(12)
Tertiary educational attainment of 25- to 64-year-olds (%)	34	(35)	Environmental management	3	(4)
Gross expenditure on R&D (% of GDP)	1.2	(2.4)	Water-related adaptation technologies	0.5	(0.4)
			Climate change mitigation technologies	10	(10)

ENVIRONMENT

Energy intensity: TPES per capita (toe/cap.)	4.4	(4.1)	Road vehicle stock (veh./100 inhabitants)	85	(59)
TPES per GDP (toe/1 000 USD, 2010 PPPs)	0.13	(0.11)	Water stress (abstraction as % of available resources)	1	(10)
Renewables (% of TPES)	40.5	(9.6)	Water abstraction per capita (m^3/cap./year)	1 195	(819)
Carbon intensity (energy-related CO_2):			Municipal waste per capita, (kg/capita)	650	(516)
per capita (t/cap.)	6.9	(9.4)	Material productivity (USD, 2010 PPPs/DMC, kg)	1.0	(1.7)
per GDP (t/1 000 USD, 2010 PPPs)	0.26	0.26	Land area (1 000 km^2)	263	(34 341)
GHG intensity:[c]			% of arable land and permanent crops	2	(12)
per capita (t/cap.)	18.0	(12.4)	% of permanent meadows and pastures	40	(23)
per GDP (t/1 000 USD, 2010 PPPs)	0.54	0.34	% of forest area	39	(31)
Mean population exposure to air pollution ($PM_{2.5}$, µg/m^3)	9	14	% of other land (built-up and other land)	19	(33)

* Values earlier than 2010 are not taken into consideration.

a) Where the OECD aggregate is not provided in the source database, a simple OECD average of the latest available data is calculated where data exist for a significant number of countries.

b) Higher-value inventions that have sought patent protection in at least two jurisdictions. Averages of latest three years.

c) Excluding emissions/removals from land use, land-use change and forestry.

Source: Calculations based on data extracted from databases of the OECD, Eurostat, IEA and Statistics NZ.

Executive summary

New Zealand is one of the most dynamic economies in the OECD and has built an international reputation as a "green" country. It fares well in terms of environmental quality of life; the country's population enjoy easy access to pristine wilderness and good air quality. However, New Zealand's growth model, largely based on exporting primary products, has started to show its environmental limits, with increased greenhouse gas (GHG) emissions, diffuse freshwater pollution and threats to biodiversity.

A long-term vision for the transition towards a low-carbon, greener economy is necessary

There are likely trade-offs between continued reliance on exporting primary products and environmental and climate change mitigation goals. Expansion of dairy farming has led to more intensive use of agricultural inputs and water, nitrogen losses and higher GHG emissions. New Zealand should build on its well-developed knowledge and innovation system for exporting higher value export products and decouple growth from natural resource use. Nearly 10% of government research spending targets environmental research, the highest share in the OECD. This has helped New Zealand acquire a competitive advantage in several environmental technologies. It should continue to lead international research efforts to find solutions that reduce the environmental impacts of agriculture.

With four-fifths of power generation sourced from renewables and nearly half of GHG emissions coming from agriculture, New Zealand faces particular challenges to meet its 2030 climate change mitigation target under the Paris Agreement. The Emissions Trading Scheme, launched in 2008, will remain the cornerstone of the country's climate change policy, but it needs to be strengthened to provide a sufficiently high and stable price signal to influence investment decisions and unlock emission mitigation solutions. Pricing or regulatory measures are needed to curb GHG emissions from agriculture. Reducing transport-related emissions also demands additional efforts: freight and people travel mostly by road; the car ownership rate is the highest in the OECD; and the fleet is relatively old and inefficient. While electric vehicles can contribute to reducing emissions, there is a need for stricter vehicle standards and a coherent system of fuel and vehicle taxes and charges.

New Zealand's advanced natural resource management system could be made more effective

The 1991 Resource Management Act (RMA) is a remarkably comprehensive piece of environmental legislation. However, with more than 20 amendments since its adoption, it has doubled in size and lost some of its coherence. Some newly adopted national environmental standards and policy statements have strengthened the regulatory framework, but significant gaps remain. Local authorities have major environmental management and land-use planning responsibilities, but have implemented the RMA requirements without national guidance in many policy areas. Resulting inconsistencies in the application of the RMA have generated an uneven playing field for economic entities and uncertainty in achieving desired environmental outcomes. New Zealand needs to conduct a comprehensive evaluation of implementation of the RMA by local authorities, establish nationally standardised requirements in several domains and provide better guidance to local authorities on how to carry out their permitting, compliance monitoring and enforcement responsibilities. It also needs to properly align the RMA with legislation on local governments and land transport infrastructure. There are ample opportunities for public participation in land-use planning and drafting environmental legislation, which need to be preserved. New Zealand needs to continue to build capacity of Maori communities to realise their consultation rights.

The much welcomed national freshwater policy reform needs to be swiftly and effectively implemented

Agricultural and urban stormwater run-off continues to put pressure on freshwater quality and ecosystems, and increased irrigation water has led to water scarcity in some areas. The adoption of the National Policy Statement for Freshwater Management in 2011 filled a long-standing policy gap; it encourages collaborative governance and stakeholder engagement and is a fundamental step to safeguard water quality and reduce water over-allocation. However, progress with implementation has been slow. Further government support is required to assist regional councils and local communities with setting ambitious goals, and to accelerate implementation of the reform to reduce investment uncertainty and the risk of further pressure on freshwater resources and ecosystems.

Economic instruments would help manage water quantity and quality more cost-effectively

New Zealand has introduced some economic instruments for water management, but there is significant scope for expanding their use. Resource rentals for water abstraction and pollution charges should be explored, as well as the wider use of trading mechanisms such as the Lake Taupo nitrogen market. Resolving Maori rights and interests in water will be necessary to move forward with the introduction of economic instruments and to improve water governance. Government grants and concessional financing for irrigation projects aim to reduce the vulnerability of pasture-based agriculture to variable rainfall patterns and to enhance water-use efficiency. However, they do not systematically consider the environmental and social costs of irrigation, and the benefits largely accrue to the agriculture and processing industries. There is a risk that financial support for irrigation further increases pressures on freshwater resources, especially if more efficient irrigation techniques simply allow an increase in irrigated volume or area. Natural capital accounting could help evaluate the costs and benefits of investment in irrigation projects and assist with resource management decisions.

New Zealand's green and liveable cities face increasing environmental pressures

New Zealand's cities feature large open green spaces, generally clean air and good water and waste services. However, population growth and urban expansion are posing increasing pressure on housing, land use, and wastewater and transport infrastructure, especially in

Auckland. With urban mobility relying heavily on private car use, congestion levels and transport-related GHG emissions are high. Further developing urban public transport systems could provide other options for commuters and improve environmental outcomes. More systematic use of user- and beneficiary-based instruments (e.g. road pricing and development charges) would help local governments finance investment in infrastructure and services, while encouraging more efficient use of resources and land, and containing urban sprawl.

Governance for sustainable urban development remains challenging

Many cities have adopted environmental performance objectives and some aim at a more compact urban development with better public transport accessibility. However, institutional fragmentation, a complex urban planning system, inconsistent local practices, policy misalignment and restrictive land-use regulations frustrate both urban growth and environmental protection objectives. In 2010, a major reform established an integrated metropolitan governance body for Auckland and required spatial planning for the region. This has helped improve institutional co-ordination and advance integrated planning for land use, housing, and transport infrastructure; it is a potential model for other cities.

Assessment and recommendations

The Assessment and recommendations *present the main findings of the* Environmental Performance Review of New Zealand *and identify 50 recommendations to help New Zealand make further progress towards its environmental policy objectives and international commitments. The OECD Working Party on Environmental Performance reviewed and approved the* Assessment and recommendations *at its meeting on 9 November 2016. Actions taken to implement selected recommendations from the 2007 OECD* Environmental Performance Review *are summarised in the Annex.*

1. Environmental performance: Trends and recent developments[1]

New Zealand's population enjoys generally high living standards and environmental quality of life. The natural environment is deeply rooted in the cultural identity of the large indigenous Maori population and of the entire country. The use of natural resources underpins New Zealand's small open economy. The products of the primary sector (including agriculture, forestry, fishery and aquaculture products, as well as oil and coal) account for over half of the country's exports. New Zealand is the world's largest exporter of dairy products and sheep meat, and among the largest exporters of forestry products. Agriculture accounts for 7% of value added, more than three times the OECD average. The country's pristine wilderness and spectacular landscapes attract millions of tourists every year.

The economy has grown faster than the OECD's as a whole since 2000. Sustained exports and construction activity have been the key drivers of growth. However, fast population growth, partly linked to large immigration flows, has increased housing shortages and costs in major cities (Section 5). Income inequality and poverty rates have risen, and disparities persist in health and education outcomes (OECD, 2015). New Zealand's growth model has been showing its environmental limits, with increased greenhouse gas (GHG) emissions, rising pressures on freshwater (Section 4) and biodiversity, and persistent bottlenecks in transport, water and waste treatment infrastructure.

Climate change mitigation and adaptation

GHG emissions continue to rise: by 2014, they had increased by 6% from 2000 levels, and by 23% from 1990 levels (Figure 1). Road transport, industry and agriculture (mainly livestock production and fertiliser use) have been the main drivers of this increase. The land use, land-use change and forestry (LULUCF) sector removed more than a third of New Zealand's GHG emissions in 2000-14. However, removals have declined in recent years as more planted forests have reached harvest maturity (MfE, 2015). While emissions have grown at a lower rate than the economy and the population, New Zealand's gross GHG emissions per capita and per unit of gross domestic product (GDP) remain among the five highest in the OECD.

New Zealand has an unusual emissions profile: nearly half of its GHG emissions come from agriculture, mainly emissions of methane from ruminant animals (enteric fermentation) and nitrous oxides from animal waste and fertilisers. This is the highest share in the OECD (Figure 1) and reflects the importance of the sector to the economy. Transport, mainly on roads, is the second largest emitting sector; it accounts for 17% of emissions (MfE, 2016a). Motor vehicles are the primary transport mode for both goods and passengers, reflecting New Zealand's dispersed population, a history of low-density urban development and the associated challenges in expanding alternative transport modes, notably public transport. As a result, motor vehicle and car ownership rates are the highest in the OECD. The number of vehicles has increased by 65% since 2000, with a rising share of diesel vehicles. The fleet is relatively old (the average age of cars is 14 years) and emission-intensive (184.8 gCO_2/km compared to 143 gCO_2/km for cars sold in Japan, where most of the New Zealand's fleet comes from).

Figure 1. **Selected environmental performance indicators**

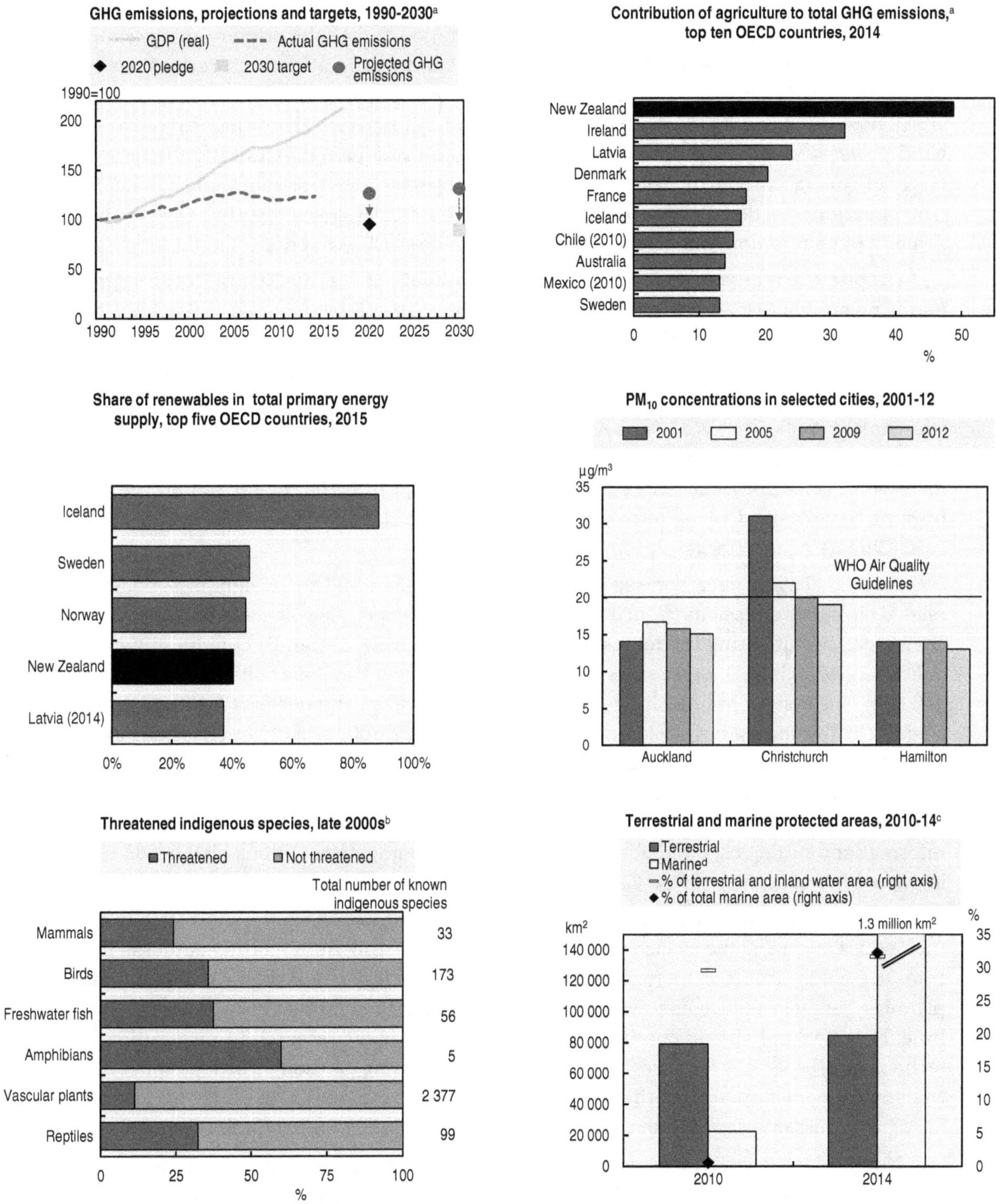

a) Excluding emissions/removals from land use, land-use change and forestry (LULUCF).
b) Threatened species according to the New Zealand Threat Classification System (NZTCS). The number of known species excludes vagrant and migrant species.
c) Data refer to information available as of 6 August 2014.
d) Include marine protected areas and marine reserves, benthic protected areas and seamount closures; exclude Sugar Loaf Island marine protected area and a range of other areas protected in consideration of domestic protected area planning. Total marine area includes the territorial sea and the Exclusive Economic Zone (EEZ).
Source: Country submission; IEA (2016), *IEA World Energy Statistics and Balances* (database); OECD (2016), *OECD Environment Statistics* (database); TheTreausury (2016), *Budget Policy Statement 2016.*

StatLink http://dx.doi.org/10.1787/888933459612

GHG emissions from power generation account for a smaller share of total emissions than in most other OECD member countries, as a result of New Zealand's clean energy mix. Renewable sources represent 80% of electricity generation and 40% of primary energy supply, among the highest shares in the OECD (Figure 1). Energy generation from renewables has increased by 60% since 2000. Most additional supply has come from geothermal sources, which now accounts for 60% of renewable energy supply (both electricity and heat); solar and wind power generation has more than tripled in the same period. Achieving the national target of generating 90% of electricity from renewables by 2025 will contribute to reducing GHG emissions (Section 3). Energy consumption increased at a slower rate than GDP, but New Zealand remains among the ten most energy-intensive OECD economies.

Despite the increase in GHG emissions, New Zealand met its Kyoto Protocol target (reducing annual GHG emissions to 1990 levels over 2008-12) by using its forest sinks and international carbon credits (Section 3). In preparation for the 2015 Paris climate conference, New Zealand announced its intended nationally determined contribution (INDC) to reduce GHG emissions by 30% below 2005 levels by 2030 (equivalent to 11% below 1990 levels). The government ratified the 2015 Paris Agreement in October 2016. Depending on the intended use of forestry sinks and carbon credits, achieving the 2030 target may effectively mean an increase in gross domestic GHG emissions. In addition, the 2030 target is not on the path towards New Zealand's long-term goal of reducing emissions by 50% below 1990 levels by 2050 (Climate Action Tracker, 2016).

Given its largely decarbonised power generation sector and the weight of agriculture-related biological emissions (from livestock and animal waste), New Zealand faces particular challenges in mitigating its domestic GHG emissions. New Zealand's climate mitigation policy largely relies on forest sinks and carbon pricing via the Emissions Trading Scheme (NZ ETS). The system has had limited effectiveness, however, and needs to be strengthened (Section 3). Expanding forest plantations remains a viable option to offset emissions in the short to medium term, while agriculture and other sectors develop and adopt new low-carbon technology. However, the expected mitigation contribution of each emitting sector and the relative role of international carbon credits and domestic actions are not clear. Information on the costs and abatement potential of mitigation options also needs to be improved (Royal Society of New Zealand, 2016).

All emitting sectors, including agriculture, need to take actions in the short term to curb their emissions using the available mitigation options, starting from phasing out fossil fuels from the energy mix and increasing the efficiency of energy use (Section 3). Better urban planning can help reduce energy use and GHG emissions in cities (Section 5). At the same time, New Zealand should continue to promote and support research in new mitigation technologies, especially for biological emissions from farming (Section 3). In September 2016, the government announced the establishment of three expert groups on agricultural biological emissions, forestry and adaptation to build the evidence base on these issues.

New Zealand is vulnerable to the effects of climate change. In some areas of the country, sea level rise and heavier rainfalls will raise the risk of coastal and river flooding; more frequent and intense droughts are expected in other areas. Overall, this will affect tourism, energy supply from hydro, irrigation, agriculture productivity, fish stocks, ecosystems and human health. National legislation requires local authorities to consider the effects of climate change in their planning decisions. However, many struggle to gather and evaluate data and to plan effectively for climate change impacts such as sea level rise (PCE, 2015a).

New Zealand has improved the evidence base of potential impacts. For example, it has developed vulnerability assessments for the tourism and transport sectors. However, these have yet to be translated into sectoral adaptation strategies; similar assessments for other key economic sectors (e.g. agriculture) are lacking.

Air quality management

With increasing road transport, industrial production and power generation, emissions of some major air pollutants (nitrogen and sulphur oxides, and non-methane volatile organic compounds) rose over 2000-14, although at a lower rate than GDP and population growth. Nonetheless, air quality has generally improved, owing mainly to a shift from wood to electricity- and gas-based home heating; national wood burner emission and efficiency standards, and the replacement of older wood burners; improved building insulation; and the introduction of standards for vehicle fuels. Air quality is generally good by international standards (Figure 1), even though short-term air quality standards are breached near busy inner-city roads and in areas with high concentrations of wood burners.

New Zealand has improved the monitoring of particulate matter (PM_{10}) pollution, but fine particulate matter ($PM_{2.5}$), which has greater health impacts, is still monitored at only a few sites in major cities. Most of the air quality standards, which are part of the 2004 National Environmental Standards (NESs) for Air Quality, follow the guidance of the World Health Organization. However, New Zealand has no national standards on $PM_{2.5}$ concentrations. A review of the NESs' particulate matter provisions is due to be completed in 2017.

Waste management

New Zealand lacks comprehensive, timely and internationally comparable data on waste generation, treatment and disposal. Available data indicate that the generation of municipal solid waste rose by 13% between 2012 and 2014, as a result of increased population and income. The majority of waste is disposed of in landfills. The 2008 Waste Minimisation Act introduced a waste disposal levy (NZD 10 per tonne on waste sent to landfill). Revenue from the levy is used to support waste minimisation activities at national and local level, partly through the Waste Minimisation Fund. However, the levy effectively covers only 30% of total landfilled waste. This hampers its effectiveness in encouraging waste minimisation and alternative forms of waste treatment. There is no national regulation of the disposal of agricultural waste, despite the large size of the sector, nor of hazardous waste landfills, storage or transportation facilities (Section 2). The size and low population density of the country make recycling an economically difficult business. To encourage recycling, the government has accredited 14 voluntary product stewardship schemes.

Waste management practices differ across local authorities. Several local councils have launched programmes and regulations aimed at promoting recycling. For example, recycling requirements have helped the Wellington region reduce the amount of waste going to landfills by 15% in five years. Some cities apply quantity- or volume-based waste charges, which provide incentives to households to reduce waste. Evidence from the Auckland region indicates that districts applying volume-based charges send nearly half of the waste volume to landfills than districts financing waste management through flat charges included in property taxes. This is consistent with experience from other countries (e.g. Germany and Korea). Quantity- or volume-based waste charges could be more extensively applied to encourage waste minimisation and recycling, and finance advanced waste management services.

Biodiversity conservation and sustainable use

Most of New Zealand's native flora and fauna species are endemic, owing to the geographic location and natural history of the country (which evolved in the absence of mammalian predators). Invasive species, predators and habitat fragmentation and degradation continue to push native species into extinction. The species extinction rates are among the highest in the world: more than half of amphibians and roughly a third of mammals, birds, fish and reptiles are under threat (Figure 1). New Zealand is a global leader in pest control methods (e.g. of mammalian predators and invasive weeds). These methods, coupled with specific recovery programmes (e.g. offshore island management), have helped improve the population status for certain species. The Predator Free New Zealand 2050 initiative, launched in mid-2016, foresees the establishment of a public-private partnership company to support large-scale predator eradication programmes.

The area under environmental protection expanded to reach 32% of New Zealand's territory and 30% of the Exclusive Economic Zone (EEZ), shares significantly higher than in most OECD member countries and well above international targets (Figure 1). Almost half of the terrestrial protected areas fall within the most stringent protection categories according to the international classification, and prioritisation of ecosystems for conservation has improved. However, not all ecosystem types are well represented in the protected area network, and some land with significant conservation value has low legal protection status (PCE, 2013a). The government's proposal of a new Marine Protected Areas Act improves the process for establishing and managing marine reserves (the current legislation dates back to 1971), but it would apply only to territorial waters (as opposed to the entire EEZ).

There are concerns that indigenous biodiversity on private land is declining (Brown, 2015). This partly reflects limited use of incentives for landowners to maintain biodiversity and ecosystem services on their land. After an unsuccessful attempt to adopt the National Policy Statement for Indigenous Biodiversity in 2011, the government plans to launch a stakeholder dialogue to develop a new national policy statement by late 2018. Inter-institutional collaboration over biodiversity policy has improved and New Zealand has successfully mobilised local communities to engage in biodiversity protection programmes. However, the separate management of species and ecosystems has led to inefficiencies in preventing biodiversity loss. A more strategic and long-term approach to biodiversity protection and sustainable use is needed. The first step is the delivery of the 2016-20 National Biodiversity Strategy and Action Plan.

New Zealand has made progress in mainstreaming biodiversity considerations into sectoral policies, but pressures from some sectors remain of concern. Agricultural production (mainly dairy farming) has intensified; fertiliser consumption increased faster than agricultural production and value added over the 2000s. This has added to large volumes of nitrogen released to soils from dairy farming, with harmful effects on biodiversity and water quality (Section 4). Organic farming is barely developed, representing less than 1% of agricultural land in 2014, compared with the OECD average of more than 2%. Commercial and customary fisheries have long been primarily managed through a transferable quota system, which has helped reduce overfishing and maintain the fish stock at sustainable levels. A suite of management tools recognises Maori customary non-commercial fishing rights and practices. Several management plans and measures address the effect of fishing methods on seabirds and other marine species, although pressures remain high. The ecological integrity of forest ecosystems is good, although pressures from invasive species and disease outbreaks are increasing. Forest plantations have expanded as a result of the NZ ETS (Section 3) and of several programmes that support afforestation and forest regeneration to provide carbon sequestration.

Recommendations on climate change, air, waste and biodiversity

Climate change

- Develop a strategic plan for the achievement of the 2030 climate mitigation target; identify the expected contribution of each sector to domestic emission mitigation and the anticipated reliance on international carbon markets; improve the knowledge base on the available mitigation options, their costs and trade-offs.
- Develop vulnerability assessments for all major economic sectors to inform sectoral climate change adaptation strategies; develop mechanisms to mainstream climate resilience into sectoral planning and investment processes; support local communities to mainstream climate resilience into land-use planning.

Air management

- Continue to strengthen the monitoring and reporting of air quality data, in particular of $PM_{2.5}$ concentrations in areas that are likely to exceed international guidelines; broaden the scope of the National Environment Standards on Air Quality to include maximum concentrations for $PM_{2.5}$.

Waste management

- Extend the waste disposal levy to cover all relevant landfill types; encourage local authorities to introduce quantity- or volume-based waste charges to help minimise waste, foster recycling and improve recovery of waste service costs.
- Improve the collection of data on the generation, disposal and treatment of waste, with a view to producing timely, comprehensive and internationally comparable information.

Biodiversity conservation and sustainable use

- Continue to improve the information base on the state of biodiversity, particularly in private lands; identify conservation priorities and formulate long-term strategies and plans for biodiversity protection and sustainable use; speed up the process for the adoption of a national policy statement on biodiversity; build on international experience in using innovative policy instruments and approaches, including payments for ecosystem services and biodiversity offsetting.

2. Environmental governance and management

Since 2007, New Zealand has made considerable progress in strengthening stakeholder collaboration and engagement with Maori communities at national and sub-national level and implementing recommendations of the previous OECD *Environmental Performance Review* in the areas of environmental information and education. However, some of the 2007 *Review* recommendations in the regulatory domain remain unaddressed, in particular with respect to hazardous waste management, integration of biodiversity considerations into land-use planning, compliance assurance and liability for environmental damage. New Zealand would benefit from introducing approaches and instruments such as integrated pollution prevention and control and strategic environmental assessment, which are widely regarded as best international practices.

Institutional framework

In New Zealand's decentralised system of environmental governance, most policies are implemented at the regional and local levels. The central and local governments are developing ways of working with Maori communities (iwi/hapu) in accordance with the Treaty of Waitangi. At the national level, the National Resources Sector (NRS) – created in 2008 – is a grouping of the eight government agencies with natural resource management responsibilities. Led by the Ministry for the Environment (MfE), the NRS co-ordinates policy making effectively in a number of areas to align economic development and sustainability goals through multiple institutional mechanisms. However, in some areas such as urban development and management of marine ecosystems, co-ordination among institutions is insufficient. This is partly due to the patchy regulatory regime in these domains and lack of clarity in the role of different government agencies (EDS, 2016).

The combination of land-use planning and environmental regulatory powers in the hands of regional and territorial authorities allows adequate consideration of local circumstances. However, with the exception of a few policy areas where National Environmental Standards (NESs) have been established, this system leads to regulatory requirements for economic activities that are inconsistent across the country and overly dependent on local development priorities. The national independent environmental regulator – the Environmental Protection Authority, which was created in 2011 – has a disparate mix of responsibilities under different statutes (e.g. to regulate hazardous substances and economic activities on the continental shelf), but only marginal powers in regulating pollution.

With declining environment-related personnel numbers, the resource capacity of smaller district and city councils is a persistent challenge. This is particularly true in compliance monitoring and enforcement, where local authorities have few dedicated staff. The central government co-ordinates general natural resource management priorities with local authorities. The National Monitoring System ensures the national government's oversight of local-level environmental policy implementation, but includes few outcome indicators.

Regulatory framework

The 1991 Resource Management Act (RMA) is a remarkably comprehensive piece of environmental legislation, governing almost every aspect of environmental management. However, over its lifetime, the RMA has been subject to 21 substantive amendments, doubling in size and inevitably losing some of its coherence. The RMA provides a framework for national environmental policy development via National Policy Statements (NPSs) and NESs; sub-national governments are responsible for implementing national directions. The RMA system presumes the use of land is permitted unless restricted by a regional or district plan.

The development of NPSs and NESs is fragmented and slow (only four NPSs and five sets of NESs adopted over 25 years). The full potential of the RMA for establishing nationwide environmental rules, therefore, has not been reached. The adoption of NESs for water bodies used as sources of drinking water supply and for assessing and managing contaminants in soil over the last decade has strengthened the regulatory framework, but significant gaps remain. New Zealand has not progressed in developing a nationwide regime and standards for managing hazardous waste or biodiversity protection. The government is aware that national consistency of environmental regulatory requirements is lacking; it plans to issue several new NPSs and NESs in the near future. There is also a lack of guidance from the central government on implementing existing national policies and standards. This leads to uncertainty in achieving desired environmental outcomes and creates an uneven playing field for economic entities. No comprehensive evaluation has analysed the performance of the RMA in order for it to deal with implementation problems and deliver its objectives (Palmer and Blakeley, 2015). More generally, *ex post* evaluation, especially at the local level, could be strengthened.

New Zealand has a complex hierarchy of land-use planning documents at the national, regional and local levels. This often leads to duplication in developing, for example, district and regional plans (Section 5). All regulations and plans are subject to an assessment of costs and benefits (including environmental and social ones) as part of the regulatory impact analysis. The *ex ante* assessment of regional and territorial plans under the RMA includes evaluation of reasonable development alternatives, but not systematic appraisal of significant and cumulative environmental effects. The integration of environmental, particularly biodiversity protection, considerations into land-use planning and management remains a significant challenge.

In a system unusual among OECD member countries, a discharge permit is required whenever an intended development or activity is not in accordance with the rules of the relevant authority's planning document. An assessment of environmental effects (AEE) is required as part of every resource consent application, irrespective of the size of the potential environmental impact. Conditions in discharge permits for air, water and waste are not set according to any nationally standardised methodology, although they must be consistent with NESs. Unlike in many other OECD member countries, there is no system for cross-media integration of discharge permits on the basis of best available techniques that addresses environmental impacts in a holistic way, although conditions may require the permit holder to adopt the best practicable option. Activities that do not require a permit because of their relatively minor impact or historic use rights contribute to cumulative environmental impacts, which are poorly accounted for (Brown, 2016).

Reform of the RMA to reduce the administrative burden on businesses is ongoing. This process includes streamlining development and amendment of policy statements or plans and consideration of resource consent and permit applications. Simplifying regulations for activities with low environmental impact is consistent with good international practices. However, the use of streamlined environmental planning with restricted public participation and no judicial control should be limited to only a few, clearly defined cases to prevent administrative abuse.

Compliance assurance

Most local authorities monitor compliance with resource consents proactively. A growing number have adopted a risk-based approach, prioritising inspections based on factors such as compliance history and the number and complexity of consent conditions. However, over a third of local authorities identified monitoring and enforcement as a "significant capability gap" (NZPC, 2016).

Non-compliance with environmental requirements remains relatively high, with 20% of inspected resource consent holders found to be non-compliant, although fines for criminal offences have been substantially increased. Local authorities lack adequate enforcement capacity, particularly at the territorial level: under half of local authorities used infringement notices entailing administrative fines in 2014/15, while district and city councils account for only 23% of all environmental enforcement actions in the country (MfE, 2016b).

New Zealand has established soil contamination standards and procedures for the identification and remediation of contaminated land. It uses innovative financial security instruments such as bonds and mitigation trusts to ensure environmental remediation and restoration of ecosystems. However, it lacks a mechanism to enforce liability with respect to past contamination of land or water bodies, or damage to ecosystems and biodiversity. The budgetary Contaminated Sites Remediation Fund administered by the MfE is the main means of addressing land contamination where no liability for the contamination can be assigned.

The central government and local authorities have concluded a number of voluntary agreements with individual companies and industry groups to promote sustainable production practices, including the major "Sustainable Dairying: Water Accord" to reduce agricultural pollution of freshwater bodies. The agreement sets clear environmental performance targets, many of which have already been achieved, and requires regular reporting and third-party auditing (Section 4). The central government also uses sustainable public procurement and corporate environmental responsibility awards to promote green business practices. However, local authorities underuse compliance promotion.

Environmental democracy

There are several opportunities for public participation in the drafting of primary and secondary legislation. In addition, the public can take part in district and regional planning, which provides the regulatory basis for local environmental management. Specific legal provisions implement the consultation rights of the Maori people. One example of collaborative consultation is the Land and Water Forum; it has been effective in bringing together multiple stakeholders to tackle the challenge of water management, including diffuse water pollution from agriculture (Section 4). The plan development process (including standard-setting) is the primary opportunity for public participation under the RMA whereas public involvement in the consent determination process is much more limited (only 4% of consents are notified to the public).

Over the last decade, the country has demonstrated progress in promoting broad access to environmental information. Specifically, it has adopted the 2015 Environmental Reporting Act and implemented the Environmental Monitoring and Reporting initiative to improve collection, management and publication of environmental data. However, unlike most other OECD member countries, New Zealand does not have a Pollutant Release and Transfer Register (PRTR), which would provide the public with industrial release and waste management data.

The Environment Court provides broad and transparent access to justice on environmental matters. The government actively facilitates access of Maori groups, community organisations and other non-governmental organisations (NGOs) to environmental judicial remedies by covering their legal costs through the Environmental Legal Assistance Fund.

New Zealand has made progress in promoting environmental education and incorporating sustainability in the national school curriculum. The national Enviroschools programme and its equivalent for Maori-speaking communities actively promotes voluntary engagement of schools in a "whole school" approach to environmental education.

Recommendations on environmental governance and management

Regulatory framework

- Conduct a comprehensive evaluation of the effectiveness of RMA implementation at the local authority level in achieving its objective of development within the limits of the environment's carrying capacity; consider a regulatory review of the RMA to evaluate whether its framework as a whole remains fit for purpose.
- Prepare new and review existing NPSs and NESs to reinforce the national-level regulatory and methodological framework for managing air and water pollution; establish national standards for hazardous waste management.
- Establish nationally standardised requirements for air and water discharge permits and waste generation and management; encourage better cross-media integration of discharge permits on the basis of best available techniques; extend consent and permit requirements to existing use rights obtained under older regulatory regimes.
- Build capacity of local authorities to carry out their permitting, compliance monitoring and enforcement responsibilities through better nationwide guidance, support and training, including interactive online support; introduce outcome indicators in the National Monitoring System to strengthen the national government's oversight and *ex post* evaluation of policy implementation and enforcement at the local level.
- Evaluate the implementation of requirements for the assessment of environmental effects (AEE) and consider defining environmental impact-based thresholds for activities above which the scope of assessment would remain comprehensive and notification to the public would be mandatory, while smaller activities could undergo simplified AEE without notification.
- Ensure coherence of regional and territorial land-use plans; require explicit assessment of cumulative environmental impacts as part of the planning process; continue efforts to integrate biodiversity protection into land-use planning, particularly on private land.

Compliance assurance

- Promote risk-based targeting and other resource-efficient inspection practices among local authorities; strengthen compliance assurance through more active use of administrative enforcement tools and better national oversight of their consistent application; enhance compliance promotion through best practice guidance.
- Establish mechanisms to enforce strict (independent of fault) liability regime for damage to water bodies and ecosystems; expand the use of bonds and mitigation trusts under the RMA to secure the remediation of potential future environmental damage.

Environmental democracy

- Continue to ensure public participation in land-use planning, limiting exemptions to a few clearly defined cases; build capacity of Maori communities to ensure their adequate participation in resource management planning.
- Establish a Pollutant Release and Transfer Register (PRTR) to collect, and facilitate the public's access to, information on environmental impacts of private companies.

3. Towards green growth

New Zealand has built an international reputation as a "green" country, both as tourism destination and as producer of natural and safe food. In 2011, the government established the Green Growth Advisory Group to advise on green growth opportunities, in line with the 2009

OECD Declaration on Green Growth, and to inform the preparation of the Business Growth Agenda (the government's economic development programme). The Agenda, launched in 2012 and revamped in 2015, considered the recommendations of the Group, but only to a limited extent. It pursues the broad goal of building a more competitive and productive economy; it sets the target of making exports account for 40% of GDP by 2025, up from about 30% in 2015. Among other things, the Agenda focuses on improving the productivity of, and the value generated by, the natural resource-based sectors (including the large export-oriented livestock production sector), while reducing their environmental impact.

Nonetheless, the Agenda is far from providing a long-term vision for the transition of New Zealand to a low-carbon, greener economy. Such transition is likely to entail increasing trade-offs with the current production and export targets. In particular, reducing GHG emissions (Section 1) and improving water quality (Section 4) would be difficult to achieve by relying only on productivity gains and without reducing agricultural output (Royal Society of New Zealand, 2016). New Zealand should accelerate its current work on exploring the economic opportunities that arise from exporting higher value products, tapping into emerging markets and investing in environmental quality improvements to reduce its reliance on natural resource use. This will help the country defend its "green" reputation, which will be increasingly essential for its competiveness and attractiveness in the global market as consumer and investor preferences shift towards sustainability and strong environmental performance.

Getting prices right

In line with the recommendations of the 2007 OECD *Environmental Performance Review*, New Zealand has extended the use of economic instruments to put a price on environmental externalities and encourage efficient use of natural resources. These include the globally unique nitrogen cap-and-trade system in the Lake Taupo catchment (Section 4), the New Zealand GHG Emissions Trading Scheme (NZ ETS) and the waste disposal levy (Section 1).

The NZ ETS, introduced in 2008, is the cornerstone of the country's climate change mitigation policy. It was designed to operate within the international Kyoto Protocol emission credits market and to cover all GHGs and emitting sectors, including agriculture and forestry – the only ETS in the world to do so. However, the system has been amended several times, which has created regulatory uncertainty for participants. The changes indefinitely postponed the inclusion of biological emissions from agriculture (nearly half of New Zealand's GHG emissions). They also added transitional measures to moderate the impact of the carbon price on participants (such as the so-called one-for-two arrangement[2] and the delay in phasing out the free allocations to emission-intensive, trade-exposed activities). These provisions, alongside the unlimited availability of cheap international credits, have contributed to weakening the carbon price signal. With the exception of a modest positive impact on afforestation, the effectiveness of the NZ ETS has been limited and is likely to remain so (Leining and Kerr, 2016).

Changes to the NZ ETS are needed if it is to provide a sufficiently high and stable price signal to influence investment decisions and unlock emission mitigation options. In 2015, the MfE launched the third review of the NZ ETS to assess its effectiveness in contributing to achieving New Zealand's INDC. The first phase of the review led to the gradual phase-out of the one-for-two arrangement. The review did not consider the possibility of bringing biological emissions from agriculture back within the NZ ETS, however. New Zealand needs to reassess the decision of indefinitely postponing the entry of these emissions in the

NZ ETS. If such a decision is confirmed, alternative pricing or regulatory measures should make agriculture contribute to achieving climate mitigation objectives. Given the significance of agricultural biological emissions, continuing to shield them from mitigation obligations would make meeting these objectives harder, place a disproportionate burden on other sectors and slow the pace of adjustment in the agriculture sector (Bibbee, 2011). To address this issue, in September 2016 the government announced the establishment of the Biological Emissions Reference Group.

Expanding the use of environmentally related taxes and charges could encourage more efficient use of energy and resources and support the government's ongoing fiscal consolidation efforts. Revenue from environmentally related taxes accounts for 1.3% of GDP and 4.2% of total tax revenue, among the lowest shares in the OECD; it has declined as a share of GDP by nearly 20% since 2000. Unlike many OECD member countries, New Zealand taxes only transport energy, and does so at comparatively low rates. At the same time, the NZ ETS put a price on CO_2 emissions from most fuel use. Overall, 68% of CO_2 energy-related emissions face a carbon price signal (in the form of energy tax or NZ ETS price), which is less than in most OECD member countries (OECD, 2016a). Despite rising emission allowance prices since mid-2015, the carbon price component of energy prices remains negligible, well below a conservative estimate of the social cost of carbon (EUR 30 tCO_2) and too low to influence behaviour (OECD, 2016a; Royal Society of New Zealand, 2016). Even if carbon prices increase further, there is scope to raise taxes on fuels used for transport, heating and industrial processes so long as the NZ ETS does not cap GHG emissions. Fuel taxes can also help take account of local air pollution and other social costs directly or indirectly linked to transport energy use (e.g. noise, congestion and accident costs) in the absence of a sophisticated (country-wide, time- and location-specific) road pricing system, which would be theoretically more efficient.

New Zealand is the only OECD member country to apply an excise duty to petrol but not to diesel; diesel vehicles are subject to a distance-based road user charge instead. As such, the road user charge does not encourage behaviours that would reduce fuel use (e.g. avoiding high-speed driving that uses up more fuel). The tax and charge rates are set based on investment needs, with no consideration for environmental externalities. The differential charging system tends to favour diesel vehicles due to their higher fuel efficiency, but does not consider the higher emissions of local air pollutants from such vehicles. As the road charges are not differentiated by the car's weight or engine size, they provide no incentive to the uptake of smaller or more fuel-efficient vehicles. In addition, New Zealand applies a favourable tax treatment to company cars and parking lots, which is a cost for the public budget and tends to encourage private car use, long-distance commuting and urban sprawl (Harding, 2014). The number of motor vehicles has increased considerably, with higher growth rates for diesel than for petrol vehicles. Lax vehicle standards have favoured the import of used vehicles; as a result, the vehicle fleet is old and relatively inefficient (Section 1). The government should consider introducing fuel efficiency and emission standards for imported (new and used) vehicles. Overall, there is a need for a coherent system of fuel and vehicle standards and charges. Introducing road pricing (tolls or congestion charges) would help improve transport demand management in large urban areas, especially in Auckland (Section 5).

Support to fossil fuel consumption is low in New Zealand in comparison to most other countries. New Zealand is a founding member of the Friends of Fossil Fuel Subsidy Reform, an informal group of non-G20 countries that advocates policy reforms of these subsidies globally.

Leading by example, in 2015, New Zealand voluntarily underwent a peer review of fossil-fuel subsidies in the context of the Asia-Pacific Economic Co-operation. The review concluded that none of the eight measures analysed encourage wasteful consumption, in part because they do not lower domestic fuel prices (APEC, 2015). OECD (2016b) estimates, however, that some of these measures cost the New Zealand government about NZD 60 million in tax breaks and budgetary transfers in 2014. In addition, the free allocations of NZ ETS emission allowances to energy-intensive, trade-exposed activities represent forgone revenue that the government could raise if it auctioned the allowances (PCE, 2016a). The government provides some tax and royalty incentives to oil and gas exploration. As OECD (2013a) indicated, these incentives can distort investment decisions in favour of fossil fuel production and potentially counteract New Zealand's efforts to address global climate change.

Investing in sustainable energy and low-carbon transport modes

Investment in renewables has increased in recent years, without the need for any direct subsidies or public support; geothermal, hydro and wind are cost-competitive. IEA (forthcoming) considers this performance a world-class success story. New Zealand already has the OECD's fourth highest shares of renewables in its energy mix (Figure 1). Renewable sources (mainly hydro) supply over 80% of its electricity (Section 1), and the government aims to bring this share to 90% by 2025. However, some factors constrain the further development of renewable sources: the vulnerability of hydro resources to droughts; their uncertain long-term availability due to climate change and water quality concerns; and the impact of growing shares of variable renewable resources (i.e. wind and solar power) on the stability of the power system.

There is scope to improve energy efficiency as the energy intensity of the economy has remained broadly stable since 2000 at levels well above the OECD average (Section 1). New Zealand's approach to energy efficiency has changed from direct financial support to a greater focus on information and partnerships. The NZ ETS has provided little incentive to invest in renewables and energy efficiency. It is not clear how much further improvement market forces will deliver. A comprehensive package of policy measures is needed to complement the NZ ETS carbon pricing. Such measures should primarily address non-pricing barriers to investing in low-carbon energy sources and adopting energy-efficient technology in industry, transport and buildings (Section 5). This will have multiple environmental, energy security and health benefits.

Investment in land transport infrastructure is significant, but heavily tilted towards roads. In 2012-15, the National Land Transport Fund (NLTF), which receives all revenue from the petrol tax and the road user charge, mostly financed investment in highways and local roads (78% of the NLTF). Public transport, cycling and walking infrastructure received only 10% of the Fund (NZTA, 2015). Additional investments in road infrastructure will be needed to meet increasing demand. However, further developing urban public transport systems and improving service quality and supply of bus services could provide other options for commuters, reduce road congestion and improve environmental outcomes.

With its large share of renewable electricity, New Zealand can use electric vehicles (EVs) effectively to mitigate transport-related GHG emissions. The transport sector is the largest final energy user and the second largest source of GHG emissions (Section 1). So far the uptake of EVs in New Zealand has been limited and growing slowly. In mid-2016, the government launched the Electric Vehicle Programme aiming to double the EV fleet every year till 2021. It foresees exempting EVs from the road user charge until they make up 2% of the light vehicle fleet. This will provide some incentive to users, but the electricity distribution system will need to be adapted and the charging infrastructure developed to accelerate the mass roll out of EVs. The central and local governments should lead by example and commit to purchase EVs for a proportion of their own fleets, which would provide a strong signal to the transport industry and the public. More advanced options such as a full electric car-sharing service could be piloted.

Promoting eco-innovation

New Zealand has a well-developed innovation system and a sound skills base. In line with an increased emphasis on innovation as a driver of economic growth, public investment in science and innovation has increased by 60% since 2007-08. However, gross domestic expenditure on research and development (R&D) has remained low at about 1.2% of GDP, about half the OECD average. Public institutions, mostly universities and Crown research institutes, conduct most of the R&D. Despite close co-operation between industry and public research, the number of patents is relatively small, and commercialisation of public research results could be improved (OECD, 2014).

The government is the main source of funding for environmental research. Environment-related R&D accounts for nearly 10% of government R&D outlays. This is the highest share in the OECD, but has declined from about 18% in 2007. The share of total energy R&D budget dedicated to renewables and energy efficiency has progressively increased; it exceeded 70% in 2014, although public funding for energy R&D is limited and should be raised (IEA, forthcoming). This has contributed to a steady increase of the number of patent applications related to climate change mitigation technology, a trend observed in many other countries and driven by global climate mitigation commitments. Overall, environment- and climate-related technologies made up nearly 12% of all patent applications in 2010-12, in line with the OECD average and more than three times the level in 2000. New Zealand has developed a specialisation and competitive advantage in some technology fields:[3] water, wastewater and waste treatment; water adaptation; and renewable energy generation.

New Zealand's innovation policy has increasingly focused on environment-related research and innovation as a way to improve the natural resource base of the economy. The Conservation and Environment Science Roadmap, under development in 2016, aims to set the future research priorities in these domains. Five out of the 11 "science challenges" included in the National Science Challenges initiative relate to the environment and natural resources. The initiative, launched in 2013, pledges to invest more than NZD 350 million over ten years to support public research on emerging and complex issues for New Zealand's future development by drawing scientists and stakeholders together across different institutions and science fields. The environment is also among the key research sectors identified by the National Statement of Science Investment (NSSI), which identifies priorities for the government's investment in research and innovation in 2015-25. The NSSI has partially shifted research funding from budget allocations for research institutions to contestable funding open to all institutions and science fields, with a view to improving the efficiency of R&D spending and support impact-driven science. However, the bidding process is time consuming and tends to increase the upfront costs of research projects. There are concerns this may negatively affect the retention of research skills and penalise environmental research, which has generally fewer market applications and has, therefore, less tangible impact. Progress has been made in reducing fragmentation of research funding across institutions and support programmes, but administration and transaction costs remain high. The economic efficiency of the environment-related innovation policy and its contribution to ultimately improving environmental performance, resource productivity and energy efficiency are not systematically evaluated.

New Zealand is a world leader in the research related to reducing the environmental impact from agriculture, primarily on GHG emissions and water quality, and has consolidated its technology specialisation and competitive advantage in this area. New Zealand led the establishment of the Global Research Alliance on Agricultural Greenhouse Gases, which groups 46 countries and fosters international co-operation and investment in research into mitigating GHG emissions from food production. The government, in co-operation with the business sector, has launched several initiatives to support agriculture-related R&D and commercialisation of research results.

Contributing to the global sustainable development agenda

New Zealand has gained a reputation as a "good global citizen", partly owing to its development-friendly approach in trade negotiations and its support to Small Island Developing States. On the basis of the OECD pilot assessment methodology (OECD, 2016c), New Zealand performs better than the OECD as a whole with regards to meeting most Sustainable Development Goals (SDGs). Spending on official development assistance (ODA) grew considerably in 2010-15; however, at 0.27% of gross national income (GNI), it remains well below the internationally agreed target of 0.7% of GNI. More than 40% of ODA targets environmental objectives (including climate change, biodiversity, desertification, renewable energy, water supply and sanitation), one of the highest shares in the OECD. An export-oriented economy, New Zealand has negotiated numerous free trade agreements, most of which include environmental provisions; it advocates the removal of trade barriers on environmental goods and services. This may support the country's efforts in developing a greener export base.

Recommendations on green growth

- Establish a whole-of-government, multi-stakeholder process to develop a long-term vision for the transition of New Zealand towards a low-carbon, greener economy, taking into account the opportunities to diversify the economy and reduce its reliance on agriculture and the use of natural resources; develop a framework for monitoring and reporting progress towards green growth objectives, based on sound indicators linking economic activity with environmental performance, as a way to build consensus around the low-carbon, green transition.

Getting prices right

- Reform the NZ ETS at the earliest opportunity to ensure a price of carbon that is consistent with New Zealand's transition to a low-carbon economy, by i) aligning the supply of NZ ETS units to the country's mitigation targets and the trajectory towards net-zero emissions; ii) auctioning domestic allocations once the stock of banked NZ ETS units is depleted, and considering the introduction of a floor price, increasing over time, on auctioned allowances; iii) avoiding the use beyond 2020 of international carbon credits that were acquired before 2015; iv) setting a limit to the quantity of international carbon credits that can be used to offset domestic emissions (if international credits become newly eligible); v) establishing a clear timeframe and schedule for phasing out the free allocations of emission allowances to energy-intensive and trade-exposed activities; vi) removing the price ceiling or, at the very least, increasing it over time.

Recommendations on green growth *(cont.)*

- Set a clear date for the inclusion of biological emissions from agriculture in the NZ ETS or introduce alternative pricing and regulatory measures to enforce emission reduction obligations; place the point of obligation at the farm level; further invest in developing tools for measuring, monitoring and reporting GHG emissions at farm level.
- Expand the use of environmentally related taxes, charges and prices, possibly within the framework of an overall reform of the tax structure, with a view to encouraging more efficient use of energy and resources and supporting the ongoing fiscal consolidation efforts: i) consider introducing an excise duty on diesel and ensure that petrol and diesel tax/charge rates take account of environmental externalities; ii) introduce water pollution charges and taxes on industrial air emissions.
- Systematically assess fossil fuel subsidies and tax exemptions, with a view to identifying those that are inefficient and encourage wasteful consumption and fossil fuel production and should, therefore, be removed.

Investing in sustainable energy and low-carbon transport modes

- Design and implement a comprehensive package of GHG emission mitigation measures to complement the NZ ETS carbon pricing and address non-pricing barriers to the adoption of low-carbon technology and solutions, including for energy generation and use in industry, transport and buildings; carefully assess the interactions between the NZ ETS and other potential GHG mitigation policy instruments.
- Ensure the consistency of investment priorities for land transport infrastructure, and the related financing model, with long-term climate and environmental objectives; reform the tax treatment of company cars and parking spaces; introduce fuel efficiency and air emission standards for new and imported used vehicles; ensure adequate public and private investment for the adaptation of the electricity distribution system and the development of charging infrastructure for electric vehicles (EVs); introduce mandatory EV quotas in the fleets of public institutions.

Promoting eco-innovation

- Develop a science and innovation roadmap to provide a long-term view of innovation policy, while maintaining the current emphasis on environmental research; continue to increase, and provide stability to, public R&D funding to attract and retain innovation capacity; further streamline the innovation and R&D funding system, with a view to reducing transaction and administrative costs; continue to invest in agriculture-related research and to lead internationally the development of technologies and practices to mitigate GHG emissions and reduce water contamination.

Contributing to the global sustainable development agenda

- Maintain the strong commitment to environment and climate change in development co-operation, while increasing the volume of official development assistance in line with international goals.

4. Water resources management

New Zealand's freshwater resources are vital to the primary sector and tourism, as well as to the country's culture. Agriculture is the dominant land use; dairy farming has intensified in recent decades in response to high global milk prices. The link between pastoral intensification and pressures on freshwater quality and quantity is increasingly being acknowledged (PCE, 2013b; MfE, 2016c). Water contamination from the cumulative effects of diffuse agricultural and urban stormwater run-off (Section 5) is a growing environmental and public health concern. For Maori, freshwater is a taonga (culturally valued resource), essential to life and identity, and they are asserting their right to co-govern water resources and be more actively involved in decision-making processes.

In recognition of the need to safeguard water quality and prevent and reduce over-allocation, New Zealand has embarked on a process of reforming national freshwater policy. Further government support is required to assist regional councils and local communities with setting ambitious goals, and to accelerate implementation of the reform to reduce investment uncertainty and the risk of further pressure on freshwater resources and ecosystems.

State and trends

New Zealand has abundant water resources, with less than 5% of renewable freshwater resources allocated for use. However, rainfall and freshwater availability vary substantially across regions and seasons. A large proportion of annual rainfall occurs in winter when demand for irrigation is relatively low. Some regions are relatively dry and suffer from periodic droughts. Three-quarters of consumptive freshwater is used for irrigation, mostly in the regions of Canterbury and Otago, where summers with low rainfall and high temperatures would otherwise limit farming (MfE and Statistics NZ, 2015). In these regions, as well as in Marlborough and Hawke's Bay, water demand is exceeding what is available and sustainable; freshwater allocated for irrigation of pastoral and arable land increased by 82% between 1999 and 2010. However, the latest data indicate that approximately 35% of the volume of water allocated is not being used, which highlights opportunities for a more efficient reallocation of water (Aqualinc, 2010). Reconciling these competing needs and providing adequate environmental flows for freshwater ecosystems is an emerging challenge, which will be further exacerbated by climate change.

Achieving water quality improvements in many New Zealand catchments will likely require significant manipulation of existing land management, given the intensive nature of the country's agricultural sector and good regulation of point source pollution in most places. Water quality in some regions (Canterbury, Otago, Southland, Waikato, Taranaki, Manawatu-Wanganui and Hawke's Bay) has suffered from diffuse pollution associated with the steady expansion of intensive farming (most notably dairy farming) and urbanisation (PCE, 2015b; see also Section 5). The pollutants of most concern are nutrients, pathogens and sediments. In particular, nitrogen levels from diffuse agricultural sources have continued to increase; between 1998 and 2009, the nitrogen balance worsened more than in any other OECD member country (OECD, 2013b). Over 1990-2012, nitrogen leaching into soil from agriculture increased by 29% and total nitrogen levels in rivers by 12% (MfE and Statistics NZ, 2015). Contamination of groundwater with nitrates and microbial pathogens is recognised as a human health risk. For example, New Zealand has relatively high rates of largely preventable enteric or gastro-intestinal disease in comparison to England, Australia and Canada (Ministry of Health, 2016).

Deteriorating water quality remains one of the biggest threats to native freshwater species, alongside habitat loss and predation from introduced species. New Zealand has some of the highest levels of threatened freshwater species in the world, with almost three-quarters of native fish threatened with extinction. Macroinvertebrate Community

Index scores are poorest in rivers located downstream of catchments where agricultural intensity and urban land cover are high (Larned et al., 2016).

The full impacts of past and present agricultural land-use practices on water quality have yet to materialise; the time lag between improved land-use practices and improved water quality can be long (up to decades), particularly for groundwater resources. There are concerns that even with best mitigation practices, recent elevated inputs from continued large-scale conversion of land to dairy farming, coupled with time lag effects, will result in more freshwater degradation (Figure 2).

Figure 2. **Large-scale land-use change to dairy farming is predicted to increase nitrogen loads**

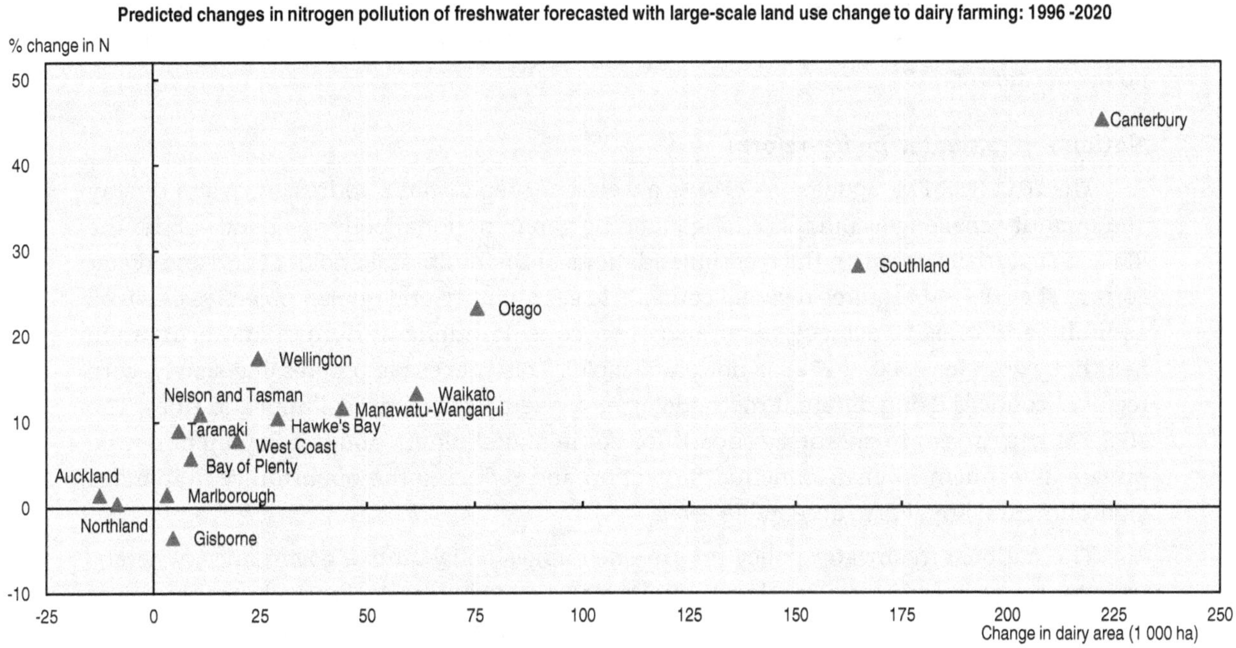

Source: PCE (2013), *Water quality in New Zealand: Land use and nutrient pollution.*

StatLink http://dx.doi.org/10.1787/888933459622

Institutional and regulatory framework

Under the 1991 Resource Management Act (RMA), regional authorities are responsible for the management of water risks – droughts, floods, water quality and freshwater ecosystem degradation – and activities that affect these risks, including water abstraction and wastewater discharges. Regional councils regulate these activities through resource consents and permits (Section 2); these include conditions to ensure that water resource use is compatible with objectives set in regional policy statements and plans. Regional councils must consult with their communities when they prepare and review water management plans. The values of iwi (indigenous communities) are important to freshwater management, and iwi play a key role in decision-making processes; co-management arrangements between iwi, regional authorities and central government are an important element of Treaty of Waitangi settlements. Central government develops national policy guidance to direct and support regional councils.

The RMA has regulated point-source pollution effectively through discharge permits, which set limits for discharging industrial and urban wastewater into water bodies. Adoption of the National Environmental Standard for Sources of Human Drinking Water

2007, along with the Health (Drinking Water) Amendment Act 2007, has strengthened drinking water legislation. However, the control of diffuse pollution and efficient water allocation remain challenging. Water is not always used, or available, for its highest value use (economic, social and environmental) primarily due to over-allocation in some regions and a "first-in, first-served" approach to issuing resource consents for water abstractions.

Until recently, the mix of regulatory and non-regulatory measures has been insufficient to address key pressures on freshwater quantity and quality, partly because of the prolonged absence of national policy guidance (Office of the Auditor-General, 2011). Decision-making processes around resource consents and freshwater management can be litigious and resource consuming, as well as create uncertainty (MfE, 2016d) (Section 2). The adoption of the 2011 National Policy Statement for Freshwater Management (NPS-FM) and the proposed amendments to the RMA are important milestones towards addressing these policy matters.

National freshwater policy reform

The 2011 NPS-FM, updated in 2014, is a welcome step towards addressing water quality and quantity challenges and fills a long-standing gap in national policy guidance under the RMA. It is partially based on the recommendations of the multi-stakeholder Land and Water Forum. The NPS-FM requires regional councils to set quantity and quality objectives, as well as limits and rules to achieve them, based on considerations of human and ecosystem health, by 2025 (or 2030, if 2025 is not practicable). This process is progressing slowly, with regional councils using different methodologies for setting objectives, limits and rules. The NPS-FM deadlines are creating concern for some stakeholders about delaying potential private investment in environmental protection and reducing the opportunity to manage environmental impacts to acceptable levels.

The national freshwater policy reform encourages collaborative governance, whereby regional councils, iwi/Maori, local communities and stakeholders collectively set objectives and limits for freshwater quantity and quality. While voluntary, the collaborative, consensus-driven process enables a shift from effect-based management of resource consents for individual landowners to integrated management of catchments. It also raises awareness of issues among stakeholders, creates buy-in and offers flexibility in achieving water quality and quantity objectives. Consensus through collaborative governance may be one of the greatest strengths of the New Zealand freshwater policy reform, but there are options to improve its effectiveness. Despite the potential benefits of collaborative governance, it is too early to evaluate the outcomes of collective action in New Zealand.

A national framework for collaborative governance, financial and technical support for collaborative groups, and incentives to improve water quality beyond the status quo may provide viable solutions for creating ambitious water quality improvement targets in a shorter period. One such incentive could be to require collaborative group discussions to start at the highest water quality level (e.g. suitable for swimming), and call for disproportionate costs (such as shutting down or reducing production, and the associated economic and social costs) to be proven to reduce water quality objectives towards, but not below, the minimum national standards (see below). This approach would consider social, economic and environmental trade-offs, while ensuring water objectives are set at the most effective level. An independent auditor, such as the Environmental Protection Authority, the Parliamentary Commissioner for the Environment or certified independent experts, could determine what is disproportionate.

The NPS-FM requires that overall freshwater quality within a region be maintained or improved, existing over-allocation phased out, and further over-allocation of water avoided. To guide regional councils and communities through the water quality objective and limit-setting process, a National Objectives Framework (NOF) provides mandatory minimum national standards for water quality (known in New Zealand as national bottom lines), with which the large majority of rivers already comply. Optional water quality guidelines beyond the minimum national standards are provided in the NOF so that objectives and limits can be customised to regional and local needs. Growing concerns about increasing nitrogen pollution and public health risks have led some parties to suggest these minimum standards need to be more ambitious to meet public expectations and to maintain the life-supporting capacity of freshwater ecosystems. For example, there is strong public support for water quality limits to be set at levels suitable for swimming (MfE, 2016c). Important work is ongoing at the national level on setting sediment, dissolved oxygen and nitrate limits to manage algal growth. Water quality parameters are also being set for estuaries, wetlands, intermittently closing and opening lakes and lagoons, and potentially groundwater. The revision or development of new water quality parameters should be expedited to minimise the need for repeated community engagement and consultation and updates of regional plans to meet new regulations.

The success of the NPS-FM will ultimately lie with regional councils and their ability to engage with the communities. There are substantial challenges to manage water within quality and quantity limits and to carry out effective collaborative governance. Guidance for regional councils, including further development of robust science and data to support limit setting and catchment management, will be critical. Improvements in analysis and reporting of environmental data are required, in particular for *Environment Aotearoa*, the national state of the environment report (PCE, 2016b). Continued progress through unambiguous national guidance and a more comprehensive NOF, coupled with holding regional councils accountable for achieving the NPS-FM and their regional plans, will be necessary to ensure success.

Getting the NPS-FM implementation right is critical for recognising the relationship between iwi/Maori and water bodies, maintaining New Zealand's environmental reputation, and reconciling agricultural production and urban development with sustainable management of natural resources. The NPS-FM ultimately aims to ensure the efficient and productive use of freshwater, and to maintain or improve freshwater quality. At the same time, in 2015 the Ministry for Primary Industries set the goal of doubling the real value of primary industry exports by 2025. To achieve both objectives would require a significant improvement in water-use efficiency (both in terms of the quantity of water used and the effects on water quality), and a shift in focus from increasing agricultural production to increasing added value/profitability. Innovations such as precision agriculture can help reduce water consumption and pollution. Ongoing agricultural advisory services and collaboration between universities, research institutes and the agriculture sector can facilitate diffusion of advanced technologies and mobility of skills.

Economic and voluntary instruments to manage water quantity and quality

New Zealand has introduced some economic instruments for water management, but there is still scope for expanding their use to manage water quantity and quality effectively, as recommended by the 2007 OECD *Environmental Performance Review*. Charges for water abstraction and discharges are minimal and cover only the administrative costs of resource consents. New arrangements are required for allocating water abstraction consents at the catchment scale, and for allocating allowances to discharge diffuse contaminants. In both instances, water use and discharge allowances should be allocated at a level that is consistent with good land management practice. Certainty around the nature of rights attached to water use and pollutant discharge allocations would promote investment certainty for water users and investors. Clarification and recognition of Maori (iwi/hapu) rights and interests in water are required before progress can be made with the introduction of economic instruments. A number of options set a precedent, including co-governance agreements, granting legal personhood to a water body, a permanent allocation of water and/or monetary settlement.

Regional councils require a set of economic instruments to maximise the efficiency of water allocation, within limits, to cater for local circumstances. The current system of "first-in, first-served" water allocation may exclude new entrants regardless of the increased value (social, cultural, economic or environmental) they may bring. Abstraction charges (or resource rentals) can encourage water users to improve water-use efficiency and provide a return to a collective resource to account for negative environmental impacts and opportunity costs. Water consent cap-and-transfer schemes can allow freshwater to move to its highest value use over time. Capping water extractions at a sustainable rate, while accounting for environmental flows and climate change impacts before catchments approach full allocation, is critical; resolving over-allocation *ex post* is more complex.

New Zealand is in a unique, advantageous position to cap and manage diffuse pollution outputs using the national model OVERSEER® (a farm-scale nutrient budgeting and loss estimation model), rather than regulating pollution through proxies such as fertiliser use and livestock numbers, which can be less effective at reducing pollution. Calculated nitrogen surplus at the farm level, and nitrogen concentrations in wastewater discharges from municipal and industrial users, could set the basis for a nitrogen pollution charge regime to internalise the full cost of pollution, in line with the polluter pays principle.

Water quality cap and transfer can allow a more efficient polluter to expand output, while ensuring that the burden of pollution remains capped. In 2011, New Zealand implemented a globally unique water quality cap-and-trade market involving diffuse sources of nitrogen pollution in the Lake Taupo catchment. It is too early to assess the impact on water quality, but the market has provided the flexibility for land to move to its highest value use, while meeting the overall nitrogen load reduction targets (Duhon et al., 2015); however, this has come at a significant cost to the public to buy back land to retire from intensive agriculture.

This bold policy experiment provides lessons for establishing similar systems in other catchments at a lower cost. Determining the current level of water quality, the assimilative capacity of water bodies and the level of water quality required to maintain ecosystem functioning while accounting for time lags will be necessary as part of setting water quality caps at the catchment level. The measurement of both environmental costs and opportunity costs is a difficult exercise, one that a natural capital accounting approach may support. Further investment in calibration and validation of the OVERSEER® is required to improve its accuracy.

Agreements between industry and government such as the "Sustainable Dairying: Water Accord" have had success in improving water quality. Thanks to this accord, environmental best practices (e.g. fencing dairy cattle off from waterways) have been put in place more rapidly than would have occurred through new regulations, which require public consultation and are open to potentially lengthy court cases.

Financing water resource management

The droughts of 2007-09 and 2012-13 demonstrated the vulnerability of New Zealand's weather-dependent and predominantly pasture-based agriculture industry and economy to variable rainfall patterns. The government is providing grants and concessional financing to help fulfil irrigation's potential to increase export earnings and accelerate New Zealand's economic development; NZD 400 million has been allocated for irrigation schemes in 2016-19. Creating greater efficiency in water use and augmenting surface and groundwater flows have the potential to reduce pressure on water resources and address over-allocation. There are economic benefits from supporting the development of irrigation; it contributed an estimated NZD 2.17 billion to the national economy in 2011/12 and this value continues to grow. However, these estimates do not include environmental and social impacts of irrigation, or the marginal benefits of individual projects, and the benefits largely accrue to the agriculture and processing industries.

Government promotion of, and financial support for, increasing irrigation and more intensive agriculture – without operational rules and regulation to protect river flows and water quality under the NPS-FM and reflected in regional plans – are likely to further increase pressures on freshwater resources. Environmental gains may be limited if more efficient irrigation techniques do not result in lower net water use, but simply allow an increase in irrigated volume or area. The government also provides funding across multiple schemes to enable greater protection of water bodies and to address historic pollution. An increase in water pollution associated with land-use intensification is recognised as a risk that needs to be managed, as it runs counter to the objectives of this water quality funding. Natural capital accounting could be explored to evaluate the costs and benefits of irrigation and clean-up projects compared to realistic alternative approaches, and assist with resource management decisions.

Greater financial support is required for regional councils, which are already struggling to manage freshwater effectively. Considerable finances will be needed to continue to fund regional collaborative groups and technical advisory groups, address historic pollution, and invest in science and innovative technologies to achieve freshwater objectives. Greater support and funding will also be required for regional councils to increase their capacity for more effective implementation, monitoring, enforcement and reporting. The government proposes to increase the ability of councils to recover costs from water users for monitoring, enforcement, research and management. The use of economic instruments could also be used as a source of revenue to recover costs for water management.

Recommendations on water resources management

- Foster coherence between water, climate and primary industry policies; develop a whole-of-government long-term strategy to increase the added value of export products within climate and freshwater quality and quantity objectives; explore options to diversify the agricultural sector, improve trade relations, tap into emerging markets.

National freshwater policy reform

- Continue partnerships with Maori/iwi in policy development and decision making at both central and local government levels; under the principles of the Treaty of Waitangi, address iwi proprietary and non-proprietary rights and interests in freshwater (quantity and quality).

Recommendations on water resources management *(cont.)*

- Increase financial support and capacity for regional councils to deliver on, and expedite implementation of, the National Policy Statement for Freshwater Management (NPS-FM); assist with the development of robust science at regional and catchment scales; encourage regional councils to make progress even without absolute science and enable flexibility in policy to periodically review water quantity and quality limits; increase investment in research and innovation to develop new water pollution abatement technologies (including OVERSEER®).
- Review implementation of the NPS-FM to ensure that water quantity and quality limits set locally are ambitious and comprehensive enough to achieve national ecosystem and human health objectives and public expectations; establish performance indicators to track and evaluate implementation of the NPS-FM by regional councils, and strengthen compliance monitoring and enforcement of resource consent conditions; ensure the revision or development of new water quality parameters is expedited to minimise the need for repeated community consultation and updates of regional plans.
- Require regional councils and collaborative groups to start discussions around water quality limits at the highest level (e.g. at water quality suitable for swimming); if necessary, the case can be made to argue away from such limits, within the bottom lines, if disproportionate costs can be proven.
- Develop a national framework for collaborative governance to ensure the appointment of collaborative groups reflect a balanced range of the community's interests, values and investments, including the unique position of Maori, as well as to clarify the process, including the ultimate line of decision making, the objectives of collaborative governance and expected use of outputs; develop indicators to test that collaborative group recommendations comply with, or give effect to, the RMA and the NPS-FM and to evaluate the cost effectiveness of collective action.

Financing water resource management

- Review government support for irrigation to ensure that funding is only provided for projects that would not proceed otherwise, and that have net community-wide benefits; conduct, and release publicly, cost-benefit analyses of irrigation projects that are eligible for financial support; any funding should seek to achieve the greatest return on investment in terms of long-term, measurable environmental, economic and social outcomes.

Economic instruments to manage water quantity and quality

- Rationalise and expand the use of water demand management measures, including volumetric pricing to recover costs of water management and reflect environmental impacts and opportunity costs associated with scarcity; strengthen and expand water markets where appropriate to encourage innovation and the efficient use of water, particularly in stressed and over-allocated catchments.
- Introduce pollution charges or enable water quality trading to internalise the environmental and opportunity costs of diffuse pollution from rural and urban sources, and promote innovation in pollution control; develop a strategic financing model for the remediation of historically contaminated water sites.
- Experiment with natural capital accounting to provide a basis for valuing water resources and freshwater ecosystems, and quantifying the costs and benefits of freshwater policy and management decisions.

5. Sustainable urban development

New Zealand is among the most urbanised countries in the world. In 2014, 86% of the population lived in cities and towns of 1 000 inhabitants or more (UN, 2014). This makes the environmental footprint of cities particularly important to national environmental performance and citizens' quality of life. Auckland, the only large city by international standards, accounts for roughly one-third (1.45 million) of the country's population and GDP. It hosts the country's major commercial and manufacturing centres, and serves as the most important logistical trade node. Other important cities are the capital Wellington and Christchurch (with nearly 400 000 residents each); another dozen towns are home to more than 50 000 inhabitants.

Most urban areas are experiencing pressures from population growth. Growth was particularly strong in Auckland and its two neighbouring cities Hamilton and Tauranga (with growth rates above 30% over 2000-15). Auckland's population is expected to increase by another 50% over the next 30 years. Urban population growth has provoked severe pressures on land use, environment, housing and water, and transport infrastructure, particularly in Auckland. The challenge for Auckland and other fast-growing cities is to accommodate a larger population in a way that makes more efficient use of space and infrastructure, and that enhances environmental sustainability, well-being and the economic viability of development. Coherent national policies promoting sustainable development and green growth are critical to support cities in achieving these objectives and to ensure coherence and consistency between national and local policies.

Key urban and environmental trends

As in many "new world" countries, cities in New Zealand have largely developed in tandem with the expansion of motorisation. As such, their urban form reflects the prevalence of private motor vehicles as the dominant transport mode, as well as a cultural preference for stand-alone houses (Howden-Chapman et al., 2015). Cities generally feature small high-density areas and large low-density peri-urban suburbs. Most have been expanding to accommodate their growing populations, with the lion's share of the new built-up area located at the city fringes and greenfields. Auckland's built-up area increased by about 10% since 2001 (Figure 3). However, with the city's population growing even faster, the city's population density has increased.

Despite expansion, housing supply has not met the demand of a rapidly growing population. House prices have risen sharply (by some 50% over 2013-16 in Auckland), eroding affordability and raising financial stability risks (OECD, 2015). The environmental performance of the housing stock in New Zealand cities is relatively poor. About 30% of New Zealand homes are poorly insulated and a quarter of homeowners and half of renters report problems with dampness or mould. This incurs significant economic costs, and is detrimental both to environmental performance (e.g. increasing energy consumption) and public health. New Zealand cities face spatial inequalities as wealthier and more educated people tend to live in suburbs nearer the city centre or with natural amenities (NZPC, 2016).

The level of public transport use has increased in most major cities, but remains low by OECD standards. In most cities, dwellers travel more than 90% of distances in private motor vehicles, facilitated by large areas devoted to roads and parking. Significant investment has expanded both Auckland's public transport and motorway capacity, which has helped accommodate population growth and keep congestion levels relatively stable over the past

Figure 3. **Population and built-up area are growing in many cities**

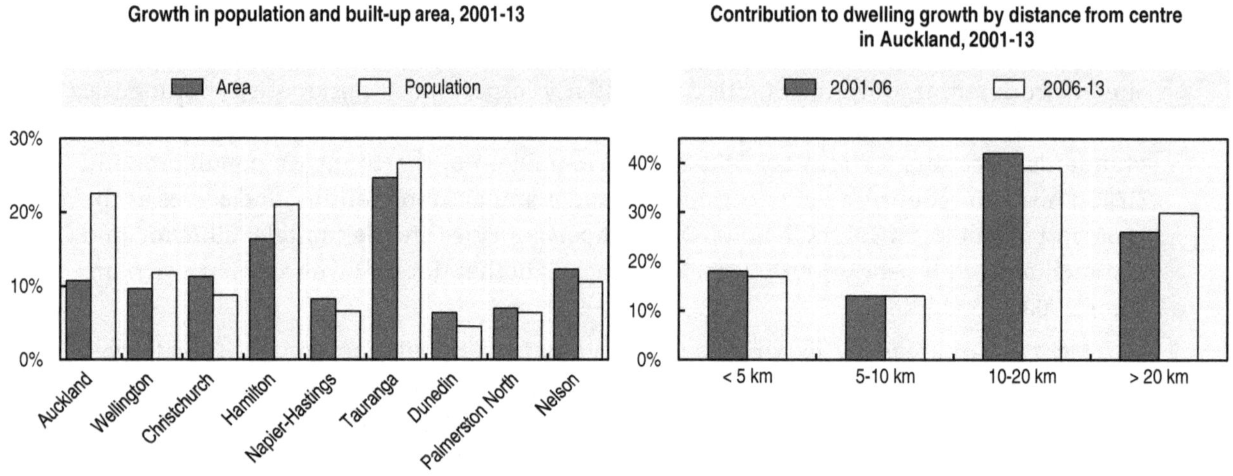

Source: Based on New Zealand Productivity Commission (2016), Better Urban Planning (draft); Nunns (2014), *Population-weighted densities in New Zealand and Australian cities: A new comparative dataset* (database).

StatLink http://dx.doi.org/10.1787/888933459632

15 years. However, the city's congestion levels remain the second highest in Oceania (TomTom, 2016). Heavy reliance on private motor vehicles results in air quality falling below required standards in areas close to highways and arterial roads (which are also heavily used by diesel-powered heavy vehicles). Transport-related energy use and greenhouse gas (GHG) emissions are high and increasing. Yet GHG emissions at city level have increased less than GDP and population growth. Auckland and Wellington have lower carbon dioxide emissions per capita than many cities in Australia, Canada or the United States.

Environmental quality of life in New Zealand cities is relatively high. Cities are relatively green, with large gardens and easy access to natural areas. Within Auckland's urban area, green spaces occupy a quarter of the land. Urban air quality has improved and is generally good compared to many cities in other OECD member countries; average concentrations of fine particulate matter and nitrogen oxides generally meet national standards or international guidelines for air quality. Further, 96% of the urban population is connected to wastewater treatment services (NZPC, 2016). However, sewerage infrastructure expansion and stormwater management have not kept pace with population growth. This has resulted in frequent overflows of sewerage systems in rainy periods, which can have severe impacts on water quality. More than half of Auckland's freshwater streams and a third of marine waters are in a degraded or poor state. In addition, urban expansion into greenfield areas has contributed to soil degradation and habitat fragmentation. A number of cities started implementing policies to reduce waste generation and encourage recycling, but data limitations hamper the tracking of progress. Many of these pressures are likely to intensify as the population and built-up area grow.

The institutional and policy frameworks for sustainable urban development

In contrast to many OECD member countries, New Zealand has no national policy, or vision, for urban development. Yet many cities, including the three largest ones, have adopted urban development strategies pursuing the goal of compact urban form. These strategies aim to reap the economic and social benefits from agglomeration, increase accessibility and public transport use and, ultimately, reduce potential environmental impacts of sprawling cities (NZPC, 2016). These cities have, therefore, adopted policies that constrain urban outward expansion and promote densification. However, several factors have prevented significant progress: institutional fragmentation; a complex planning system; insufficient national guidance; poor integration of land use, transport and infrastructure decisions; and lack of community support.

As in many countries, administrative boundaries do not match the extent of built-up areas in several New Zealand cities, which undermines coherent and integrated urban planning. To facilitate integrated decision making, a national law agglomerated all local authorities in the Auckland region (seven local councils and a regional council) into one single metropolitan governance body (named Auckland Council) in 2010 and required it to develop a spatial plan. The reform enabled the council to tackle issues beyond the capacity of previously individual councils (such as advancing network investments in the area of sewerage and wastewater management) and improved vertical co-ordination. Several smaller cities have, at their own initiative, established looser forms of inter-municipal collaboration, such as mayoral forums and joint working groups, but institutional co-ordination remains weak. The multiplicity of interlocutors for city governments at the national level, and insufficient co-ordination among them, limit an integrated approach to urban planning. In the absence of formal structures to co-ordinate large urban infrastructure projects, ad hoc collaborative processes try to resolve long-standing tensions between the central government and Auckland government in transport and housing (NZPC, 2016).

Three core pieces of legislation (Resource Management Act or RMA, Local Government Act and Land Transport Management Act) govern urban planning through a hierarchy of plans from the national to the local level. The different procedures, criteria and timeframes for planning and decision making required by these acts have led to a proliferation of local planning documents, duplication of efforts and considerable investment of time and resources by all parties involved.

National guidance is lacking on how to implement the RMA (the primary land-use legislation) in urban settings and on how to reconcile different planning instruments. This has led to inconsistencies across plans, misalignment of policy and application of unnecessarily restrictive and complex land-use regulations, which have ultimately frustrated both the objectives of urban growth and environmental protection. In a welcome step, the government announced that the National Policy Statement (NPS) on Urban Development Capacity would come into effect in December 2016. However, the NPS focuses heavily on land supply and capacity for housing and business development. While it requires the integration of infrastructure, business and residential planning, it misses the opportunity to provide city councils with guidance on how to manage urban growth in a way that would enhance urban environmental performance.

Spatial plans (i.e. plans integrating land use, housing, transport, infrastructure and other urban planning issues) are not mandatory in New Zealand cities, with the exception of Auckland. In 2012, the Auckland Council adopted the Auckland Plan, a comprehensive spatial plan that established a clear vision and strategic direction for the region's development over 30 years, accompanied by objectives and measurable targets. Land use, housing, transport and infrastructure planning documents are to be explicitly aligned to the Auckland Plan for prioritising resource allocation. Some cities (or groups of neighbouring authorities) have also moved towards strategic spatial planning on a voluntary basis. However, these strategies have limited legal weight and no formal links with statutory planning and budgeting processes under the three core acts mentioned above, which hampers their implementation.

Despite recent reforms to streamline decision-making processes (Section 2), processes to establish or change land-use rules and regulations are complex and slow; it can take more than eight years on average to develop a new land-use plan and four years for councils to amend an existing one. This is in part related to the resistance of land- and homeowners to urban development that could affect the value of their properties and the character of their neighbourhoods. Local interest groups have often used the extensive rights of appeal under the RMA to thwart development of wider public interest (NZPC, 2016). Against this background, special legislation was passed for the development of Auckland's land-use plan (the Auckland Unitary Plan). The process combined extended public publication at the early stages of the process with limited rights of appeal once the plan is approved. The 2015 Resource Legislation Amendment Bill (under discussion at the time of writing) envisages a similar collaborative process. Information campaigns and demonstration projects could be used to influence the prevailing risk aversion and conservative attitudes.

A common set of urban environmental and economic indicators (e.g. housing density, housing quality, water and waste management, access to green spaces) would help benchmark cities and compare best practices, both within New Zealand and internationally. It would also improve transparency, support decision making and allow better evaluation of urban development and planning. Some cities collect and publish data on selected variables (such as water consumption and GHG emissions); however, these data are neither collected systematically nor compiled at national level. The newly-formed Auckland Council published its first comprehensive State of the Environment Report in 2010.

Land use and building regulations

In the context of legislative uncertainty and limited national guidance, many local authorities have struggled to develop effective tools to guide land use. Land use is predominantly managed through regulatory measures, taking the form of urban growth boundaries and zoning. To date, these tools have shown limited success in guiding urban form (e.g. achieving compact development objectives), while indirectly contributing to rising land and house prices in fast-growing cities. Land prices inside Auckland's urban growth boundary are nearly ten times higher than outside, while a suite of complex and restrictive land-use rules (e.g. building heights, minimum lot sizes, etc.) has made inner-city development more difficult and expensive (NZPC, 2016; OECD, 2015; Zheng, 2013). Some rules, such as parking requirements, may run counter to sustainability objectives (e.g. they favour private car use over other transport modes).

To ease pressures on housing supply, the proposed Auckland Unitary Plan would substantially revise land-use rules. Specifically, they would allow for significant intensification in some districts, while enlarging the urban area through a new, more flexible growth boundary. In addition, an accord between the government and Auckland Council established some 100 Special Housing Areas for new development with reduced consenting times and limitations for appeals. However, most of these areas are situated in greenfield areas, potentially frustrating intensification objectives. Any regulatory measure used to increase housing supply should be carefully assessed against its effects on urban form and its contribution to reducing fossil fuel consumption and related emissions from private car use and buildings, and soil and habitat degradation. At the same time, tackling the housing shortage will also require actions beyond land supply, including addressing bottlenecks in the construction industry and reviewing tax provisions that favour real estate investment over other forms of long-term wealth accumulation.

The government has taken significant action to improve the quality of the built environment. Subsidies under *Warm Up New Zealand: Healthy Homes* retrofitted about 15% of the national housing stock. However, 30% of homes remain uninsulated, many of which are rental buildings. The government recently strengthened insulation requirements for rental properties (which will take effect in 2019). To avoid retrofitting needs for new housing, the government should consider modernising national building standards, which are below standards required in many other OECD member countries. New Zealand operates different voluntary building performance rating tools. Making assessments (e.g. for energy performance) mandatory for certain buildings, and gradually rolling out requirements to a larger share of the housing stock, would encourage the market to factor in energy efficiency into property prices. Building performance could also be linked to fiscal instruments (e.g. development contributions in Wellington are lower for buildings with strong environmental performance), or ease regulatory requirements (e.g. granting additional floor area for high-performing buildings).

Economic instruments for sustainable urban development

New Zealand should consider more systematic use of pricing instruments to achieve urban policy objectives. Some cities introduced pricing instruments in water and waste management, with positive results. Water charges helped per capita water consumption drop by roughly 30% since the introduction of universal metering and volumetric charging in Auckland, Tauranga and Nelson. Water consumption remains significantly higher in cities that do not charge for water supply by volume (e.g. Christchurch and Wellington). Current legislation limits the ability of cities to apply volumetric charges to wastewater services and make greater use of road tolls and congestion charges (NZPC, 2016).

There is also wide scope to make better use of pricing instruments to encourage efficient land use. Development contributions (levied to finance infrastructure) do not reflect the true cost of providing infrastructure to a specific area. This makes inefficient land use artificially cheap (e.g. "leapfrog development" that takes place away from existing infrastructure) and potentially accelerates urban sprawl. Limited distinctions between development contributions across building types and characteristics (e.g. size or energy efficiency) translate into weak incentives for developers to build high-performance buildings or low-impact infrastructure. Financial contributions (levied to reflect costs of development on the environment) are often charged at a fixed rate, rather than being based on the marginal environmental damage of development, and the Resource Legislation Amendment Bill proposed to remove them entirely. Property taxes (called *rates*) are mostly levied on the basis of capital value (rather than land value), which may favour greenfield over infill developments insofar as they are permitted.

Expansion of pricing instruments would also diversify funding options available to city councils; many councils need significant investment to accommodate population growth, including in water and wastewater, roads and public transport infrastructure. The central government finances about half of local roads or public transport, but entirely finances state highways; this creates incentives for local government to opt for state highway over local road and public transport solutions (PCE, 2016a). Funding heavily relies on property taxation (i.e. general rates), which implies large cross-subsidies from the general public and weakened incentives for councils to accommodate growth (as infrastructure investment may lead to a higher tax burden on the community). User- and beneficiary-based funding (e.g. through road and water pricing and better targeted development contributions) would reduce the burden on the public budget; at the same time, it would contribute to better demand management and more efficient use of land and resources. There may be room for the tax system to capture windfall gains accruing to landowners from infrastructure improvement (e.g. betterment levies) and rezoning land for urban use (land-value capture) to pay for required infrastructure.

Recommendations on sustainable urban development

The policy and planning framework

- Examine how to improve procedures, criteria and timeframes for planning and decision making to allow for more integrated and timely management of natural resources and urban environment while preserving the ability for effective local participation.
- Consider making spatial planning mandatory for all urban areas with population over 100 000, while simplifying infrastructure and transport planning requirements; provide greater recognition and legal weight to spatial planning initiatives in smaller urban areas, and guidance on how spatial planning should be conducted; at the very least, clarify the hierarchical relationships and linkages across planning instruments for land use, infrastructure and transport and, where possible, align planning horizons and review periods.
- Broaden the scope of the National Policy Statement on Urban Development Capacity, or develop other legally binding measures to ensure that local planning processes and instruments i) recognise and encourage good urban design outcomes and principles for sustainable urban development; ii) identify and appropriately manage important or sensitive environmental systems; and iii) incorporate climate change mitigation goals and resilience against climate change and natural hazards.
- Facilitate the decision-making process to change existing land-use plans and reduce the scope for vested interests to thwart development of wider public interests (e.g. by front-loading public consultations and ensuring an independent expert review of proposed plans and suggestions from the public).
- Create a common set of urban environmental and economic indicators to increase transparency on cities' environmental performance, facilitate benchmarking and identification of best practices, inform decision making and allow for better policy evaluation.

Institutional framework and multi-level governance

- Establish a national co-operative structure comprising national institutions with responsibilities for urban-related matters (e.g. on the model of the Natural Resources Sector), with a view to improving horizontal and vertical policy co-ordination.
- Consider replicating the Auckland institutional reform in other major urban areas, with the necessary adjustments, and encourage partnerships among smaller municipalities with a view to overcoming institutional and land-use planning fragmentation.

Regulations and economic instruments for sustainable urban development

- Ensure that regulations in land-use plans pass robust cost-benefit analyses that consider environmental outcomes (including effects on transport, green spaces, etc.), as well as economic and social outcomes (including distributional consequences and intergenerational equity).

Recommendations on sustainable urban development *(cont.)*

- Make more systematic use of development contributions and rates to guide efficient and sustainable urban land use by: i) differentiating development contributions along the location and type of development to reflect the true cost of development on infrastructure and service provision; ii) considering adjusting development contributions and rates where development yields positive effects on the environment; and considering maintaining financial contributions or develop other instruments to reflect the environmental costs of developments.
- Remove barriers to road pricing (e.g. road tolls and congestion charging) and encourage councils to introduce volumetric charging for drinking water supply, with a view to foster efficient use of infrastructure and resources, while reducing the burden on local government budgets.
- Consider the use of betterment levies (e.g. through targeted rates) as an additional cost-recovery mechanism for infrastructure and services provision, especially where development and financial contributions do not apply; and explore alternative instruments to finance urban infrastructure, including taxing windfall gains occurring to landowners following rezoning of urban land (value capture).
- Review whether the current design of property taxation is aligned with land-use objectives and assess the potential benefits of shifting the property tax structure towards a land tax or to split rates.
- Assess the environmental, social and economic implications of the funding model for roads and public transport; promote innovation encouraging alternative options for public transport (e.g. car-sharing, demand-responsive transport in small or low-density cities), while continuing to expand and improve conventional public transport services.

Sustainable housing

- Improve the environmental performance of the building stock to reduce health impacts from poor insulation and the emission of air pollutants from inefficient heating by: i) modernising and strengthening national building standards; ii) establishing supplementary incentives to promote investment in insulation and modern heating in rental buildings; and iii) encouraging new housing to meet best practice urban design and sustainable housing principles.
- Ensure that areas of fast-track residential development (notably those created under the Special Housing Act) are screened against environmental impacts, especially against cumulative and irreversible impacts.

Notes

1. See Section 4 for water management.
2. The one-for-two arrangements (removed in mid-2016) had allowed non-forestry sector participants to surrender one emission allowance for every two tonnes of CO_2 emission, thereby halving the number of allowances needed.
3. The revealed technological advantage index measures the share of an economy's patents in a specific technology relative to the share of total patents owned. The index is equal to zero when the economy has no patents in a given field, equals one when the economy's share in the technology field is equivalent to its share in all fields (no specialisation) and rises above one when specialisation is observed.

References

APEC (2015), "Peer review on fossil fuel subsidy reforms in New Zealand", *Final Report*, September, 2015, Asia-Pacific Economic Co-operation, Singapore.

Aqualinc (2010), "Update of water allocation data and estimate of actual water use of consented takes 2009-10", report commissioned by the Ministry for the Environment, No. H10002/3, Aqualinc Research Ltd, Christchurch.

Bibbee, A. (2011), "Green growth and climate change policies in New Zealand", *OECD Economics Department Working Papers*, No. 893, OECD Publishing, Paris, *http://dx.doi.org/10.1787/5kg51mc6k98r-en*.

Brown, M.A. (2016), *Pathways to Prosperity: Safeguarding Biodiversity in Development*, Environmental Defence Society, Auckland.

Brown, M.A. (2015), *Vanishing Nature: Facing New Zealand's Biodiversity Crisis*, Environmental Defence Society, Auckland.

Climate Action Tracker (2016), Countries: New Zealand website, (last updated 2 November 2016), *http://climateactiontracker.org/countries/newzealand.html* (accessed November 2016).

Duhon, M., H. McDonald and S. Kerr (2015), "Nitrogen trading in Lake Taupo: An analysis and evaluation of an innovative water management policy", *Working Paper*, No. 15-07, Motu Economic and Public Policy Research, Wellington.

EDS (2016), *Evaluating the Environmental Impacts of the RMA*, Environmental Defence Society, Auckland.

Harding, M. (2014), "Personal tax treatment of company cars and commuting expenses: Estimating the fiscal and environmental costs", *OECD Taxation Working Papers*, No. 20, OECD Publishing, Paris, *http://dx.doi.org/10.1787/5jz14cg1s7vl-en*.

Howden-Chapman, P. et al. (2015), "Survey of sentiments about cities", in Early, L., P. Howden-Chapman and M. Russell (eds.), *Drivers of Urban Change*, e-book, Steele Roberts, Wellington.

IEA (forthcoming), *Energy Policies of IEA Countries: New Zealand Review*, IEA/OECD Publishing, Paris.

Larned, S.T. et al. (2016), "Water quality in New Zealand rivers: Current state and trends", *New Zealand Journal of Marine and Freshwater Research*, Vol. 50/3, Royal Society of New Zealand, Taylor & Francis and Routledge, pp. 389-417.

Leining, C. and S. Kerr (2016), "Lessons learned from the New Zealand Emissions Trading Scheme", *Motu Working Paper*, No. 16-06, Motu Economic and Public Policy Research, Wellington.

MfE (2016a), *New Zealand's Action on Climate Change*, September 2016, Ministry for the Environment, Wellington.

MfE (2016b), *National Monitoring System for 2014/15* (database), Ministry for the Environment, Wellington, *www.mfe.govt.nz/rma/rma-monitoring-and-reporting/reporting-201415* (accessed 10 July 2016).

MfE (2016c), Feedback on Freshwater Reforms – 2016 website, *www.mfe.govt.nz/fresh-water/reform-programme/freshwater-reforms-2016/feedback-fresh-water-reforms-2016* (accessed 12 July 2016).

MfE (2016d), *Next Steps for Fresh Water: Consultation Document*, Ministry for the Environment, Wellington.

MfE (2015), *New Zealand's Second Biennial Report under the United Nations Framework Convention on Climate Change*, Ministry for the Environment, Wellington.

MfE and Statistics NZ (2015), *New Zealand's Environmental Reporting Series: Environment Aotearoa 2015*, Ministry for the Environment and Statistics New Zealand, Wellington.

Ministry of Health (2016), "Drinking-water legislation", webpage, *www.health.govt.nz/our-work/environmental-health/drinking-water/drinking-water-legislation* (accessed May 2016).

NZPC (2016), *Better Urban planning: Draft Report*, New Zealand Productivity Commission, Wellington.

NZTA (2015), "National Land Transport Fund Annual Report", provided to the Minister of Transport and presented to the House of Representatives pursuant to section 11 of the Land Transport Management Act and section 150 of the Crown Entities Act 2004 for the year ended 30 June 2015, New Zealand Transport Agency.

OECD (2016a), *Effective Carbon Rates: Pricing CO_2 through Taxes and Emissions Trading Systems*, OECD Publishing, Paris, *http://dx.doi.org/10.1787/9789264260115-en*.

OECD (2016b), *Inventory of Support Measures for Fossil Fuels* (database), *www.oecd.org/site/tadffss/data/* (accessed September 2016).

OECD (2016c), *Measuring Distance to the SDGs Targets: A Pilot Assessment of where OECD Countries Stand*, OECD Publishing, Paris, *www.oecd.org/std/OECD-Measuring-Distance-to-SDGs-Targets-Pilot-Study.pdf*.

OECD (2015), *OECD Economic Surveys: New Zealand 2015*, OECD Publishing, Paris, *http://dx.doi.org/10.1787/eco_surveys-nzl-2015-en*.

OECD (2014), *OECD Science, Technology and Industry Outlook 2014*, OECD Publishing, Paris, *http://dx.doi.org/10.1787/sti_outlook-2014-en*.

OECD (2013a), *OECD Economic Surveys: New Zealand 2013*, OECD Publishing, Paris, *http://dx.doi.org/10.1787/eco_surveys-nzl-2013-en*.

OECD (2013b), *OECD Compendium of Agri-environmental Indicators*, OECD Publishing, Paris, *http://dx.doi.org/10.1787/9789264181151-en*.

Office of the Auditor-General (2011), *Managing Freshwater Quality: Challenges for Regional Councils*, Office of the Auditor-General, Wellington.

Palmer, G. and R. Blakeley (2015), "Submission on New Zealand Productivity Commission's better urban planning inquiry", *Issues Paper*, Submission 007, March 2016, New Zealand Productivity Commission, Wellington.

PCE (2016a), "Emissions Trading Scheme Review 2015/16: Other matters", Submission to the Minister for Climate Change Issues, Parliamentary Commissioner for the Environment, Wellington.

PCE (2016b), *The State of New Zealand's Environment: Commentary by the Parliamentary Commissioner for the Environment on Environment Aotearoa 2015*, 29 June 2016, Parliamentary Commissioner for the Environment, Wellington.

PCE (2015a), "Preparing New Zealand for rising seas: certainty and uncertainty", report prepared for the Ministry for the Environment, November 2015, Parliamentary Commissioner for the Environment, Wellington.

PCE (2015b), *Water Quality in New Zealand: Land Use and Nutrient Pollution, Update Report*, Parliamentary Commissioner for the Environment, Wellington.

PCE (2013a), *Investigating the Future of Conservation: The Case of Stewardship Land*, Parliamentary Commissioner for the Environment, Wellington.

PCE (2013b), *Water Quality in New Zealand: Land Use and Nutrient Pollution*, Parliamentary Commissioner for the Environment, Wellington.

Royal Society of New Zealand (2016), *Transition to a Low-carbon Economy for New Zealand*, Royal Society of New Zealand, Wellington.

TomTom (2016), TomTom Traffic Index website, *www.tomtom.com/en_nz/trafficindex/* (accessed 18 July 2016).

UN (2014), *World Urbanization Prospects: The 2014 Revision*, United Nations, New York.

Zheng, G. (2013), "The effect of Auckland's metropolitan urban limit on land prices", *Research Note*, March 2013, New Zealand Productivity Commission, Wellington.

ANNEX

Actions taken to implement selected recommendations from the 2007 OECD *Environmental Performance Review of New Zealand*

RECOMMENDATIONS	ACTIONS TAKEN
Chapter 1. Environmental performance: Trends and recent developments	
Increase regulatory support for recovery or recycling (including deposit-refund systems) of priority waste, such as end-of-life vehicles and electronic goods, building on the extended producer responsibility principle.	The Waste Minimisation Act 2008 requires product stewardship schemes to be developed for certain "priority products" where there is a high risk of environmental harm from the waste or significant benefits from recovering the product (no priority products have been declared to date). It also establishes a process for government accreditation of voluntary product stewardship schemes with businesses and organisations (14 voluntary schemes have been accredited to date).
Issue national policy guidance concerning conservation of biodiversity on private land, and ensure that nature conservation objectives are fully reflected in spatial and coastal plans.	The National Coastal Policy Statement was promulgated in 2010. It will guide the next generation of coastal plans. The government held consultations for a proposed National Policy Statement for Indigenous Biodiversity, but this did not pass into law. The government plans to re-launch a stakeholder dialogue to develop a new national policy statement for biodiversity by late 2018.
Strengthen and harmonise monitoring of major pressures on biodiversity and ecosystems, both within and outside protected areas.	The Department of Conservation (DOC) has implemented a national system for monitoring of overall trends, trends for specific species and effect of management actions in protected areas, as well as a national database of freshwater ecosystems.
Finalise and implement the ocean policy and pursue the further expansion of marine reserves and the strengthening of regional co-operation for the management of high seas fish stocks.	Several marine reserves have been created. The Marine Reserves Act is being revised to provide for a greater variety of protected areas. The 2012 Exclusive Economic Zone and Continental Shelf (Environmental Effects) Act promotes the sustainable management of natural resources in the Exclusive Economic Zone. New Zealand participates in international marine protection measures (such as the International Plan of Action for Conservation and Management of Sharks) and organisations (such as the Commission for the Conservation of the Antarctic Living Resources, the Western and Central Pacific Fisheries Commission, and the Commission for the Conservation of Southern Bluefin Tuna).
Adopt and implement a clear and comprehensive package of climate change policy measures (e.g. economic instruments, flexible mechanisms) to meet New Zealand's international commitments, giving consideration to setting sectoral targets; develop strategies for future climate protection commitments in line with guidelines of the Intergovernmental Panel on Climate Change.	The 2002 Climate Change Response Act (and its subsequent amendments) remains the framework legislation addressing New Zealand's climate-related international obligations. New Zealand set the targets of reducing greenhouse gas (GHG) emissions by 5% below 1990 levels by 2020, by 30% below 2005 levels by 2030 (nationally determined contribution or NDC), and by 50% below 1990 levels by 2050. Sectoral targets have not been set. Climate mitigation policy has largely relied on forest sinks and carbon pricing via the Emissions Trading Scheme, but a clear and comprehensive policy package has not been developed. In September 2016, the government announced the establishment of three expert groups on agricultural biological emissions, forestry and adaptation to build the evidence base on these issues.

RECOMMENDATIONS	ACTIONS TAKEN
Define and implement measures to reduce net GHG emissions from the agriculture and forestry sectors, prioritising those that also meet other environmental objectives (e.g. flood protection, nature conservation) so as to capture "win-win" opportunities. Give consideration to allocating carbon sink credits and liabilities to forest owners, and ensure that the agriculture sector reduces its GHG emissions through low-cost practice changes and efficiency gains (e.g. energy efficiency improvements, increased biogas recovery).	Forestry was the first sector to enter the New Zealand Emissions Trading Scheme (NZ ETS) in 2008; emission allowances are issued against eligible emission removals from forest management. The Afforestation Grant Scheme (first established in 2008) promotes carbon sequestration and sustainable land use; other grant schemes are in place to encourage afforestation and carbon storage, reduce soil erosion, and improve water quality. In the agriculture sector, mitigation options have focused on increasing the productivity per animal and overall efficiency of farms, as well as on investment in research in new technology to reducing biological GHG emissions. The government, in co-operation with the business sector, has launched several initiatives to support research and development in reducing the environmental impact from agriculture, primarily on GHG emissions and water quality. New Zealand participates in research networks such as the Global Research Alliance on Agricultural Greenhouse Gases.
Chapter 2. Environmental governance and management	
Develop national regulations specifically concerning the management of hazardous waste and introduce mandatory and comprehensive systems for tracking its transport, treatment and disposal.	No action taken.
Clarify liability arrangements for the remediation of contaminated sites, and develop financing mechanisms that apply the polluter pays principle as fully as possible.	In 2011, the Ministry for the Environment reviewed the liability arrangements for contaminated land. Liability is limited to contamination created after the Resource Management Act (RMA) came into effect (1991) and rests with the current landowner who can pursue actual responsible parties. The government's Contaminated Sites Remediation Fund (CSRF) was established in 2003 to assist landowners subject to eligibility and assessment criteria to remediate their contaminated land.
Ensure that national sustainable development objectives are reflected in territorial development plans and resource consents.	Since 2007, New Zealand has adopted four National Policy Statements (NPSs) and four National Environmental Standards (NESs). In accordance with the RMA, regional and territorial policies and plans must give effect to NPSs (i.e. national objectives and policies) and comply with NESs (i.e. technical rules).
Strengthen compliance with the environmental conditions set in resource consents and permits (e.g. concerning disposal of dairy effluents, timber harvest in private indigenous forests) through increased inspection and enforcement.	In 2014/15, compliance monitoring covered 60% of resource consents that required monitoring according to their conditions. More than 20% of resource consents were found to be non-compliant. The use of administrative enforcement tools is rather limited, corresponding to 30% of non-compliance cases in 2014/15. In the area of criminal enforcement, the Resource Management Amendment Act (2009) raised the maximum fine for convictions under the RMA from NZD 200 000 (for both companies and individuals) to NZD 300 000 for individuals and NZD 600 000 for companies (with an additional daily fine for a continuing offence).
Assure independent evaluation of the effectiveness of voluntary agreements and covenants in reducing environmental pressures from agriculture and forestry activities. Assure the effectiveness of voluntary agreements, requiring clear environmental performance targets, regular reporting and third-party auditing.	The "Sustainable Dairying: Water Accord", concluded between the government and the dairy industry, establishes several measurable targets (e.g. for exclusion of livestock from waterways, installation of water meters at farms, and collection of nutrient management information). The multi-stakeholder Dairy Environment Leadership Group (DELG) oversees the accord's implementation. An independent third party audits annual reports. DairyNZ and the Dairy Companies Association of New Zealand report to DELG annually on progress against accord commitments. Around 71% of the plantation forestry estate is under third party sustainable forest management certification. Forest Stewardship Council certification includes regular audits.
Expand availability of quantitative indicators and time series data related to environmental quality, assuring policy relevance and public access. Strengthen monitoring of air and water quality, and waste generation and treatment, assuring baseline consistency of methods used at local level to facilitate data aggregation and periodic reporting of key environmental indicators at national level.	The Environmental Reporting Act (2015) provides a legal framework for national-level reporting. A first comprehensive *Environment Aotearoa* report was published in 2015. The Ministry for the Environment has partnered with local government to take forward the EMaR (Environmental Monitoring and Reporting) initiative, which aims to improve the collection, collation, publication and reuse of environmental data. Its public interface, the Land, Air, Water Aotearoa (LAWA) data discovery portal, has published freshwater and coastal water information to date. EMaR is also co-ordinating programmes of work to develop and implement National Environmental Monitoring Standards (NEMS). Multiple NEMS have been completed, and more are in progress.
Continue to promote the integration of environmental education in school curricula and in occupational training.	The Ministry of Education has issued guidelines for environmental education in schools. The national Enviroschools programme has continued to expand, now covering nearly 1 000 establishments.

RECOMMENDATIONS	ACTIONS TAKEN
Chapter 3. Towards green growth	
Strengthen and extend measures to decouple environmental pressures from economic growth, where possible using market-based approaches to ensure that environmental costs are reflected in prices.	New Zealand has extended the use of economic instruments to put a price on environmental externalities. It launched a GHG emissions trading system in 2008, piloted a nitrogen cap-and-trade system in the Lake Taupo catchment and introduced some new environmentally related taxes, namely the waste disposal levy and a levy on goods containing synthetic GHGs. Some local authorities use volume-based waste charges and volumetric water charges.
Further strengthen measures to promote energy efficiency in the transport, energy and industrial sectors (e.g. energy taxation and pricing, product standards, building codes).	The NZ ETS is the main pricing instrument to encourage energy efficiency improvements in the transport, energy and industrial sectors. Other measures include: support programmes for building insulation (Warm Up New Zealand programmes), voluntary energy performance rating for building (NABERSNZ, Home Star and Green Star), fuel economy labelling for vehicles, and road user charge exemption for electric vehicles.
Augment measures to encourage improved emission performance of motor vehicles and to internalise the environmental costs of road transport (e.g. fuel taxes, fuel quality standards, inspection of in-use motor vehicles, road user charges).	New Zealand has strengthened vehicle exhaust regulations and fuel quality standards. It applies fuel economy labelling for light vehicles and a voluntary heavy vehicle fuel efficiency programme, but there are no mandatory standards for vehicle fuel efficiency and emissions. Electric vehicles are exempt from the road user change. Vehicle taxes are not differentiated according to vehicles' environmental and energy performance, and fuel tax rates do not take into account environmental costs of road transport.
Increase levels of official development assistance and continue to mainstream environmental concerns into ODA.	Spending on official development assistance (ODA) increased in 2010-15, and the government plans to increase the assistance to USD 1.2 billion over three years starting from 2015/16. In 2015, net ODA disbursement were 0.27% of gross national income (GNI), compared to the internationally agreed target of 0.7% of GNI. More than 40% of total ODA directly or indirectly targets environmental objectives. The Aid Programme Strategic Plan for 2015-19 integrates environment and climate change as cross-cutting issues.
Chapter 4. Water resources management	
Further expand the knowledge base concerning sustainable abstraction levels of key aquifers, and strengthen regulatory control of total allowable abstraction.	In 2015, GNS Science (a government-owned research company) mapped New Zealand's aquifers and estimated groundwater volumes. The Resource Management (Measuring and Reporting of Water Takes) Regulations 2010 require consented water abstractions over 5L/s to be metered and reported from November 2016. The National Policy Statement for Freshwater Management requires regional councils to set sustainable abstraction limits and to phase out any existing over-allocation. Information about interconnectivity between groundwater and surface water remains limited.
Issue a national policy statement on freshwater quality, establish national environmental standards for drinking water sources and strengthen national approaches for protecting receiving water quality.	A National Policy Statement for Freshwater Management was issued in 2011, and subsequently amended in 2014, to provide additional guidance to regional councils, including minimum standards for water quality in lakes and rivers. The National Environmental Standard for Sources of Human Drinking Water 2007 and the Health (Drinking Water) Amendment Act 2007 have strengthened drinking water legislation and the protection of drinking water sources.
Introduce market-based instruments to internalise the environmental costs of non-point source discharges from agriculture (e.g. run-off of fertilisers, urine from grazing stock).	The Lake Taupo cap-and-trade nitrogen market was launched in 2011 to address diffuse source pollution. There are no other examples of economic instruments such as pollution charges and water quality trading.
Consider introducing cap-and-trade systems and other regulatory and market-based instruments to rationalise the allocation of water abstraction rights in water-stressed regions.	Water is allocated on a first-in, first-served basis. The transfer of water permits is permitted under section 136 of the RMA, but not used widely in practice. The 2016 *Next steps for freshwater: Consultation document* includes a proposal to better enable the transfer of water permits. There are no resource rental fees (abstraction charges) that reflect the environmental or scarcity costs.
Further apply sustainable land and forest management approaches (e.g. environmental farm planning, nutrient budgeting, application of sustainable forest management practices) and assess their effectiveness in reducing pressures on the environment.	Industry representatives (dairy, horticulture, and sheep and beef) offer a range of environmental advisory services. Some regional councils require nutrient budgeting and farm environmental management plans. The Freshwater Improvement Fund, established in 2014, helps water users move to managing within environmental water quantity and quality limits. The Sustainable Farming Fund, launched in 2000, funds collaborative projects for improved water management. The environmental effectiveness of these initiatives has not been assessed. The "Sustainable Dairying: Water Accord" 2014 (a voluntary agreement between government and the dairy industry) has encouraged the uptake of environmental best practices (e.g. fencing dairy cattle off from waterways) more rapidly than would have occurred through new government regulations.

RECOMMENDATIONS	ACTIONS TAKEN
Chapter 5. Sustainable urban development	
Expand measures to reduce health risks associated with poor indoor air quality, substandard housing and unsafe heating.	The *Warm Up New Zealand* programmes have provided subsidies to households for improving insulation and heating systems, and have contributed retrofitting nearly 20% of the housing stock. As from 2016, the *Warm Up New Zealand: Healthy Home* programme focuses on rental properties occupied by low-income tenants in high health needs. Regulations for ventilation of buildings have been strengthened. The 2016 Residential Tenancies Amendment Act strengthened floor and roof insulation requirements for social housing and rented homes (which will take effect in 2019). The National Environmental Standards on Air Quality include a design standard for new wood burners installed in urban areas; several regions impose stricter standards.
Review systems for charging users for waste and wastewater services, identifying opportunities to strengthen economic incentives for resource conservation and efficiency.	The Waste Minimisation Act 2008 established the Waste Disposal Levy, which is imposed on waste disposed in landfills (currently at NZD 10 per tonne, limited to landfills accepting household waste). Volume-based waste charges are applied in some cities.
Strengthen and expand the use of water demand management measures (e.g. volumetric metering, pricing for full recovery of water management costs, water efficiency standards).	The 2010 Resource Management (Measurement and Reporting of Water Takes) Regulations requires water takes (of 5 litres/sec or more) to be measured and reported from November 2016. Some cities apply volumetric water pricing and established water-use efficiency goals (e.g. Auckland).
Expand and upgrade waste treatment and disposal facilities (e.g. landfills, hazardous waste platforms, wastewater treatment plants), promoting co-operation among territorial authorities where this will lead to economies of scale, and applying the polluter pays principle.	Agglomeration of eight local authorities to the Auckland Council provided preconditions for integrated waste management in the region. No other actions have been taken.

Source: Country submission.

PART I

Progress towards sustainable development

PART I

Chapter 1

Environmental performance: Trends and recent developments

New Zealand's population enjoys a high environmental quality of life, although strong economic growth has intensified energy and resource use and exerted increasing environmental pressures. This chapter examines the country's progress in decoupling economic activity from environmental pressures, focusing on the period since 2000. It presents the key socio-economic developments and reviews New Zealand's progress in moving towards i) an energy-efficient and low-carbon economy; ii) resource efficiency in material consumption waste management; iii) sustainable management of the natural asset base; and iv) a high environmental quality of life for its citizens.

The statistical data for Israel are supplied by and under the responsibility of the relevant Israeli authorities. The use of such data by the OECD is without prejudice to the status of the Golan Heights, East Jerusalem and Israeli settlements in the West Bank under the terms of international law.

1. Introduction

New Zealand is a remote island state in the South Pacific Ocean, comprising two main islands (the North and South Islands) and many smaller islands. It is one of the most dynamic economies in the OECD. Since 2000, vigorous economic growth has helped raise the living standards of the small, but increasing, population. Natural resources have been a pillar of this growth, with agriculture, forestry, fishery and tourism accounting for a larger share of gross domestic product (GDP) and exports than in many OECD member countries. At the same time, the natural environment is deeply rooted in the country's cultural identity. Environmental quality of life is generally high, but the strong reliance on natural resources, along with rising income and consumption, has resulted in increased emissions of greenhouse gases (GHGs) and some air pollutants, higher waste generation and stronger pressures on freshwater and biodiversity.

This chapter provides an overview of New Zealand's main achievements, as well as remaining challenges on the path towards green growth and sustainable development. Drawing on indicators from national and international sources, it reviews progress against national policy goals, as well as international commitments and targets, focusing on the period since 2000. To the extent possible, it compares the state of the environment and key environmental trends with those of other OECD member countries. The chapter sketches out major policy developments in relevant environmental sectors, including air, climate, waste, water and biodiversity.

2. Key economic and social developments

2.1. Economic structure and performance

New Zealand is a small, open and fast growing economy. The highly efficient agricultural sector continues to be a mainstay of the economy and to dominate the country's exports; it accounted for 7% of value added in 2015, more than three times the OECD average (Figure 1.1). New Zealand is the world's largest exporter of dairy products and sheep meat. Dairy and other animal products and meat accounted for about 40% of total goods exports in 2014 (with dairy products alone representing nearly three-quarters of these exports). Fast rising milk prices spurred the conversion of land mostly from sheep and beef farming to dairy in the last two decades (Chapter 4). New Zealand is also among the largest exporters of forestry products in the OECD. Overall, in 2014, wood products accounted for 7% of exports.

New Zealand's economy has a sizable and expanding service sector, accounting for 71% of GDP in 2015, some large-scale manufacturing industries (notably aluminium and metal production, and food processing) and high-tech manufacturing (Figure 1.1). The diverse, and sometimes spectacular, landscapes underpin the growing film industry and tourism sectors. The number of overseas visitors increased by about 13% over 2012-15, and is expected to grow further. In 2015, tourism accounted for nearly 5% of GDP, 7% of employment and 17% of total export revenue (second only to revenue from dairy exports) (Statistics NZ, 2016a).

Figure 1.1. **The New Zealand economy is growing faster than the OECD area**

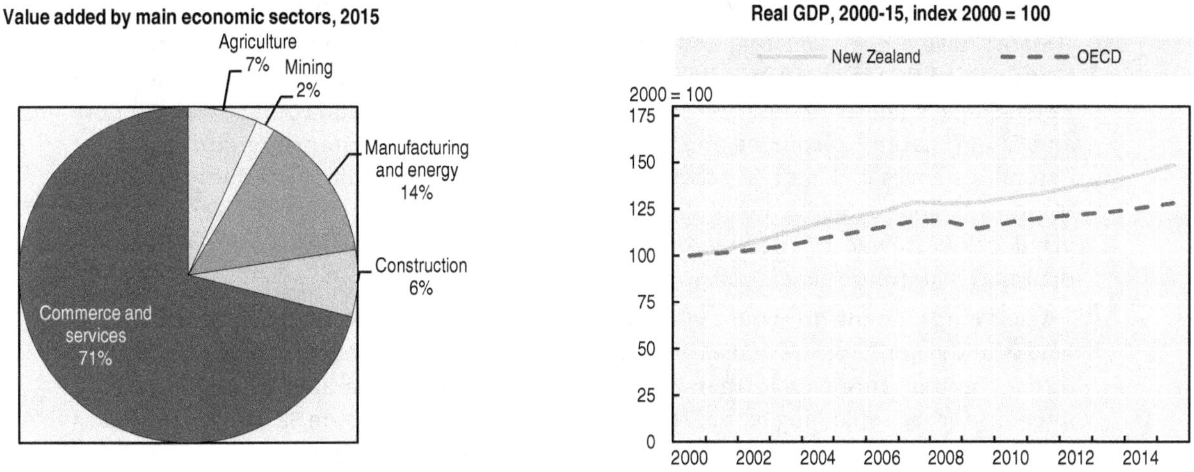

Source: OECD (2016), "OECD Economic Outlook No. 99 (Edition 2016/1)", *OECD Economic Outlook: Statistics and Projections* (database); Statistics NZ (2016), *Infoshare* (database).

StatLink http://dx.doi.org/10.1787/888933459642

New Zealand's economy grew by about 50% in real terms in 2000-15, faster than the OECD average (Figure 1.1). Exports have been the main engine of this growth. Further impulse came from the construction sector, given the reconstruction activities following the 2011 earthquake that destroyed large parts of the city of Christchurch.[1] Residential and infrastructure building in Auckland have also enjoyed sustained growth in response to strong population growth and housing demand (OECD, 2015a; also see Section 2.2 and Chapter 5). The strong economic expansion helped reduce unemployment to 5.8% in 2015, well below the OECD average (see Basic Statistics). After peaking to 3.4% in 2015, annual growth is expected to decelerate to about 3% per year in 2016/17 due to the decline of post-earthquake reconstruction activities, the decrease in the agricultural output caused by severe droughts and the decline in dairy prices (OECD, 2016a, 2015a).[2] Bottlenecks in housing, urban infrastructure and skills, inequalities in living standards and rising environmental pressures pose further risks to sustaining growth (OECD, 2016a, 2015a).

The country's fiscal position is strong. Government debt is low compared to other OECD member countries and the government budget is nearly balanced. Government spending and revenue are below the respective OECD averages (see Basic Statistics). The central government budget for environmental protection activities represented about 1% of total government expenditure in 2015 (Chapter 3). In 2014, revenue from environmentally related taxes amounted to 1.3% of GDP and 4.2% of total tax revenue, well below the corresponding OECD averages (see Basic Statistics; Chapter 3).

2.2. *Well-being and quality of life*

Sustained economic growth has helped further improve the well-being of New Zealand's small, but increasing, population. Between 2000 and 2015, New Zealand's population increased by 19%, partly owing to large net immigration flows (at rates of around 1% of the total population per year). In 2015, total population was 4.6 million, about three-quarters of which is of European descent. Maori, the second largest ethnic group accounting for 16% of the population, have a deep cultural relationship with the environment (Box 1.1). Other

Box 1.1. **Maori culture and the natural environment**

Maori have a deep spiritual and cultural relationship with the entire landscape of New Zealand that is based on a holistic view of the environment. Traditional values such as whakapapa (ancestral lineage) place Maori in an environmental context with all flora and fauna, natural resources and ecological systems. Kaitiakitanga (guardianship of natural resources by Maori, in accordance with custom and tradition) defines the role of Maori as temporary guardians of the richness of all life and matter. Maori recognise that privileges bestowed by the environment go hand-in-hand with the responsibility to maintain it for future generations.

Maori land amounts to about 15 000 km^2, or about 6% of the total land area. Most Maori land is in the north, centre and east of the North Island. Ownership of that land is divided into 2.7 million interests (ownership records), a figure comparable to the number of interests for the remaining part of the country. On average, there are 98 owners per Maori land block; a block average size is 0.5 km^2 (Maori Land Court, 2016).

Maori continue to assert claims of ownership and customary rights over natural resources within their tribal areas through the courts and the Waitangi Tribunal, which handles claims by Maori that the government has breached the treaty. Maori values are systematically taken into account by decision makers in New Zealand and have a strong influence on natural resource management (Chapter 2).

Source: Maori Land Court (2016); OECD (2007).

major ethnic groups include Asian and Pacific peoples (Statistics NZ, 2015a). Population is projected to reach about 5 million in 2025 and 5.8 million in 2050 (Statistics NZ, 2015b).

New Zealand's citizens enjoy high living standards, with all the components of the Better Life Index above the OECD average, with the exception of "income and wealth" (Figure 1.2). Per capita income increased by 25% in 2000-15, nearly closing the gap to the OECD average and further reducing regional disparities.[3] Yet, as in many other countries, income inequality and poverty have increased. Income inequality (as measured by the Gini coefficient) increased from below the OECD average in the mid-1980s to slightly above it in the mid-2010s (Figure 1.3; see Basic Statistics). This was largely due to increases in the inequality of market incomes, but also in part to policy reforms that reduced the redistributive capacity of the tax-benefit system (with lower progressivity of the tax system and social benefits). The poverty rate (measured as the number of people whose income is less than half of the median household income) is about 10%, in line with the OECD average. Nonetheless, child poverty is a concern,[4] and an increasing share of the population report they cannot afford to buy enough food (OECD, 2014; Simpson et al., 2015).

Poverty concerns are linked to the rising burden of housing costs on low-income households (OECD, 2015a). Housing costs represent on average almost one-fourth of household disposable income, the eighth highest value in the OECD. Rapid population growth and a low responsiveness of supply have led to housing constraints and a sharp rise in housing prices, notably in Auckland. The largest New Zealand city and major economic hub, Auckland attracted most of the immigration flows and accounted for one-third of the country's total population growth in 2000-15 (Statistics NZ, 2016b). Some other major cities have been experiencing similar pressures, as well as transport, water and waste infrastructure bottlenecks (Chapter 5).

Figure 1.2. **Well-being perception is generally higher in New Zealand than in the OECD**

Better Life Index, 2016 or latest available year

Note: The OECD Better Life Index framework is based on 11 topics considered a good measure of the concept of well-being. Each dimension is based on one to three indicators with equal weights and then normalised to range between 0 (worst performance) and 10 (best performance). The environment dimension of the well-being indicator focuses on citizens' satisfaction with local water quality and on annual population exposure to fine particulates ($PM_{2.5}$).
Source: OECD (2016), OECD Better Life Initiative 2016.

StatLink http://dx.doi.org/10.1787/888933459652

Figure 1.3. **Income inequality is slightly above the OECD average**

Gini coefficient before and after taxes and transfers, 2013 or latest available year

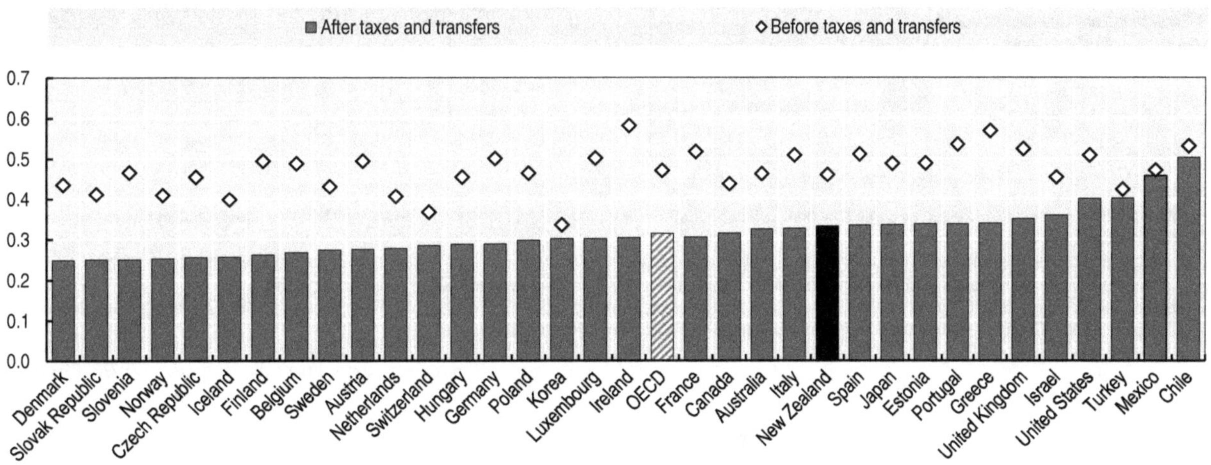

Note: The Gini coefficient is a common measure of income inequality that scores 0 when everybody has identical incomes and 1 when all the income goes to only one person.
Source: OECD (2016), "Income Distribution", *OECD Social and Welfare Statistics* (database).

StatLink http://dx.doi.org/10.1787/888933459667

New Zealand stands out in many other dimensions of life satisfaction, according to the Better Life Index (Figure 1.2). It scores the highest for social network support and health status, and performs well in terms of education and skills. Life expectancy at birth is higher than the OECD average and has improved over time (see Basic Statistics). The level of education attainment of the population is generally high. More than a third of the working-age population (25-64 years) has completed tertiary education, in line with the OECD average (see Basic Statistics). However, disparities persist in health and education outcomes. A higher proportion of Maori and Pacific Islands peoples live in chronic poverty, underperform in employment and education, are overrepresented in prison and as victims of crime, and have poorer health and access to care (OECD, 2015a).

New Zealanders are also more satisfied with environmental quality (as measured by exposure to fine particles and local water quality) than the OECD average (Figure 1.2). Regular surveys since 2000 by Lincoln University confirm the general satisfaction of New Zealanders with environmental quality and the management of natural resources. However, according to the latest survey, about half of respondents are concerned with water pollution and noise (Figure 1.4). In fact, water-related issues were rated as the most important environmental issue facing New Zealand, reflecting deteriorating water quality in some regions (Section 5.5; Chapter 4). Two-thirds of respondents were concerned or very concerned with the effects of climate change, both individually and for society as a whole (Figure 1.4).

Figure 1.4. **Water is a major environmental concern to New Zealand citizens**

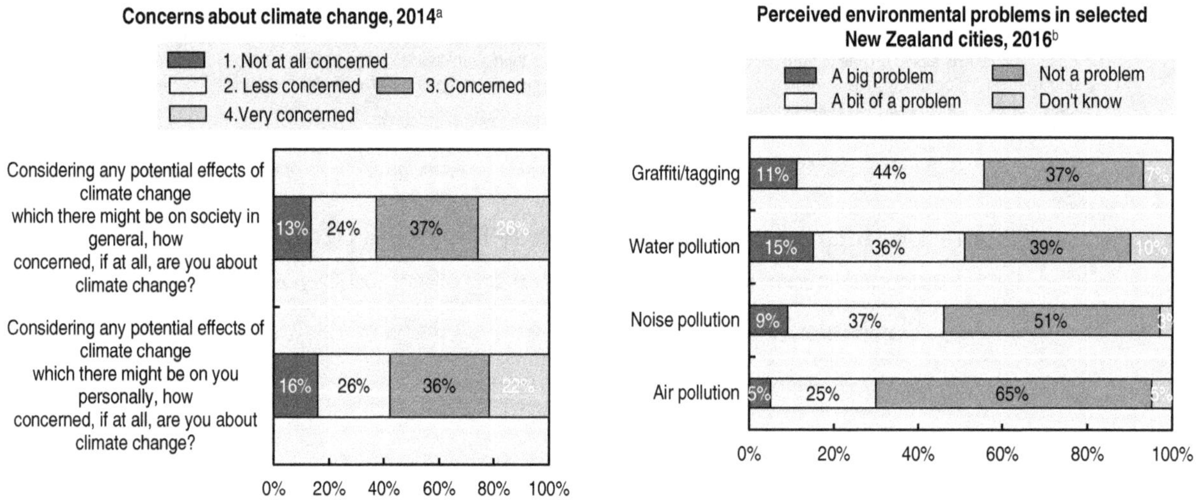

a) Percentage of responses to a survey carried out from July to September 2014 and inviting respondents to rate their concern about climate change on a scale of 1-4.

b) Percentage of responses to the 2016 Quality of Life Survey involving more than 7 000 citizens living in seven New Zealand cities. Respondents were asked to indicate the more worrying environmental issues and to what extent these had been a problem in the last 12 months.

Source: Colmar Brunton (2016), *Quality of Life Survey 2016: Topline report;* Leining, C. and S. White (2015), "From Fact to Act: New Zealanders' Beliefs and Actions on Climate Change", *Motu Note,* No.19, Motu Economic and Public Policy Research.

StatLink http://dx.doi.org/10.1787/888933459677

3. Transition towards a low-carbon and energy-efficient economy

3.1. *Energy structure and intensity*

New Zealand is endowed with a wide variety of fossil fuels and renewable energy sources. Its gas reserves are sufficient to entirely meet domestic consumption. New Zealand is a net exporter of coal, although parts of the large mining sites are closing down.[5] It exports most of the domestically produced, high quality oil, but remains a net importer of oil (IEA, forthcoming).[6] Located along the Pacific "Ring of Fire", the country has world-class geothermal resources, mostly in the North Island, while most of the hydropower resources are in the South Island.

New Zealand has a clean, low-carbon energy mix in international comparison. In 2015, renewable energy sources accounted for 40% of the total primary energy supply (TPES), among the highest shares in the OECD. Oil accounts for a third of TPES, with natural gas and solid fuels making up the remainder (Figure 1.5). Renewable primary energy supply increased by about 60% since 2000, mainly driven by an increase in geothermal power generation (see below); over the same period, solar and wind energy supply more than tripled, although starting from a very low base. Almost 60% of New Zealand's renewable primary energy supply comes from geothermal sources (the second highest share in OECD after Iceland), followed by hydro, biofuels, solar and wind (Figure 1.5).

Figure 1.5. **A high and increasing share of energy is sourced from renewables**

Renewables (RES) in total primary energy supply (TPES) and power generation, top ten OECD countries, 2015

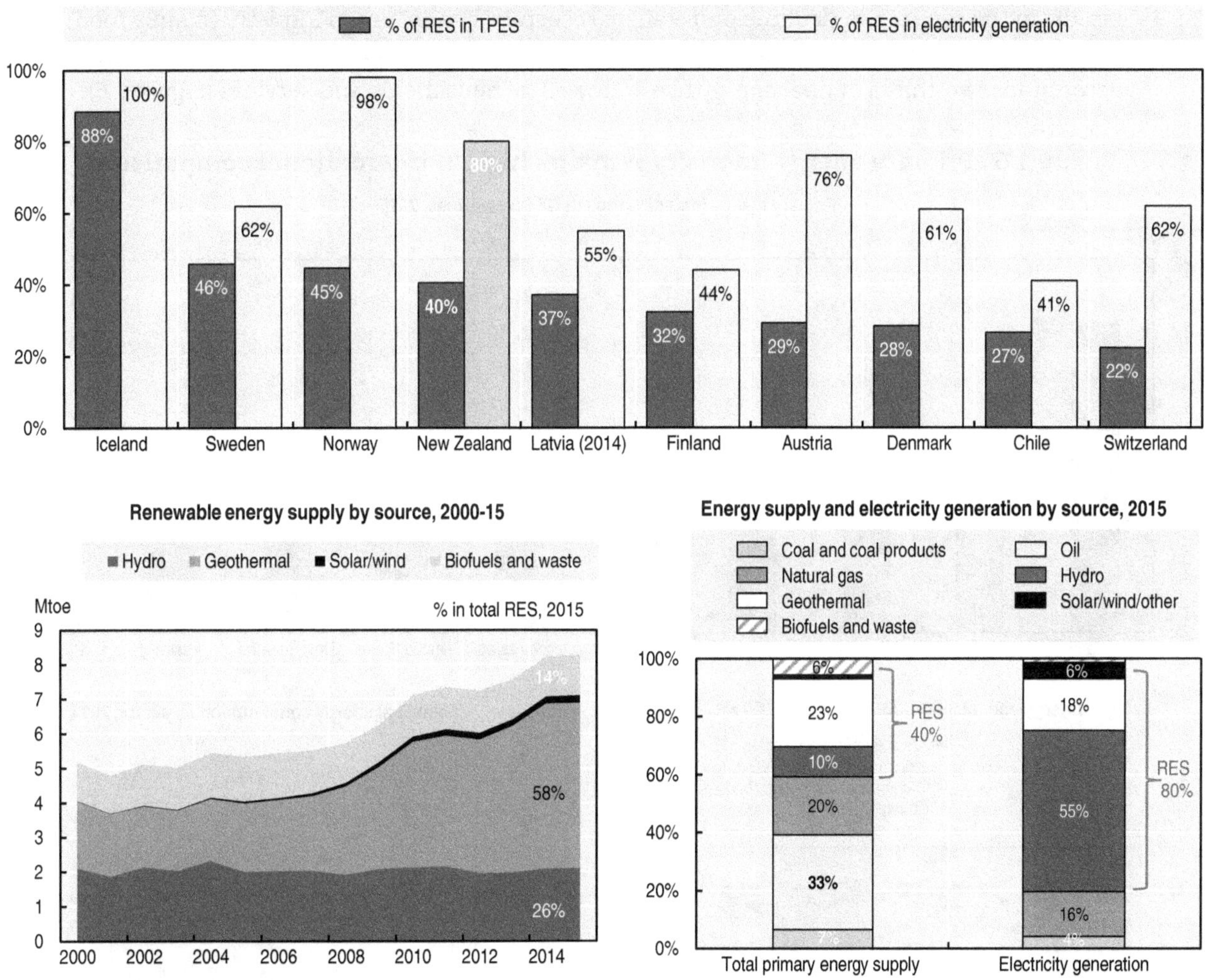

Source: IEA (2016), *IEA World Energy Statistics and Balances* (database).

StatLink http://dx.doi.org/10.1787/888933459687

Renewables accounted for 80% of electricity generation in 2015, up from 72% in 2000. This is the third highest share in the OECD (Figure 1.5). Hydropower has historically accounted for the bulk of electricity output from renewables (more than two-thirds in 2015; see Figure 1.5). Geothermal has increased to reach 18% of power generation, compensating for reduced electricity generation from natural gas and coal (which will come to an end by 2018). In 2008, New Zealand set the target of producing 90% of its electricity from renewable sources by 2025. Taking into account projected growth in power demand, renewable generation levels would need to increase by about 20% (IEA, forthcoming). The target is expected to be met without direct government intervention or financial support, as many renewables are cost-competitive with thermal generation in New Zealand (Chapter 3).

New Zealand remains among the ten most energy-intensive OECD economies (Figure 1.6). Despite the departure of large industry from the country, energy intensity (TPES per unit of GDP) remained virtually stable between 2005 and 2012, and then started to rise moderately. As a result, New Zealand has not met the target of reducing energy intensity by 1.3% per year, as set by the New Zealand Energy Efficiency and Conservation Strategy 2011-16 (IEA, forthcoming; see Chapter 3). Between 2000 and 2014, energy consumption increased rapidly in the services, agriculture and transport sectors; energy use in industry (mainly food processing and non-metallic minerals) has risen since 2010. Transport and industry together account for two-thirds of final energy use, followed by households and services (Figure 1.6).

Figure 1.6. **Primary energy intensity remains high in international comparisons**

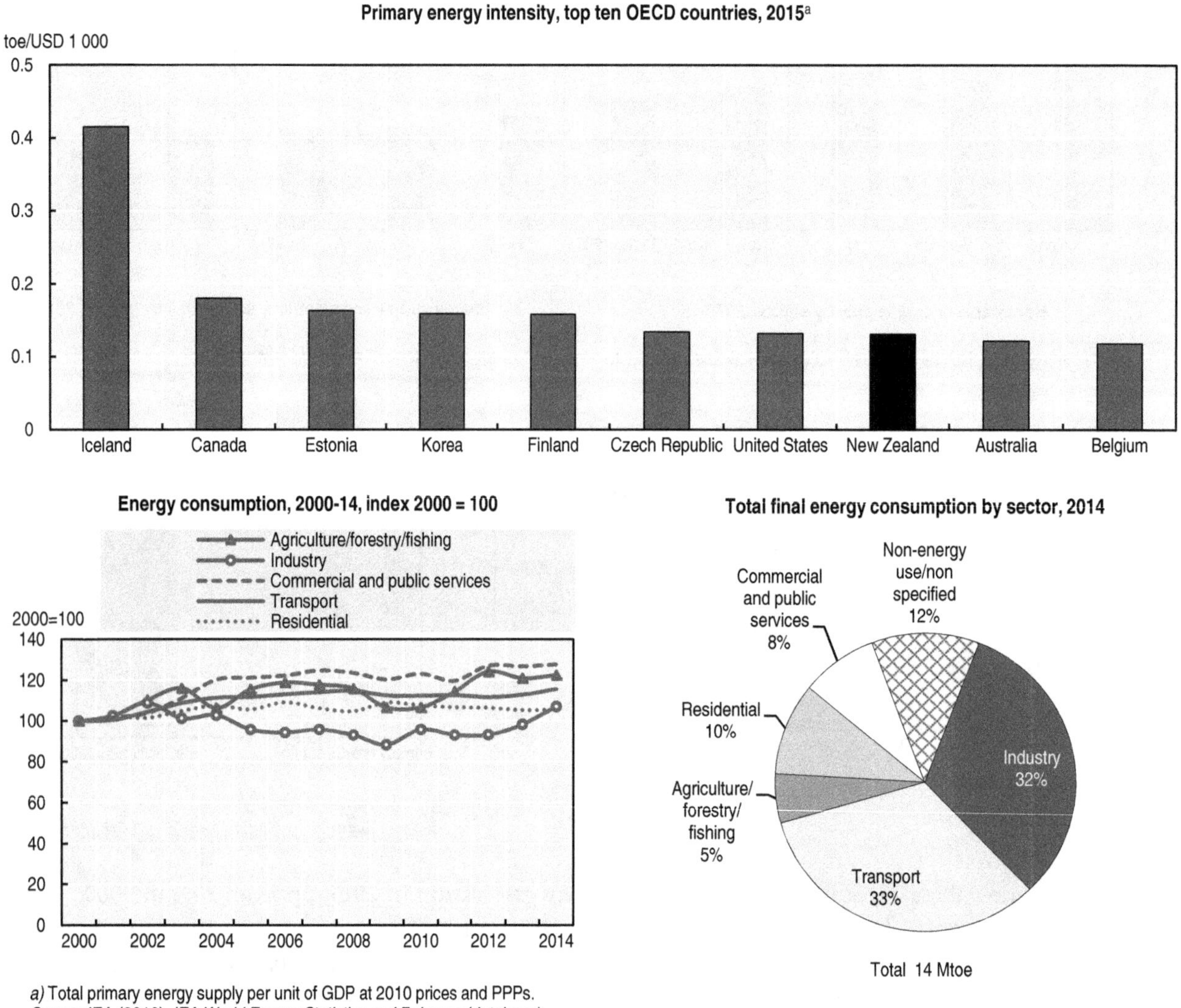

a) Total primary energy supply per unit of GDP at 2010 prices and PPPs.
Source: IEA (2016), *IEA World Energy Statistics and Balances* (database).

StatLink http://dx.doi.org/10.1787/888933459693

3.2. Transport

Transport is the main energy user and a major source of GHG emissions. Increased transport demand associated with sustained GDP growth has resulted in rising energy use and GHG emissions from the sector (Figures 1.6 and 1.8; Section 3.3). As in all OECD member countries, road transport accounts for the bulk of energy use for the transport sector (over 90% in 2014). Motor vehicles are the primary transport mode for both goods and passengers, reflecting New Zealand's dispersed population, a history of low-density urban development and the insufficient development of alternative transport modes, notably rail and public transport. Given its geographical remoteness, New Zealand relies on aviation to connect to the rest of the world, and between islands and distant regions. Domestic aviation accounts for nearly 6% of energy use for the transport sector, one of the highest shares among OECD member countries.

Motor vehicle and car ownership rates are the highest in the OECD: 85 vehicles (including trucks) and 66 passenger cars per 100 inhabitants. The number of vehicles has increased considerably (by 65%) since 2000. The number of diesel vehicles, which emit more particulate matter and nitrogen oxides per litre of fuel burned than vehicles running on petrol, continue to increase (notably light diesel vehicles). In 2014, diesel vehicles made up 17% of the fleet, up from 12% in 2000. The number of electric (EVs) and hybrid vehicles boomed in 2014-16, although they still represent about 0.5% of total light vehicle fleet (Chapter 3).

The mix of vehicle standards and taxes does not provide sufficient incentives to renew the fleet towards cleaner, more fuel-efficient vehicle technologies (IEA, forthcoming; Chapter 3). New Zealand does not have mandatory standards for vehicle fuel efficiency and emissions, but it applies vehicle exhaust regulations, fuel economy labelling for light vehicles and a voluntary heavy vehicle fuel efficiency programme. Electric vehicles are exempt from the road user charge, but otherwise vehicle taxes are not differentiated according to vehicles' environmental and energy performance (Chapter 3).

The vehicle fleet is relatively old and emission-intensive. The car fleet consists mainly of re-sold foreign cars, primarily from Japan, as there is no car manufacturing in New Zealand. The average age of the car fleet is 14 years (and 17 years for trucks and buses). The average fuel efficiency of the vehicle fleet has stabilised at 10 litres/100vkm, compared to 8 litres/100vkm in Japan (IEA, forthcoming). The average CO_2 emissions per kilometre of newly registered vehicles declined between 2005 and 2014 from 223 to 184.8 gCO_2/km, but remains above the average of the European Union (119.6 gCO_2/km in 2015) and of Japan (143 gCO_2/km in 2013). As a result, New Zealand has the highest or among the highest road-transport emissions per capita of nitrogen and sulphur oxides, carbon monoxide, non-methane volatile organic compounds and CO_2 in the OECD (Figure 1.7).

3.3. Climate change mitigation and adaptation

GHG emission trends

New Zealand has an unusual emissions profile, with nearly half of its emissions coming from agriculture (Figure 1.8). This is the highest share in the OECD, reflecting the importance of agriculture, including food and livestock production, in the economy. Most of the agriculture-related emissions are biological emissions, mainly methane (CH_4) from ruminant cattle (enteric fermentation) and nitrous oxides (N_2O) from animal waste and fertilisers. Overall, methane and N_2O emissions from all sources contribute 54% of total emissions, compared to 16% in the OECD as a whole. Transport, mainly on roads, is the second largest

Figure 1.7. **New Zealand's road transport emissions are among the highest in the OECD**

Air pollutant emissions per capita from road transport, top ten OECD countries, 2014

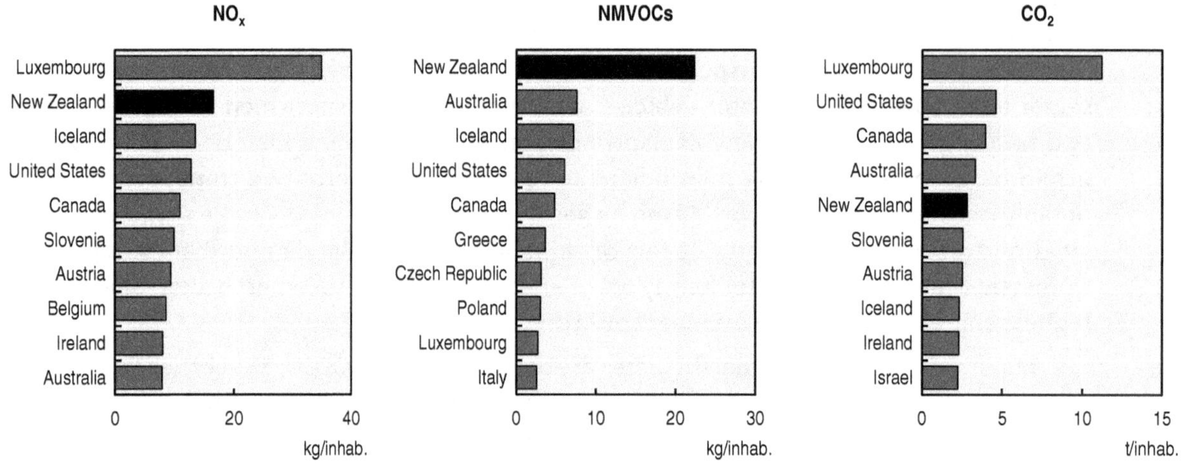

Source: IEA (2016), *IEA CO_2 Emissions from Fuel Combustion Statistics* (database); OECD (2016), "Air emissions by source", *OECD Environment Statistics* (database).

StatLink http://dx.doi.org/10.1787/888933459700

emitting sector; it accounts for 17% of emissions. GHG emissions from power generation account for a smaller share of total emissions than in most other OECD member countries, as a result of the large share of renewables in the energy mix (Figures 1.5 and 1.8).

GHG emissions have continued to rise: by 2014, gross emissions (i.e. excluding land use, land-use change and forestry, LULUCF) had increased by 6% from 2000 levels and by 23% from 1990 levels. The LULUCF sector contributed to removing more than a third of New Zealand's GHG emissions in 2000-14. However, removals have declined in recent years as more planted forests have reached harvest maturity (MfE, 2015). In 2014, taking into account emission removals from LULUCF, net GHG emissions were more than 20% above 2000 levels and about 54% above 1990 levels (Figure 1.9).

The main drivers of GHG emission growth were the agricultural sector (primarily due to increased dairy production and fertiliser use), road transport, manufacturing industries (particularly minerals and metals, chemicals and food processing) and construction (MfE, 2016a). In the agriculture sector, increased productivity has resulted in a considerable decline of GHG emissions per unit of farm product, but overall emissions have grown, and are projected to continue to grow, because of increased total output. Despite the increasing waste generation, emissions from waste management decreased, owing to better management systems of landfilled waste (improved methane recovery) (Figure 1.9). While emissions have grown at a lower rate than the economy (+ 44%) and the population (+ 17%) in 2000-14, New Zealand's gross GHG emissions per capita and per unit of GDP remain among the five highest in the OECD (Figure 1.9).

GHG emission reduction targets and mitigation policy

While New Zealand accounts for a minor share of global GHG emissions (0.16%), it has been active in international discussions about climate change, acknowledging that all small emitters together generate 30% of global emissions and need to share responsibility for their reduction (MfE, 2016b). The 2002 Climate Change Response Act (and its subsequent amendments) is the framework legislation addressing the country's obligations in the

Figure 1.8. **New Zealand has a unique GHG emissions profile**

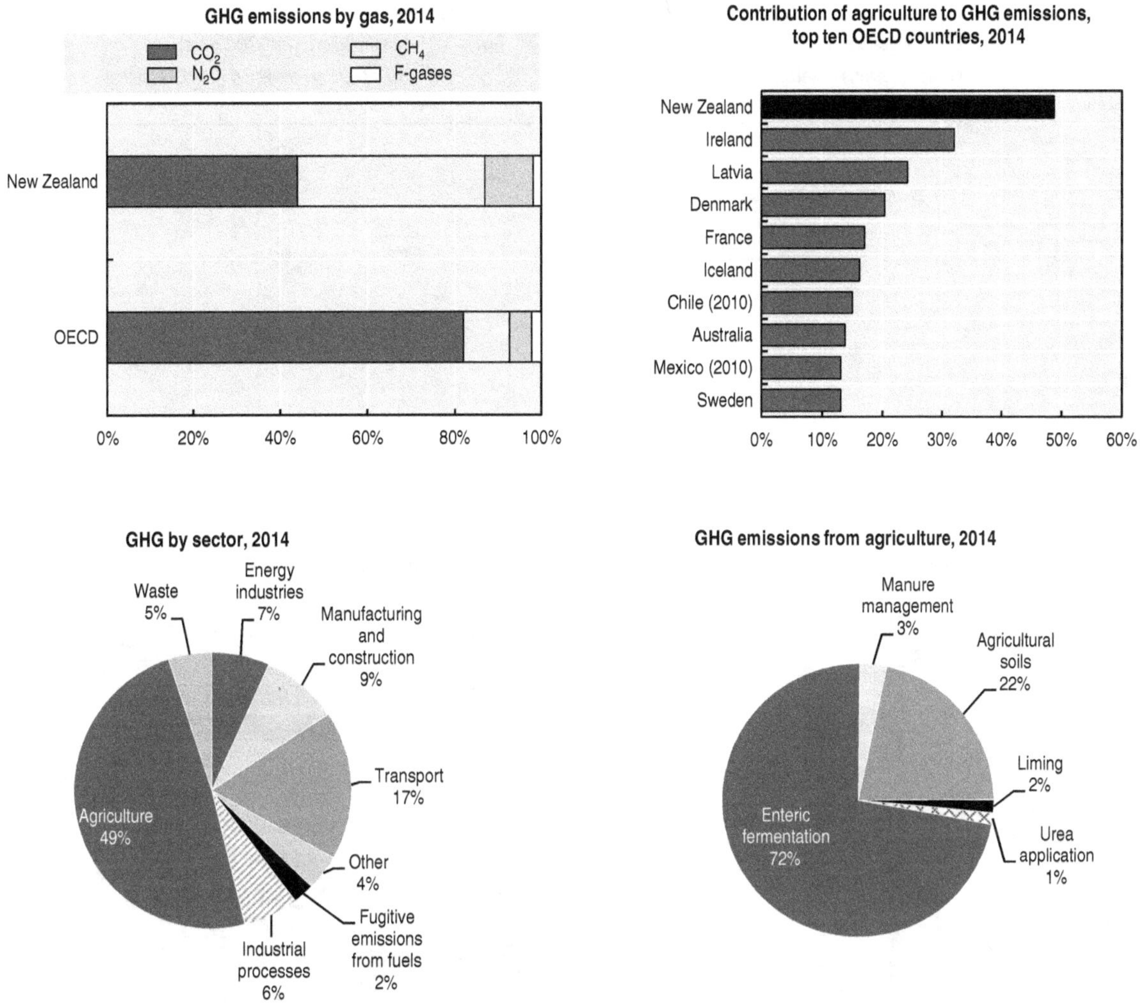

Note: Excluding emissions/removals from land use, land-use change and forestry.
Source: MfE (2016), *New Zealand's Greenhouse Gases Inventory 1990-2014*; OECD (2016), "Greenhouse gas emissions by source", *OECD Environment Statistics* (database).

StatLink http://dx.doi.org/10.1787/888933459714

context of the United Nations Framework Convention on Climate Change (UNFCCC). Under the Kyoto Protocol, New Zealand committed to reducing its average annual net GHG emissions over the first commitment period (2008-12) to 1990 levels. Despite the increase in gross GHG emissions, the country over-achieved its Kyoto Protocol target by using its forest sinks and international carbon credits (Chapter 3). New Zealand did not make a commitment for 2013-20 under the Kyoto Protocol, but it set an unconditional target to reduce emissions by 5% below 1990 levels by 2020, as well as a long-term target of a 50% emission reduction below 1990 levels by 2050. Projections indicate New Zealand is on track to meet the 2020 target, using a combination of forestry removals, domestic abatement and the surplus Kyoto units acquired during the first commitment period (MfE, 2016c; see Figure 1.9).

In preparation of the 2015 Paris Climate Conference, New Zealand announced its intended nationally determined contribution (INDC) to reduce GHG emissions to 30% below 2005 levels by 2030 (Figure 1.9). This is equivalent to a reduction of 11% with respect to 1990 levels. The government ratified the 2015 Paris Agreement on 4 October 2016.

Figure 1.9. **GHG emissions continue to increase**

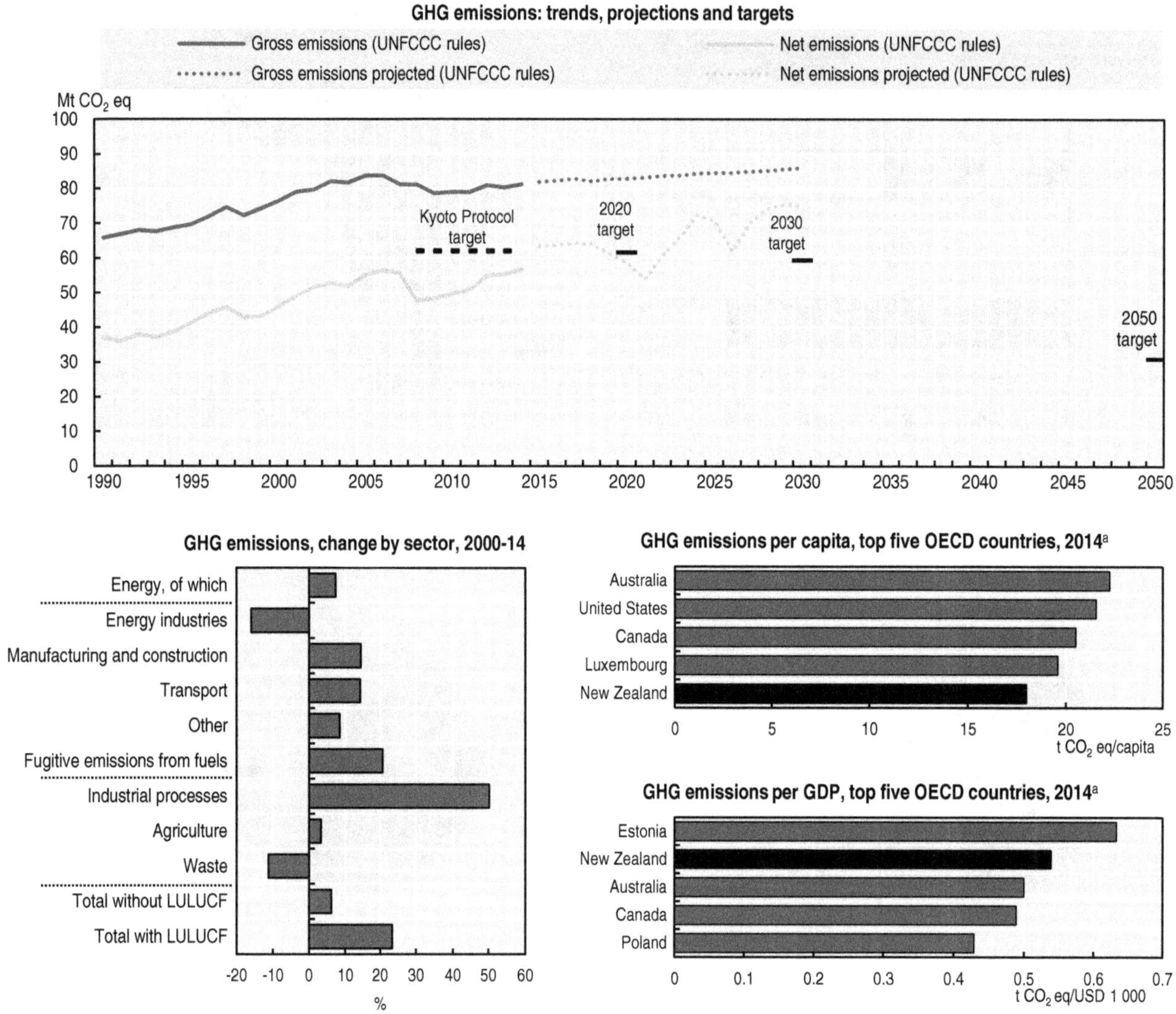

Notes: Gross emissions exclude LULUCF. Projections are based on current guidance and are subject to change as updated information become available.
a) Excluding emissions from land use, land-use change and forestry sector (LULUCF).
Source: MfE (2016), *New Zealand's Greenhouse Gases Inventory 1990-2014*; MfE (2015), *Second Biennial Report under the UNFCCC;* OECD (2016), "Greenhouse gas emissions by source", *OECD Environment Statistics* (database).

StatLink http://dx.doi.org/10.1787/888933459727

New Zealand intends to achieve the 2030 target through a combination of domestic mitigation actions, emission removals from forestry and purchase of international carbon credits. The expected contribution of each domestic sector to emission reductions and the relative role of international carbon credits and carbon sinks are not yet clear. Depending on the intended use of forestry sinks and carbon credits, achieving the 2030 target may effectively increase gross domestic GHG emissions. In addition, this target is not on the path to New Zealand's long-term goal, which would require reducing emissions by 45% below 2005 levels (or by 30% below 1990 levels) by 2030 (Climate Action Tracker, 2016).

New Zealand's climate mitigation policy has largely relied on forest sinks and carbon pricing via the Emissions Trading Scheme (NZ ETS). As Chapter 3 discusses, the system has had limited effectiveness, however, and needs to be strengthened. Expanding forest plantations remains a viable option to offset emissions in the short to medium term while the other sectors develop and adopt new low-carbon technology. However, forest sinks cannot be the only option, as eventually all available land-based sinks, including forests, become saturated. A few other measures are in place to promote energy efficiency; use of renewable energy; and reduction of emissions from transport, including voluntary energy performance standards for building, fuel economy labelling for vehicles and tax incentives for electric vehicles. In the agriculture sector, mitigation options have focused on increasing the productivity per animal and overall efficiency of farms, as well as on investment in research in new technology to reducing biological emissions (Chapter 3).

Given its largely decarbonised power generation sector and the weight of agricultural emissions, New Zealand faces particular challenges in mitigating its domestic GHG emissions. While potential technological solutions for reducing agriculture-related biological emissions exist (e.g. nitrification inhibitors and productivity-enhancing farm management practice), further research is needed to develop them; one or two decades may be required to reach commercial viability (Royal Society of New Zealand, 2016). As this occurs, other measures such as regulations or pricing instruments are needed to encourage farmers to adopt cutting-edge technology.

Short- and medium-term mitigation options are available in all other emitting sectors, starting with further reducing reliance on fossil fuels and increasing the efficiency of energy use, especially in building, industry and transport (IEA, forthcoming; PCE, 2015a; see also Chapter 3). However, there is a need to improve information on the costs and abatement potential of mitigation options (Royal Society of New Zealand, 2016). New Zealand should identify the expected contribution of each sector to the achievement of the 2030 and 2050 targets, and design a comprehensive package of climate mitigation measures to complement the NZ ETS (Chapter 3). In September 2016, the government announced the establishment of three expert groups on agricultural biological emissions, forestry and adaptation to build the evidence base on these issues (MfE, 2016b).

Impact of climate change and adaptation policy

According to the latest national climate projections, average temperatures in New Zealand will increase by about 0.7-1°C by 2040 and by 0.7-3°C by 2090, depending on the global emission scenario (MfE, 2016d). The temperature increase is projected to bring more intense rainfall to most areas of the country (notably where average annual rainfall also increases, such as the West Coast of the South Island), raising the risk of river flooding. At the same time, most areas of the country are projected to see more dry days per year, while droughts become more frequent and intense. Droughts represent one of the biggest risks to energy security, given the strong reliance on hydropower for energy supply (IEA, forthcoming). New Zealand is also vulnerable to sea level rise, as most cities are within a few kilometres of the coast.[7] Sea level rise is expected to cause more frequent and severe coastal flooding and more widespread soil erosion (a longstanding problem in some coastal areas); groundwater linked to the sea is also expected to rise, potentially causing groundwater to become brackish (PCE, 2015b).

Under the Resource Management Act, local authorities are required to consider the effects of climate change in their planning decisions. The central government supports this process by providing guidance (e.g. through provisions in the New Zealand Coastal Policy Statement) and information (e.g. through a four-year research programme on community vulnerability). However, the Parliamentary Commissioner for the Environment (PCE, 2015b) noted that better direction and guidance are needed on the critical issue of sea level rise, including on the evaluation, planning and data gathering for rising sea levels, the assessment of coastal hazards and the elaboration of coastal plans with local communities. The government has invested in building the evidence base for climate change adaptation and prepared resilience and vulnerability assessments for the tourism and transport sectors. New Zealand should develop vulnerability assessments for all major economic sectors and translate these into policy strategies and responses. No national adaptation strategy has been developed to date.

4. Transition towards a resource-efficient economy

4.1. *Material consumption*

Domestic material consumption (DMC)[8] decreased by 13% over 2008-12, driven by the economic slowdown following the global economic crisis and structural changes in the economy (with stronger growth in the service sector). The decrease in DMC helped bring down the material intensity of the economy (DMC/GDP) and per capita consumption, but New Zealand remains more resource-intensive than the OECD average (Figure 1.10). This reflects the importance of agriculture and forestry to the economy. In 2012, biomass accounted for nearly 50% of domestic consumption, 60% of domestic extraction and 80% of material resource exports (compared to respective OECD averages of around 20%). Recent years saw a notable increase in wood extraction and exports, with increases of 40% and 80%, respectively, over 2008-12 (OECD, 2016b). The recent strong increase in the construction of housing and infrastructure will likely boost the consumption of construction minerals.

Figure 1.10. **Material intensities improved, but remain high in international comparison**

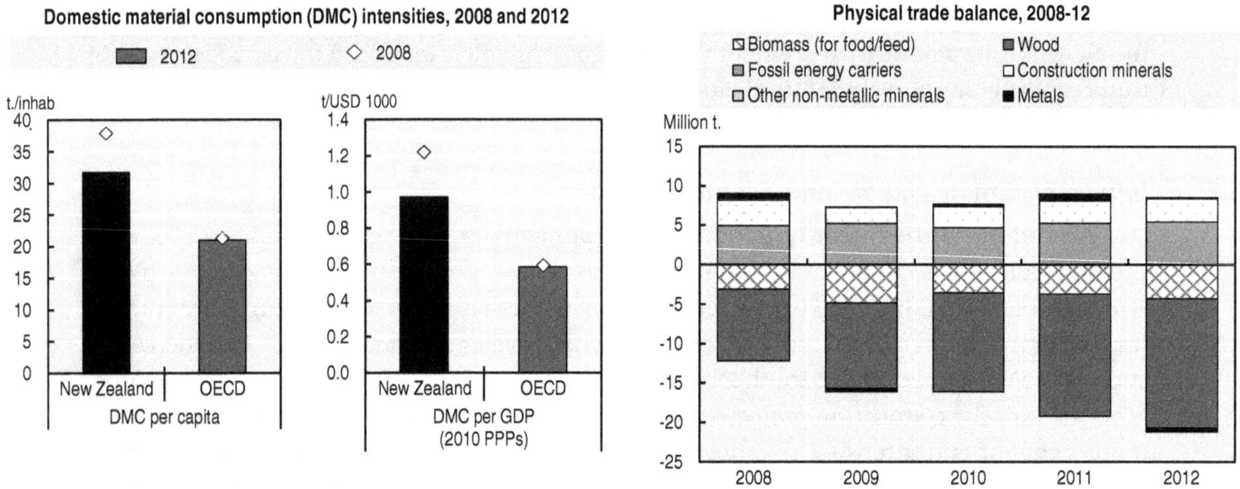

Note: Domestic material consumption (DMC) refers to the sum of domestic extraction of raw materials used by an economy and their physical trade balance (imports minus exports of raw materials and derived products).

Source: OECD (2016), "Material resources", *OECD Environment Statistics* (database).

StatLink http://dx.doi.org/10.1787/888933459736

4.2. *Waste management*

New Zealand lacks comprehensive, timely and internationally comparable data on waste management. Reliable data are only available for waste volumes disposed of in certain landfills; no data are available on recycling or other types of waste recovery.[9] Available data suggest the generation of municipal solid waste (MSW) has increased alongside population, GDP and private final consumption (Figure 1.11). Per capita MSW generation appears to be

Figure 1.11. **Landfilled municipal waste increased alongside private final consumption**

Landfilled municipal waste and private final consumption, 2012-14[a]

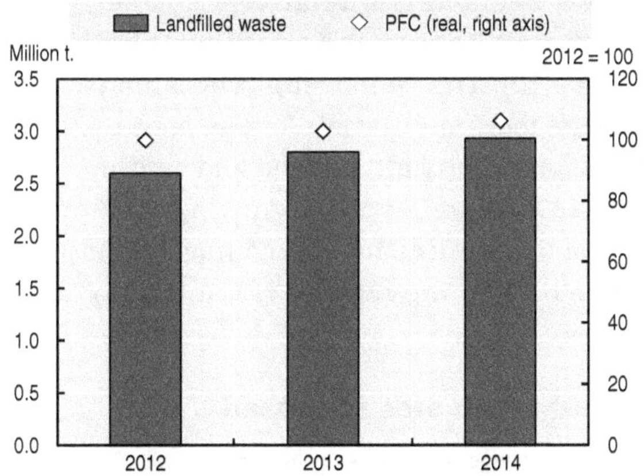

Estimated landfilled waste by type of landfill, 2013[b]

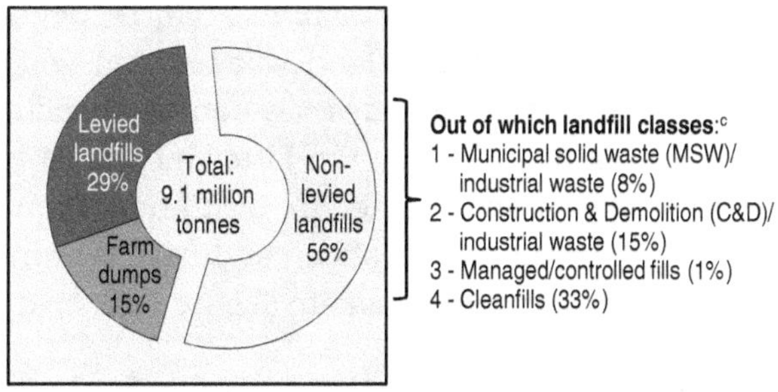

a) Partial data referring to waste disposed of at levied landfills as defined in the 2008 Waste Minimisation Act. Data include minor amounts of construction and demolition waste.
b) Estimates based on survey conducted for the Ministry for the Environment. A new study has been commissioned to better understand number of fills and the compostion and quantity of waste being disposed of at these fills.
c) The landfill classes are defined under the 1991 Resource Management Act on the basis of the materials accepted and related consent conditions:
1 - MSW landfills accept household and similar wastes; industrial landfills are usually monofills associated with a specific industry;
2 - C&D waste landfills receive mainly wood products, asphalt, insulation and other materials;
3 - Managed landfills accept inert materials and C&D waste with light contaminants;
4 - Cleanfills accept only virgin natural material such as clay, soil and rock.
Source: OECD (2016), "Municipal Waste", *OECD Environment Statistics* (database); OECD (2016), *OECD National Accounts Statistics* (database); MfE (2016), "Types of landfills", Waste (website); MfE (2014), *Review of the effectiveness of the waste disposal levy;* Tonkin & Taylor (2014), *New Zealand Non-Municipal Landfill Database.*

StatLink http://dx.doi.org/10.1787/888933459743

among the highest in the OECD. It is estimated that the majority of MSW is landfilled. All local authorities offer drop-off collection services for recycling, and some have adopted recycling requirements or quantity-based waste charges, which helped reduce waste volumes going to landfill. However, many authorities still lack strong incentives to change household behaviour (see Chapter 3 and 5).

The 2008 Waste Minimisation Act established a levy on waste disposed of in landfills, with the aim to generate funding to local governments, help minimise waste and promote alternative forms of waste treatment. To ease implementation, the levy was limited to landfills that accept municipal waste, with the intention to expand it to other landfills over time. However, this has not yet happened. In 2013, the majority of landfilled waste was disposed of at non-levied landfills (which include cleanfills and temporary soil dumps) (Figure 1.11). The levy's limited coverage, its relatively low level (NZD 10 per tonne) and the practice of levy avoidance hamper the instrument's effectiveness (MfE, 2014a). New Zealand should extend the levy obligation to all relevant landfill types so as to reduce opportunities for levy avoidance and to provide greater incentives to minimise waste (see also Chapter 3). The Ministry for the Environment has commissioned a study to better understand the quantity and composition of waste disposed of at landfills. To encourage recycling among industry and businesses, the government has accredited 14 voluntary product stewardship schemes; however, the limited data on waste recovery make the evaluation of these schemes difficult. New Zealand has no national regulation for disposal of agricultural waste, despite the large size of the sector; it is one of the few OECD member countries without national regulation of hazardous waste management within the country (Chapter 2). The 2010 New Zealand Waste Strategy sets out the government's long-term priorities for waste management and minimisation, but does not include any quantitative targets.

5. Natural asset base

5.1. *Land use*

With 17 inhabitants per square kilometre, New Zealand is a relatively sparsely populated country by OECD standards (see Basic Statistics). Forests and agricultural land cover about 40% of land area, respectively (Figure 1.12). The remaining land area is occupied by scrub land, wooded land, wet open land, bare rocks and glaciers, or else built-up. The past two decades saw noticeable increases in forest area, horticultural land and built-up area (Figure 1.12); the latter increased by 10% over 1996-12, reflecting a growing urban population (Chapter 5). In addition, high international dairy prices have encouraged land conversion from sheep and beef farming to dairy, mainly in the regions of Canterbury, Southland and Waikato (Figure 1.12; also see Chapter 4).

Figure 1.12. **Cropland, planted forest and urban area increased**

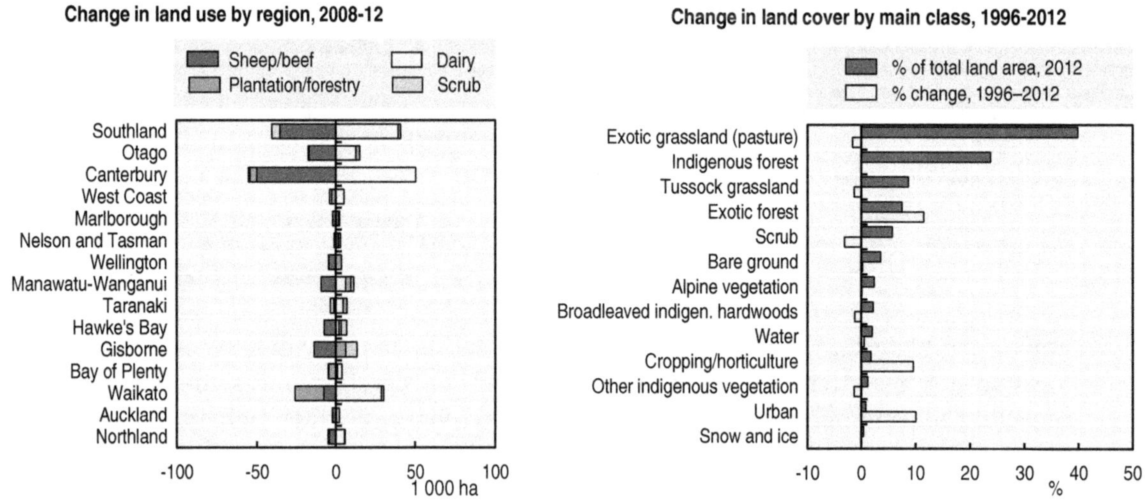

Source: MfE (2014), *New Zealand's Fifth National Report to the United Nations Convention on Biological Diversity;* PCE (2015), *Update Report - Water quality in New Zealand: Land use and nutrient pollution.*

StatLink http://dx.doi.org/10.1787/888933459752

5.2. *Forest resources*

New Zealand's forest area expands over more than 10 million ha. In 2013, forests covered 39% of total land area, the ninth-highest rate in the OECD. Natural forests cover 80% of total forest area (nearly one third of the country); the remaining 20% is planted forest. Total forested area has increased slightly since 2000, in part due to significant expansion of planted forests with exotic tree species. New Zealand offers grants for reforestation to address soil erosion; 55% of new planting since 2008 has received grants through either the East Coast Forestry Project or the Afforestation Grants Scheme. The inclusion of forestry into the NZ ETS has encouraged some investment in forest plantation (Section 3.3; Chapter 3). Nearly two-thirds of forests planted after 1989 have been voluntarily registered in the NZ ETS. The forestry sector is an important pillar of New Zealand's economy: it contributes to approximately 3% of GDP, nearly 1% of employment and 7% of exports. Despite its small size, New Zealand is the world's second largest exporter of industrial round wood (after the Russian Federation) (Government of New Zealand, 2014; FAO, 2016).

The ecological integrity of forest ecosystems is generally good, although pest, disease outbreaks and woody invasive species have emerged as concerns (Clifford et al., 2013). Nearly two-thirds (60%) of natural forest is protected in public conservation land, one of the highest shares in the OECD. Less than 0.1% of natural forest is harvested per year. Commercial timber from privately owned natural forest can only be harvested if sourced under sustainable forest management plans and permits; no harvesting is permitted on public conservation land (Government of New Zealand, 2014). The forest area certified under the Forest Stewardship Council (FSC) scheme increased considerably over the last decade and reached 15% of total forest area in 2012 (FAO, 2016). In addition, initiatives have been launched to ensure sustainable forestry production of indigenous forest in private lands and in planted forest involving the Maori population, civil society and the business sector.

5.3. *Fish resources*

Total fish production has declined by 20% since 2000, driven by a gradual decline in fish catches. Aquaculture has been constantly growing (by 28% over 2000-14); it accounted for 20% of total fish production in 2014. New Zealand's fish production relies mainly on deep water fishing and is highly export-oriented; the country exports about 90% of its seafood production (OECD, 2015b).

Commercial and customary fisheries have been primarily managed through a transferable quota system since 1986 (Chapter 3).[10] With 100 species and 628 covered fish stocks, the system is one of the largest in the world (MPI, 2016), helping to reduce overfishing and maintain the fish stock at sustainable levels. Nevertheless, 17% of fish stocks (of known status) were deemed to be overfished in 2015; 6% were deemed to be collapsed (MPI, 2016). The Fisheries Act and the Fisheries 2030 strategy include environmental obligations and aim at strengthening environmental and economic performance of the sector. In addition, the Ministry for Primary Industry has made considerable efforts to monitor and enforce compliance with the regulation; large parts of the Exclusive Economic Zone (EEZ) have been put under some form of protection (Section 5.4). Bycatch and the use of harmful fishing methods (notably seabed trawling) has therefore decreased over the past few years, but remain a pressure on marine species and seabirds. Little is known about the impact of aquaculture on the marine environment (MfE and Statistics NZ, 2015).

Following the Treaty of Waitangi Fisheries Claims Settlement Act of 1992, a suite of management tools has been introduced to recognise customary use and management practices of Maori in the exercise of non-commercial fishing rights. These include establishment of traditional fishing grounds (mataitai reserves) to provide for customary management practices and food gathering and exclude commercial fishers; adoption of local management practices for both commercial and non-commercial fishing in an area of particular significance to an iwi/hapu (so-called taiapure); and temporary closure of an area to fishing to enable the local indigenous community (Tangata Whenua) to exercise their customary rights.

5.4. *Biodiversity*

Biodiversity and threatened species

Due to its geographic location and its natural history (which evolved in the absence of mammalian predators), New Zealand has a unique wealth of biodiversity, with one of the world's highest rates of endemic flora and fauna species.[11] At the same time, New Zealand has one of the world's highest shares of threatened species (Brown, 2016). About a quarter of native mammals, a third of birds, fish and reptiles and some 60% of native amphibians are threatened (Figure 1.13); some sources point to even higher risks of extinction.[12] The

Figure 1.13. **The share of threatened native flora and fauna species is high**

Threatened indigenous species,[a] late 2000s

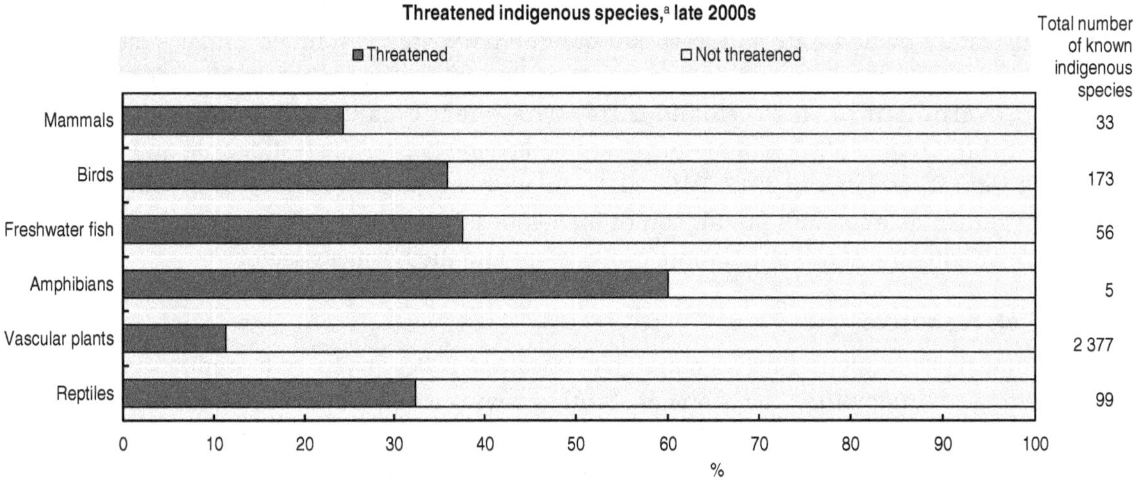

a) Threatened species according to the New Zealand Threat Classification System (NZTCS), which includes "nationally critical", "nationally endangered" and "nationally vulnerable" species, i.e. species that are at greatest risk of extinction. Excludes vagrant and migrant species.
Source: OECD (2016), "Threatened species", *OECD Environment Statistics* (database).

StatLink http://dx.doi.org/10.1787/888933459769

risk of extinction worsened for 7% of indigenous species (59 of 799) between 2005 and 2011, while improving for 1.5% of these species. The main drivers of biodiversity loss are biological invasion, including by mammalian predators, weeds, pests and diseases; habitat removal and modifications; and pollution.

While indigenous biodiversity has declined generally, efforts for species recovery have increased significantly since 2000. New Zealand is a global leader in species recovery programmes (such as offshore island management) and pest control methods. These efforts helped eradicate predators from more than 100 islands and improved the population status of some species (including the kiwi, brown teal, kokako and yellowhead). New Zealand has also increased efforts to suppress or eradicate invasive mammalian predators on the mainland, including through fenced bird sanctuaries and landscape-scale pest control, notably through aerial application of a toxin known as "1080" (sodium monofluoroacetate). The Predator Free New Zealand 2050 initiative, launched in mid-2016, aims to eradicate key pests responsible for biodiversity loss (rodents, mustelid and possums) by 2050. It foresees the establishment of a public-private partnership company to support the refinement of existing techniques (e.g. GPS-guided aerial application of 1080) and research in new techniques (e.g. self-resetting traps and predator-specific toxins) (DOC, 2016).

Better institutional collaboration across government agencies, including through establishment of the Natural Resources Sector (Chapter 2), improved the mainstreaming of biodiversity into sectoral policies, including agriculture. New Zealand has also strengthened collaboration with Maori communities, and successfully mobilised local communities and philanthropic partners to engage in biodiversity protection programmes (Brown, 2016). However, data limitations (particularly on the state of biodiversity on private lands), as well as lack of clarity and clear implementation pathways for biodiversity laws and policy goals, continue to hamper effective protection and sustainable use of biodiversity. Methods to protect indigenous biodiversity on private land are generally based on voluntarism (Brown, 2016, 2015). A National Policy Statement for Indigenous Biodiversity was proposed in 2011, but did not pass into law largely because of opposition from private landowners

(Chapter 2). The government is planning to launch a stakeholder dialogue to develop a new National Policy Statement by late 2018. This is one component of the recently launched 2016-20 National Biodiversity Strategy and Action Plan, which outlines planned actions to implement international targets of the UN Convention on Biological Diversity.

Terrestrial protected areas

Terrestrial protected areas have increased by 15% since 2000 and covered almost one-third of New Zealand's territory in 2014 (85 000 km^2), a share significantly higher than in most other OECD member countries. Almost half of these areas fall within the most stringent categories of protection of the International Union for Conservation of Nature (IUCN) (i.e. nature reserve and wilderness areas, and national parks) (Figure 1.14), and prioritisation of ecosystems for conservation has improved. The Department of Conservation (DOC) provides extensive tracks, huts and other infrastructure within protected areas (public conservation land), many of which host natural attractions and spectacular landscapes. The number of international tourists visiting major national parks increased over the 2000s (Figure 1.14). In 2012, more than 1.7 million international visitors walked or trekked on public conservation land, more than twice as many as in 2000 (DOC, 2013). Walking and trekking are also the most popular activities undertaken by New Zealand tourists. Visitor numbers to national parks are expected to double over the next six years; this may increase pressures on ecosystems. Setting a precedent at the international scene, New Zealand granted legal personhood to a protected area in 2014 as a key part of the Treaty of Waitangi settlement negotiated between Tuhoe iwi and the Crown (Box 1.2).

Figure 1.14. **New Zealand has large national parks, which attract an increasing number of tourists**

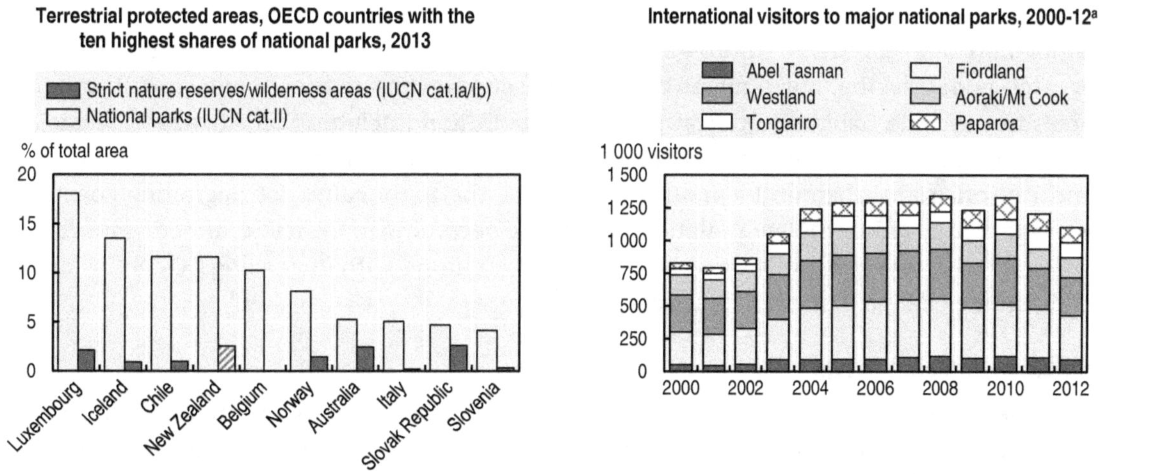

a) Estimates rounded to the nearest hundred obtained from the International Visitor Survey conducted by the Ministry of Business, Innovation and Employment. Fiordland data include Fiordland National Park, Milford Sound, Milford Track and Manapouri. Westland data include Tai Poutini National Park (Fox Glacier and Franz Josef Glacier).

Source: Department of Conservation (2016), National parks visitor statistics (website); OECD (2016), *OECD Environment Statistics* (database).

StatLink http://dx.doi.org/10.1787/888933459779

Marine environment

New Zealand's marine environment is one of the world's most diverse. It encompasses both sub-Antarctic and sub-tropical waters and hosts a wide range of habitats and marine life. More than 17 000 marine species have been identified in New Zealand waters to date;

Box 1.2. **Te Urewera – granting a national park legal personhood**

Te Urewera is a forested, sparsely populated area in the east of the North Island, which for centuries has been home to Ngai Tuhoe iwi (an indigenous tribe). Since 1954, a large part of this area has been protected as a national park. Up until 2014, Te Urewera was the largest national park on the North Island (covering more than 2 100 km^2) and managed as Crown land by the Department of Conservation (DOC).

In 2014, the park was granted legal personhood under the Te Urewera Act. The act transformed the park into a unique legal entity named "Te Urewera" and provided it with "all the rights, powers, duties and liabilities of a legal person". The lands would remain protected, with public use like in national parks, but would maintain their own separate identity. They would be governed with Tuhoe involvement, thereby strengthening respect for Tuhoe cosmology and relationship with the lands. The Te Urewera Act shifted management responsibilities from the DOC to the Te Urewera Board, which comprises joint Tuhoe and Crown membership. The board can file lawsuits on behalf of Te Urewera and represent it in court.

The innovative concept of "legal personhood" was devised to break a stalemate over the question of ownership between the Tuhoe (who wished to retain their own sovereignty and control over their lands) and the government (which was unable to agree to transferring ownership of a national park to a tribe). Granting the area legal personality meant that nobody owns the park. As such, the Te Urewera Act may provide a precedent to settlement negotiations between other Maori/iwi and the Crown. In a similar spirit, the government and iwi have agreed to create a new legal entity for the Whanganui River (Chapter 4).

Source: Ruru (2014); Logan (2016).

and it is estimated that another 17 000 to 65 000 are yet to be identified. Most marine birds and more than one-quarter of marine mammals are threatened with extinction; population data for other marine organisms are limited (MfE and Statistics NZ, 2016). Fishing bycatch is decreasing, but remains a major pressure on the marine environment; other pressures include habitat modification or loss, pollution (including oil extraction waste), exotic species and competition for food from commercial fishing. Excess sedimentation and run-off from urban and agricultural land are the main cause for degrading coastal ecosystems. In addition, New Zealand's oceans are becoming more acidic, affecting marine species and ecosystems; this trend is expected to continue with increasing CO_2 emissions and climate change (MfE and Statistics NZ, 2016).

Marine protected areas

The network of marine areas under some form of protection has expanded to cover about 30% of New Zealand's marine area (almost 1.3 million km^2). In 2007, the government passed regulations closing nearly one-third of New Zealand's EEZ to harmful fishing practices (e.g. dredging and bottom-trawling) to protect seabed biodiversity. However, many ecosystem types are represented in the marine protected area network only to a limited extent (Brown, 2015). The 2005 Marine Protected Areas Policy and Implementation Plan provided a framework for collaborative stakeholder-led processes to identify networks of possible marine reserves and close gaps in protection. However, by 2014, only three processes had been established. Stakeholder agreement has been difficult to achieve, which has been attributed to the limited array of protection options available under the 1971 Marine Reserves Act, as well as concerns of commercial industries (Brown, 2015). The government's proposal of a new Marine Protected Areas Act aims to provide a wider variety of protection options and improves the process for establishing and managing marine reserves. However, it would apply only to territorial waters (as opposed to the entire EEZ).

5.5. *Freshwater resources*

Freshwater resources are crucial to New Zealand: they are home to a wide variety of indigenous flora and fauna, support key economic activities such as agriculture, hydropower generation and tourism, and are deeply rooted in the culture of the indigenous population (Chapter 4). The country has a natural abundance of freshwater and hence low water stress at the national level (see Basic Statistics). However, freshwater availability varies substantially across regions and seasons. On per capita terms, freshwater abstraction is significantly above the OECD average (see Basic Statistics), reflecting the importance of irrigated agriculture and hydropower generation, as well as a relatively small population. New Zealand ranks among the top five OECD member countries for the highest rates of water abstraction for both agricultural purposes and public water supply (Figure 1.15).[13]

Figure 1.15. **Per capita water abstraction is high in international comparison**

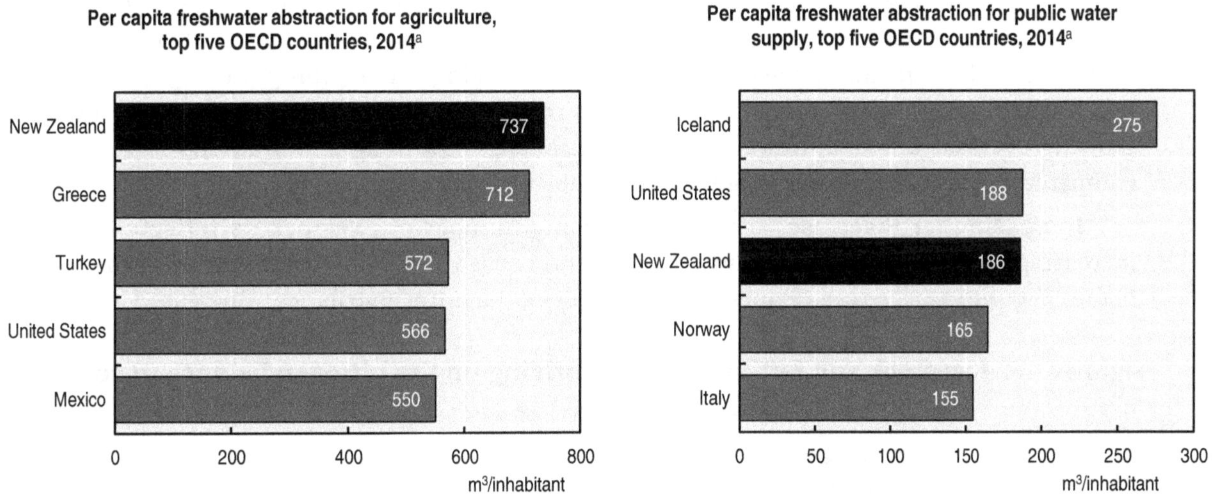

a) Or latest available year.
Source: OECD (2016), "Water: Freshwater Abstractions", *OECD Environment Statistics* (database).

StatLink http://dx.doi.org/10.1787/888933459781

Total consented water abstraction increased by 6% over 2006-10, driven mainly by growing water intakes for manufacturing (+26%) and irrigation (+11%). The latter reflects a continuous increase in the actual irrigated area (it has increased by almost 50% since 2002). Irrigation accounts for three-quarters of consumptive freshwater use (Chapter 4). The abstraction pressure is uneven across regions, with Canterbury, Southland and Otago alone accounting for about 90% of estimated water use. In these and some other parts of the country, water demand is exceeding what is available and sustainable, leading to increased competition among users and pressure on freshwater ecosystems (Chapter 4). Population growth, projected irrigation expansion and climate change are likely to further increase pressure on the resource. In recognition of the need to prevent further over-allocation and phase out existing over-allocation, the government has embarked on a process of reforming national freshwater policy (Chapter 4).

Water quality is variable, depending on the dominant land use in a catchment (MfE and Statistics NZ, 2015). Point-source water pollution from industrial and urban wastewater discharges has declined. However, water quality in some regions has suffered from diffuse pollution associated with the steady expansion of intensive farming and urbanisation. The pollutants of most concern are nutrients, pathogens and sediment (PCE, 2012). In particular, nitrogen levels from diffuse agricultural sources continued to increase, causing environmental and public health concerns. In recognition of the need to safeguard water quality from further deterioration, recent government freshwater policy reform requires water quality limits to be set in every catchment to maintain or improve water quality (Chapter 4).

Agricultural inputs and nutrient balances

The expansion of intensive agriculture (primarily dairy production) has triggered an increase in consumption of nitrogen fertilisers, which outpaced the growth in agricultural production. As a consequence, the nitrogen intensity (fertiliser used per agricultural area) has increased by 25% since 2002 (OECD, 2013a). Use of phosphorus fertilisers has decreased, albeit at a slower rate than in many other OECD member countries. Sales of pesticides increased by 22% over 2002-09, mainly driven by the increase in herbicides for livestock husbandry and forestry. Pesticides have been detected in 17% of sampled groundwater wells, though only one well exceeded the maximum acceptable value for drinking water (Humphries and Close, 2015). The area of organic agricultural land has more than doubled since 2005, driven by growing overseas demand; however, it remains small (0.9% of agricultural land in 2014) compared to the OECD average (more than 2%) (FiBL and IFOAM, 2016).

Increasing fertiliser use, and the increasing number of livestock, is reflected in increasing nitrogen levels in agricultural soils, and consequently surface and groundwater bodies (Figure 1.16; also see Chapter 4). Over 2000-10, the nitrogen balance[14] increased both

Figure 1.16. **Livestock and fertiliser use are driving up the nitrogen balance in soils**

Selected agricultural trends, 2000-14, index 2000 = 100[a]

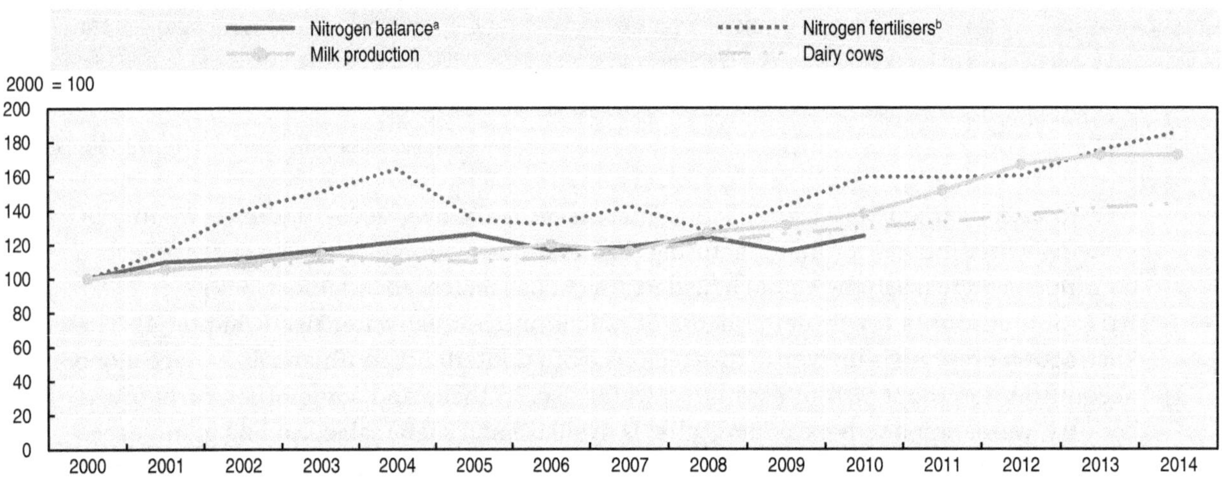

a) The gross nitrogen balance calculates the difference between the nitrogen inputs entering a farming system (i.e. mainly livestock manure and fertilisers) and the nitrogen outputs leaving the system (i.e. the uptake of nitrogen for crop and pasture production).

b) Apparent consumption of fertilisers expressed in tonnes of active ingredients.

Source: Dairy NZ (2015), *New Zealand Dairy Statistics 2014-15*; IFAD (2016), *Fertilisers statistics* (database); OECD (2016), "Environmental Performance of Agriculture (Edition 2013)", *OECD Agriculture Statistics* (database).

StatLink http://dx.doi.org/10.1787/888933459797

in absolute terms (25%) and in terms of quantities applied per unit of agricultural land (41%). Not only is this the largest increase in the OECD, it contrasts with declining trends in most other countries (OECD, 2013). Like nitrogen, the phosphorous surplus is among the highest in the OECD (OECD, 2013). However, phosphorous levels in soils and water bodies have decreased over the past decade, reflecting reduced phosphorus fertiliser use, riparian planting, stock exclusion from waterways and soil conservation efforts. Recent government freshwater policy reform requires water quality limits to be set for all catchments to ensure that freshwater quality is maintained or improved (Chapter 4).

6. Environmental quality of life

6.1. Air emissions and air quality

Air emissions

New Zealand stands out as one of the few OECD member countries that saw emissions of major air pollutants increase since 2000, although at a slower pace than population and GDP growth.[15] Transport and industry were the main drivers behind the increase. In 2014, New Zealand ranked within the top ten OECD member countries showing the highest emissions intensities for nitrogen oxides (NO_x), sulphur oxides (SO_x) and non-methane volatile organic compounds (NMVOC), both in per capita and per GDP terms (OECD, 2016c). No estimates on national emissions of particulate matter (PM) are available, even though this pollutant is of most concern in New Zealand. PM emissions from wood- and coal-based home heating – the main sources – are estimated to have decreased by 24% between 2006 and 2010. The decrease was driven by a gradual switch from wood and coal to electricity- and gas-based heating systems, national wood burner emission and efficiency standards, the replacement of older wood burners and better insulation systems (MfE and Statistics NZ, 2015). Recent modelling suggests that PM emissions from on-road transport have decreased since 2001 (alongside other pollutants), following the introduction of standards for vehicle fuels and improvements in the vehicle fleet.[16]

Air quality

Air quality in New Zealand is generally good by international standards. According to OECD estimates, the annual average exposure of New Zealand citizens to fine particulate matter ($PM_{2.5}$) is among the lowest in the OECD (Figure 1.17). This reflects the country's economic structure (i.e. reliance on natural resource use and a small heavy industry base), as well as geographic and climatic conditions (most cities benefit from strong winds that help disperse emitted air pollutants). However, even low exposure to air pollution can significantly damage human health. OECD calculations indicate the number of premature deaths due to outdoor air pollution in New Zealand could nearly double by 2060, while the costs of premature deaths could nearly triple (Figure 1.17).

Annual average PM_{10} concentrations fell by 8% over 2006-12 following adoption of the 2004 National Environmental Standards (NESs) for ambient air quality, as well as for regulating major sources of air pollution.[17] Lower emissions from home heating and road transport were the main drivers behind improved air quality. In 2012, most monitoring sites (87%) remained below the World Health Organization (WHO) guideline for average annual particulate matter (PM_{10}) exposure, including in the population centres of Auckland, Wellington and Christchurch (Chapter 5). However, half of monitored sites exceeded the NES for short-term PM_{10} exposure, mostly due to the burning of wood and coal for domestic

Figure 1.17. **Air quality is good in international comparison, but health impacts are projected to rise**

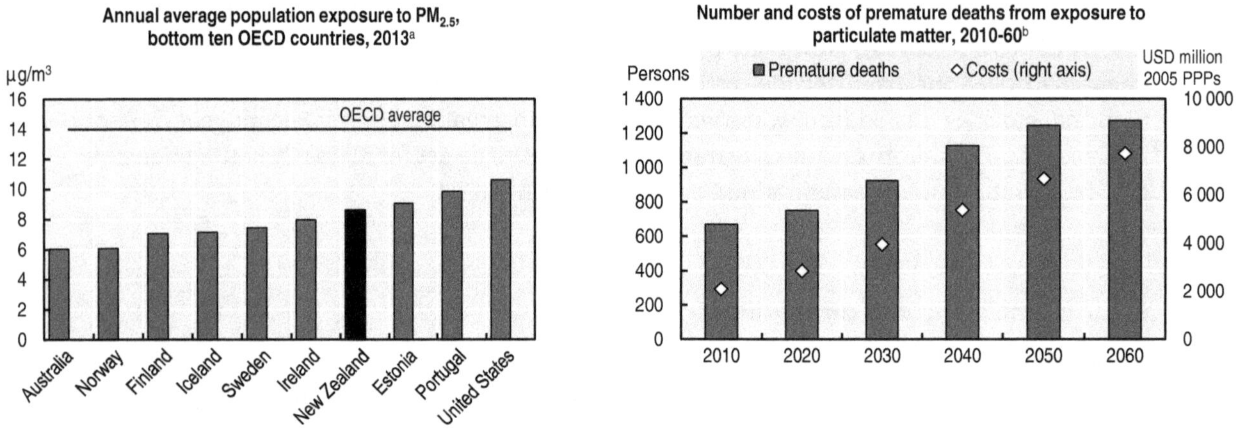

a) $PM_{2.5}$ data are based on a hybrid approach based on remotely sensed satellite data calibrated with ground-based measurement. $PM_{2.5}$ values for ground-based measurements have been converted from PM_{10} and should be considered with care as conversion factors are approximative. This approach may result in differences between the estimates presented here and New Zealand official national statistics.

b) Non-linear function, which assumes that the incremental numbers of deaths decreases as concentrations become higher. 2010 data are based on Global Burden Disease work.

Source: OECD (2016), "Air quality and health: Exposure to $PM_{2.5}$ fine particles - countries and regions", *OECD Environment Statistics* (database); based on OECD (2016), *The Economic Consequences of Outdoor Air Pollution.*

StatLink http://dx.doi.org/10.1787/888933459806

heating. National air quality standards are also exceeded in urban areas near busy roads (MfE, 2014b). Monitoring of PM_{10} pollution improved, but only a few sites in major cities monitor concentrations of fine particular matter ($PM_{2.5}$), which have greater health impacts. In contrast to many other OECD member countries, New Zealand has no national standards on $PM_{2.5}$ concentrations. A review of the NESs particulate matter provisions is due to be completed in 2017.

6.2. *Ozone depletion: Contribution and vulnerability*

New Zealand has ratified the Vienna Convention on the Protection of the Ozone Layer and the related Montreal Protocol combating ozone-depleting substances (ODSs). The country successfully phased out ODS consumption through a progressive reduction on the permits to import substances not produced domestically. Methyl bromide, used mainly as pesticides in crops, was phased out in 2007; it can now only be used for quarantine and pre-shipment fumigation. The phase-out of hydrochloroflurocarbons (HCFCs) was completed in January 2015, in advance of the 2030 international target (MfE, 2013).

New Zealand is vulnerable to ozone-layer depletion due to its proximity to Antarctica, where this phenomenon is more pronounced. The country has high levels of ultraviolet (UV) in international comparisons; extreme UV thresholds are often exceeded.[18] The reduction of the ozone concentration, and consequent over-exposure to UV radiation, can have severe implications for natural ecosystems and for human health, notably skin cancers and cataracts. New Zealand has the highest incidence and mortality rates of melanoma cancer in the world; it was the fourth most-common cause of cancer and the sixth most-common cause of death in the country (Figure 1.18).

Figure 1.18. **New Zealand's rates of melanoma incidence and mortality are the highest in the world**

Melanoma's incidence and mortality rates, 2012

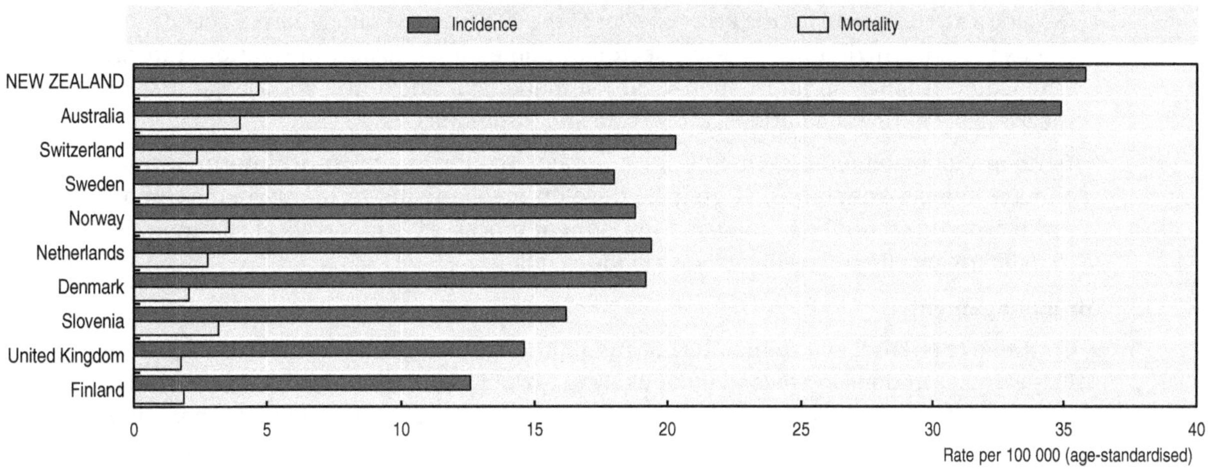

Source: Centre for Public Health Research (2016), *Environmental Health Indicators* (database); WHO-International Agency for Research on Cancer (2016), *Cancer Mortality* (database).

StatLink http://dx.doi.org/10.1787/888933459819

6.3. *Access to water supply, sanitation and wastewater treatment*

In 2014, 82% of the population was connected to public wastewater treatment plants, an increase of 1.2% since 2000; an additional 10% was connected to independent treatment (OECD, 2016d). Urban expansion and associated infrastructure development drove the increase in connection rates. Recent data on access to wastewater treatment by treatment type are not available; in 2000, the connection rates of the population to tertiary and secondary wastewater treatment were 40% and 26% respectively, followed by 14% for primary treatment (OECD, 2015c).

6.4. *Environmental quality of housing*

New Zealand's building stock is often poorly insulated and thus energy performance is relatively poor; nearly two-thirds of homes were built before adoption of requirements for thermal insulation in new homes in 1978. In addition, the residential housing stock is frequently damp, cold in winter and mouldy: about a quarter of homeowners and half of renters report problems with dampness or mould. These issues are more frequently reported by some population subgroups, namely people in one-parent families with children, people of prime working age, and Maori and Pacific peoples (Statistics NZ, 2015c). Dampness and mould have detrimental effects on public health; New Zealand has the highest rate of respiratory illness in the OECD, with one out of four people suffering from asthma (IEA, forthcoming). Despite significant government efforts in recent years, an estimated 600 000 homes remain inadequately insulated, which tend to be occupied by low-income families. Better insulation of houses would bring significant health benefits, alongside environmental benefits associated with energy savings (Chapter 3).

Recommendations on climate change, air, waste and biodiversity

Climate change

- Develop a strategic plan for the achievement of the 2030 climate mitigation target; identify the expected contribution of each sector to domestic emission mitigation and the anticipated reliance on international carbon markets; improve the knowledge base on the available mitigation options, their costs and trade-offs.
- Develop vulnerability assessments for all major economic sectors to inform sectoral climate change adaptation strategies; develop mechanisms to mainstream climate resilience into sectoral planning and investment processes; support local communities to mainstream climate resilience into land-use planning.

Air management

- Continue to strengthen the monitoring and reporting of air quality data, in particular of $PM_{2.5}$ concentrations in areas that are likely to exceed international guidelines; broaden the scope of the National Environment Standards on Air Quality to include maximum concentrations for $PM_{2.5}$.

Waste management

- Extend the waste disposal levy to cover all relevant landfill types; encourage local authorities to introduce quantity- or volume-based waste charges to help minimise waste, foster recycling and improve recovery of waste service costs.
- Improve the collection of data on the generation, disposal and treatment of waste, with a view to producing timely, comprehensive and internationally comparable information.

Biodiversity conservation and sustainable use

- Continue to improve the information base on the state of biodiversity, particularly in private lands; identify conservation priorities and formulate long-term strategies and plans for biodiversity protection and sustainable use; speed up the process for the adoption of a national policy statement on biodiversity; build on international experience in using innovative policy instruments and approaches, including payments for ecosystem services and biodiversity offsetting.

Notes

1. A 6.3 magnitude earthquake hit Christchurch on 22 February 2011, killing 185 people and causing widespread damage to the city's infrastructure, which had already been weakened by a 7.1 magnitude earthquake in September 2010. A significant number of dwellers were displaced, and much of the city's infrastructure and assets had to relocate and be rebuilt.
2. After the record high of 2013, dairy prices continued to decline, following the weaker import demand from the People's Republic of China and increased global production (OECD-FAO, 2016). Dairy production in New Zealand is largely based on pasture and therefore prone to extreme weather events. Recent forecasts indicate these events may reduce New Zealand's dairy production by 6.8% (OECD-FAO, 2016).
3. In 2013, GDP per capita in the wealthiest region was 2.3 times higher than in the poorest region; this is among the lowest values among OECD member countries (OECD, 2014). The relatively small regional spread is explained by a relatively mobile workforce and a strong agricultural sector, which has boosted per capita income in rural areas.
4. The share of 0-17 year olds living below the poverty line (defined at 60% of the median income after housing costs) increased from 24% to 29% between 2013 and 2014 (Simpson et al., 2015).
5. The Pike River mine was closed in November 2010 as a consequence of a methane explosion; other mining activities have been suspended at the Spring Creek mine on the west coast of the South Island.

6. New Zealand crude oil is high quality with low density and sulphur content, which has a premium price advantage on the international market (IEA, forthcoming).
7. The International Panel on Climate Change (IPCC) projects the sea around New Zealand will rise about 30 cm in the next 50 years.
8. DMC is the sum of domestic raw materials extraction used by an economy and its physical trade balance (imports minus exports of domestic raw materials and manufactured products).
9. Data on waste management are limited to waste disposed of in levied landfills that accept municipal solid waste (as defined by the New Zealand Waste Minimisation Act 2008). This is estimated to account for nearly 30% (2.7 million tonnes) of total waste disposed of to land (in addition, about 6.5 million tonnes are disposed of in non-levied landfills and farm dumps) (MfE, 2014a).
10. Aboriginal fisheries are regulated by specific regulations as customary-non-commercial fishing and excluded from the other schemes.
11. For example, 100% of frogs, lizards, bats and coders; 96% of freshwater fish and spiders; 81% of flowering plants; and 56% of birds are endemic (found nowhere else in the world) (Brown, 2016).
12. Using a different classification, which includes threatened and at risk species, the Ministry for the Environment estimates that 81% of bird species, 72% of freshwater fish, 88% of reptiles, 100% of frogs and 27% of resident marine mammal species face extinction (MfE and NZ Statistics, 2015).
13. New Zealand does not regularly collect data on water abstraction; data are estimated on the basis of water allocations (about half of allocated water is actually abstracted). International comparison thus needs to be treated with caution.
14. The nutrient balance is defined as the difference between nutrient inputs entering a farming system (mainly livestock manure and fertilisers) and nutrient outputs leaving the system (the uptake of nutrients for crop and pasture production). A nutrient deficit indicates declining soil fertility; a nutrient surplus indicates a risk of polluting soil, water and air (OECD, 2014).
15. Nitrogen oxides (NO_x) emissions increased by 13% over 2000-14, sulphur oxides (SO_x) emissions by 5% and non-methane volatile organic compounds (NMVOC) emissions by 8% (OECD, 2016c).
16. Between 2001 and 2012, estimated emissions from on-road transport decreased for carbon monoxide (CO) (-39%), NO_x (-35%), PM_{10} (-24%), $PM_{2.5}$ (-25%) and volatile organic compounds (VOC) (-50%) (MfE and Statistics NZ, 2015).
17. The NES on Air Quality includes five standards for ambient (outdoor) air quality (on PM_{10}, NO_2, O_3, SO_2 and CO); standards banning activities that discharge significant quantities of dioxins and other toxics into the air; a design standard for new wood burners installed in urban areas; and a requirement for landfills with over 1 million tonnes of refuse to collect greenhouse gas emissions. The standard for PM_{10} concentrations requires that daily average concentrations do not exceed 50µg/m^3 more than one day per year. It is based on the WHO guideline for short-term exposure, which requires that daily average concentrations do not exceed 50µg/m^3 more than three days per year.
18. The UV index or sun index is an indicator of the level of exposure to UV radiation; WHO developed it to inform the public on the risks of excessive UV exposure and advise on the need of protective measures. The scale of the indicator is open-ended and values vary in relation to exposure risk according to the following classification: 1-2: low; 3-5: moderate; 6-7: high; 8-9: very high; 11+: extreme.

References

Brown, M.A. (2016), *Pathways to Prosperity. Safeguarding Biodiversity in Development*, Environmental Defence Society, Auckland.

Brown, M.A. (2015), *Vanishing Nature: Facing New Zealand's Biodiversity Crisis*, Environmental Defence Society, Auckland.

Clifford, V. et al. (2013), "Quantifying the change in high country fire hazard from wilding trees", *New Zealand Fire Service Commission Research Report*, No. 127, New Zealand Forest Research Institute.

Climate Action Tracker (2016), "New Zealand", webpage, *http://climateactiontracker.org/countries/newzealand.html* (accessed 3 October 2016).

DOC (2016), Predator Free New Zealand 2050, website, *www.doc.govt.nz/our-work/predator-free-new-zealand-2050*, Department of Conservation, Wellington (accessed 15 October 2016).

DOC (2013), *Visitor Trends Report*, Department of Conservation, Wellington.

FAO (2016), *The Global Forest Resources Assessment: How are the world's forests changing?*, Second edition, The Food and Agriculture Organization of the United Nations, Rome.

FiBL and IFOAM (2016), *The World of Organic Agriculture 2016*, Research Institute of Organic Agriculture and International Federation of Organic Agriculture Movements, Frick and Bonn.

Government of New Zealand (2014), *New Zealand's Fifth National Report to the United Nations Convention on Biological Diversity. Reporting period: 2009-2013*, Government of New Zealand, Wellington.

Humphries, B. and M. Close (2015), *National Survey of Pesticides in Groundwater 2014*, Environmental Science and Research Limited (ESR), report prepared for New Zealand regional councils.

IEA (forthcoming), *Energy Policies of IEA Countries: New Zealand*, IEA/OECD Publishing, Paris.

Logan, H. (2016), Looking Back – Looking Forward? Institutional aspects of New Zealand approaches to nature conservation, *Policy Quarterly*, Vol. 12, No. 1, pp. 42-49.

Maori Land Court (2016), Maori Land Update, June 2016, Ministry of Justice.

MfE (2016a), *New Zealand's Greenhouse Gases Inventory 1990-2014*, Ministry for the Environment, Wellington.

MfE (2016b), *New Zealand's Action on Climate Change*, September 2016, Ministry for the Environment, Wellington.

MfE (2016c), Latest Update on New Zealand's 2020 Net Position, webpage, Ministry for the Environment, Wellington, *www.mfe.govt.nz/climate-change/reporting-greenhouse-gas-emissions/latest-2020-net-position* (accessed October 2016).

MfE (2016d), *Climate Projections for New Zealand: Snapshot*, June 2016, Ministry for the Environment, Wellington.

MfE and Statistics NZ (2016), *New Zealand's Environmental Reporting Series: Our Marine Environment 2016*, Ministry for the Environment and Statistics New Zealand, Wellington.

MfE (2015), *New Zealand's Second Biennial Report under the United Nation Framework Convention on Climate Change*, Ministry for the Environment, Wellington.

MfE and Statistics NZ (2015), *New Zealand's Environmental Reporting Series: Environment Aotearoa 2015*, Ministry for the Environment and Statistics New Zealand, Wellington.

MfE (2014a), *Review of the Effectiveness of the Waste Disposal Levy*, Ministry for the Environment, Wellington.

MfE (2014b), *Air Domain Report 2014*, Ministry for the Environment, Wellington.

MfE (2013), *Stratospheric Ozone Indicator Update*, October 2012, Info 652, Reviewed July 2013, Ministry for the Environment, Wellington, *www.mfe.govt.nz/more/environmental-reporting/reporting-act/atmosphere/levels-stratospheric-ozone-indicator*.

MPI (2016), The Status of New Zealand's Fisheries 2015, February 2016, Ministry for Primary Industry, Wellington.

OECD (2016a), *OECD Economic Outlook*, Volume 2016/1, OECD Publishing, Paris, *http://dx.doi.org/10.1787/eco_outlook-v2016-1-en*.

OECD (2016b), "Material resources (Edition 2015)", *OECD Environment Statistics* (database), *http://dx.doi.org/10.1787/data-00695-en* (accessed 5 October 2016).

OECD (2016c), "Emissions of air pollutants", *OECD Environment Statistics* (database), *http://dx.doi.org/10.1787/data-00598-en* (accessed 7 October 2016).

OECD (2016d), "Water: Wastewater treatment (Edition 2016)", *OECD Environment Statistics* (database), *http://dx.doi.org/10.1787/af447570-en* (accessed 15 October 2016).

OECD (2015a), *OECD Economic Surveys: New Zealand 2015*, OECD Publishing, Paris, *http://dx.doi.org/10.1787/eco_surveys-nzl-2015-en*.

OECD (2015b), "New Zealand", in *OECD Review of Fisheries: Policy and Summary Statistics 2015*, OECD Publishing, Paris, *http://dx.doi.org/10.1787/rev_fish-2015-29-en*.

OECD (2015c), *Environment at a Glance 2015: OECD Indicators*, OECD Publishing, Paris, *http://dx.doi.org/10.1787/9789264235199-en*.

OECD (2014), Society at a Glance 2014 Highlights: New Zealand, OECD Social Indicators, *www.oecd.org/newzealand/OECD-SocietyAtaGlance2014-Highlights-NewZealand.pdf*.

OECD (2013), "Environmental Performance of Agriculture (Edition 2013)", *OECD Agriculture Statistics* (database), *http://dx.doi.org/10.1787/data-00660-en* (accessed 5 October 2016).

OECD (2007), *OECD Environmental Performance Reviews: New Zealand*, OECD Publishing, Paris, *http://dx.doi.org/10.1787/9789264030589-en*.

OECD-FAO (2016), *OECD-FAO Agricultural Outlook 2016-2025*, OECD Publishing, Paris, *http://dx.doi.org/10.1787/agr_outlook-2016-en*.

PCE (2015a), "New Zealand's contribution to the new international climate change agreement", Submission to the Minister for Climate Change Issues and the Minister for the Environment, Parliamentary Commissioner for the Environment, Wellington.

PCE (2015b), "Preparing New Zealand for rising seas: certainty and uncertainty", report prepared for the Ministry for the Environment, November 2015, Parliamentary Commissioner for the Environment, Wellington.

PCE (2012), *Water Quality in New Zealand: Understanding the Science*, Parliamentary Commissioner for the Environment, Wellington.

Royal Society of New Zealand (2016), *Transition to a Low-carbon Economy for New Zealand*, April 2016, Royal Society of New Zealand, Wellington.

Ruru, J. (2014), Tuhoe-Crown settlement – Te Urewera Act 2014, *Maori Law Review*, October 2014.

Simpson, J. et al. (2015), "Child Poverty Monitor 2015",Technical Report, NZ Child and Youth Epidemiology Service, University of Otago, Dunedin.

Statistics NZ (2016a), *Tourism Satellite Accounts: 2015* (database), Statistics New Zealand, Wellington (accessed 28 September 2016).

Statistics NZ (2016b), "Estimated Resident Population for Urban Areas, at 30 June (1996+) (Annual-Jun)", Statistics New Zealand, Wellington (accessed 18 August 2016).

Statistics NZ (2015a), *New Zealand in Profile 2015*, Statistics New Zealand, Wellington.

Statistics NZ (2015b), "Area unit population projections, by age and sex, 2013(base)-2043", Statistics New Zealand, Wellington (accessed 15 June 2016).

Statistics NZ (2015c), "Perceptions of housing quality in 2014/15", Statistics New Zealand, Wellington (accessed 16 June 2016).

PART I

Chapter 2

Environmental governance and management

New Zealand has significantly strengthened stakeholder collaboration in environmental management and established nationwide environmental requirements in several key areas. However, insufficient human and technical capacity of local authorities, along with remaining regulatory gaps, generate implementation challenges. This chapter analyses New Zealand's environmental governance system, including horizontal and vertical co-ordination mechanisms. It reviews the regulatory framework for environmental impact assessment and permitting, as well as measures to ensure compliance with environmental law. The chapter also assesses progress in promoting public participation in decision making and access to environmental information, education and justice.

1. Introduction

New Zealand's system of environmental governance is unique in many respects. Although it is a unitary state, the country has largely decentralised regulatory and compliance assurance functions to regional and territorial authorities; national environmental standards and rules cover only a limited number of issues. Most environmental impacts are governed by a single comprehensive piece of legislation – the 1991 Resource Management Act (RMA) – which closely integrates land-use planning and environmental regulation. Uncommonly among OECD member countries, the legislation requires individual activity consents or permits only when the activity is not generally permitted under a local plan or by a national environmental standard or regulation. This system was designed to balance the interests of local development and environmental protection. However, since it has often led to inconsistent policy implementation, establishing a regulatory level playing field has become one of the central government's priorities.

2. Institutional framework for environmental governance

In New Zealand's decentralised system of environmental governance, most policy implementation responsibilities are at the regional and local levels. Responsibilities for land-use planning and environmental permitting have, in general, been devolved to the community most closely affected by the use of land and natural resources, in accordance with the RMA. Local authorities identify the environmental risks in their area and develop policy statements and plans (within a defined hierarchy) to regulate activities in response to those threats.

2.1. *National institutions and horizontal co-ordination*

Since 2007, when the previous OECD *Environmental Performance Review* was released, New Zealand has substantially improved horizontal co-ordination on environmental management at the national level. The Natural Resources Sector (NRS) – a grouping of the eight government agencies under nine ministers with natural resource management responsibilities – was created in 2008 to build a coherent and integrated approach to policy making in this field. The NRS agencies are: Ministry for the Environment (MfE); Ministry of Business, Innovation and Employment; Ministry for Primary Industries, with responsibilities for agriculture and fisheries; Land Information New Zealand; Department of Conservation (DOC); Department of Internal Affairs; Ministry of Transport; and Te Puni Kokiri, the public service department advising the government on policies and issues affecting Maori.

The NRS co-ordinates work in several focus areas to align economic development and sustainability goals. These include, for example, issues of freshwater allocation; energy efficiency and use of renewable energy; and urban land management. This unique model of horizontal co-ordination (equally followed in the social sector, security and intelligence, and other areas) has allowed the government to reduce inter-ministerial tensions, pursue a more holistic approach to natural resource management and work towards an integrated customer service perspective in relation to non-government stakeholders and Maori communities. At the same time, there is still a lack of institutional co-ordination on aquaculture, fisheries and marine biodiversity protection, as well as urban development (Chapter 5). This is partly due to the patchy regulatory regime in these domains and lack of clarity in the role of different government agencies (EDS, 2016).

The NRS has several co-ordination mechanisms: the Business Growth Agenda Natural Resources Ministers Group (for ministers, meets monthly), the NRS Leadership Board (for Chief Executives of member agencies, meets quarterly) and the NRS Programme Governance Group (for mid-level management representatives, meets monthly). The NRS Support Unit, housed in the MfE and jointly staffed through secondments from NRS agencies, ensures day-to-day collaboration across the sector. The Parliamentary Commissioner for the Environment (PCE), who has broad powers to investigate environmental concerns, ensures general oversight of resource management nationwide. The PCE is independent of the government and issues high-quality reports to Parliament.

The MfE has been the principal national policy-making authority on environmental matters since 1986. The DOC is mainly concerned with management of the conservation estate (i.e. protected areas) and issues permits for activities that could potentially harm biodiversity. The Environmental Protection Authority (EPA) was established in 2011 by a special act. The EPA primarily regulates production and use of hazardous substances and new organisms, environmental effects of activities on New Zealand's continental shelf and transboundary movements of hazardous waste, as well as advises on development proposals of national significance. The EPA's remit covers a mixture of provisions of different statutes, but is only limited to supporting independent decision makers (such as Boards of Inquiry) in permitting major infrastructure projects under the RMA, which is uncommon for a national environmental regulator.

2.2. Sub-national institutions and vertical co-ordination

There are three types of sub-national (local) authorities: territorial authorities (which include city and district councils); regional councils (which have jurisdiction covering multiple territorial authorities)[1] and unitary authorities (which have powers of both a regional council and a territorial authority). There are 11 regional councils, 61 territorial authorities (made up of 11 city councils and 50 district councils) and 6 unitary authorities, together constituting 78 local authorities. While the idea of merging territorial authorities does not have local political support, local councils are interested in achieving economies of scale through sharing services (e.g. waste management) among neighbouring districts.

All local authorities have planning responsibilities, which are closely intertwined with their regulatory powers (Section 3.3). Regional councils and unitary authorities have regulatory and enforcement powers for the management of fresh, ground and coastal water; soil conservation; and control of emissions to air, land and water. Territorial and unitary authorities are in charge of land use and have regulatory and enforcement powers in the areas of solid waste management, water supply and wastewater treatment – topics that commonly belong to local authorities' responsibilities in OECD member countries. Giving effect to the Treaty of Waitangi requires close collaboration between local authorities and Maori communities (iwi/hapu) over specific important natural resources. All local authorities are primarily accountable to their electorates.

The issue of resource capacity of local authorities (particularly smaller councils) is a persistent challenge.[2] Environment-related staff numbers have recently been decreasing in all three sub-national authority types: between 2011 and 2013 alone, they dropped by between one-quarter and one-third. In 2012/13, only 20 of 78 local authorities had dedicated environmental inspectors, while 10 councils had dedicated general enforcement officers who prepared sanction decisions. One unitary authority and nine territorial authorities had no compliance monitoring or enforcement staff at all (MfE, 2016a). Although regional councils have comparatively greater capacity assigned to compliance monitoring and enforcement, 80% of all district and city councils believe they lack sufficient human resources to exercise their duties (MfE, 2014). Over a third of local authorities identified monitoring and enforcement as a "significant capability gap" (NZPC, 2016).

The capacity building Making Good Decisions Programme operated by the Opus Environmental Training Centre trains councillors, community board members and independent commissioners on issue resource consents and making other decisions under the RMA. However, only 38% of regional and territorial councils agree they receive the training and information required to implement new national environmental policies and regulations (NZPC, 2016). New Zealand should make better use of its participation in the Australasian Environmental Law Enforcement and Regulators Network (AELERT), which aims to build relationships between sub-national jurisdictions to facilitate the sharing of information and improve the regulatory compliance capacity of member agencies.

Local Government New Zealand, an association of regional and territorial authorities headed by a National Council, supports co-ordination among local authorities. The Upper North Island Strategic Alliance and the Central New Zealand Alliance gather several neighbouring councils in the respective geographic areas. Together, they support collaboration on economic development, transport, tourism, and water and waste management services. However, these organisations do not promote the harmonisation of environmental policy instruments used by individual authorities.

To ensure vertical co-ordination, the Chief Executives Environment and Economy Forum brings together chief executives of the national NRS agencies and regional councils each quarter to discuss key natural resource management issues and priorities. However, this co-ordination does not involve district and city councils, which are likely to be in even greater need of national policy implementation guidance. Establishing a co-ordination body following best practices in other OECD member countries (Box 2.1) may facilitate capacity building for local authorities.

Box 2.1. **Multi-level co-ordination between environmental authorities in Sweden**

The Swedish Enforcement and Regulations Council (ToFR) is a body for co-operation between Swedish public authorities on regulation and enforcement matters with respect to implementation of the country's Environmental Code. Established by Parliament, with members appointed by the government, ToFR is chaired by a representative of the Swedish Environmental Protection Agency (EPA) and includes representatives of several other national authorities (e.g. the Chemicals Agency), the Swedish Association of Local Authorities and Regions, two County Administrative Boards and one municipality.

The council's activities are mainly organised around time-limited projects with participation from various member authorities. Its secretariat regularly holds seminars on

Box 2.1. **Multi-level co-ordination between environmental authorities in Sweden** *(cont.)*

topics of common interest for member authorities, covering inspection planning based on the environmental quality objectives, linkages between environmental management systems and compliance monitoring, enforcement methods, quality of enforcement, etc. These seminars act as forums for discussing common viewpoints and promoting integration between sectors and levels of government.

ToFR maintains an electronic Supervision Guidance Network – a "listserv" open to all civil servants working at the central environmental authorities and in environmental departments of County Administrative Boards. It allows individuals to ask their colleagues questions and e-mail answers to all participants. In addition, the Swedish EPA operates a "legal support service" (help desk) available by telephone for two hours every working day. This service offers advice and interpretation on legal issues. It is used not only by regional and local environmental authorities, but by other stakeholders as well.

Source: Mazur (2011).

Several central government bodies (Ministry for the Environment, Auditor General, Department of Internal Affairs, Ministry of Business Innovation and Employment, and Ministry of Health) oversee local governance functions. The Ministry for the Environment (MfE) oversees local authorities' environmental management activities. Between 1995 and 2014, it carried out 11 national surveys of local authorities for this purpose. The surveys have now been replaced by the National Monitoring System (NMS). The NMS requires local authorities, the EPA and the MfE itself to provide detailed data each year on the functions, tools and processes for which they are responsible under the Resource Management Act (RMA).

3. Setting of regulatory requirements

Three main statutes govern environmental management in New Zealand: the 1991 RMA, the 1996 Hazardous Substances and New Organisms Act (HSNO Act) and the 2012 Exclusive Economic Zone and Continental Shelf (Environmental Effects) Act (EEZ Act).[3] The RMA – a remarkably comprehensive piece of environmental legislation – provides a framework for national and regional environmental policy development, as well as regional and local (district) planning and permitting (Box 2.2). Environmental issues are also integrated into many other statutes that incorporate sustainable development ideas and principles. There are some discrepancies across these laws, in particular between RMA provisions and those of the Local Government Act (2002) and the Land Transport Management Act (2003); these create regulatory barriers to sustainable urban development (Chapter 5).

Over its lifetime, the RMA has been subject to 21 substantive amendments, doubling in size and inevitably losing some of its coherence. The Resource Management Amendment Act 2009 represented the biggest review of the RMA since its inception in 1991. Among other measures, it improved the resource consent process to reduce the cost and time faced by applicants and increased the size of criminal fines for environmental offences (Section 4.2). The 2013 RMA amendments further streamlined resource consent applications. The Resource Legislation Amendment Bill 2015 is under consideration in Parliament. Among its aims, the bill seeks to provide more choice over plan making processes and create a more consistent and efficient consent process.

Box 2.2. **The RMA: Balancing national direction and decentralisation in integrated resource management**

Prior to 1991, New Zealand had complex regulation for resource management characterised by process duplication and a plethora of decision-making bodies with high compliance and transaction costs. With its adoption in 1991, the RMA tried to replace this complex landscape with a "one-stop shop" consent (permitting) system. The RMA was intended to install a regulatory regime establishing non-negotiable "bio-physical bottom lines" to ensure development occurred within the capacity of the environment that supported it. Beyond those bottom lines, resource users would be left to make their own decisions.

The RMA's setup is hierarchical and decentralised, having radically altered the historic resource management responsibilities at all administrative levels. Bottom lines are set at the national level, while regional and territorial authorities implement national directions in the form of National Policy Statements (NPSs), National Environmental Standards (NESs) and regulations. The RMA was designed as a framework (for land, air, freshwater and coastal zone management), not a blueprint. It gave local authorities wide discretion to identify the most efficient means of achieving the act's purpose and meeting community needs. The following are the current and forthcoming NPSs and NESs:

National Policy Statements	National Environmental Standards
Existing	
Electricity transmission (2008) Coastal Policy (2010) Renewable electricity generation (2011) Freshwater management (2011, updated in 2014)	Air quality (2004) Sources of human drinking water (2008) Telecommunication facilities (2008) Electricity transmission activities (2009) Assessing and managing contaminants in soil to protect human health (2012)
Planned	
Urban development capacity Biodiversity	Plantation forestry

Under the RMA's hierarchy, regional and territorial policies and plans must give effect to NPSs (i.e. national objectives and policies) and comply with NESs (i.e. technical rules).

Other national direction priorities include developing regulations on stock exclusion from water bodies, pest control, aquaculture, natural hazards, end-of-life tyres and dam safety, as well as updating the NPS on freshwater management and NESs on air quality soil contaminants and telecommunication facilities.

Source: EDS (2016); MfE (2016b, 2013a).

These legislative changes should be seen as part of the trend towards reducing the administrative burden for businesses. The regulatory debate in recent years has largely focused on compliance costs borne by small and medium-sized enterprises (SMEs) and the need to reduce regulatory pressure on them. For example, the Ministry of Business, Innovation and Employment is leading an SME "Good Regulation" project. In addition, a Business Compliance Cost Panel within government looks for ways to relieve the administrative burden; a Small Business Advisory Group represents the SME community in these deliberations. At the same time, both non-governmental organisations (NGOs) and the PCE (2016a) criticise these developments for giving economic development precedence over environmental protection.

Under the RMA, National Policy Statements (NPSs) require regional and territorial authorities to implement certain policy objectives through regional policy statements[4] and regional and district plans. However, only four NPSs have been issued over the 25 years since the RMA's adoption. The government is planning to use this instrument more extensively to strengthen the basis for national environmental policy (Box 2.2).

3.1. *Evaluation of policies and legislation*

Undertaking regulatory impact analysis (RIA) during the development of regulatory proposals has been a formal requirement for all central government agencies since 1998. Among other goals, the Regulatory Impact Statement (RIS) must do the following:

- Assess efficiency and effectiveness of the proposal's provisions in achieving its objectives.
- Identify other reasonably practicable options for achieving the proposal's objectives.
- Identify expected benefits and costs (environmental, economic, social and cultural), including preparation of a Business Compliance Cost Statement.
- Assess the risk of acting or not acting if there is uncertain or insufficient information about the subject matter of the provisions.

Also at the central government level, various analytical methods, including cost-benefit-analysis and multi-criteria analysis, are part of the Natural Resource Framework – a system of approaches and tools, intertwined with Maori cultural values, to analyse the interrelationships between people and the environment and to assess policy options.

At the local level, all proposed plans, standards, policy statements and regulations under the RMA are required to undergo an *ex ante* evaluation and internal government review. The RMA also requires councils to monitor the efficiency and effectiveness of policies, rules and methods in their plans. Indeed, there are positive examples of this practice (e.g. the Auckland Plan foresees comprehensive triennial evaluations of delivery against targets; Chapter 5). However, the *ex post* policy evaluation remains underdeveloped. The MfE's new National Monitoring System has substantially improved collection and management of local authorities' environmental performance data, but includes few outcome indicators (e.g. the rate of non-compliance with resource consents, characterising the effectiveness of policy implementation). While the RMA requires public release of efficiency and effectiveness monitoring results at least every five years, only seven local authorities published such results in 2014/15 (MfE, 2016a). Local authorities may be at different stages of their reporting cycle, but this is still a significant decline from the 36 councils that published performance results in 2012/13 and the 51 that did so in 2010/11 (MfE, 2014). The absence of standard report formats and performance metrics seriously constrains meaningful comparison of performance outcomes across councils or against key indicators (NZCID, 2015). However, the MfE should use this performance information to design targeted capacity building programmes for local authorities.

While surveys and research on plan making and consenting have been carried out, no comprehensive empirical research has been undertaken to analyse the performance of the RMA. Such analysis could help identify remedies to deal with demonstrated implementation problems. A lot of data has been collected, but there has been no systematic evaluation of how well the act has delivered on its objectives (Palmer and Blakeley, 2015).

3.2. *Environmental standards*

National Environmental Standards (NESs) are regulations issued under the RMA that apply nationally. NESs can prescribe technical standards, methods or other requirements for environmental matters. Each regional, city or district council must enforce the same standard, and amend its policy statements and plans to be consistent with NESs. As the number of NESs is likely to increase in the future, changing all local authority plans may become a cumbersome process. In some circumstances, councils can impose stricter standards than the NES: this has occurred, for example, in several regions with respect to standards for wood burning in households and for discharges from vessels.

In addition to the NES for Air Quality (2004), New Zealand has established four more NESs in line with a recommendation of the previous EPR (Box 2.2). While NES development has accelerated since 2008, it is still slow and largely fragmented, depriving the regulatory framework of unequivocal national minimum requirements. In the coming years, the government intends to significantly expand the realm of national direction: priorities include developing NPSs on urban development capacity (Chapter 5) and biodiversity, an NES on plantation forestry and regulations on several other topics (Box 2.2).

The NES for Air Quality is made up of 14 separate, but interlinked, standards that generally follow guidance from the World Health Organization (WHO). These include seven standards banning emissions of significant quantities of toxic air pollutants and five standards for ambient air quality. These standards, implemented through regional air quality plans, include regulatory and promotional measures to address emissions from domestic heating and permitting for industrial emissions; limit values for major industrial sources are usually set by using dispersion modelling.

The NES for Sources of Human Drinking Water applies to source water before it is treated and only when the sources supply water to communities, not individual households. The NPS for Freshwater Management requires regional councils to maintain or improve water quality and to set quality objectives and pollutant input limits by 2025 (or by 2030 if it is not practicable to do so by 2025) for individual water bodies based on considerations of human and ecosystem health. This process is slow, with regional councils using different methodologies for allocating pollution loads among dischargers (Chapter 4). Although the 2007 EPR recommended that New Zealand develop regulatory measures to reduce diffuse water pollution, principally from agriculture, there are no national regulatory nutrient limits, and politically sensitive discussions continue at the regional level on how to set them. Discharges from ships and offshore installations into coastal marine waters in accordance with the RMA.

New Zealand is one of the few OECD member countries without national regulation of hazardous waste management. The EPA regulates transboundary movements of hazardous waste under the 2011 Import and Export (Restrictions) Act. There are no technical standards for hazardous waste landfills, storage or transportation facilities, either. Disposal of hazardous waste is managed through consents by regional councils using several non-regulatory guidelines from the government. There has been no progress in implementing the 2007 EPR recommendation to introduce national regulations for mandatory and comprehensive domestic tracking of hazardous waste transport, treatment and disposal.

3.3. Environmental impact assessment and permitting

Consent regime under the RMA

The system of resource consents integrates environmental impact assessment (which New Zealand calls an assessment of environmental effects, AEE), permitting and land use. Resource consents are a general term that encompasses land use and land subdivision consents, water (abstraction) permits, discharge permits (covering air,[5] water and waste) and coastal permits. Over 80% of all resource consents deal with land use and subdivision issues (Figure 2.1).

Figure 2.1. **Land-use issues dominate the resource consent regime**

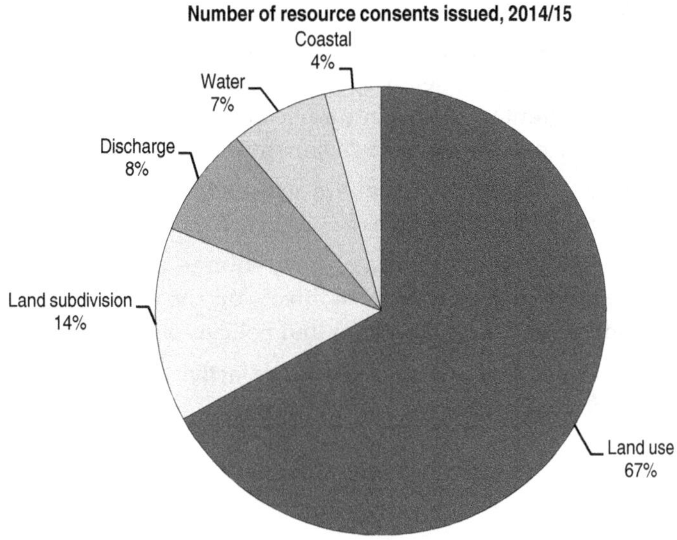

Source: MfE (2016), *National Monitoring System for 2014/15* (database).

Local government authorities issue most of the resource consents. At the national level, the EPA assesses RMA-related applications for a resource consent on matters of national significance, such as major infrastructure projects.[6] It recommends to the Minister for the Environment whether the application should be determined by a board of inquiry (established on a case by case basis) or the Environment Court.

Most OECD member countries would define categories of activities requiring a permit in a national or sub-national regulation. New Zealand, conversely, requires a resource consent whenever an intended development or activity is not in accordance with the rules of the relevant authority's planning document (e.g. a district plan; see Section 3.4). Plans, usually through rules, state whether an activity is permitted or whether it requires a resource consent (Box 2.3). Permitted activities may still be subject to conditions such as operating standards, but compliance is rarely monitored. The system was originally intended to reduce the need for authorisations. However, due to the absence of standard requirements for obtaining a consent, the same activities (e.g. effluent discharges from dairy farms) may require a consent in one region, but not in another; this leads to national inconsistency.

The RMA explicitly provides for certain existing land uses that were lawfully established to continue without need for additional authorisation. Local councils are reluctant to challenge existing use rights even when they have legal grounds to do so, which results in inherent favouring of incumbent users of resources (EDS, 2016). Permitted activities and existing uses contribute to cumulative environmental impacts that are not always well accounted for (Brown, 2016).

In 2014/15, over 40 000 consent applications were processed, which is higher than in 2012/13, but still significantly lower than in the 2000s (Figure 2.2). The decrease in

Box 2.3. **Resource consent requirements under the RMA**

Controlled activity: Resource consent is required. The consent authority (council) must grant a consent if the application contains all information necessary to meet the requirements. Conditions may be imposed only for matters specified in an NES or the jurisdiction's resource management plan.

Restricted discretionary activity: Resource consent is required. The consent authority's discretion is restricted to matters clearly specified in the jurisdiction's resource management plan. Where consent is granted, the activity must comply with the requirements, conditions and permissions specified in the relevant documents.

Discretionary activity: Resource consent is required. The consent authority has broad discretion over whether to grant or refuse the consent. If granted, conditions may be included.

Non-complying activity: Resource consent is required and may only be issued if the consent authority is satisfied that adverse effects on the environment from the activity will be minor or not conflict with objectives and policies of the relevant plan.

No resource consent is required for a ***permitted activity***, while an explicitly ***prohibited activity*** may not be issued a consent.

Source: NZPC (2016).

Figure 2.2. **The total number of resource consent applications is declining**

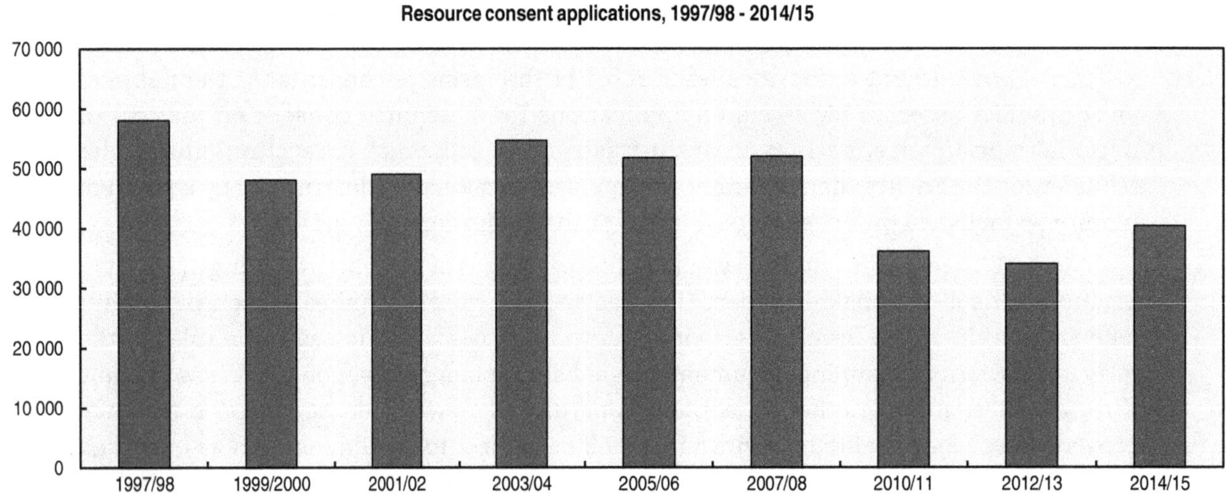

Source: MfE (2016), *National Monitoring System for 2014/15* (database).

StatLink http://dx.doi.org/10.1787/888933459823

applications may be linked to overall economic performance, but could also reflect changes in regional plans to allow more permitted activities. Where an industrial activity requires consents of the same type from both territorial and regional councils, the RMA allows these consents to be bundled together and determined at a joint hearing.

Every resource consent application must include an AEE, which contains a plan to avoid, mitigate or remedy the identified risks and adverse impacts. The scope of the AEE does not depend on the size of the potential impact, contrary to practice in many other OECD member countries. In addition to the MfE's 2006 guidance on how to prepare and evaluate an AEE, some councils have issued standards for AEEs, and in 2015 the Environmental Institute of Australia and New Zealand released voluntary guidance on ecological impact assessment for New Zealand. However, many of these documents do not provide sufficient depth and detail; where they do, they recommend assessment tools that may be too costly and time-consuming for the scale of many activities (Brown, 2016).

Approvals are frequently provided with conditions attached (Box 2.3), including, where warranted, monitoring of impacts. There is no system for cross-media integration of discharge permits for air, water and waste, as in many other OECD member countries. For discharge permits, the regional authority may impose the "best practicable option" test for mitigation measures (Reeves, 2015). However, unlike the criterion of best available techniques in EU countries, this test does not require cross-media, process-oriented solutions to minimise impact. Permit conditions may be bound to comply with other requirements, such as a water conservation order (for water bodies in their natural state) granted by a special tribunal appointed by the Minister for the Environment. Overall, there is a lack of national-level regulatory guidance on setting conditions in resource consents and permits, which often makes such conditions unclear and difficult to enforce (Brown, 2016).

The maximum term of discharge permits is 35 years. Long-term consents can and often do include review conditions to allow consent holders to keep up with the pace of change in technology that may help minimise environmental impacts. However, it is advisable to limit the validity of permits to eight to ten years or require their periodic review, as is commonly done in EU member states.

Applications for resource consents may be either publicly notified (involving broad public participation), limited-notified (with notices sent only to directly affected parties) or non-notified. The share of notified consents has been declining steadily in recent years and accounts for only 4% of the total (primarily for large development projects). In 2014/15, 56% of district councils did not notify any of the resource consents that they processed (MfE, 2016a). According to the 2009 amendments to the RMA, councils are no longer required to publicly notify a resource consent application if the potential environmental impacts are minor. This considerably limits public participation in the AEE and permitting processes, contrary to the dominant practice in OECD member countries and the OECD Council recommendation on the matter.[7] This issue could be addressed by introducing activity-size or impact-based thresholds above which AEE should be fully fledged and subject to mandatory public participation; smaller activities could undergo simplified AEE without notification.

Many businesses complain about the complexity and length of the consent application process. In fact, 96% of new resource consents were processed within the statutory time limits of up to 60 working days for an application process without a public hearing in 2014/15 (MfE, 2016a); less than 1% of consent decisions are appealed to the Environment Court. However, the Rules Reduction Taskforce recently singled out the RMA as the piece of legislation imposing the highest administrative burden on businesses: it accounts for 32% of all administrative applications in New Zealand (DIA, 2015), which is natural considering its vast scope. Still, to address these concerns, the Resource Legislation Amendment Bill 2015 would, among other measures, introduce a new fast-tracked process (with a ten-day limit) for simple applications and impose certain restrictions on public notification and appeals.

Other consent regimes

Under the EEZ Act, the EPA issues consents for environmental impacts of activities on New Zealand's continental shelf and its Exclusive Economic Zone. Since its establishment in 2011, the EPA has granted four consents for oil and gas extraction and rejected two consent applications for seabed mining due to lack of information on the potential environmental impacts.

In addition, under the HSNO Act, the EPA regulates pesticides, dangerous goods, household chemicals and other dangerous substances, as well as the importation, development, field test and release of new organisms. New Zealand's chemical safety regulations are different from most other OECD member countries. It has defined a number of group standards, which are descriptions of specific uses and hazard profiles of chemical substances. If a chemical that complies with one of these standards is produced or imported, then its use is authorised. If it does not comply, then the importer or manufacturer has to perform a risk assessment and request an authorisation from the EPA. That way, only chemicals that pose a potential risk have to go through a resource-intensive administrative process. The government is considering proposals to revise this scheme; there is no incentive to review the risks of chemicals that have been on the market for a long time and for which new knowledge is available, unless the government itself initiates a costly procedure to do this.

The DOC reviews applications (with compulsory AEE) and issues permits for activities involving the use of public conservation land and waters other than for personal recreation purposes.

3.4. Land-use planning and strategic environmental assessment

The RMA establishes a hierarchy of planning documents with split responsibility between the central government and local authorities. All lower-tier RMA documents are required to be consistent with higher-tier documents. Land use is regulated by district plans, which in some regions are complemented by regional spatial strategies. Regional councils must consider how Maori values apply to regional and local circumstances as part of their planning process. There are also separate regimes for managing state-owned land (8% of the total land area), overseen by Land Information New Zealand. Regional coastal plans manage activities in coastal marine areas. However, there is no spatial planning for marine areas, with the exception of an ongoing "Sea Change" pilot project in the Hauraki Gulf (*www.seachange.org.nz*).

There is often duplication of efforts in developing city/district, unitary and regional plans (MfE, 2013a). Each document is distinct, typically goes through a separate planning process and may contain different provisions to those of even adjacent jurisdictions. The Environment Court has to resolve quite a few inconsistencies between regional and district plans. To address this issue, the Resource Legislation Amendment Bill 2015 proposes a national planning template to reduce "unnecessary variation" between council plans. It would also expand the MfE's right to give direction to councils in land-use planning matters, which will contribute to greater nationwide consistency of environmental planning.

Private interests and environmental protection priorities are generally addressed at the local or regional level through often cumbersome and costly planning processes that take many years (Chapter 5). District and regional plans assign different statuses to development activities. The accompanying rules depend on the potential impact of activities on the environment, including biodiversity. Rules usually include restrictions on the clearing of vegetation, as well as damming and diversion of waterways; limits on fertiliser application; requirements for erosion control; and other land-use controls to minimise potential environmental harm. However, there is broad recognition that these planning instruments fail to address cumulative environmental impacts and long-term consequences of human development on the environment (Brown, 2016).

Under the Resource Legislation Amendment Bill 2015, councils can formally ask the Minister for the Environment for a streamlined plan-making process that would suit local circumstances. At the end of such a process (aimed primarily at facilitating housing development, see Chapter 5), the minister must approve or decline the council's proposed plan change. That decision could not be appealed; this proposed change has been criticised as opening the door to administrative abuse (PCE, 2016a). The bill also envisages a collaborative planning process, which would encourage greater public engagement at an early stage (with the resulting plan decisions exempt from appeal); however, there are no incentives for councils to choose this process over the streamlined one. While restricting judicial control for a collaborative process seems justified, doing so for an administrative approval would deprive the public of any oversight and recourse options. The PCE recommended limiting and better defining the types of plan changes that may undergo the streamlined process.

All regulations and plans are subject to an evaluation of alternatives, assessment of costs and benefits (including environmental and social costs) and public review as part of regulatory impact analysis (Section 3.1). However, there is no systematic evaluation of significant and cumulative effects on the environment of every proposed plan or programme. A requirement to consider environmental and sustainability issues is part of several statutes, including those related to transport planning. Practical implementation, however, is challenging (Box 2.4).

Box 2.4. **Challenges of integrating environmental considerations into transport planning**

Transport policies and plans in New Zealand are developed through a combination of national, regional and local processes. The regional land transport strategy (RLTS), for example, provides guidance on the transport development in a region for the next 30 years. The process of developing an RLTS is not explicitly defined, but the Land Transportation Management Act (2003) aims to achieve sustainable land transport by avoiding, "to the extent reasonable in the circumstances", adverse effects on the environment and taking into account the views of affected communities.

The incorporation of environmental and sustainability principles into transport planning and decision making has been challenging. The main barriers include:

- limited use of environmental data
- insufficient development and analysis of different transport options
- limited explicit consideration of environmental impacts of different transport options
- heavy focus of monitoring on intended outcomes, often at the expense of wider environmental consequences
- lack of external integration with other (non-transport) regional and national policies
- difficulties engaging a wide group of stakeholders.

Source: McGimpsey and Morgan (2013).

There are particular issues with the integration of biodiversity protection into land-use planning. The 2007 EPR recommended that New Zealand fully reflect nature conservation objectives in land-use and coastal plans. In 2011, the government held consultations for a proposed NPS for Indigenous Biodiversity. However, this NPS did not pass into law because of opposition from private landowners; they considered the policy for identifying sites for biodiversity protection to be disproportionately restrictive (Brown, 2016). The government is looking to establish a collaborative group of stakeholders to work through key issues of biodiversity management and protection on private land in view of preparing a draft NPS on biodiversity by the end of 2018.

4. Compliance assurance

The 2007 EPR recommended that New Zealand strengthen compliance with environmental conditions set in resource consents and permits through increased inspection and enforcement. While the enforcement tools have been strengthened, local authorities still lack resources to monitor and enforce compliance adequately (Section 2.2); this contributes to relatively high non-compliance with environmental requirements. Compliance promotion is underused by local authorities. The lack of national guidance on compliance assurance (compliance promotion, monitoring and enforcement) not only reduces opportunities for councils to focus on compliance priorities, but also exposes their inconsistent practices to criticism from the regulated community. To address this problem, regional councils have established a Compliance and Enforcement Special Interest Group. It has produced a Regional Sector Strategic Compliance Framework 2016-18 (CESIG, 2016) that encourages the risk-based approach to compliance promotion and monitoring, and peer review across regional councils.

4.1. *Environmental inspections*

Local authorities must carry out inspections to monitor compliance with resource consent conditions and their impact on the environment. In 2014/15, compliance monitoring covered 58 449 of 97 210 resource consents that required monitoring according to their conditions. This is a fairly high compliance monitoring rate (60%) by international standards. However, a significant share (20.7%) were found to be non-compliant (MfE, 2016a).

Most local authorities have developed monitoring and enforcement strategies and conduct proactive compliance monitoring of resource consents. However, only 16% aim to monitor all resource consents they issue. Less than 5% of local authorities, due to limited staff resources, do not routinely monitor compliance with consents and only act in response to complaints about related offences (MfE, 2014). Few local authorities had a database for recording compliance monitoring information (MfE, 2016a).

A small, but growing, share of local authorities has adopted a risk-based approach to compliance monitoring. They set priorities based on factors such as compliance history and the number and complexity of consent conditions, which corresponds to good international practices in this domain. The Regional Sector Strategic Compliance Framework recommends benchmarking of monitoring frequencies against other regional and unitary authorities once every three years to ensure a consistent approach to inspections nationwide (CESIG, 2016). However, only 10% of local councils use electronic systems to schedule and track monitoring and enforcement; the same percentage of local authorities co-ordinate compliance monitoring of resource and building consents to avoid duplication of effort (e.g. by having a building inspector verify compliance with both for minor activities) (MfE, 2014). The MfE needs to do more to explain the benefits of risk-based targeting and other resource-efficient inspection practices to local authorities.

4.2. Enforcement tools

The RMA provides for punitive (infringement notice, prosecution) and directive (abatement notice, enforcement order) enforcement tools. Infringement notices are mostly imposed for non-compliance with abatement notices that had been issued earlier and ordered specific corrective actions. Infringement notices may carry an administrative fine of up to NZD 1 000 (about USD 700). Local authorities may also ask the Environment Court for an enforcement order to cease an activity or prescribe actions to prevent or remediate environmental damage.

Administrative enforcement

The use of administrative enforcement tools is rather limited. In 2014/15, 3 667 enforcement actions were taken, corresponding to 30% of non-compliance cases (MfE, 2016a). Local authorities most commonly use abatement notices (52% of enforcement cases in 2014/15), while almost never using enforcement orders. The issuance of infringement notices, used primarily by regional councils and unitary authorities, represented 39% of enforcement cases in 2014/15. Across all enforcement tools, district and city councils account for only 23% of all environmental enforcement actions in New Zealand. In 2014/15, 14 territorial authorities did not undertake any formal enforcement action (MfE, 2016a) due both to lack of enforcement resources and the unwillingness of local councils to put too much pressure on business actors.

One example of the limited use of administrative enforcement tools is the response by Environment Canterbury (exercising the functions of the regional council) to complaints about pollution of waterways by livestock. It took enforcement actions in response to only 15 of 382 complaints in 2011-15, issuing infringement notices in just 6 cases (Fish & Game New Zealand, 2016). Other evidence (Brown et al., 2013) confirms that compliance assurance is weakest in the agricultural sector.

Over two-thirds of enforcement cases are related to land-use issues, while about one-quarter are connected to discharge of contaminants to land (Figure 2.3). One key compliance issue is that consent holders regard a consent simply as an operating licence and either do not understand or disregard its conditions (MfE, 2014).

Enforcement actions depend on factors such as the seriousness of the breach, the attitude and past compliance record of the offender, and whether the violation was deliberate. All regional councils, half of unitary authorities and 43% of territorial authorities have written policies on appropriate enforcement decision making. Still, some local councils are concerned about consistency of enforcement for different activities within their respective jurisdictions; a few even use enforcement decision groups to evaluate recommendations from enforcement officers (MfE, 2014). To improve nationwide consistency of compliance assurance, national templates could be used for resource consents, and national guidance could be issued on targeting of compliance monitoring (as in the Netherlands) and on criteria for using different enforcement tools (as in Sweden) (Mazur, 2011).

Figure 2.3. **Enforcement efforts are focused on land use and soil contamination**

Abatement and infringement notices by environmental domain, 2012/13

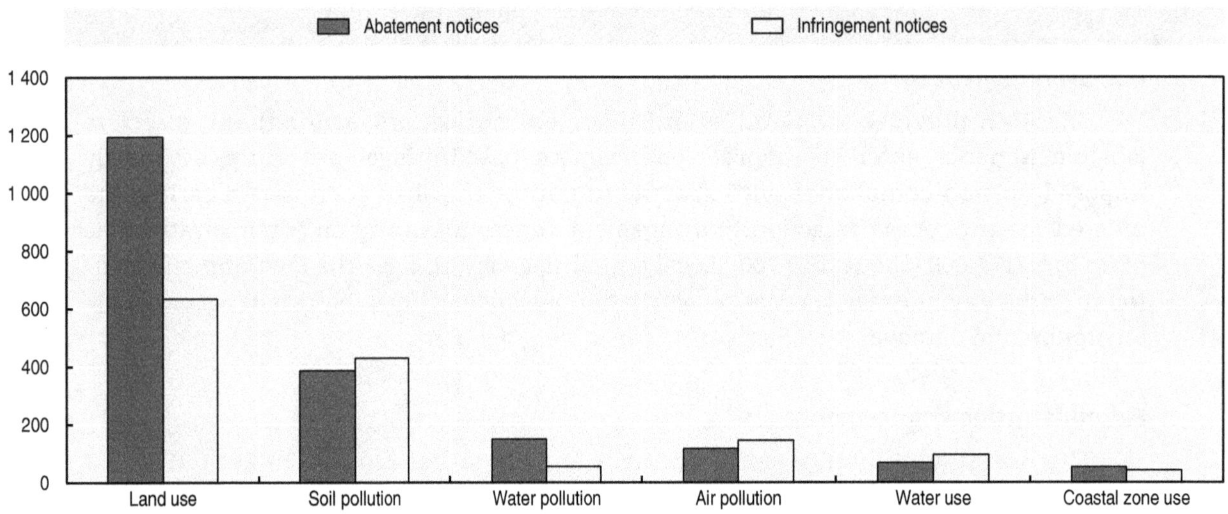

Source: MfE (2014), *Resource Management Act: Survey of Local Authorities, 2012/2013.*

StatLink http://dx.doi.org/10.1787/888933459834

Criminal enforcement

Prosecutions are undertaken for the most serious offences. The Resource Management Amendment Act 2009 raised the maximum fine for convictions under the RMA from NZD 200 000 (for both companies and individuals) to NZD 300 000 for individuals and NZD 600 000 for companies (with an additional daily fine for a continuing offence). This amendment intended to improve the deterrent effect of enforcement and compliance mechanisms under the act. In the three years following the 2009 amendments, the average criminal fine imposed increased slightly to NZD 28 800, but in individual cases fines seldom exceed NZD 100 000 (MfE, 2013b).

Local authorities have direct prosecutorial powers under the RMA. In 2012/13, regional councils approved 60 prosecutions, 37 of which related to discharge of contaminants to land; unitary authorities approved 20 prosecutions. Territorial authorities use prosecutions more rarely than regional councils (24 cases), with most related to land use (MfE, 2014). The cost and time associated with prosecution strains local councils' already limited resources.

Courts take into account a number of factors in sentencing offenders under the RMA. They base decisions on the precedent of the Court of Appeals case Machinery Movers Ltd. vs. Auckland Regional Council (1994), including the deliberateness of the offence, the offender's corporate environmental policies and compliance record (Price, 2003). The vast majority of court decisions on RMA-related cases result in convictions. Regional councils achieve the highest conviction rate as they have the greatest capacity to properly prepare such criminal enforcement cases.

The EPA has enforcement powers with respect to the HSNO Act, the EEZ Act, the Climate Change Response Act (2002) and the Ozone Layer Protection Act (1996). Its prosecution policy sets out guidelines and standards to be followed by EPA staff when deciding whether to prosecute, and in conducting prosecutions (EPA, 2014).

4.3. Environmental liability and remediation

The RMA establishes strict liability (independent of fault) by stating that "every person has a duty to avoid, remedy, or mitigate any adverse effect on the environment arising from an activity carried out by or on behalf of that person, whether or not the activity is in accordance with a rule in a plan [or] resource consent". The liability regime does not cover pollution that occurred before the RMA came into effect in 1991.

The liability regime is implemented through abatement notices or court-issued enforcement orders that impose remediation actions on the responsible party. New Zealand uses innovative financial security instruments such as bonds and mitigation trusts to ensure environmental remediation and restoration of ecosystems related to potential future damage (Box 2.5). Many insurance companies in New Zealand offer premises pollution liability insurance, as well as comparable insurance for contractors. These policies cover liability resulting from gradual, as well as accidental, pollution. Insurance policies generally cover traditional liability (bodily injury, property damage, etc.), as well as remediation costs related to damage to the environment. However, unlike in most OECD member countries, the government has no way to recover costs from responsible parties if it takes a remediation action itself.

Box 2.5. **Using innovative financial security instruments**

In accordance with the RMA, bonds may be required where compliance will likely take a long time to demonstrate (e.g. in replanting affected vegetation) or where there is significant risk to the community. Bonds may be relatively small (e.g. several thousand dollars to secure a small-scale ecosystem restoration project) or comprise millions of dollars for high-risk activities. For example, the Waikato Regional Council holds a bond of NZD 40 million to secure compliance with certain permit conditions of the Newmont Waihi gold mine.

Mitigation trusts are independent entities that carry out conservation work or distribute funding to address adverse environmental impacts. They are usually established in response to a large-scale project with diffuse effects over a wide area (e.g. the Waikato Catchment Ecological Enhancement Trust) or by an agency to manage impacts of several projects (e.g. the Taranaki Tree Trust). When a consent or a permit is granted, agreement is normally reached on the objectives of the trust and its annual disbursements.

However, the costs of setting up and running a mitigation trust are often significant, including legal fees, reimbursement of trustees, distribution of funds, liaison with stakeholders and monitoring of outcomes. As a result of these high administrative costs, mitigation trusts are not as effective as they might be in implementing ecosystem restoration measures.

Source: Brown (2016).

The NES for Assessing and Managing Contaminants in Soil to Protect Human Health (2012) sets soil contamination standards and provides for the identification and remediation of contaminated land. Regional councils and unitary authorities investigate land to identify and monitor contamination. Territorial authorities are in charge of preventing or mitigating any adverse effects of the development or use of contaminated land. While management or remediation works are underway at dozens of sites, the time, effort and expertise required for these activities appear to substantially exceed the capacity of territorial authorities (MfE, 2014).

New Zealand does not have the means to enforce liability with respect to past (pre-1991) contamination of land or water bodies, or to damage to ecosystems and biodiversity. The 2007 EPR recommended that New Zealand clarify liability arrangements for the remediation of contaminated sites and develop financing mechanisms that apply the polluter pays principle as fully as possible. Under the existing arrangement, liability rests with the current landowner, who in theory can identify the actual responsible party and sue it in court.

In practice, the responsible party seldom pays for remediation. The Contaminated Sites Remediation Fund (CSRF) administered by the MfE provides NZD 2.63 million in annual budgetary funding to regional councils and unitary authorities to address sites that pose a risk to human health and the environment. Regional councils and unitary authorities apply for funding to the MfE on behalf of landowners that are seeking financial assistance to remediate their contaminated sites. Based on these applications, the MfE prioritises funding to sites that pose the greatest risk to human health and the environment through the CSRF Priority List of ten confirmed contaminated sites (updated bi-annually) that pose a significant risk to human health and the environment. As of 2013, there were almost 20 000 sites with potential land contamination, including many with historic arsenic and heavy metal contamination from abandoned gold mines and pesticide contamination of old horticultural land.

4.4. *Promotion of compliance and green practices*

While the central government uses a number of tools to encourage good environmental performance, local authorities are only starting to give compliance promotion the attention it deserves. Government promotion of compliance can reduce costs for businesses by allowing them to achieve and maintain compliance as efficiently as possible. It may also reduce regulatory costs by increasing the efficiency of compliance monitoring and enforcement. Compliance promotion is particularly effective when targeted at the SME community.

Voluntary agreements

The central government and local authorities have concluded a number of voluntary agreements with individual companies and industry groups to promote sustainable production practices. The "Sustainable Dairying: Water Accord" – by far the largest one – was put in place in July 2013 (replacing the "Dairying and Clean Streams Accord" of 2003). It establishes national good management practice benchmarks to improve management of risks to freshwater bodies posed by the dairy industry by (Box 2.6; see also Chapter 4). As recommended by the 2007 EPR, this accord sets clear environmental performance targets and requires regular reporting and third-party auditing. It has achieved tangible results ahead of the adoption of relevant government regulation.

Box 2.6. A voluntary agreement with the dairy industry to protect water bodies

The "Sustainable Dairying: Water Accord" was concluded between DairyNZ (an industry organisation representing New Zealand's dairy farmers), the Dairy Companies Association of New Zealand, the country's five largest dairy companies, the Fertiliser Association of New Zealand and several other relevant organisations. The accord's "friends", which contribute

Box 2.6. **A voluntary agreement with the dairy industry to protect water bodies** *(cont.)*

to its success, include the MfE, the Ministry for Primary Industries, 13 regional councils, 3 district councils and the Federation of Maori Authorities. The accord was put in place in view of the forthcoming national regulation of environmental impacts of intensive farming, which has been under consideration since 2011, but has still not been issued.

The accord establishes measurable targets in several policy areas, including:

- 100% exclusion of livestock from all waterways (over 1 metre wide), lakes and significant wetlands by May 2017
- preparation of riparian (borderline between land and waterway) management plans by all participating farms by May 2020
- collection and benchmarking of nutrient management information from all participating dairy farms by November 2015
- assessment of all participating dairy farms' compliance with relevant regional council rules and/or resource consents by May 2014
- installation of water intake meters by 85% of the farms by 2020.

The Dairy Environment Leadership Group, which includes representatives of all the engaged stakeholders, oversees the accord's implementation. An independent third party audits annual reports.

According to the second annual implementation report, 90% livestock exclusion had been achieved by the end of 2015; the government's draft regulation aims at full exclusion by mid-2017. While the number of prosecutions related to farm effluents is declining, the nutrient management target has not yet been achieved.

Source: DairyNZ (2016, 2013).

Providing information and advice to the regulated community

Several regional councils (such as one for the Bay of Plenty) initiate pollution prevention audits in small businesses and disseminate information on best practices in the most problematic activity sectors. The Regional Sector Strategic Compliance Framework (CESIG, 2016) also promotes engagement and education of the regulated community. Many regional councils hold stakeholder forums in key economic activity sectors. In addition, the EPA has developed a "toolbox" to raise awareness among SMEs and Maori communities about the use of hazardous chemicals. Other useful tools to provide guidance to the business community include free-access webpages (where best practices include the US Environmental Protection Agency's online National Compliance Assistance Centers and NetRegs in the United Kingdom), as well as concise printed materials (Mazur, 2012).

Sustainable public procurement and eco-labelling

The New Zealand government worked closely with its Australian counterpart to produce a joint framework for sustainable procurement (APCC, 2007). In 2013, the two countries signed an Australia-New Zealand Government Procurement Agreement to create and maintain a single government procurement market. The New Zealand government's Guide to Sustainable Procurement (MED, 2010) suggested compliance with environmental standards as one of the key procurement criteria, largely inspired by the UK model. With support from the New Zealand Business Council for Sustainable Development, a wide range of New Zealand's government agencies are using these criteria.

For sustainable public procurement, government agencies largely rely on the Environmental Choice New Zealand eco-labelling scheme to identify green products and services. The number of companies and products licensed to use this voluntary eco-label has steadily increased over the last decade. Around 2 000 products and services are eligible to carry the eco-label.

Green certification and awards

The number of companies operating in New Zealand certified to the ISO 14001 Environmental Management System (EMS) standard has doubled since 2007 (Figure 2.4). Enviro-Mark Solutions Ltd., a government-owned research institute, has programmes for environmental and energy/carbon certification of both company management and products. Still, with 294 ISO 14001 certificates in 2014, certification levels remain very low. For comparison, Estonia (which has less than a third of New Zealand's population) had 492 such certificates in 2014 and Ireland (which has roughly the same population as New Zealand and a large agricultural sector) had 666. The main reasons for low environmental certification levels are absence of demand for it in Chinese and other Asian markets where many New Zealand companies export, but also lack of regulatory incentives (e.g. in terms of inspection frequency) for EMS-certified companies. The government can do more to promote EMS certification: certified operators may be eligible for less prescriptive permits (as in the Netherlands), less onerous reporting requirements (in Italy and Slovakia), reduced penalties in case of non-compliance (in the United States and Austria) or lower permit fees (in the United Kingdom) (Mazur, 2012).

Figure 2.4. **More businesses adopt environmental management systems**

Number of ISO 14001 EMS certificates issued in a given year, 2003-14

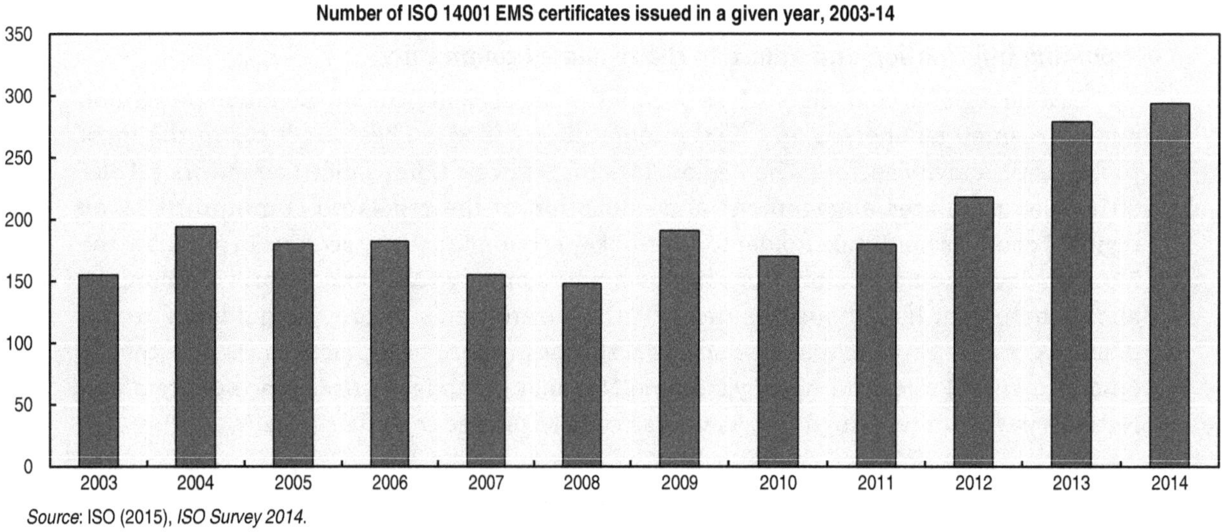

Source: ISO (2015), *ISO Survey 2014.*

StatLink http://dx.doi.org/10.1787/888933459847

Several corporate environmental responsibility awards promote green business practices. The Green Ribbon Awards administered by the MfE recognise outstanding contributions by individuals, organisations, businesses and communities to protecting and enhancing New Zealand's environment. The Energy Efficiency and Conservation Authority

(EECA) Awards are given to organisations and individuals who have demonstrated excellence and innovation in energy efficiency or renewable energy projects. Most regional councils run their own environmental award programmes.

5. Promoting environmental democracy

Environmental democracy has particular importance in New Zealand given that the Treaty of Waitangi (1840) guarantees special rights for the Maori people. Over the last decade, the country has demonstrated progress in promoting access to environmental information, justice and education for everyone. There are multiple opportunities for public participation in policy making, while public engagement in individual permitting decisions is more limited.

5.1. *Public participation in environmental decision making*

The government is legally required to consult the public on changes to legislation by inviting submissions of any interested persons on the content of draft laws. There are also public consultation provisions for most secondary (subordinate) legislation.

District and regional planning processes allow the public significant participation rights. A local council must publish a notice on the proposed policy statement or plan or changes to an existing one in newspapers, on its website and/or by sending affected persons information directly. Any person can make a written submission, and a hearing should be held upon request. A person who made a submission and is unhappy with the decision may appeal to the Environment Court. The role of the public is much more limited in the consent determination process (the requirement for their notification has been scaled back through the 2009 and 2013 RMA amendments); it is assumed that consultations on the plan providing justification for consents were comprehensive (Section 3.3). However, the RMA amendments proposed in 2015 would limit notification of plan changes by giving enhanced review and approval powers to the Minister for the Environment (Section 3.4).

Specific provisions in the legislation refer to mandatory consultations with the Maori people. Natural Resources Sector agencies are required to work with Maori communities (iwi/hapu) to implement principles of the Treaty of Waitangi through relationship agreements or formal settlements. Three-quarters of local councils have entered into 117 iwi/hapu agreements, including joint management agreements (MfE, 2016a). Maori groups were involved in the development of the 2014 NPS for Freshwater Management (Fox and Bretton, 2014). In addition, iwi/hapu management plans must be taken into account in preparing or changing regional and district plans: 190 iwi/hapu plans have been lodged with local authorities throughout New Zealand. More than half of local authorities make explicit budgetary commitments to Maori participation in resource management planning (MfE, 2016a).

Almost every local authority routinely determines within the consent evaluation process whether the proposed activity affects local Maori people (tangata whenua); many local authorities established Maori standing or advisory committees (Fox and Bretton, 2014). Almost a third of local authorities involve Maori in compliance monitoring activities, especially in cases where the resource consent included a specific provision for Maori participation (MfE, 2014).

The Land and Water Forum (LAWF) established in 2009 brings together a range of industry groups, environmental and recreational NGOs, iwi, scientists and other organisations with a stake in freshwater and land management. The 54 member organisations are joined by active observers from local and central governments. The LAWF aims to develop a shared vision among all those with an interest in water through stakeholder-led collaboration. It has been instrumental in the development of the NPS for Freshwater Management and continues to play an important role in this domain, having produced four reports with 218 recommendations as of early 2016 (Chapter 4). However, several NGOs have criticised the LAWF's decision making as biased towards agricultural interests.[8]

The MfE has published a number of guides to ensure effective participation in resource management processes at the local and regional levels. The MfE also administers the Community Environment Fund (CEF), which encourages community participation in environmental initiatives. The CEF provides NZD 10 000 to NZD 300 000 to local initiatives that help reduce GHG emissions, protect biodiversity and improve freshwater management, coastal management, air quality, etc.

5.2. Access to environmental information

An Environmental Reporting Framework was developed via the Environment Domain Plan 2013, which described over 150 initiatives to improve and manage environmental statistics (Statistics NZ, MfE, DOC, 2013). A pilot air domain report was published in 2014, followed by a first comprehensive *Environment Aotearoa* report in October 2015.

The Environmental Reporting Act (2015) provides a legal framework for national-level reporting in New Zealand. It requires the MfE and Statistics New Zealand to produce "synthesis reports" on the state of the environment every three years, as well as report every six months on one of the five environmental domains (air, climate, freshwater, land and marine issues). In this way, at least one "domain report" is published every three years for each domain. The adoption of this act addresses the 2007 EPR recommendation to expand the availability of quantitative environmental quality indicators. In response to recommendations by the PCE, Statistics New Zealand has developed a "Good Practice Guide" (not published at the time of writing) for preparing state of the environment reports (PCE, 2016b). However, the reporting framework suffers from insufficient data quality and lack of "response" indicators (that would characterise government actions to address environmental problems).

The MfE has partnered with local authorities to take forward the Environmental Monitoring and Reporting (EMaR) initiative, which aims to improve the collection, collation, publication and reuse of New Zealand's environmental data. EMaR is also engaging regional councils to develop and implement National Environmental Monitoring Standards and to improve the quality of environmental information at the national and regional levels. In 2014/15, only 22 local authorities (including as few as 7 territorial authorities) monitored the state of the environment in their jurisdiction; 42 local authorities did so in 2010/11 (MfE, 2016a). The shortage of reliable and nationally uniform data is particularly acute in such key environmental policy areas as waste management and biodiversity protection.

The government has improved public access to environmental information through the Government Open Access and Licensing framework (NZGOAL). The Land, Air, Water Aotearoa (LAWA) data portal publishes freshwater and coastal water information and scientific data. It plans to publish more data on air quality, land, biodiversity and marine issues. However, unlike all other OECD member countries, New Zealand neither has a

Pollutant Release and Transfer Register (PRTR)[9] nor plans to develop one. Establishing such a register would provide the public with access to a database of industrial releases to air, water and soil, and of waste transported to treatment and disposal sites.

5.3. *Access to justice*

The Environment Court is a single national court with permanent locations in Wellington, Auckland and Christchurch. Environment judges from the three main centres go on circuit to other locations as needed. Most of the court's workload is generated by appeals brought against decisions of local authorities involving regional and district plans, as well as resource consents. The Environment Court jurisprudence also demonstrates an increasing sophistication in taking into account Maori interests in environmental matters (Fox and Bretton, 2014). All Environment Court decisions are published online.

The government actively helps civil society access judicial remedies. The Environmental Legal Assistance (ELA) Fund provides Maori groups, community organisations and other NGOs with financial assistance to defend public interests in resource management cases at the Environment Court, as well as at boards of inquiry (Section 3.3). The ELA Fund reimburses the costs of legal representatives and expert witnesses to help prepare, mediate and present the group's case. Since May 2013, it has also been available to fund appeals to the Environment Court and board of inquiry proceedings. The ELA Fund has an annual budget of NZD 600 000 and offers grants of up to NZD 50 000 per group, per application, for any one case. However, ELAF is not available to individuals.

5.4. *Environmental education*

Over the last decade, New Zealand has made further progress in promoting environmental education and incorporating sustainability into the national school curriculum, as recommended by the 2007 EPR. The Ministry of Education's guidelines for environmental education in schools help teachers identify opportunities within the existing national curriculum statements to plan and provide education in, about and for the environment. The ministry also supports a professional development programme for teachers and many learning-outside-the-classroom projects. A range of programmes run by community groups and environment centres support child and adult sustainability skills education under the MfE's Community Environment Fund and the Department of Conservation's Community Fund. Furthermore, the DOC, MfE and Ministry of Education are jointly developing a national strategy for Environmental Education for Sustainability.

The national Enviroschools and Te Aho Tu Roa (for Maori-speaking communities) programmes actively promote voluntary engagement of schools in a "whole school" approach to environmental education; these programmes are co-funded by the MfE, local authorities, local trusts and schools. Since its launch as a national programme in 2001, Enviroschools has continued to grow and expand. To date, over a third of schools and early childhood centres have joined the Enviroschools programme – nearly 1 000 educational establishments covering 250 000 pupils. According to a 2014 nationwide survey of Enviroschools (Enviroschools, 2015), most of them actively engage in actions for water quality and conservation (75% of the schools), waste minimisation plans and actions (99%) and energy projects, including actions for sustainable transport and energy conservation actions (69%).

Recommendations on environmental governance and management

Regulatory framework

- Conduct a comprehensive evaluation of the effectiveness of RMA implementation at the local authority level in achieving its objective of development within the limits of the environment's carrying capacity; consider a regulatory review of the RMA to evaluate whether its framework as a whole remains fit for purpose.
- Prepare new and review existing NPSs and NESs to reinforce the national-level regulatory and methodological framework for managing air and water pollution; establish national standards for hazardous waste management.
- Establish nationally standardised requirements for air and water discharge permits and waste generation and management; encourage better cross-media integration of discharge permits on the basis of best available techniques; extend consent and permit requirements to existing use rights obtained under older regulatory regimes.
- Build capacity of local authorities to carry out their permitting, compliance monitoring and enforcement responsibilities through better nationwide guidance, support and training, including interactive online support; introduce outcome indicators in the National Monitoring System to strengthen the national government's oversight and *ex post* evaluation of policy implementation and enforcement at the local level.
- Evaluate the implementation of requirements for the assessment of environmental effects (AEE) and consider defining environmental impact-based thresholds for activities above which the scope of assessment would remain comprehensive and notification to the public would be mandatory, while smaller activities could undergo simplified AEE without notification.
- Ensure coherence of regional and territorial land-use plans; require explicit assessment of cumulative environmental impacts as part of the planning process; continue efforts to integrate biodiversity protection into land-use planning, particularly on private land.

Compliance assurance

- Promote risk-based targeting and other resource-efficient inspection practices among local authorities; strengthen compliance assurance through more active use of administrative enforcement tools and better national oversight of their consistent application; enhance compliance promotion through best practice guidance.
- Establish mechanisms to enforce strict (independent of fault) liability regime for damage to water bodies and ecosystems; expand the use of bonds and mitigation trusts under the RMA to secure the remediation of potential future environmental damage.

Environmental democracy

- Continue to ensure public participation in land-use planning, limiting exemptions to a few clearly defined cases; build capacity of Maori communities to ensure their adequate participation in resource management planning.
- Establish a Pollutant Release and Transfer Register (PRTR) to collect, and facilitate the public's access to, information on environmental impacts of private companies.

Notes

1. Regions are delineated along water basin boundaries, but may comprise several basins (Chapter 4).
2. Councils are funded by a combination of local taxes and central government funding (primarily in the form of road and public transport subsidies).

3. The EEZ Act provides for an environmental consent regime for oil and gas exploration and drilling, seabed mining and other potentially harmful activities on the country's continental shelf.
4. Regional policy statements may cover topics for which no NPS has been issued.
5. Discharges of contaminants into air by agricultural users are exempt from permit requirements. The use of agrichemicals is addressed by non-binding industry guidelines and codes of practice, as well as by district and regional plans.
6. In 2011-13, the EPA processed 60 resource consents and 2 regional plans.
7. C(79)116 – Recommendation of the Council on the Assessment of Projects with Significant Impact on the Environment.
8. Fish & Game, the country's leading environmental and recreation non-profit organisation, left the LAWF in November 2015 (Brower, 2016).
9. The OECD Council Recommendation C(96)41/FINAL, amended by C(2003)87, recommends that OECD member countries establish and maintain a PRTR.

References

APCC (2007), *Australian and New Zealand Government Framework for Sustainable Procurement*, Australasian Procurement and Construction Council, Deakin West.

Brower, A.L. (2016), "Is collaboration good for the environment? Or, what's wrong with the Land and Water Forum?", *New Zealand Journal of Ecology*, Vol. 40/3, New Zealand Ecological Society, Christchurch, pp. 390-397.

Brown, M.A. (2016), *Pathways to Prosperity: Safeguarding Biodiversity in Development*, Environmental Defence Society, Auckland.

Brown, M.A. et al. (2013), "Ecological compensation: An evaluation of regulatory compliance in New Zealand", *Impact Assessment and Project Appraisal*, Vol. 31/1, Fargo, International Association for Impact Assessment, pp. 34-44.

CESIG (2016), *Regional Sector Strategic Compliance Framework 2016-2018*, Compliance and Enforcement Special Interest Group.

DairyNZ (2016), *Sustainable Dairying: Water Accord: Two Years on…*, March 2016, DairyNZ, Hamilton.

DairyNZ (2013), *Sustainable Dairying: Water Accord*, DairyNZ, Hamilton.

DIA (2015), "The loopy rules report: New Zealanders tell their stories", *Rules Reduction Taskforce Report to the Minister of Local Government, Department of Internal Affairs*, August 2015, Department of Internal Affairs, Wellington.

EDS (2016), *Evaluating the Environmental Impacts of the RMA*, report by the Environmental Defence Society, Wellington, June 2016.

Enviroschools (2015), *Enviroschools: Key Findings from the Nationwide Census*, Toimata Foundation, Hamilton.

EPA (2014), *EPA Compliance: Our Approach*, Environmental Protection Authority, Wellington, May 2014.

Fish and Game New Zealand (2016), *An Analysis of Environment Canterbury's Enforcement of Waterway Protection Rules*, Fish & Game New Zealand, April 2016.

Fox, C. and C. Bretton (2014), "Maori participation, rights and interests", presentation at the Resource Management Law Association 2014 conference, 26 September 2014, Dunedin.

ISO (2015), *ISO Survey 2014*, International Organization for Standardization, Geneva.

Mazur, E. (2012), "Green transformation of small businesses: Achieving and going beyond environmental requirements", *OECD Environment Working Papers*, No. 47, OECD Publishing, Paris, *http://dx.doi.org/10.1787/5k92r8nmfgxp-en*.

Mazur, E. (2011), "Environmental enforcement in decentralised governance systems: Toward a nationwide level playing field", *OECD Environment Working Papers*, No. 34, OECD Publishing, Paris, *http://dx.doi.org/10.1787/5kgb1m60qtq6-en*.

McGimpsey, P. and R.K. Morgan (2013), "The application of strategic environmental assessment in a non-mandatory context: Regional transport planning in New Zealand", *Environmental Impact Assessment Review*, Vol. 43, November 2013, Elsevier, Amsterdam, pp. 56-64.

MED (2010), *Guide 1 to Sustainable Procurement: Identifying Sustainable Procurement Priorities*, A guide for agencies, Ministry of Economic Development, Wellington, June 2010.

MfE (2016a), *National Monitoring System for 2014/15* (database), Ministry for the Environment, Wellington, *www.mfe.govt.nz/rma/rma-monitoring-and-reporting/reporting-201415* (accessed 10 July 2016).

MfE (2016b), Priorities for National Direction website, Ministry for the Environment, Wellington, *www.mfe.govt.nz/rma/rma-legislative-tools/priorities-national-direction* (accessed 28 September 2016).

MfE (2014), *Resource Management Act: Survey of Local Authorities, 2012/2013*, Ministry for the Environment, Wellington, April 2014.

MfE (2013a), *Improving Our Resource Management System*, Ministry for the Environment, Wellington, February 2013.

MfE (2013b), *A Study into the Use of Prosecutions under the Resource Management Act 1991, 1 July 2008 – 30 September 2012*, Ministry for the Environment, Wellington, October 2013.

NZCID (2015), *Integrated Governance Planning and Delivery: A Proposal for Local Government and Planning Law Reform in New Zealand*, New Zealand Council for Infrastructure Development, Auckland, August 2015.

NZPC (2016), *Better Urban Planning*, draft report, New Zealand Productivity Commission, Wellington.

Palmer, G. and R. Blakeley (2015), "Submission on New Zealand Productivity Commission's better urban planning inquiry, *Issues Paper*, Submission 007, March 2016, New Zealand Productivity Commission.

PCE (2016a), *Resource Legislation Amendment Bill 2015: Submission to the Local Government and Environment Committee*, Parliamentary Commissioner for the Environment, 14 March 2016.

PCE (2016b), *The State of New Zealand's Environment: Commentary by the Parliamentary Commissioner for the Environment on Environment Aotearoa 2015*, 29 June 2016, Parliamentary Commissioner for the Environment, Wellington.

Price, K. (2003), *New Zealand: Environmental Liability: Risk and Compliance*, 18 June 2003, *www.mondaq.com/NewZealand/x/21635/Health+Safety/Environmental+Liability+Risk+And+Compliance*.

Reeves, S. (2015), *Environmental Law of New Zealand*, Fourth Edition, Kluwer Law International BV, The Netherlands.

Statistics NZ, MfE, DOC (2013), *Environment Domain Plan 2013: Initiatives to Address our Environmental Information Needs*, Statistics New Zealand, Ministry for the Environment and Department of Conservation, Wellington.

PART I

Chapter 3

Towards green growth

New Zealand experienced strong economic growth for most of 2000-15. The Business Growth Agenda aims to continue improving the productivity and environmental performance of the natural resource-based sectors to support the country's growth. This chapter reviews New Zealand's efforts to promote green growth and sustainable development at the domestic and global levels. It analyses progress in using economic and tax policies to pursue environmental objectives and in reforming potentially harmful incentives. The chapter also discusses policies to promote low carbon energy and transport infrastructure and services, and reviews the country's eco-innovation performance.

The statistical data for Israel are supplied by and under the responsibility of the relevant Israeli authorities. The use of such data by the OECD is without prejudice to the status of the Golan Heights, East Jerusalem and Israeli settlements in the West Bank under the terms of international law.

1. New Zealand's economy and the environment

New Zealand is a small open economy with one of the highest living standards in the OECD (Figure 1.2). The economy grew faster than the OECD as a whole in 2000-15, at an annual rate of 2.7% (Figure 1.1; Chapter 1). Key drivers of growth over the decade include a sharp increase in the international prices of dairy products, the main exports; a booming tourism sector; and housing and infrastructure construction (OECD, 2015a). Rapid population growth, partly linked to large net immigration flows, and low responsiveness of housing supply have exacerbated housing constraints, notably in Auckland, and increased pressures on transport, water and wastewater infrastructure (Section 5; Chapter 5).

New Zealand has built an international reputation as a "green" country, both as tourism destination and as producer of natural and safe food. Natural resources are a major contributor to growth: the products of the primary sector (including agriculture, forestry, fishery and aquaculture, as well as oil and coal) account for over half of the country's exports. New Zealand is the world largest exporter of dairy products and sheep meat, which account for more than 40% of total exports. Overall, agriculture accounts for 7% of gross domestic product (GDP), a much larger share than in most OECD member countries. At the same time, tourism and other services have grown rapidly, representing more than a quarter of exports in 2015. The country's pristine wilderness and spectacular landscapes attract millions of tourists every year (Chapter 1).

New Zealand's growth model has begun to show its environmental limits, with increased greenhouse gas (GHG) emissions and waste generation, freshwater contamination (Chapter 4) and threats to biodiversity (Chapter 1). The country has benefited from the increase in international dairy prices, which has encouraged a large conversion of land from forestry and other types of farming to dairy over the last two decades (Chapter 1). This has also led to a more intensive use of agricultural inputs (such as fertilisers and feed) and higher water demand for irrigation. Such changes have generated adverse environmental impacts, including nitrogen losses to water bodies, soil compaction, biological GHG emissions and reduced variety in pastoral landscapes (Baskaran, Cullen and Colombo, 2009). Foote, Joy and Death (2015) estimate that the cost of some environmental impacts exceeded the dairy export revenue in 2012.

A 2016 OECD study estimate that adjusting New Zealand's GDP growth for the cost of total pollution abatement would reduce growth over 2000-13 by 0.03 percentage points on average per year (Cárdenas Rodríguez, Haščič and Souchier, 2016; Figure 3.1).[1] While this is a very low loss in GDP growth, accounting for pollution abatement leads to an increase in economic performance in three-quarters of other OECD member countries. This may indicate that New Zealand's strong growth has come partly at the expense of environmental quality, a dynamic that puts the country's "green" reputation at risk. This could be detrimental to the competitiveness and attractiveness of the economy in a global market as consumer and investor preferences shift towards sustainability and strong environmental performance.

Figure 3.1. **Economic growth in New Zealand is lower when accounting for pollution**

Pollution adjustment of GDP growth, top and bottom six OECD countries, percentage points of output growth, annual average 2000-13

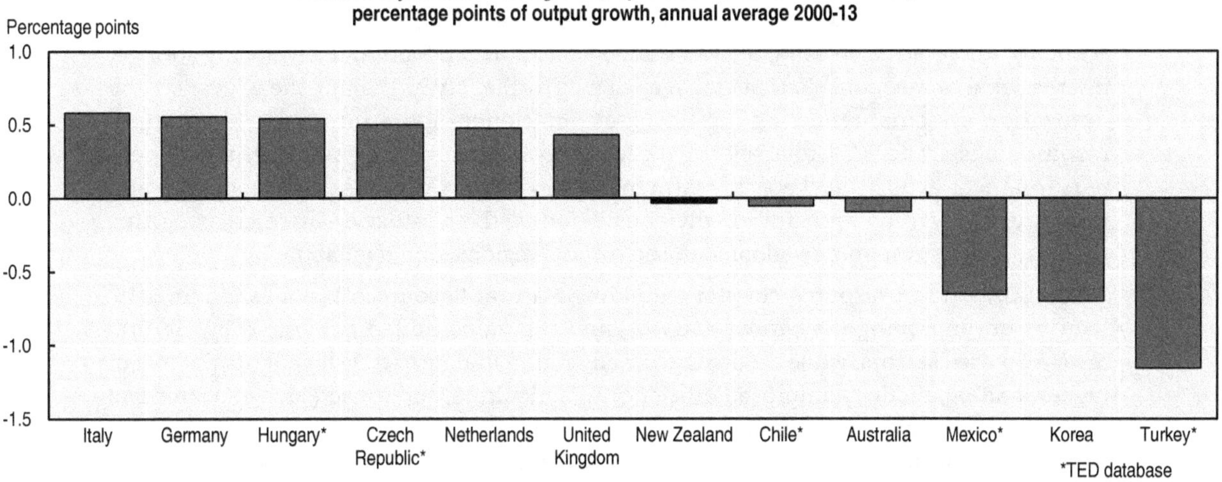

Note: The indicator shows to what extent a country's GDP growth should be corrected for pollution abatement efforts. It adds what has been undervalued due to diversion of resources to pollution abatement, or deduces the "excess" growth which is generated at the expense of environmental quality. The chart compares the six countries at the top and at the bottom of the range.

Source: Cárdenas Rodríguez, M., I. Haščič and M. Souchier (2016), "Environmentally adjusted multifactor productivity: Methodology and empirical results for OECD and G20 countries", *OECD Green Growth Papers*, No. 2016/04; Conference Board (2014), *The Conference Board - Total Economy Database* (TED database), www.conference-board.org/data/economydatabase/.

StatLink http://dx.doi.org/10.1787/888933459852

2. Building a green growth strategy

New Zealand has strengthened the institutional and policy arrangements for ensuring environmental and economic policy coherence (Chapter 2). In 2009, it signed the OECD Declaration on Green Growth; in 2011, the government established the Green Growth Advisory Group to advise on green growth opportunities and support preparation of the Business Growth Agenda (the government development programme). The group recommended that "green growth enablers become part of the core platform in the government's overall economic management", as opposed to suggesting a stand-alone strategy for green growth.

The Business Growth Agenda (BGA), launched in 2012 and revamped in 2015, considered the group's recommendations, but only to a limited extent. The BGA pursues the broad goal of building a more competitive and productive economy, with a strong focus on international markets and innovation. It sets the target of making exports account for 40% of GDP by 2025 (from about 30% in 2015). The improvement of the natural resource base is one of its six pillars, as natural resources are an input to key economic sectors, especially the large export-oriented livestock production sector (Box 3.1).

Nonetheless, the BGA is far from providing a long-term vision for the transition of New Zealand to a low-carbon, greener economy. Such transition is likely to entail increasing trade-offs with the current production and export targets. In particular, reducing GHG emissions and improving water quality would be difficult with a strict reliance on productivity gains and no reductions in agricultural output (Royal Society of New Zealand, 2016). At the same time, growing tourism exports can pose risks to natural and cultural resources, especially if the number of tourists increased rapidly and concentrated in a few places in national parks and conservation areas. New Zealand should consider establishing a collaborative (whole-of-government, multi-stakeholder) process to develop a long-term vision for the country's transition towards a low-carbon, greener economy. This vision

Box 3.1. **The Business Growth Agenda: A green growth strategy framework?**

The Business Growth Agenda (BGA) aims to encourage a more productive and competitive economy. It foresees increasing the value added of export products and developing stronger international connections. To that end, it envisions further strengthening the education and innovation systems, removing infrastructure bottlenecks and improving the natural resource base. The BGA focuses on six key areas or inputs for successful business performance: export markets, investment, innovation, skills, natural resources and infrastructure, which are additionally considered in the context of three cross-cutting themes – Maori economic development, sectors and regions, and regulation.

The BGA natural resource chapter ("Building Natural Resources"), published in 2015, focuses on improving the productivity of, and the value added generated by, natural resource-based sectors, while reducing their environmental impact. It highlights the role of higher land productivity, improved efficiency in agricultural input use (such as water and fertilisers) and advanced technologies in enabling a lighter environmental footprint and ensuring the most productive use of resources. The chapter puts forward 74 projects that revolve around seven principal drivers of growth: maximising the productivity of agricultural and horticultural land, while reducing environmental effects; providing more flexible governance options for Maori land, and assisting Maori trusts and landowners to improve the productivity of their land; encouraging regional economic development with certain and timely processes for allocating access to resources; freeing up urban land supply and accelerating access and use of it; improving the efficiency of freshwater allocation and usage within limits and encouraging investment in water storage and irrigation; developing aquaculture, fisheries and other marine resources, while maintaining marine biodiversity and sustainability; and improving energy efficiency and use of renewable energy to raise productivity, reduce carbon emissions and promote consumer choice.

Over the past four years, 35 projects have been completed in the Natural Resources workstream. Their scope has been broad, ranging from commissioning detailed economic growth studies for selected regions to reducing nitrogen discharge into Lake Taupo (Chapter 4).

Source: Government of New Zealand (2015a, 2015b).

should take into account the economic opportunities arising from exporting higher value products, tapping into emerging markets and investing in environmental quality improvements. This will ultimately help the country reduce its reliance on agriculture and the use of natural resources, and withstand the risks of dairy price fluctuations.

New Zealand has many opportunities for a transition towards a low-carbon, greener economy. Vivid Economics and University of Auckland (2012) identified several green growth opportunities, including exporting green products and technology such as sustainable agricultural products and services, geothermal energy, biotechnology, second-generation biofuels and forestry products; importing new technologies and ideas to enhance domestic environmental policies, and resource and energy efficiency; improvements in building and transport energy efficiency; and electricity grid technology. As Section 5 discusses, the latter should be given priority, alongside raising investment in research and development (Section 6).

As the Green Growth Advisory Group (2011) acknowledged, New Zealand would benefit from a framework for monitoring progress towards green growth objectives. This framework should be based on sound indicators that link economic activity with environmental performance; it should include indicators on the effectiveness of the policy response in addressing environmental challenges and generating eco-innovation and green business opportunities. New Zealand could build on the OECD green growth indicators framework and on the experience of other OECD member countries that have customised it to their national circumstances (e.g. Chile, Denmark, Germany, Korea, the Netherlands) (OECD, 2014a). Systematic reporting on progress would help create a common understanding in society and build consensus and ownership about the low-carbon, green transition.

3. Greening the system of taxes, charges and prices

In line with recommendations of the 2007 OECD *Environmental Performance Review*, New Zealand has extended the use of economic instruments to put a price on environmental externalities and encourage efficient use of natural resources. It launched a GHG emissions trading system in 2008, discussed in Section 3.5, and piloted a nitrogen cap-and-trade system in the Lake Taupo catchment. This internationally unique policy experiment has proved a cost-effective way to address nitrogen pollution from diffuse sources (Box 4.7). A tradable quota system has long been in place to manage fisheries (Section 3.6). New Zealand also introduced some new environmentally related taxes, namely the waste disposal levy (described in Section 3.3) and a levy on goods containing synthetic GHGs (Section 3.1). Some local authorities used new pricing instruments in water and waste management, with positive results. Quantity- or volume-based waste charges have encouraged households to limit waste generation, and volumetric water charges have helped reduce per capita water consumption in some cities (Chapters 1 and 5). However, current legislation limits the ability of cities to apply volumetric charges to wastewater services and make greater use of road tolls and congestion charges (NZPC, 2016).

3.1. *Environmentally related taxes: An overview*

New Zealand has a competitive and efficient tax system. Tax-to-GDP ratio stood at 32% in 2014, lower than the OECD average of 34%; the government is committed to keep it low. Over 55% of tax revenues are collected through income and profits – the third highest share after Denmark and Australia. The central government collects nearly 90% of general government revenues (only Ireland and the United Kingdom have comparable shares), which indicates local governments have relatively limited fiscal autonomy (Chapter 5).

Revenue from environmentally related taxes is low in international comparison. It accounts for 4.2% of total tax revenue and 1.3% of GDP (data 2014), among the lowest shares in the OECD (Figure 3.2). Environmentally related taxes are defined as any compulsory, unrequited payment to general government levied on tax bases deemed to be of particular environmental relevance. As in all other OECD member countries, most environmentally related tax revenue is collected through taxes on consumption of energy products (54%) and vehicle ownership and use (45%).

Since the mid-2000s, environmentally related tax revenue (in real terms) has increased by almost 15%, with a dip in 2008-09 linked to the economic recession. Revenue from energy taxes has grown since 2012, owing to tax rate hikes. It had declined between 2005 and 2011 following less use of petrol and the shift to diesel, which is exempt from the excise duty and is indirectly taxed via a distance-based tax on diesel vehicles (see next section).[2] The expanding vehicle fleet, especially of those running on diesel (Chapter 1),[3] has resulted in increased revenue from vehicle taxes. This combination of factors meant that

Figure 3.2. **Revenue from environmentally related taxes is low in international comparison**

Environmentally related tax revenue as percentage of GDP and total tax revenue, OECD countries, 2014[a]

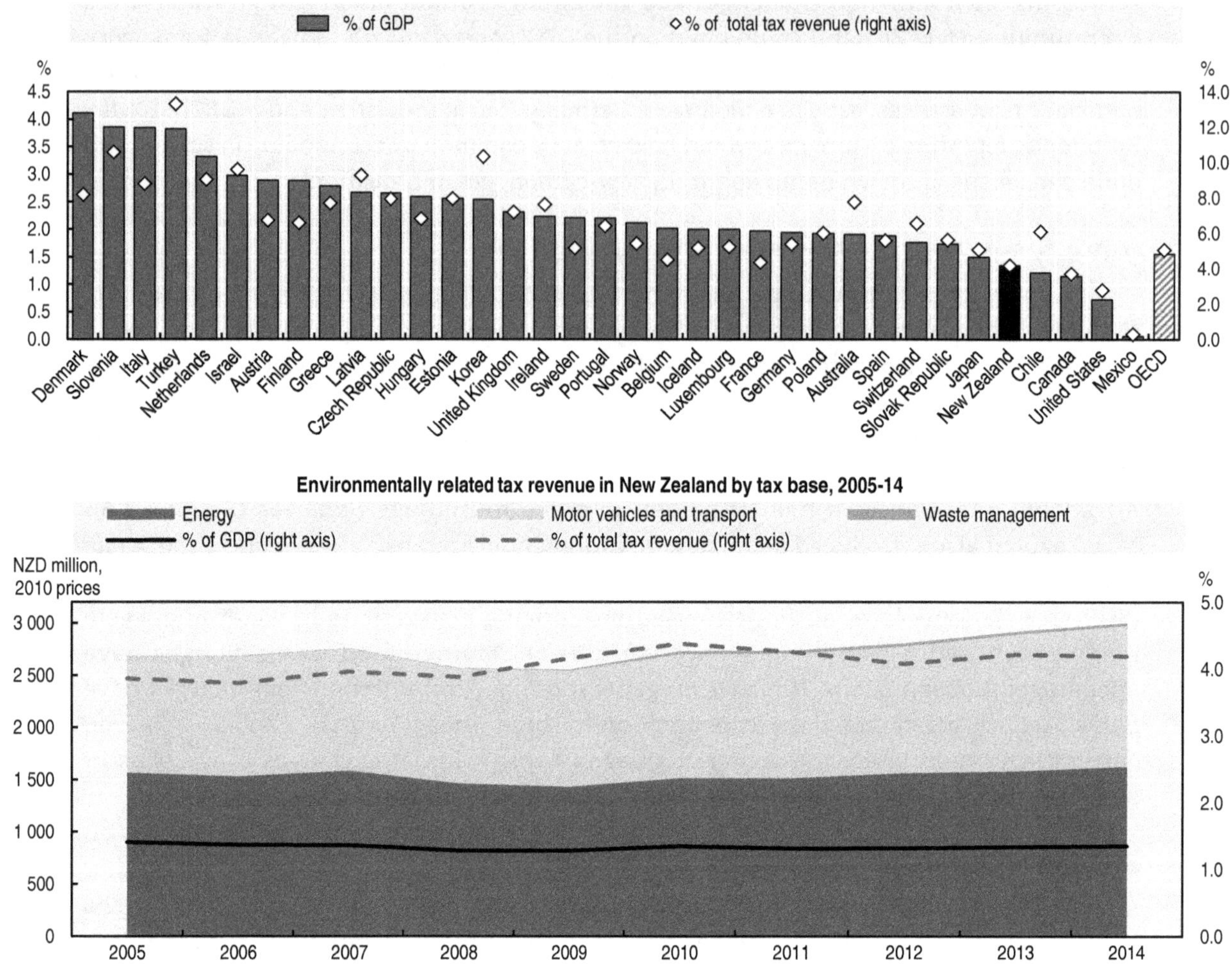

a) Australia, Japan and the Netherlands: 2013 data for percentage of total tax revenue; Poland: 2013 data.

Source: Eurostat (2016), *Environmental taxes* (database); OECD (2016), "Environmental policy instruments", *OECD Environment Statistics* (database).

StatLink http://dx.doi.org/10.1787/888933459868

environmentally related tax revenue grew at a slower rate than GDP: indeed, its ratio on GDP has declined by nearly 4% since 2005 (Figure 3.2).

Taxes on pollution and resource use are virtually limited to the waste disposal levy, which accounts for a negligible share of revenue (Section 3.4). In 2013, New Zealand introduced the Synthetic Greenhouse Gas (Goods) Levy on imported products containing hydrofluorocarbons (HCFCs) and perfluorocarbons (PFCs) such as fridges, freezers, heat pumps, air-conditioners and refrigerated trailers. Rates are linked to the price of carbon in the NZ Emissions Trading Scheme (ETS) (Section 3.5) and vary across products to reflect the amount, type and global warming potential of the gas they contain. Rates have been low – e.g. around NZD 1 or less per household air conditioning system – and revenue is negligible.

While a low tax burden is conducive to growth, New Zealand could boost environmentally related taxes and charges by reforming fuel taxes, raising their rates and introducing new instruments such as taxes on industrial emissions and water pollution, as well as congestion charges. This could provide the government with some flexibility to lower other taxes that may be detrimental to growth; taxes on corporate income, for example, account for nearly 14% of total tax revenue, the second highest in the OECD.

Furthermore, expanding the use of environmentally related taxes and charges could help the government in its fiscal consolidation efforts. While New Zealand enjoys a solid fiscal position, with a near-balanced budget and low government debt in international comparison, the government is planning fiscal consolidation measures to reduce the Crown's net debt from 25% to 20% of GDP over 2015-20 (OECD, 2015a).[4] Much of the consolidation is expected to be achieved through spending cuts. However, New Zealand needs to ensure that reduced spending does not delay needed investment in infrastructure (Section 5; Chapter 5) or impede efforts to improve the well-being of the most vulnerable groups (OECD, 2015a). Additional revenue may, therefore, be necessary.

3.2. Energy and vehicle taxes and charges

Energy taxes account for a lower share of environmentally related tax revenue than on average in the OECD (54% compared to 70%). New Zealand is almost unique in the OECD in taxing only transport energy. It is also the only OECD member country that does not apply a fuel excise duty on diesel; a distance-based charge applies instead (see below). The fuel excise duty applies to all other transport fuels, i.e. mainly to petrol, but ethanol is exempt. Other levies – the Petroleum or Engine Fuel Monitoring Levy and the Local Authorities Fuel Tax – apply to nearly all fuels. The government raised the excise rate in 2012-15, seeking to increase infrastructure funding. However, the petrol price and tax rate remain low by international standards, and even more so those of diesel. New Zealand presents the largest tax gap between petrol and diesel when tax rates are converted per unit of energy (Figure 3.3).

Figure 3.3. **Tax rates on road fuels are among the lowest in the OECD**

Tax rates on road fuels on an energy basis, 2012

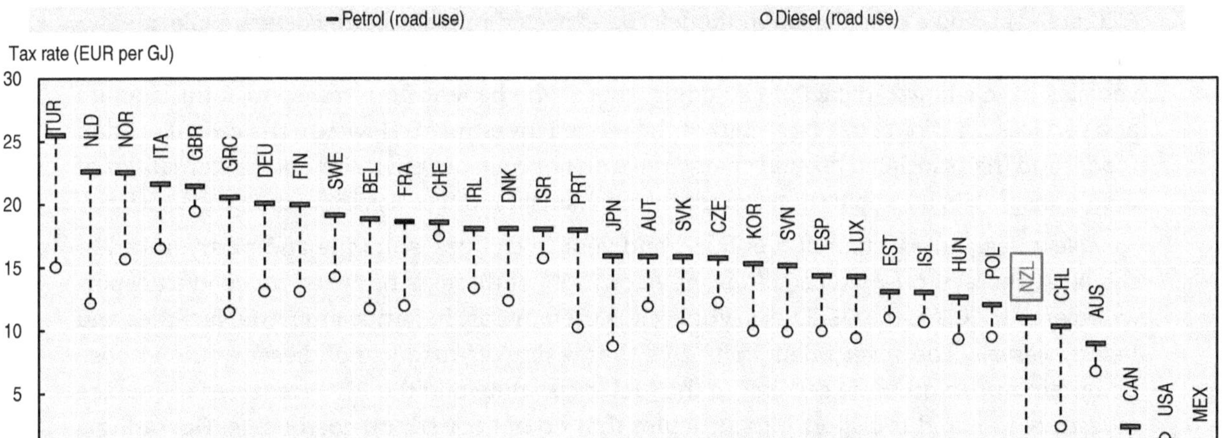

Note: Tax rates are as of 1 April 2012, except 1 July 2012 for AUS. Figures for CAN and USA include only federal taxes. NZL applies a road-user charge to diesel that is not included in the figure. Tax rates converted using standard carbon emission factors from the Intergovernmental Panel on Climate Change and energy conversion factors from the IEA.
Source: Adapted from OECD (2015), *Taxing Energy Use.*

StatLink http://dx.doi.org/10.1787/888933459876

All road vehicles are subject to a one-off registration fee and a periodic licensing fee, which vary according to the weight of the vehicle and the fuel it runs on, but not on environmental performance parameters.[5] All vehicles that run on a fuel not subject to fuel excise duty, which comprise mostly diesel vehicles, must have a road user charge (RUC) licence. RUCs, which are distance based, can be purchased in multiples of 1 000 km. The cost of a licence varies, depending on the type of vehicle and its weight:[6] heavy vehicles (over 3.5 tonnes) face a higher RUC, on the premise they cause more damage to roads and require pavement and roads to be built to a higher standard. All light vehicles (weighing less than 3.5 tonnes), including passenger cars, face the same rate, on the assumption they cause little road damage. This provides no incentive to move towards smaller, low-emission and more fuel-efficient vehicles. However, electric vehicles (EVs) have been exempt from the charge since 2009. The exemption, initially granted up to 2013, was recently extended until EVs reach 2% of the vehicle fleet (Section 5.2).

In theory, the rates of the petrol excise duty and the RUC rates are set so that, on average, petrol and diesel vehicle users pay the same tax amount (either in fuel tax or in RUC). However, the different charging systems favour diesel vehicles due to their lower fuel consumption per kilometre driven.[7] This is not justified from an environmental perspective, as diesel has a higher carbon content per litre and diesel cars are generally considered to have worse local air pollution effects than petrol (diesel vehicles emit more particulate matter and nitrogen oxides per litre) (Harding, 2014a). This tax differential is even less justified in New Zealand, which has no mandatory vehicle fuel efficiency or emission standards. The vehicle fleet is relatively old, with a large share of second-hand, emission-intensive cars.[8] While petrol light vehicles account for the vast majority of New Zealand's fleet, the share of diesel light vehicles increased to 17% in the mid-2010s (Chapter 1). New Zealand has the highest, or among the highest, road-transport emissions per capita of nitrogen oxides, non-methane volatile organic compounds and CO_2 in the OECD (Figure 1.7).

Revenue from fuel excise duty and road user charges is allocated to the National Land Transport Fund (NLTF). It is used to finance investment in land transport infrastructure and services, mostly in the road network (Section 5.2). The rates of the fuel excise duty and the RUC are set using a cost allocation model: the expected infrastructure costs are allocated to different vehicles depending on each vehicle's estimated impact on those costs (heavy vehicles have a larger impact). In so doing, those who benefit from transport infrastructure and services contribute to a large part of the related investment. However, the cost allocation model and the associated tax and charge rates do not consider environmental externalities of road transport. In addition, the earmarking mechanism reduces flexibility of fiscal decisions.

New Zealand's system of fuel taxes and vehicle charges is unique and partly linked to the large share of off-road use of diesel. About 33% of diesel is not used for road transport (compared to 30% in the OECD as a whole); it is used mainly in farms, industrial facilities and fishing vessels. The government considers that taxing off-road use of diesel would impose an unfair burden on these sectors, as the fuel excise duty and the RUC are levied to finance investment in land transport infrastructure that do not benefit off-road users. Operating a refund system would be administratively costly and potentially non transparent or vulnerable to abuse (e.g. fraudulent refund claims). However, in practice, the differential tax treatment of diesel and petrol vehicles implicitly encourages off-road use of diesel. This is partly common to other countries, where fuel use in the agriculture and fishing sectors benefits from tax exemption or partial refunds, but industrial use of fuels is generally taxed.

In addition to the absence of an excise duty on diesel, use of fossil fuels for heating, industrial processes and electricity generation is not taxed or else benefits from refund schemes. As a result, New Zealand taxes only slightly more than 40% of CO_2 emissions from energy use, below the share in all OECD-Europe countries, and above the share in all non-European OECD countries but Japan (OECD, 2016a). This does not take into account the carbon price emerging from the NZ ETS, discussed in Section 3.5. OECD (2016a) estimates that, when accounting for both energy taxes and emission allowance price, a higher share (68%) of CO_2 emissions from energy use face a carbon price signal in New Zealand. However, this share is still below that of CO_2 energy-related emissions priced in many other OECD member countries (Figure 3.4).

Figure 3.4. **A relatively low share of CO_2 energy-related emissions face a carbon price signal**

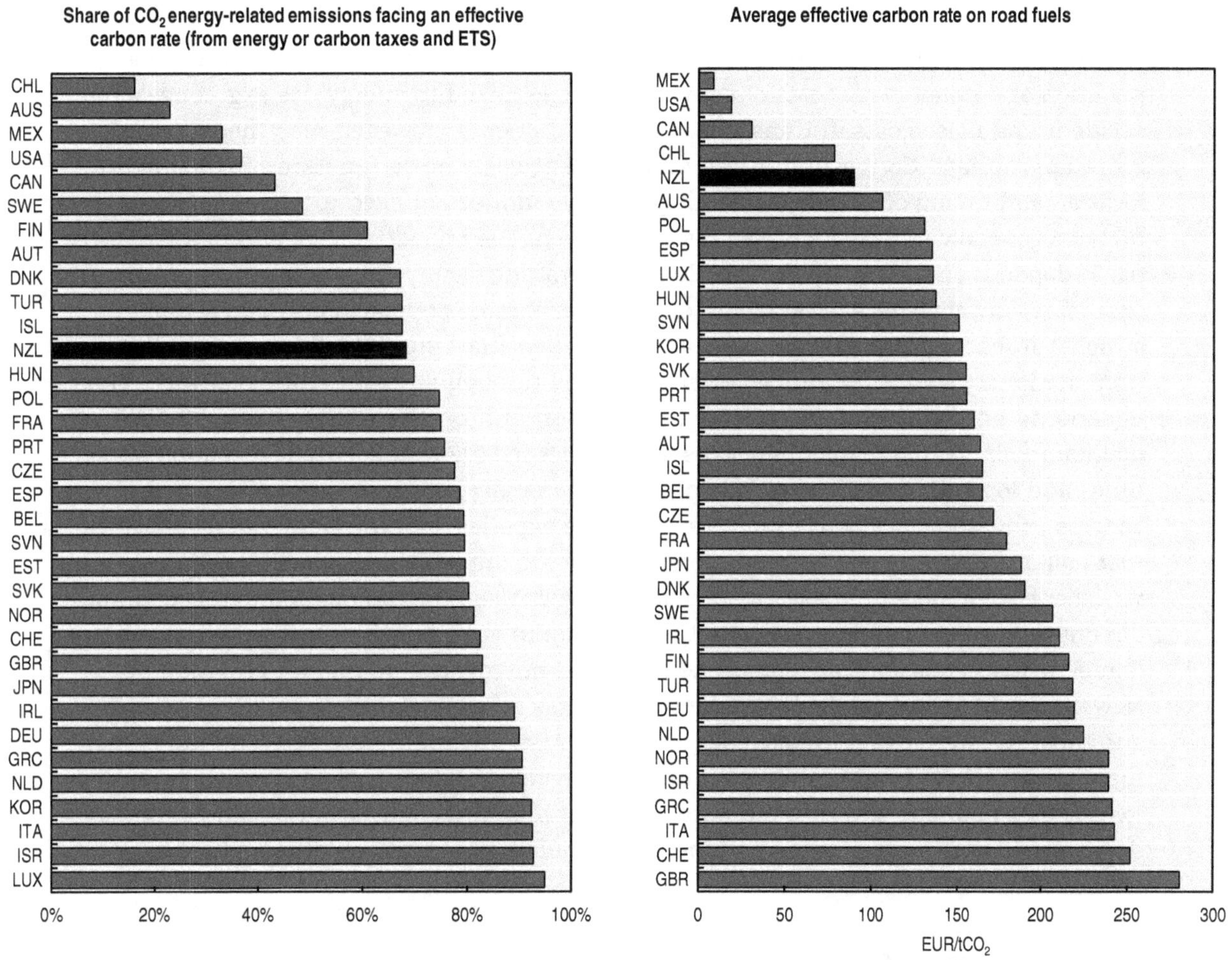

Notes: CO_2 emissions from biomass included. Effective carbon rates resulting from specific energy taxes, carbon taxes and emission trading systems (ETS). Tax rates are as of 1 April 2012, based on OECD (2015), *Taxing Energy Use 2015: OECD and Selected Partner Economies*. ETS prices are from several years (2012, 2014 and 2015).
Source: OECD (2016), *Effective Carbon Rates: Pricing CO_2 through Taxes and Emissions Trading Systems*.

StatLink http://dx.doi.org/10.1787/888933459880

The carbon price offers limited incentives for more efficient use of fossil fuels, especially in the transport sector. Only 56% of emissions from fuels used in road transport face a form of carbon price (either tax or ETS) above EUR 30 tCO_2, which is a conservative estimate of the climate cost of emissions (OECD, 2016a). This is the third lowest share in the OECD (before Mexico and the United States). New Zealand was one of the few OECD member countries with average effective carbon rates faced by road transport below EUR 100 tCO_2 in 2012. Despite rising emission allowance prices since mid-2015, the carbon price component of petrol and diesel prices remains at around NZD 0.01 per litre, too low to influence behaviour (Royal Society of New Zealand, 2016).

Even if carbon prices in the NZ ETS increase further, there is scope to raise taxes on fuels used for transport, heating and industrial processes, to the extent that the NZ ETS will continue to operate without an actual cap on domestic GHG emissions (Section 3.5). If such a domestic cap is ultimately introduced, the interactions between the NZ ETS and fuel taxes should be carefully assessed to ensure fuel taxes address environmental effects other than CO_2 emissions. In particular, New Zealand should consider the introduction of an excise duty on diesel or otherwise remove the tax treatment disparity between petrol and diesel use.

In addition to the social costs of CO_2 emissions, fuel taxes can help account for local air pollution and other social costs directly or indirectly linked to energy use (e.g. congestion, accident and noise costs in transport). Other instruments, however, may theoretically be more appropriate. Congestion, noise and accident costs are a function of the amount, location and timing of vehicle traffic; they are only indirectly linked to fuel use, as greater fuel use generally reflects increased distance driven. The impact of local air pollution also partly depends on the location of vehicle use or emitting facility: higher pollution in remote or rural regions may have lower health effects than in more populated or urban regions, but a higher impact on natural resources and vegetation (Harding, 2014a). Local air pollution from stationary sources could be better addressed through a tax on emissions with rates depending on the size of the affected population and on the social costs of different pollutants, similar to the tax Chile plans to introduce in 2017 (OECD, 2016b). A country-wide, time- and location-specific road pricing would generally be a more cost-effective tool to address congestion, accidents and noise. Still, the experience of the Netherlands indicates that political economy reasons are a serious barrier to implementation (OECD, 2015b). With its experience in distance-based road charging, New Zealand is well placed to move in this direction (Road User Charges Review Group, 2009). In the meantime, in the absence of a domestic GHG emission cap, comprehensive road pricing system and air emission taxes, New Zealand should consider broadening the fuel tax base and ensure that the excise duties and the RUC rates are set to take adequate account of environmental externalities. Higher fuel tax rates would provide an incentive for drivers to reduce fuel consumption; to the extent this happens through reductions in distance travelled, other social costs may decrease. Any adverse impact on vulnerable population groups could be addressed with targeted benefit schemes.

3.3. Tax treatment of company cars and commuting expenses

Like many other OECD member countries, New Zealand favourably taxes benefits deriving from the personal use of company cars. According to an OECD study, the New Zealand tax system captures slightly more than 40% of a benchmark for neutral tax treatment of company car benefits relative to cash wage income (Harding, 2014b). This is a relatively low share compared to the other 25 OECD member countries covered in the study (Figure 3.5). This is because company cars used for private purpose increase an employee's annual taxable income by only 20% of the vehicle's acquisition value. In addition, the fuel costs paid by employers do not increase the employee's taxable income. As a result, there is no incentive for employees to limit the use of company cars or choose more fuel-efficient vehicles. This tax treatment results in an annual subsidy of more than USD 2 500 per year,

Figure 3.5. **New Zealand could improve its tax treatment of company car benefits**

Proportion of the benchmark tax system captured by countries' tax systems (midpoint estimate)
Assuming a three-year useful life of company cars

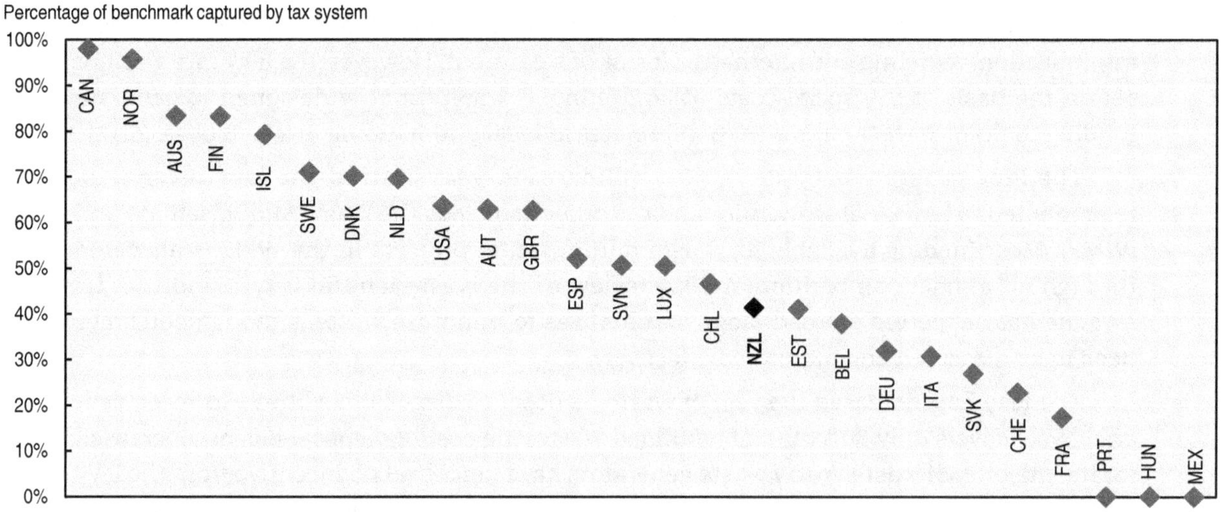

Source: OECD (2015), Updated OECD calculations based on Harding (2014), "Personal Tax Treatment of Company Cars and Commuting Expenses: Estimating the Fiscal and Environmental Costs", *OECD Taxation Working Papers, No. 20.*

StatLink http://dx.doi.org/10.1787/888933459890

the third highest among the OECD member countries surveyed. Therefore, it is attractive for employees to be paid part of their salary in the form of company cars. Assuming about 30% of newly registered vehicles were company cars in 2012, this favourable tax treatment led to approximately USD 205 million in revenue forgone, or about 20% of the tax revenue from vehicle-related taxes, in the same year.

Employees cannot deduct expenses related to commuting between home and work from their taxable income, and public transport expenses paid by employers are considered fully as taxable income to employees. This leaves the employee neutral in choosing between commuting options: it encourages neither long driving distances that can trigger additional peak-hour traffic, nor use of public transport (as would be the case if only expenses for public transport use were deductible). However, free or subsidised parking spaces provided on the employer's premises are not considered to be taxable income for employees. Given the increasing financial cost of parking, this can be a benefit of substantial value; it decreases the cost of driving to work relative to other forms of transport and thereby distorts decisions about the form of commuting (Harding, 2014b).

In addition to be a cost for the public budget, the favourable tax treatment of company cars and parking lots tend to encourage private car use, long-distance commuting and urban sprawl. It can result in increasing fuel consumption, emissions of GHGs and local air pollutants, noise, congestion and risk of accidents (Roy, 2014). As Chapter 5 notes, major New Zealand cities are expanding at their fringes, rather than in inner-city areas, to host a growing population. Despite more use of public transport, driving remains the main urban transport mode; for example, in Auckland, nine out of ten dwellers drive to work. New Zealand should, therefore, reconsider the taxation system of company cars and parking spaces, which runs against its climate mitigation goals and the sustainable urban development objectives of major cities.

3.4. Waste disposal levy and waste charges

The 2008 Waste Minimisation Act introduced a disposal levy (NSD 10 per tonne on waste sent to landfill). The levy aims to increase the cost of waste disposal, thereby changing the price signals associated with waste disposal and potentially promoting waste minimisation, recycling and alternative forms of treatment. However, the levy rate was not set on the basis of the social costs of landfilling; it was primarily designed to generate funding to finance waste minimisation projects at local and national levels (Bibbee, 2011).

The levy generates about NZD 25 million each year. Half of the levy revenue is redistributed to territorial authorities and the other half feeds the Waste Minimisation Fund (WMF). Most funding available for waste minimisation projects in the WMF is allocated through an annual competition. A 2014 review of the waste landfill levy found that its revenue has supported a broad range of initiatives to minimise waste, although outcomes need to be measured and monitored effectively.

The levy has increased the cost of waste disposal to disposal facilities. However, as it effectively covers only 30% of total landfilled waste, the cost of disposal has not increased for the majority of waste; many waste generators have perceived no incentive from the levy (MfE, 2014a). Extending the levy obligation to a larger number of waste disposal facilities would help improve its effectiveness.

Expanding the use of a pricing system for waste collection services would also help increase the levy's effectiveness, encourage waste minimisation and recycling, and finance advanced waste management services (Chapter 5). Some territorial authorities apply quantity- or volume-based waste charges (weight-based, pay-per-bin or pay-per-bag), which provide incentives to households to reduce waste. Evidence from the Auckland region indicates that districts applying volume-based charges send nearly half of the waste volume to landfills than do districts financing waste management through flat charges included in property taxes. This is consistent with experience from other countries (e.g. Germany and Korea).

The NZ ETS (Section 3.5), which covers the waste management sector, obliges landfill operators to surrender emission allowances with the aim of encouraging them to invest in any landfill gas-collection system and to separate organic from non-organic waste to reduce methane emissions. However, the low NZ ETS carbon price has provided little incentive to do so to date. The interactions between the NZ ETS and the waste landfill levy should be examined.

3.5. GHG emissions trading scheme

The New Zealand Emissions Trading Scheme (NZ ETS), launched in 2008, represents the cornerstone of the country's climate change mitigation policy and the main instrument to achieve its emission reduction targets. Several unique features differentiate the NZ ETS from other emissions trading systems worldwide. These reflect New Zealand's distinct emissions profile (namely, a high proportion of agriculture-related biological emissions and a large amount of forest carbon sinks; see Chapter 1), as well as carbon leakage concerns and the aim of linking the NZ ETS to other markets.

The NZ ETS was designed to be a comprehensive scheme that included all gases covered by the Kyoto Protocol and all emitting sectors.[9] It was the first carbon market in the world to include emissions and removals from forestry and agriculture. Forestry entered the NZ ETS at its inception for fear that an announced later entry would encourage deforestation.[10]

However, subsequent amendments indefinitely postponed the inclusion of biological emissions from agriculture (methane and nitrous oxide) until technologies are available to reduce these emissions in a cost-effective way and international competitors take sufficient action on their emissions.[11] Stationary energy supply, liquid fossil fuel supply, industrial processes and waste management have all gradually joined the system. As a result, the NZ ETS covers 52% of national emissions (i.e. excluding biological emissions from agriculture). This compares to 45% of the European GHG emissions in the EU ETS and 85% of the GHG emissions in the California and Quebec cap-and-trade systems (ICAP, 2016).

The NZ ETS obliges participants to report on their GHG emissions and surrender emission units that correspond to their obligations. There is no domestic cap on emissions. This differs from other ETSs in the world, which set annual absolute emission caps (ICAP, 2016). The NZ ETS was originally designed to operate within the international Kyoto Protocol emission cap and credits market. It allowed participants to surrender either New Zealand Units (NZUs, each corresponding to 1 tonne of carbon dioxide equivalent, or tCO_2-eq) or international Kyoto-compliant units (certified emission reduction units, or CERs, emission reduction units, or ERUs, and removal units, or RMUs).[12] Until June 2015, when the NZ ETS stopped accepting international credits (see below), there had been no limit on the purchase of international carbon credits, contrary to all other ETSs in the world. As a result, the carbon price in the NZ ETS was determined by the international carbon markets, rather than by the domestic supply of NZUs. In 2011-14, most of the units surrendered by NZ ETS participants came from international sources. A relatively small share of the supply and units surrendered came from free allocations to some activities (see below) and NZUs issued against eligible emission removals from forest management (Leining and Kerr, 2016). The NZ ETS allows the government to auction allowances, but this option has not been used yet.

The NZ ETS design was intended to expose participating companies to the international carbon price. It lets them make economically efficient decisions on whether to reduce their own emissions or invest in mitigation elsewhere in the world, thereby minimising GHG abatement costs. This would allow domestic production and associated emissions to expand efficiently and New Zealand to still contribute to global mitigation efforts through the carbon market, thereby avoiding carbon leakage.[13] The system was also intended to shift the purchasing of emission units for Kyoto compliance from the government to market participants, thereby ensuring least-cost compliance with international obligations (Leining and Kerr, 2016).

The NZ ETS has been reviewed and amended several times, which has created uncertainty for participants. Some of the amendments aimed to moderate the impact of the carbon price on participants. Twenty-six emission-intensive trade-exposed activities receive free allocations based upon their historical emission intensity.[14] These free allocations were to be gradually phased out by 2030, but successive amendments have indefinitely postponed their removal out of competitiveness and carbon leakage concerns. However, evidence from carbon pricing systems implemented in other countries indicates the impact on competitiveness is generally limited and does not substantially differ between the firms that benefit from preferential treatment (such as free allocations) and those that do not (Arlinghaus, 2015). The free allocations are effectively a transfer to receiving companies and should be removed on the basis of a predetermined schedule; if allowances were auctioned instead, the government could raise NZD 50 million in revenue (at the 2016 emission allowance prices) (PCE, 2016). In addition, all participating companies have the option to pay the government a NZD 25 fixed price per unit, rather than surrender eligible units, which effectively sets a price ceiling. Prices have never exceeded the ceiling since the NZ ETS introduction, but are likely to rise in the future. New Zealand should consider removing the price ceiling or, at the very least, increasing it over time. In a welcome move, in mid-2016 the government decided to gradually phase out the so-called one-for-two arrangement, which had allowed non-forestry sector participants to surrender 1 NZU for every 2 tonnes of CO_2 emission, thereby halving the number of permits needed.[15]

The NZ ETS has made little contribution to domestic GHG emission mitigation. The one-for-two obligation (until mid-2016), the free allocations to some sectors and the lack of quantity limits on the use of Kyoto units (until mid-2015) have blunted the carbon price signal and undermined the effectiveness of the system. The NZ ETS moderately encouraged afforestation in the first few years of implementation, when the emission unit price was higher (around NZD 20/tCO_2-eq). Businesses have rarely considered the carbon price in their decisions and have not invested in reducing their emissions (MfE, 2016a). Companies have mostly purchased and surrendered to the government cheap ERUs and CERs, while banking massive amounts of the allocated NZUs (both those allocated for free and against emission removals from forestry) to meet future liabilities (Leining and Kerr, 2016).[16] This contributed to depress the NZU price in line with the price of international units until it reached nearly zero.

At the same time, thanks to the accumulated surplus of Kyoto units, the NZ ETS has helped New Zealand over-achieve its Kyoto target of bringing its average annual GHG emissions over 2008-12 back to 1990 levels (Figure 1.9). However, the overflow of Kyoto units has undermined the integrity of the NZ ETS, as many ERUs were of questionable environmental integrity (i.e. they did not represent real emission reductions beyond business-as-usual). New Zealand was the top buyer of Kyoto credits, mostly ERUs, in proportion to domestic emissions (Simmons and Young, 2016). The government has carried over this surplus of units from the first commitment period for meeting the 2020 target to reduce emissions by 5% below 1990 levels. As the Parliamentary Commissioner for the Environment recommended, the government should not carry any international units over beyond 2020. This would restore the integrity of the system and ensure that New Zealand's contribution to the goals of the Paris Agreement is real (PCE, 2016).

Since mid-2015, the NZ ETS has functioned as a purely domestic emissions trading system, de-linked from the Kyoto market. As New Zealand did not make a commitment for 2013-20 under the Kyoto Protocol, international credits are no longer eligible for compliance within the system. While prices have been increasing since, the stock of banked NZUs from the previous commitment period is sufficient to cover more than four years of emissions from participating sectors (MfE, 2015a). In this context, the price is driven by market expectations about future policy stringency rather than by the costs of mitigating domestic emissions. It thus has limited value as a long-term price signal (Leining and Kerr, 2016). The unclear relationship between the number of units available in the NZ ETS and the national emission reduction targets makes determining the supply of units, and the GHG emission mitigation outcome, highly uncertain. OECD (2013a) recommended New Zealand set a domestic cap on emissions. At the very least, New Zealand should align the supply of units in the NZ ETS with its climate mitigation targets. The government should also introduce auctioning of domestic allocations as soon as possible once the stock of banked NZUs is depleted. Further, it should consider introducing a price floor, increasing over time, on auctioned allowances. This would prevent the carbon price from plummeting to near-zero levels, as was the case in the past, and would help stabilise the price signal.

Current projections indicate that existing measures will not be sufficient to reduce emissions consistently with the nationally determined contribution (NDC) target to cut GHG emissions by 30% below 2005 levels by 2030 (MfE, 2016b, 2015b; Figure 1.9). New Zealand will need to find new ways of offsetting its domestic emissions by funding mitigation efforts in other countries, with a view to minimise abatement costs. It is likely that international emission offsets will be made newly eligible in the NZ ETS (MfE, 2015a). As the Parliamentary Commissioner for the Environment recommended, there should be a clear limit to the quantity of international credits that can be used to offset domestic emissions. This would help preserve the domestic mitigation efforts and avoid the perverse outcomes of the first commitment period.

The NZ ETS can contribute effectively to achieve New Zealand's climate mitigation objectives, provided that some changes are made. Despite some complexities, it is a well-functioning, well-managed and transparent carbon market, which does not entail excessive costs for participating companies. The government regularly provides information about market transactions (MfE, 2016a). In 2015-16, the Ministry for the Environment conducted the third review of the NZ ETS, which addressed issues such as protective measures, auctioning and restricting access to international credits. The review, still ongoing at the time of writing, led to the phase out of the one-for-two arrangement (see above). It did not consider the possibility of bringing agriculture back within the system, however.

New Zealand needs to reconsider the decision of indefinitely postponing the entry of biological emissions from farming in emission trading. If such a decision is confirmed, alternative pricing or regulatory measures should be taken to make agriculture contribute to achieving New Zealand's climate mitigation objectives. Setting a clear date for the inclusion of agriculture in the NZ ETS or for the introduction of alternative measures would provide much-needed policy certainty, help the sector prepare for the policy change, encourage investment and accelerate innovation. It would also enhance New Zealand's environmental credentials on the international scene. Continuing to exempt nearly half of domestic emissions from the NZ ETS or other emission mitigation obligations would make achieving the New Zealand NDC target harder; it could place a disproportionate burden on other sectors of the economy and slow the pace of adjustment in the agriculture sector (Bibbee, 2011). At the same time, putting a price on biological emissions from agriculture can help address nitrogen water contamination (Box 3.2).

Box 3.2. **Potential co-benefits of stacking nutrient and carbon credits**

Efforts to reduce agricultural GHG emissions and measures to reduce nitrogen pollution in water can provide environmental co-benefits. For example, a price on carbon advanced the achievement of nitrogen reductions as part of the Lake Taupo Nitrogen Market (Box 4.7) by promoting land-use change from pasture to forestry. Lankoski et al. (2015) show that allowing stacking of carbon and water quality credits can encourage farmers to adopt environmental practices that reduce both GHG emissions and nutrient pollution. Agricultural climate mitigation practices that increase nutrient and water retention and prevent soil degradation (such as soil carbon sequestration) can also increase resilience to droughts and flooding.

However, climate policies may also send the wrong signal to farmers. For example, the NZ ETS required owners of forests that existed prior to 1990 to pay for carbon credits upon any land conversion to other uses such as pasture. In the upper Waikato River catchment,

Box 3.2. Potential co-benefits of stacking nutrient and carbon credits *(cont.)*

this triggered some landowners to clear their forests before the NZ ETS started in 2008. The amendment to the NZ ETS that delayed surrender obligations for agriculture *de facto* indefinitely postponed the price restraint on land-use conversion from forestry (carbon sinks) to pastoral farming. This ultimately led to additional clearing of forested land in the Waikato River catchment and increased nutrients leaching to the river (Dickie, 2016).

Source: Dickie (2016); Lankoski et al. (2015).

Some mitigation technologies are available or will be commercially viable in the near future as a result of the considerable investment in research (Emissions Trading Scheme Review Panel, 2011; Section 6); a carbon price is needed to make them cost-competitive with current practices and encourage farmers to adopt them. Free allocations and other measures could be used to allow farmers to gradually adjust to the carbon market and protect vulnerable small, family-run farms, provided they are strictly time-bound and phased out on the basis of a clear timeline. If agriculture is to be included in the ETS, the point of obligation should be shifted from the processor level, as in the current design, to the farm level in order to ensure farmers directly perceive the price incentive. Concerns about the high costs of measuring on-farm GHG emissions could be addressed by further investing in monitoring and reporting tools such as OVERSEER®, which provides on-farm information about nutrient use and leaching (Royal Society of New Zealand, 2016; Chapter 4).[17]

The NZ ETS is likely to be insufficient on its own to drive New Zealand towards a low-emissions economy and its long-term goal of reducing emissions by 50% below 1990 levels by 2050. There are already viable emission mitigation options in all sectors of the economy (Royal Society of New Zealand, 2016), and a sufficiently high and stable carbon price is essential to unlock them. However, despite their increase, prices remain too low to influence behaviour. In mid-2016, the NZU price was NZD 17.8 or USD 12.5;[18] this compares with the estimated social cost of carbon of USD 32 tCO_2eq that is commonly used in cost-benefit analyses in New Zealand (Smith and Braathen, 2015). Even if prices increase further, other market failures and non-price barriers (such as split incentives between those making the investment and those benefiting from it, transaction and information costs, difficult access to capital, risk aversion) may prevent investment in emission abatement (Hood, 2013). Hence, the NZ ETS needs to remain the main climate mitigation policy instrument for reducing domestic emissions as part of a wider and coherent package. Managing the interactions between the emission trading and other GHG mitigation measures (such as in the electricity supply and transport sectors) will be essential to the effectiveness of the package.

3.6. *Tradable fishing quotas*

New Zealand has had an effective system of tradable fish quotas since 1986 to manage commercial and customary fisheries, a model replicated in many countries (Bibbee, 2011). Each year, the government determines a total allowable commercial catch (TACC) for each species and region based on the maximum sustainable yield, net of an allowance for recreational fishing and customary Maori uses (Chapter 1).[19] Individual fishing quotas are distributed among commercial fishers; the quotas entitle them to a given percentage of the TACC, determined on an annual basis, and can be subsequently traded within given regions and species (OECD, 2015c).

Allocating individual catch entitlements reduces the incentives to maximise catch at the opening of the fishing season (OECD, 2007). The quota system has helped reduce overfishing and maintain the fish stock at sustainable levels (Chapter 1); temporary reductions in the quotas have allowed some species populations to recover within or above their target range (OECD, 2015c). Between its inception and 2016, quota system coverage has increased from 26 to 100 species, including more than 630 fish stocks; it has become one of the largest such schemes in the world.

The government provides financial transfers for general fisheries management and conservation services. In 2013, the amount of these transfers was 12% above their 2005-10 average (OECD, 2015c). The costs of these transfers are recovered through levies charged to commercial fishing companies.[20] In the framework of the World Trade Organization (WTO) negotiation, New Zealand has supported elimination of certain forms of subsidies that contribute to overcapacity and overfishing (OECD, 2015c).

4. Greening financial support to the energy and agriculture sectors

4.1. *Fossil fuel subsidy reform*

New Zealand is a founding member of the Friends of Fossil Fuel Subsidy Reform, an informal group of non-G20 countries established in 2010 working to build political consensus on the importance of fossil-fuel subsidy reform.[21] To lead by example, in 2015, New Zealand voluntarily underwent a fossil-fuel subsidies peer review in the context of Asia-Pacific Economic Co-operation (APEC).[22] The APEC panel reviewed eight measures that could be considered to support fossil fuels: motor spirit excise duty refund; funding of international treaty obligation to hold oil stocks; non-resident drilling rig and seismic ship tax exemption; indemnity for mining land remediation; research and development funding for the oil industry; tax deductions for petroleum-mining expenditures; financial restructure of solid energy; petroleum tax and royalty regime. Some of these measures cost the New Zealand government about NZD 60 million in tax breaks and budgetary transfers in 2014 (Figure 3.6; OECD, 2016c). The peer review concluded that none of these measures were "inefficient subsidies that encourage wasteful consumption" of fossil fuels. This was partly because the subsidies do not lower domestic fuel prices as New Zealand is a price taker on world oil market (i.e. it pays market prices for its petroleum products) (APEC, 2015).

New Zealand provides some of the lowest amounts of support to fossil fuel consumption in both absolute and relative terms. This can be seen in Figure 3.6, which expresses total consumer support for fossil fuels as a share of the revenue from energy-related taxes. In particular, off-road users of fuels (petrol, liquid and compressed natural gas) can obtain refunds for excise duty payments. Total refunds (and revenue forgone) have been relatively modest in the last decade, amounting to about NZD 30-40 million annually or about 3-4% of the revenue collected through the excise duty (Figure 3.6; OECD, 2016d).

A competitive tax and royalty regime is in place to attract investment in oil and gas exploration (IEA, forthcoming). For example, investors can deduct some exploration and development expenditures for tax and royalty purposes in the year they are incurred, rather than over the lifetime of the well; since 2005, non-resident companies exploring and developing offshore have benefited from income tax exemptions (this tax concession was extended until 2019). As OECD (2013a) notes, these incentives can distort investment decisions in favour of fossil fuel production over more sustainable sources of energy; they counteract New Zealand's efforts to address global climate change and should thus be discontinued.

Figure 3.6. **Fossil fuel support is among the lowest in the OECD**

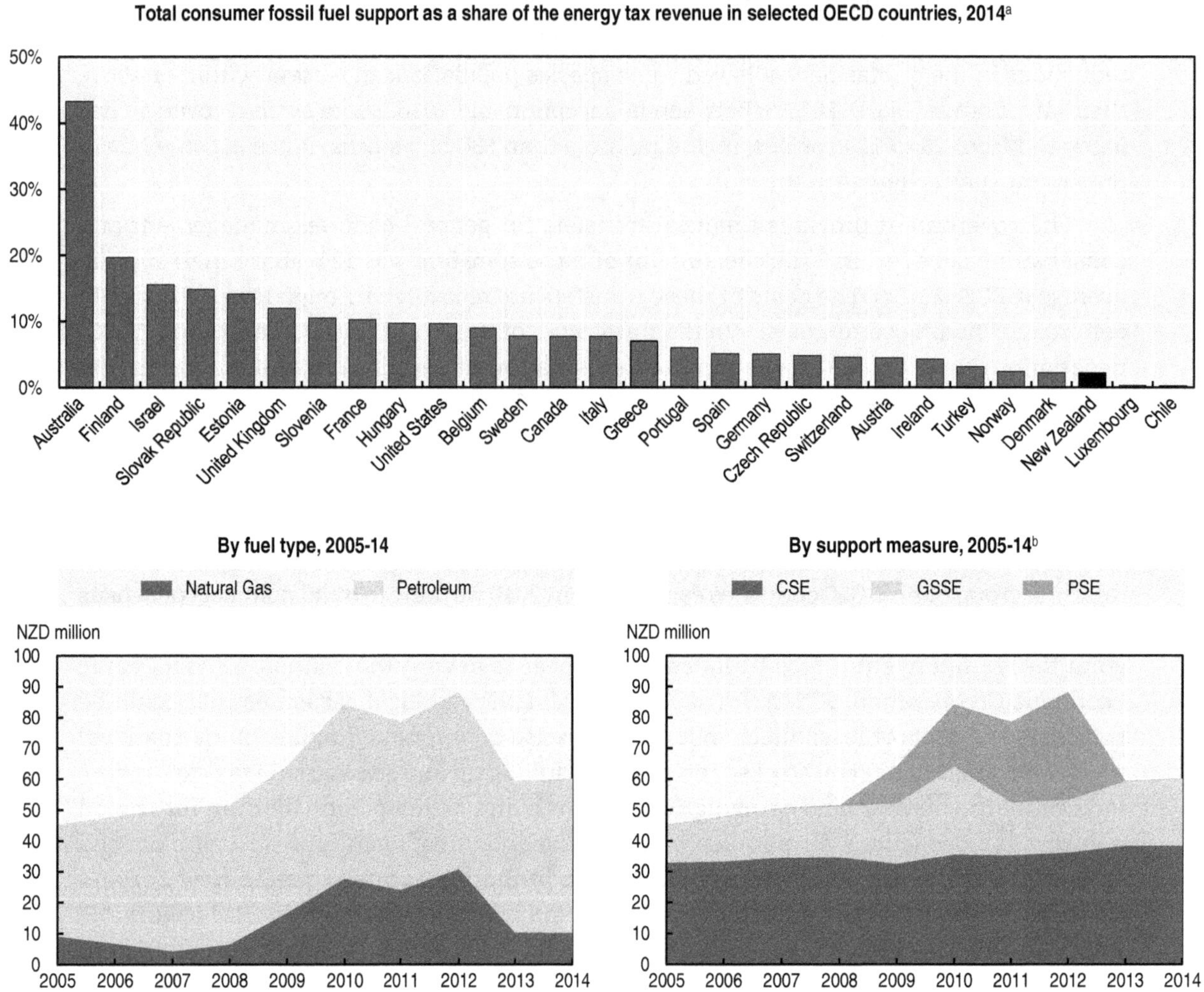

a) Data for Australia include the country's large Fuel Tax Credits, which alone explain the relatively high ratio observed for that particular country. This measure serves to rebate some of the excise taxes that businesses pay on their purchases of fuel there. Data for Greece are for the period 2010/11 only.
b) CSE=Consumer Support Estimate; GSSE=General Services Support Estimate; PSE=Producer Support Estimate (data available only for the period 2008-2013).
Source: OECD (2016), "OECD Inventory of Support Measures for Fossil Fuels", *OECD Environment Statistics* (database); OECD (2015), "Green Growth Indicators (Edition 2015)", *OECD Environment Statistics* (database).

StatLink http://dx.doi.org/10.1787/888933459900

4.2. Financial support to agriculture

Total support to agriculture represented 0.3% of GDP in 2013-15, the vast majority of which was channelled to general services such as agricultural innovation, inspection and control, and infrastructure maintenance. This includes the Sustainable Farming Fund, which supports projects aimed at improving the environmental performance of agriculture (Box 3.3). Since the reforms of agricultural policies in the mid-1980s, production and trade distorting policies supporting agriculture in New Zealand have virtually disappeared. For more than 25 years, the level of support to farmers has been the lowest among OECD member countries. Agricultural support in the form of transfers to farmers, as measured by the producer support estimate (PSE), was less than 1% of gross farm receipts in 2013-15[23] – the lowest in the OECD. However, the majority of such low support to producers is based on output and variable input use without input constraints: in 2013-15, this support represented

80% of the PSE, up from about 50% in the mid-1990s (OECD, 2016e; Figure 3.7). This form of support reduces the cost of capital and other purchased inputs; it indirectly encourages agricultural production and increases risk of overuse or misuse of inputs such as pesticides and fertilisers, with potentially negative environmental impacts.

Figure 3.7. **Agricultural producer support is low, but mostly tied to output and input use**

Producer support estimate level and composition by support categories, 2000-14

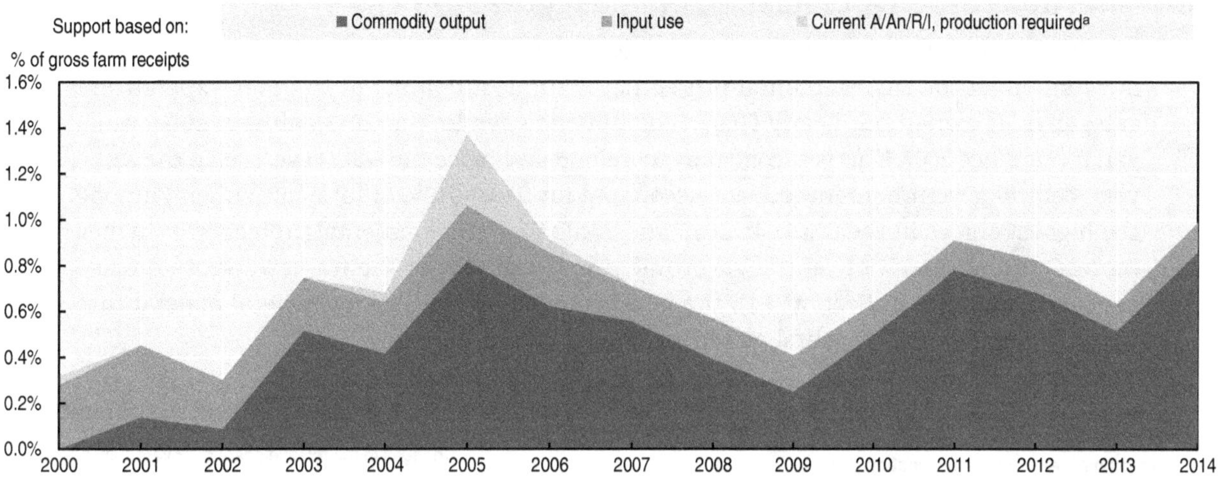

a) A: Area planted; An: Animal number; R: Receipts; I: Income.
Source: OECD (2016), "Producer and Consumer Support Estimates", *OECD Agriculture Statistics* (database).

StatLink http://dx.doi.org/10.1787/888933459919

Box 3.3. **The Sustainable Farming Fund (SFF)**

The SFF, set up in 2000, supports community- and industry-driven projects aimed at improving the productive and environmental performance of agriculture, forestry and aquaculture. The maximum total grant available for individual projects is NZD 600 000 over three years. At least 20% of project costs must be met by non-government sources, although most successful projects are able to leverage a high proportion of other funding or in-kind support to complement an SFF grant. The SFF funds a wide variety of projects, including projects focusing on sustainable land management, organic farming, improved water management, climate change mitigation and adaptation and Maori agribusiness. The expected contribution to sustainability or climate change objectives is one of the criteria used to assess applications. The fund has invested up to NZD 9 million per year and backed 948 projects over 15 years.

Source: Ministry for Primary Industries (2016); OECD (2016e, 2013b).

The Irrigation Acceleration Fund (IAF), in place since the 2011/12 financial year, and Crown Irrigation Investments Limited (CIIL), established in 2013, provide grant funding and concessional financing to community and regional irrigation-related and water storage projects. To be eligible for funding, the projects need to promote efficient use of water, environmental management and demonstrate a commitment to good industry practice (OECD, 2016e). In addition, to help address the vulnerability of agricultural production to variable rainfall patterns, investment in irrigation can help enhance efficiency in water use and augment surface and groundwater flows. However, as Chapter 4 discusses, financial support to irrigation projects indirectly encourages intensification of agriculture, which is likely to further increase pressures on freshwater resources. Environmental gains may be limited if more efficient irrigation techniques do not result in lower net water use, but simply lead to an increase in irrigated volume or area. New Zealand would benefit from systematically assessing the effectiveness of transfers to farmers and financial support for irrigation against their socio-economic objectives and potential environmental impact.

5. Investment in the environment to promote green growth

The New Zealand central government generally plays a dominant role in public finance, but its budget for environmental protection is modest compared to other expenditure categories. It carried out nearly 90% of total public spending in 2013, without substantial variations since 2007. This is second only to Ireland and twice the OECD average. In the same year, central government investment accounted for nearly 19% of total investment, among the highest shares in the OECD. In 2015, the budget for environmental protection activities represented about 1% of central government expenditure. In the framework of its fiscal consolidation efforts (Section 3.1), the government has cut back on several expenditure items, including environmental protection (Figure 3.8).

Figure 3.8. **Central government spending in environmental protection has decreased**

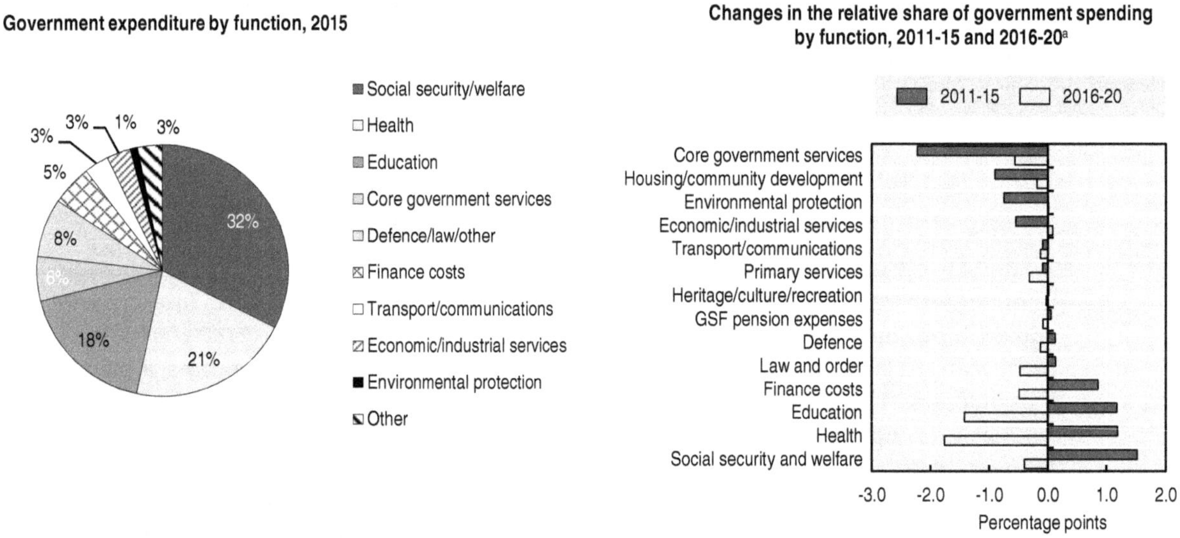

a) Based on data expressed as percentage of total government expenditure.
Source: Treasury (2016), "Half Year Economic and Fiscal Update 2015 (YEFU)", *Budget Policy Statement 2016*.

StatLink http://dx.doi.org/10.1787/888933459925

As in many other OECD member countries, local governments have major responsibilities in providing environment-related infrastructure and services, which account for a large share of their expenditure. In 2015, local governments spent 14% of their budgets on water supply and sanitation, 13% on public transport and 4% each on waste management and general environmental protection (Figure 5.10). At the same time, local governments have limited fiscal autonomy; revenue sources are largely limited to property taxes (Figure 5.8). Many local authorities identify lack of funding as a significant barrier to expand and upgrade infrastructure, including as it relates to the environment (NZPC, 2016).

Capital spending on infrastructure has increased considerably since 2000 (OECD, 2015a). Yet the quality of infrastructure is perceived to be low relative to local expectations. Firms surveyed continue to report an inadequate supply of infrastructure as the most important barrier to doing business (World Economic Forum, 2015). Large investment is still needed in transport infrastructure to meet the growing demand of good and passenger transport (Section 5.2). Growing urban populations have exerted increasing pressures on water supply and wastewater treatment infrastructure (Chapter 5).

Given the central government's fiscal consolidation objective and the limited resources of local authorities, meeting these infrastructure needs will require diversifying funding sources (OECD, 2015a). Local and national roads could make greater use of tolls, and public-private partnerships could make more efficient use of resources (Section 5.2). As Chapter 5 discusses, there is scope to expand the use of water supply and wastewater charges to better cover the costs of these services and provide incentives to use water more efficiently. Legislation, however, limits the ability of local authorities to introduce volumetric wastewater charges (based on volume of water used or discharged).

5.1. *Investing in renewable energy and energy efficiency*

Investment in renewables has increased in recent years, without the need for any direct subsidies or public support; geothermal, hydro and wind are cost-competitive. IEA (forthcoming) considers this performance a world-class success story. New Zealand has already one of the highest shares of renewables in its energy mix among OECD member countries. Renewable sources (mainly hydro) supply 80% of its electricity (Chapter 1), and the government aims to bring this share to 90% by 2025. Taking into account projected growth in power demand, current renewable generation levels would need to increase by about 20%. Renewable energy potential is largely sufficient to achieve the target, if the current hydropower generation is maintained. However, hydro resources are vulnerable to droughts, and their long-term availability is uncertain due to climate change and water quality concerns. At the same time, as IEA (forthcoming) notes, growing shares of variable renewable resources (i.e. wind and solar power) may affect the operational security of the power system and require adjustments in the electricity market rules.

There is scope to improve energy efficiency, as the energy intensity of the economy has remained broadly stable since 2000 at levels well above the OECD average (Chapter 1). New Zealand's approach to energy efficiency has changed from direct financial support to a greater focus on information and partnerships. The NZ ETS has not provided sufficient incentives for investing in renewables and energy efficiency. It is also not clear how much further market forces can improve efficiency. A comprehensive package of policy measures is needed to complement the NZ ETS carbon pricing and address non-pricing barriers to investing in low-carbon energy sources and adopting energy efficient technology in industry, transport and buildings. This will have multiple environmental, energy security and health benefits.

Energy efficiency in buildings

New Zealand has taken action to address the relatively poor energy performance of the building stock through public funding, local tax incentives, awareness-raising and voluntary labelling (Box 3.4). In 2009-16, the flagship *Warm Up New Zealand* programmes ("Heat Smart" and "Healthy Homes") provided subsidies to households for improving house insulation and heating systems (with an overall budget of about NZD 420 million). In 2016, "Healthy Homes" was extended for two years to support insulation of rental properties occupied by low-income tenants with priority health needs related to cold and damp housing; it targets about 20 000 homes for insulation. As of 2016, the *Warm Up* programmes had contributed to retrofit nearly 300 000 homes (or nearly 20% of the housing stock), about half of which were occupied by low-income households. However, these programmes have not leveraged private sector funding or encouraged households to refurbish beyond simple ceiling insulation and heating retrofits. About 2 500 homes were retrofitted at their owners' expense using voluntary targeted rates (VTR), i.e. adding the energy efficiency refurbishment costs to their rates bill (property taxes) and paying it off over a certain period of time (often ten years).

Despite progress, an estimated 30% of the housing stock remains uninsulated. The 2016 Residential Tenancies Amendment Act introduced stricter floor and roof insulation requirements for rented homes and social housing. Additional measures may be needed to encourage insulation in the untreated homes not covered by the legislation; the Building Code is below the standards required in many other OECD member countries (IEA, forthcoming) and local regulation cannot go beyond the code requirements (NZPC, 2015). The authorities should consider strengthening the standards for newly built homes under the Building Code, while minimising the risk of delaying needed growth in the housing stock (Chapter 5). They could also introduce stricter emission and efficiency requirements and more systematic control procedures for wood heating appliances, as part of the ongoing review of the National Environmental Standard on Air Quality; wood burning provides over 10% of residential heat, but is a major source of air pollution (Chapter 1; IEA, forthcoming). Additional measures (e.g. grants, subsidies and tax credits) may also be needed to provide landlords with incentives to take up more efficient heating systems, draught proofing, ventilation and moisture prevention, particularly for rentals to low-income households.

New Zealand operates three voluntary rating tools for sustainable buildings (Box 3.4). To improve the environmental performance of buildings, energy performance ratings could be made mandatory for large public buildings, and be further rolled out across the commercial and industrial sectors over time. This approach, adopted in many other OECD member countries, would encourage the housing market to factor energy efficiency into property prices (IEA, forthcoming). Ratings could be extended (or complemented) to include other sustainability dimensions such as water efficiency, waste or indoor environmental quality, building on existing voluntary rating initiatives.

5.2. Investing in low-carbon transport modes

The transport sector is the largest final energy user and the second largest source of GHG emissions (Figure 1.8). Motor vehicles are the primary transport mode for both goods and passengers, reflecting New Zealand's dispersed population, a history of low-density urban development and insufficient development of alternative transport modes (Chapter 1). While the use of public transport has increased, it remains limited: households made less than 5% of their trips in public transport over 2012-14 (Figure 5.4). Road freight has continued to increase; it is projected to increase by around 48% over the next 30 years (in tonne-kilometres), in particular around the Auckland region (Ministry of Transport, 2014). This will likely put considerable pressure on the existing road network and on the environment.

Investment in land transport infrastructure is significant, but heavily tilted towards roads. It amounted to around 1.3% of GDP in 2012-15; the authorities plan to spend around 1.5% of GDP annually on land transport infrastructure over the next decade. However,

Box 3.4. **Voluntary building rating initiatives**

- NABERSNZ is an energy efficiency rating tool for office buildings, which New Zealand adapted from the National Australian Built Environment Rating System (NABERS) model. While the tool is mandatory throughout Australia, it is voluntary in New Zealand. It is licensed to New Zealand's Energy Efficiency and Conservation Authority (EECA) and is administered by the non-governmental New Zealand Green Building Council (NZGBC). Trained assessors carry out ratings.
- Home Star is an independent, voluntary rating tool for the sustainability performance of residential buildings. It awards points across seven categories: energy, health and comfort; water; waste; materials; site; home management; and an optional innovation category. So far, agreements are in place for 700 certifications across New Zealand and 16 000 completed self-assessments online. Homes that are designed and built to meet the Building Code standard typically rate 3 or 4 on the Home Star rating scale (out of 10 for best-performing buildings).
- Green Star is a sustainability rating tool for non-residential buildings, including offices, industrial and education buildings, hospitals and libraries. It awards points across nine categories: energy, water, materials, indoor environment quality, transport, land use and ecology, management, emissions and innovation. So far, about 100 certifications have been delivered across New Zealand.

Source: NZGBC (2015, 2014).

public transport would receive only about 11%. This is a moderately higher share than in 2012-15, when 9% of the National Land Transport Fund (NLTF) was invested in public transport systems and 1% in cycling and walking infrastructure; 78% went to highways and local roads (Government of New Zealand, 2015c; NZTA, 2015). Additional investments in road infrastructure will be needed to meet increasing demand. However, further developing the rail urban public transport system, improving service quality and supply of bus services, and accelerating the roll-out of electric vehicles (see below) could provide other options for commuters, reduce road congestion and help lower GHG emissions. New Zealand should ensure investment priorities for land transport infrastructure, and the related financing model, are consistent with long-term climate and environmental objectives.

While local governments are responsible for providing part of transport infrastructure and services in their regions, funding of transport investment is highly centralised. Resources come from the NLTF, which is mostly fed by the revenue of road fuel and vehicle taxes (Section 3.2). The funding mechanism favours state highways and can discourage municipalities to invest in local roads or public transport. This is because the NLTF fully finances state highways – which are therefore virtually free for local governments – but only funds about half the cost of urban, suburban and rural roads and of public transport. As the Parliamentary Commissioner for the Environment noted, asking councils to co-finance even a small share of state highways could encourage councils to better consider alternative options, including public transport (PCE, 2016).

Giving a more prominent role to local governments in infrastructure investment and maintenance would require increasing their accountability and resources, as local fiscal autonomy remains limited (Sections 3.1). Further use of joint public procurement procedures and additional private investor participation, e.g. through public-private partnerships (PPPs) in local infrastructure provision could lead to higher investment efficiency (NZPC, 2016;

OECD, 2015d). Many local governments lack in-house capacity to conduct large complex projects; setting-up standardised procurement specifications would ease local collaborations and allow local authorities to share the costs, as well as best practices (Hodges, Proctor and King, 2013). PPPs should be carefully designed to avoid cost overruns, limit renegotiation risks and contain future fiscal liabilities; they should be systematically subject to *ex post* assessment (OECD, 2015d). Funding of national and local infrastructure should aim to recover the full costs of the investment, maintenance, use and associated environmental and social impacts to ensure competitive neutrality between transport modes. Road pricing could help place a cost on travel during peak periods and encourage more carpooling and use of public transport (Section 3.2; Chapter 5). In areas poorly serviced by public transport, or where concerns over equity arise, transfers could provide a partial offset of the charges. However, legislation restricts the application of road pricing to new roads where an alternative toll-free route is available.

Electric vehicles

With its large share of renewable electricity, New Zealand can use EVs to mitigate transport-related GHG emissions and reduce reliance on imported oil. Most car owners in New Zealand have access to off-street parking and park their vehicles overnight at private homes. This allows good charging possibilities, even in the absence of an extensive public charging infrastructure system. Commuters also travel relatively short distances, suitable for EVs with limited driving range (IEA, forthcoming). Nonetheless, so far the uptake of EVs in New Zealand has been very limited (around 2 000 vehicles in 2016) and growing slowly; the main barriers have been the high capital costs of the vehicles, limited availability of EV models, insufficient awareness and consumer confidence in the EV technology, and a lack of widespread public charging infrastructure (Ministry of Transport, 2016).

In mid-2016, the government launched the Electric Vehicle Programme to address these barriers. The programme aims at doubling the EV fleet every year until 2021. It foresees exempting EVs from the road user charge until they make up 2% of the light vehicle fleet. Further, the programme plans information campaigns, access to bus lanes and high-occupancy vehicle lanes on the highways and local roads, and investment in research and development (R&D) for low-emission vehicles. These measures will provide users with some incentive to switch to EVs, but their widespread adoption in the short term is unlikely without some additional policy measures. Experience from other countries suggests that fuel efficiency and emission standards are effective in encouraging the uptake of cleaner vehicles (IEA, forthcoming), but New Zealand is one of few OECD member countries without such standards. The central and local governments should lead by example and commit to purchase EVs for a proportion of their own fleets, which would provide a strong signal to the transport industry and public. More advanced options such as full electric car sharing service could be piloted. New Zealand will also need to adapt its electricity distribution system and develop the necessary charging infrastructure for accelerating the mass rollout of EVs (IEA, forthcoming).

6. Promoting eco-innovation

New Zealand has a well-developed innovation system and a sound skills base. In line with an increased emphasis on innovation as a driver of economic growth, public investment in science and innovation has increased by 60% since 2007-08. However, gross domestic expenditure on R&D has remained low at about 1.2% of GDP, about half the OECD average. Public institutions, largely universities and Crown research institutes, conduct most of the

R&D. This is linked to New Zealand's economic structure, with a large base of small and medium-sized enterprises and its remote geographic location. Distance from world markets presents an ongoing challenge to scaling-up innovative businesses and it also affects integration into global science and innovation networks. Despite close co-operation between industry and public research, the number of patents is relatively small and commercialisation of public research results could be improved (OECD, 2014b).

The government is the main source of funding for environmental research. Environment-related R&D accounts for nearly 10% of government R&D outlays. This is the highest share in the OECD, but it has declined from about 18% in 2007 (Figure 3.9). The share of the total energy research, development and demonstration (RD&D) budget dedicated to renewables and energy efficiency has progressively increased; it exceeded 70% in 2014, though funding for energy R&D remains overall limited to around 1% of public R&D spending (Figure 3.9). Increased R&D funding has contributed to a steady rise in patent applications

Figure 3.9. **A large share of public R&D spending goes to environmental research**

R&D budgets for energy and the environment as % of total government budgets, top ten OECD countries, 2015[a]

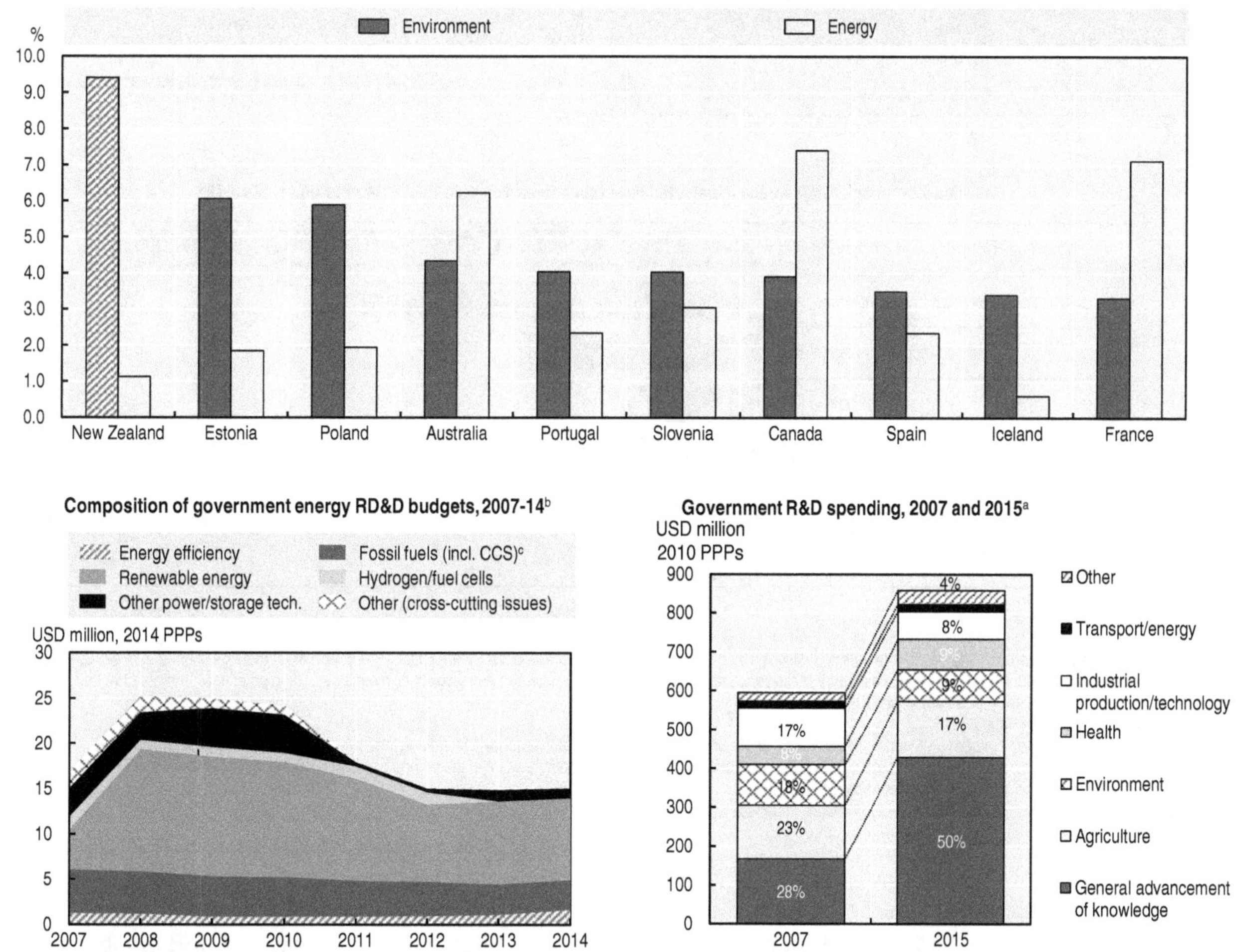

a) Government budget appropriations or outlays for R&D; breakdown according to the NABS 2007 classification. Estonia, Iceland, Poland and Spain: 2014 data; Canada: 2013 data.

b) Government budgets for research, development and demonstration (RD&D).

c) Carbon capture and storage.

Source: IEA (2016), *IEA Energy Technology and RD&D Statistics* (database); OECD (2016), *OECD Science, Technology and R&D Statistics* (database).

StatLink http://dx.doi.org/10.1787/888933459935

related to environmental management and climate-change mitigation technologies (Figure 3.10). The latter is a trend observed in many other countries and driven by global climate mitigation commitments. Overall, environment- and climate-related technologies made up for nearly 12% of all patent applications in 2010-12, in line with the OECD average and more than three times the level in 2000.

Figure 3.10. **More and more environment- and climate-related patents are filed**

Green patents applications, 1999-2012[a]

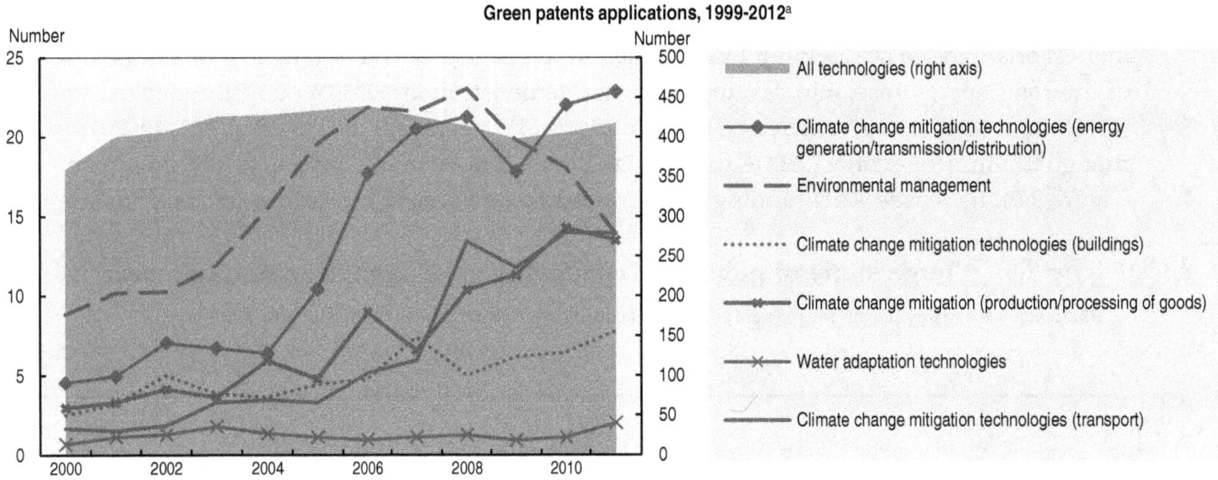

Revealed technological advantage in selected environment- and climate-related technologies, 2010-12[b]

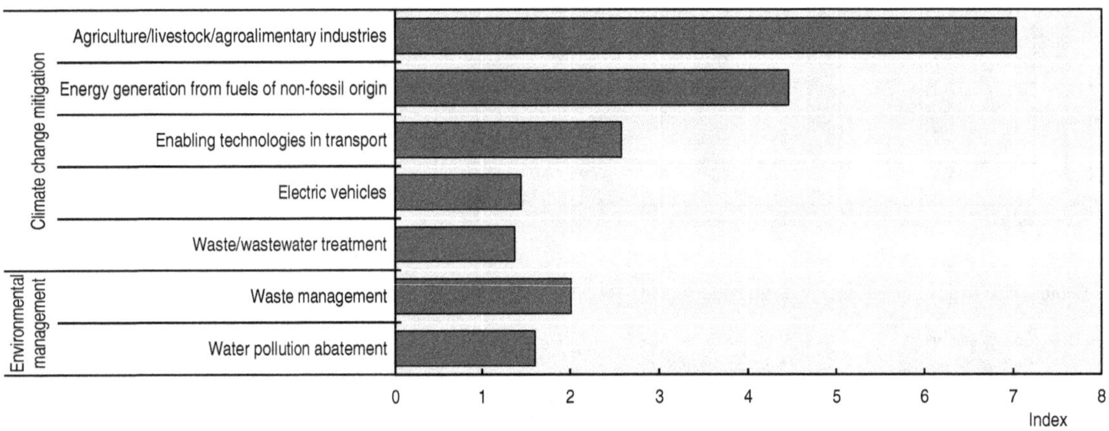

Note: Patent statistics are taken from the Worldwide Patent Statistical Database (PATSTAT) of the European Patent Office (EPO), with algorithms developed by the OECD. Data refer to patent applications filed in the inventor's country of residence according to the priority date and apply solely to inventions of high potential commercial value for which protection has been sought in at least two jurisdictions.

a) Three-year moving average data.

b) The revealed technological advantage (RTA) index measures the share of an economy's patents in a specific technology relative to the share of total patents owned. The index equals 0 when the economy has no patents in a given field, equals 1 when the economy's share in the technology field is equivalent to its share in all fields (no specialisation), and rises above 1 when specialisation is observed.

Source: OECD (2016), "Patents", *OECD Environment Statistics* (database).

StatLink http://dx.doi.org/10.1787/888933459943

New Zealand has developed a specialisation and competitive advantage in some technology (OECD, 2014b),[24] including water pollution abatement, wastewater and waste treatment, and renewable energy generation (Figure 3.10). It is a world leader in research related to reducing the environmental impact from agriculture, primarily on GHG emissions and water quality. New Zealand led the establishment of the Global Research Alliance on Agricultural Greenhouse Gases, which groups 46 countries and fosters international co-operation and investment in research into mitigating GHG emissions from food production. The government, in co-operation with the business sector, has launched several initiatives to support agriculture-related R&D and commercialisation of research results (Box 3.5). Partly as a result of these policy and investment efforts, New Zealand has consolidated its technology specialisation and competitive advantage in climate change mitigation technology in the agriculture and food industry (Figure 3.10), as well as in biotechnologies,[25] which is second only to Denmark (OECD, 2015e).

Box 3.5. **Promoting eco-innovation in agriculture**

The Pastoral Greenhouse Gas Research Consortium (PGGRC) is a partnership, formed in 2003, between the government, the dairy and fertiliser industries, and research organisations. It has invested about NZD 5 million per year in research on mitigation solutions for GHGs from pastoral agriculture (e.g. microbiology, genomics, animal nutrition, genetics and farm systems), with the ultimate goal of decreasing on-farm GHG emissions by 1.5% per year over business-as-usual. A significant area of investment for the PGGRC has been a three-year trial of nitrification inhibitors. The PGGRC works closely with the New Zealand Agricultural GHG Research Centre.

The Primary Growth Partnership (PGP) programme, launched in 2009, is a government-industry partnership that invests in research and innovation programmes to boost agricultural productivity and sustainability. Investments cover the whole of the value chain, from R&D to product commercialisation and technology transfer. PGP programmes are up to seven years in length and industry contributions must be at least equal to Crown funding. As of end-2015, the total PGP funding commitment from government and industry in these programmes was around NZD 724 million (USD 505 million).

The New Zealand Agricultural GHG Research Centre (NZAGRC), established in 2010, is a partnership between the PGGRC and leading New Zealand organisations engaged in research on agricultural GHG emissions. The centre is fully funded through the PGP, which has invested about NZD 48.5 million in the centre over ten years. The NZAGRC is a "virtual" centre: researchers carry out the work from within their own organisations.

Pastoral Genomics is an industry-led research partnership between the dairy, meat and animal feed industries and research organisations. It aims to provide pastoral farmers with better forage cultivars with improved nutritional content and higher resilience to drought and disease, while increasing productivity, profitability and environmental sustainability of New Zealand's pastoral farming systems. The partnership intends to use non-regulated biotechnologies. Available funding includes NZD 7.3 million (USD 5.1 million) of government funding over five years; industry will match this funding. Investment in the partnership is expected to ultimately increase the value of exports of pastoral farms and contribute to the Business Growth Agenda goal of increasing the ratio of exports to GDP.

Source: OECD (2016e, 2013b).

The innovation policy increasingly focuses on environment-related research and innovation as a way to improve the natural resource base of the economy. The Conservation and Environment Science Roadmap, under development in 2016, aims to set future research priorities in these domains. The environment is among the key research sectors of the National Statement of Science Investment (NSSI), which identifies priorities for the government's investment in research and innovation in 2015-25. The NSSI has partially shifted research funding from budget allocations for research institutions to contestable funding open to all institutions and science fields. In this way, it aims to improve efficiency of R&D spending and support impact-driven science. In particular, 5 of the 11 "science challenges" included in the National Science Challenges initiative, launched in 2013, relate to the environment and natural resources. The initiative pledges to invest over NZD 350 million in ten years to support public research on emerging and complex issues for New Zealand's future development, drawing scientists and stakeholders together across different institutions and science fields.

Implementation of this innovation and research strategy remains challenging, in particular for energy and environmental R&D. The research funding system is fragmented across institutions and support programmes, and entails relatively high administration and transaction costs. For example, the funding of the Crown research institutes is partly uncertain. Its dependence on competitions for funding can negatively affect researchers' career development, acquisition of specific skills and retention of human resources for science and technology. Moreover, the bidding process is time consuming and tends to increase the upfront costs of research projects. There are concerns that this may penalise environmental research, which has generally fewer market applications and has, therefore, less tangible impact. In addition, the economic efficiency of the environment-related innovation policy and its contribution on ultimately improving environmental performance, resource productivity and energy efficiency are not systematically evaluated.

7. Contributing to the global sustainable development agenda

7.1. Progress towards the Sustainable Development Goals

New Zealand is committed to contributing to sustainable development on a global level. In 2015, it participated in the adoption of the 2030 Agenda for Sustainable Development and of its 17 Sustainable Development Goals (SDGs) by the United Nations.[26] According to the Augmented SDG Index for OECD countries developed by Sachs et al. (2016), New Zealand ranks 16th among OECD member countries for its performance towards these internationally agreed objectives in the economic, environmental and social sphere.

The OECD developed a pilot assessment of OECD member countries' "starting positions" towards the SDGs (OECD, 2016f). On the basis of the same methodology, New Zealand performs better or much better than the OECD as a whole with regards to eight goals, including the environment-related goals on affordable and clean energy, and conservation and sustainable use of oceans and seas (Figure 3.11). Indicators related to five goals are in line with the OECD as a whole, including those on clean water and sanitation, and responsible consumption and production. More effort is needed to catch up with the OECD on four goals, including climate change mitigation and adaptation, and protection and sustainable use of terrestrial biodiversity (Figure 3.11).

As for all other OECD member countries, the consequences of New Zealand's domestic and trade policies can go – intentionally or unintentionally – beyond the country's borders, thereby influencing – positively or negatively – the ability of other countries to achieve their SDGs. New Zealand provides official development assistance (ODA) to help other countries meet some SDGs. A preliminary assessment based on OECD (2016f) methodology indicates that New Zealand scores slightly above the OECD as a whole in providing ODA (although below the average of the OECD Development Assistance Committee (DAC) member countries; see Section 7.3). In addition, as Section 4.2 discusses, New Zealand provides

Figure 3.11. **New Zealand is doing its share to achieve the SDGs**

New Zealand's starting position on each sustainable development goal (SDG) relative to the OECD average

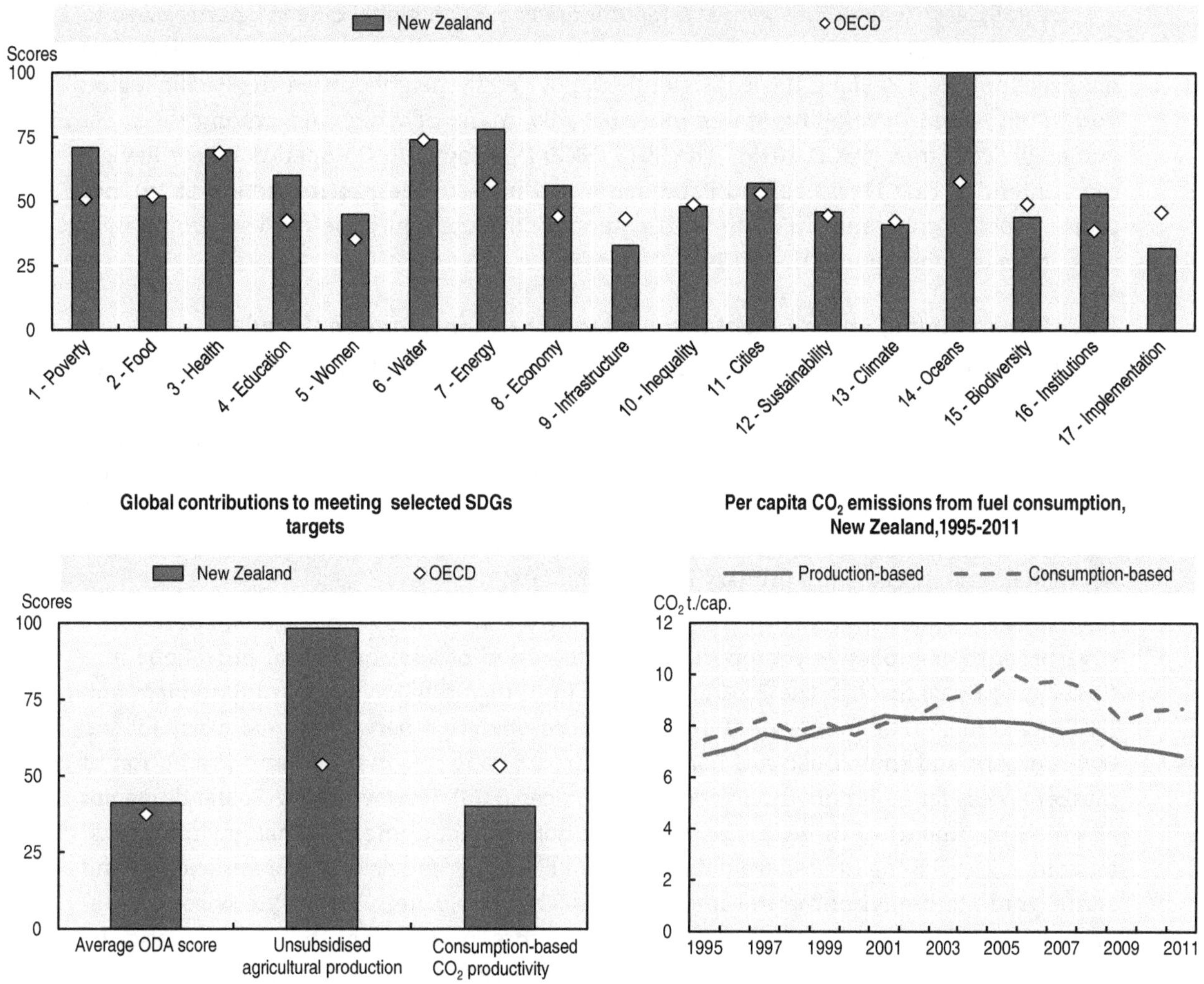

Note: All indicator scores are placed on a common scale running from 0 to 100: 100 corresponds to the target or end value as referred to in SDGs, international agreements, best international practices or other sources; 0 corresponds to the value that only 10% of OECD countries failed to reach in the base year (2010). See Table 1 in OECD (2016), *Measuring Distance to the SDGs Targets.*

Source: Based on OECD (2016), *Measuring Distance to the SDGs Targets*; IEA (2016), *IEA CO_2 Emissions from Fuel Combustion* (database); OECD (2015), *OECD Production- and Consumption-based CO_2 Emission Estimates* (database).

StatLink http://dx.doi.org/10.1787/888933459955

limited support to domestic agricultural producers (i.e. nearly all domestic agriculture production is unsubsidised, compared to only about half in the OECD as a whole; Figure 3.11); this implies little impact on world agricultural prices and market barriers for developing countries. At the same time, New Zealand's demand-based CO_2 productivity is significantly below the OECD average; this indicates that a large share of goods imported and consumed in the country embed CO_2 emissions generated by using fossil energy in other parts of the world, which affects the global climate. Consumption-based CO_2 emissions from fuel use quickly increased at the beginning of the 2000s; in 2011, they were more than 25% higher than the conventional measure of production-based CO_2 emissions (Figure 3.11; Wiebe and Yamano, 2016). Many factors underlie this trend, including increasing domestic energy generation from renewables (Figure 1.5); the expansion of dairy production (which mostly emits other GHGs than CO_2) and services; and an increasing share of imports from CO_2-intensive trade partners.

Overall, New Zealand has gained a reputation as a "good global citizen", partly owed to its environment and development-friendly approach in, for example, trade negotiations (see next section). New Zealand has consistently supported its neighbours in the Pacific region and Small Island Developing States more broadly, many of which are among the most vulnerable countries (OECD, 2015f). The 2015 OECD Development Co-operation Peer Review recommended that New Zealand establish a medium- to long-term agenda to further promote policy coherence in areas with potential development benefits. This would help support its commitment to the SDGs.

7.2. Mainstreaming environmental considerations in international trade

An export-oriented economy, New Zealand performs better than most OECD member countries as regards trade facilitation indicators such as low fees and charges, streamlining of border procedures, external border agency co-operation, governance and impartiality (OECD, 2016g). Numerous free trade agreements (FTAs) and low trade barriers lifted international trade to around 55% of GDP in 2014, despite the country's relative distance from the world's main export markets and global value chains. The ten FTAs in force account for nearly half of New Zealand's primary industry exports.

All New Zealand's recent FTAs include environment provisions (MFE, 2014b). The government has proactively supported the integration of environmental provisions into trade agreements through the 2001 Framework for Integrating Environment Standards and Trade Agreement. The framework foresees close co-operation between the Ministry for the Environment and the Ministry of Foreign Affairs in trade negotiations and promotion of market access for environmental goods and services (EGS). However, New Zealand has not assessed the impact of these arrangements on domestic and international environmental outcomes. Developing *ex post* evaluation would help target provisions more efficiently and shape trade and environmental negotiations. This could help identify environmental pressures arising from expanding productive sectors, particularly those that cannot be identified through project-focused environmental impact assessments, and to prevent or respond to these pressures.

The authorities have developed strategies to limit the potentially negative international environmental effects of exports. For example, New Zealand's trade support schemes integrate environmental aspects, in line with the OECD recommendations on officially supported export credits.[27] The export credit office performs an environmental assessment of all applications for large export credit guarantees; it has not supported any project assessed with medium- or high-potential environmental and/or social impacts (NZECO, 2016).

International trade agreements may also help develop a greener export base. Environmental goods and services (EGS) exports are growing, but remain limited. Their share in total exports was still slightly above 1.1% in 2011, despite the rapid development of wastewater management and water treatment, management of solid and hazardous waste, and recycling systems. As an active player within the APEC Environmental Goods List process, New Zealand has reduced its tariffs to 5% or less on some environmental goods. It is also involved in the negotiations of the broader Environmental Goods Agreement (EGA), which began in 2014. The EGA aims to reduce tariffs and other trade barriers on a broad range of environmental goods among a wider group of countries. A rapid end to negotiations could boost New Zealand's export potential and integration into global value chains of EGS. More generally, higher regulatory convergence and co-operation on regulations, standards, testing and certification procedures could eliminate non-tariff barriers. This, in turn, would help develop emerging green technologies.

7.3. Mainstreaming environmental considerations in development co-operation

New Zealand increased its spending on ODA considerably in 2010-15, although spending remains below internationally agreed targets. In 2015, net ODA disbursements reached USD 515 million, equivalent to 0.27% of gross national income (GNI) (Figure 3.12). This share, which has remained relatively constant since 2005, is considerably below the internationally agreed target of 0.7% of GNI and the average effort of OECD DAC member countries (0.4%). The assistance directed specifically to least developed countries remains at less than 0.1% of GNI, below the UN target of 0.15%. As OECD (2015f) notes, with its good economic and fiscal performance, New Zealand has an opportunity to increase ODA volume in line with international goals. It should establish a plan to increase its aid programme consistently with this purpose. To improve performance, the government plans to increase ODA expenditure to USD 1.2 billion over the three years starting from 2015/16.

In 2013/14, 42% of total ODA was directly or indirectly targeting environmental objectives such as those related to climate change, biodiversity, desertification, renewable energy, water supply and sanitation (Figure 3.12). This is more than 1.5 times above its 2007/08 level. It is also one of the five largest shares in the OECD-DAC and nearly double the OECD average. Most of the environment-focused ODA goes to the energy, agriculture and water sectors (Figure 3.12). Aid flows supporting climate change mitigation and adaptation objectives increased considerably in 2010-14. This reflects New Zealand's aid focus on the Pacific region and on addressing the environmental challenges of the Small Island Developing States in the region, including improving access to renewable energy. Aid flows supporting biodiversity-related objectives also grew, but to a lesser extent (Figure 3.12). In 2012-15, New Zealand's development assistance helped partner countries to increase the value of their agricultural produce, install solar power capacity, and upgrade infrastructure and facilities to improve their resilience to natural disasters and climate change effects (MFAT, 2016).

The 2011 International Development Policy Statement emphasises the importance of the environment in pursuing sustainable, equitable growth, and in fulfilling the UN Development Goals. The statement commits New Zealand to engage in a coherent policy that takes into account political, security, climate change and development objectives. The Aid Programme Strategic Plan for 2015-19 integrates environment and climate change as cross-cutting issues, and identifies renewable energy, fisheries and resilience to climate change and disasters as investment priorities. In addition, the plan highlights the need for New Zealand to better engage the private sector in supporting sustainable development (MFAT, 2015).

New Zealand has consistently stated the objective of mainstreaming the cross-cutting issues of environment and climate, gender and human rights in planning, design, implementation and evaluation of aid initiatives. Despite its efforts, however, there is limited evidence it has met this objective. OECD (2015f) recommended that New Zealand continue to focus on developing staff capability and management accountability to mainstream these cross-cutting issues into development projects effectively. In 2016, New Zealand launched a strategic evaluation of cross-cutting issues and a capability review.

Figure 3.12. **Official development assistance has increased, but remains low**

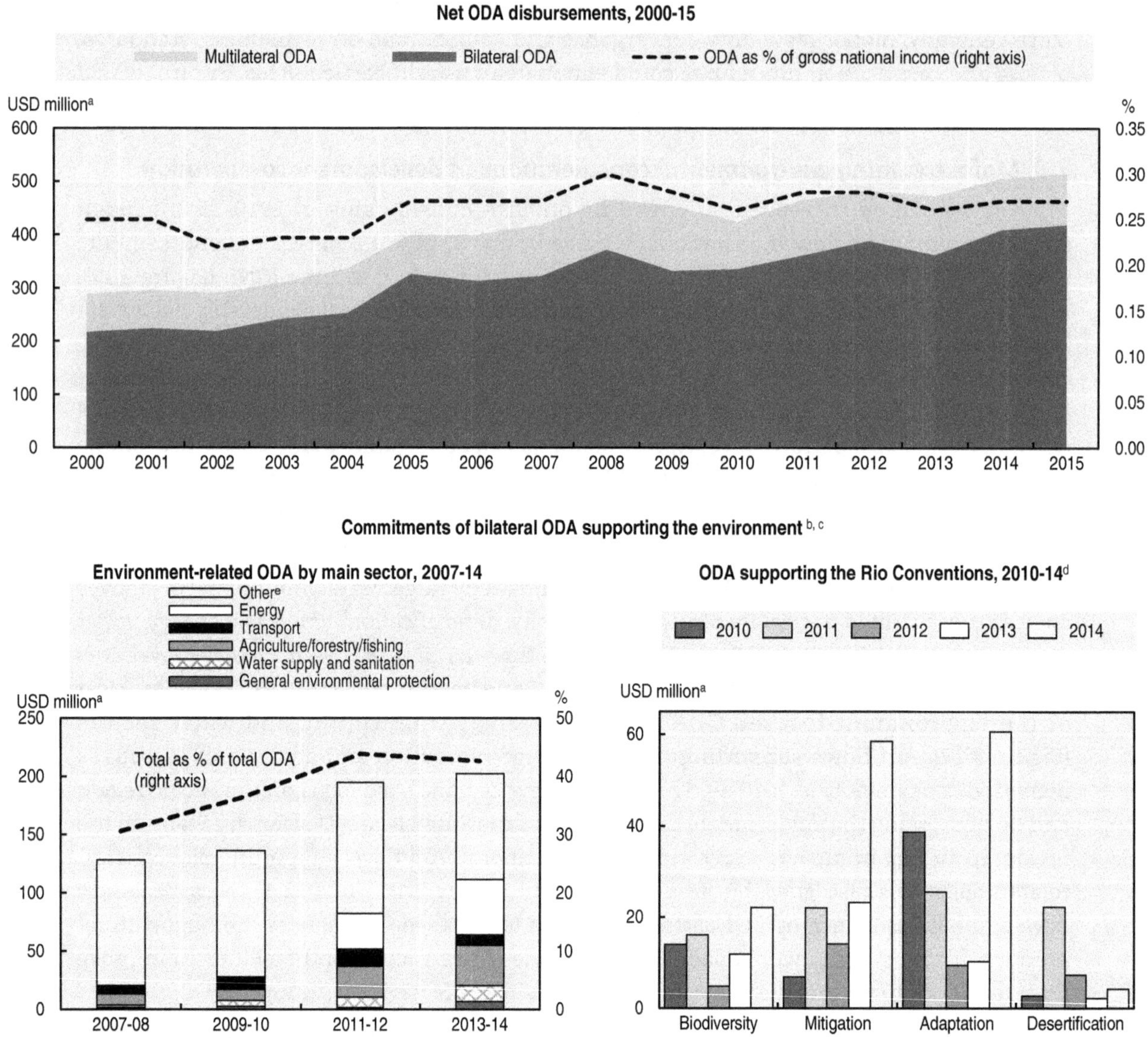

a) At 2014 prices.

b) Data refer to activities that are marked with at least one of the environment and/or Rio policy markers. They include activities targeting the environment, climate change mitigation or adaptation, biodiversity conservation and sustainable use and/or desertification control either as explicit and fundamental objective of the activities or as important but secondary objective.

c) The marker data do not allow exact quantification of amounts allocated or spent in support of the environment. They give an indication of such aid flows and describe the extent to which donors address these objectives in their aid programmes.

d) An activity can target the objective of more than one convention, thus ODA flows should not be added.

e) Mainly administrative costs of donors, unallocated and other multisector activities.

Source: OECD (2016), *OECD International Development Statistics* (database); OECD calculations.

StatLink http://dx.doi.org/10.1787/888933459964

Recommendations on green growth

- Establish a whole-of-government, multi-stakeholder process to develop a long-term vision for the transition of New Zealand towards a low-carbon, greener economy, taking into account the opportunities to diversify the economy and reduce its reliance on agriculture and the use of natural resources; develop a framework for monitoring and reporting progress towards green growth objectives, based on sound indicators linking economic activity with environmental performance, as a way to build consensus around the low-carbon, green transition.

Getting prices right

- Reform the NZ ETS at the earliest opportunity to ensure a price of carbon that is consistent with New Zealand's transition to a low-carbon economy, by i) aligning the supply of NZ ETS units to the country's mitigation targets and the trajectory towards net-zero emissions; ii) auctioning domestic allocations once the stock of banked NZ ETS units is depleted, and considering the introduction of a floor price, increasing over time, on auctioned allowances; iii) avoiding the use beyond 2020 of international carbon credits that were acquired before 2015; iv) setting a limit to the quantity of international carbon credits that can be used to offset domestic emissions (if international credits become newly eligible); v) establishing a clear timeframe and schedule for phasing out the free allocations of emission allowances to energy-intensive and trade-exposed activities; vi) removing the price ceiling or, at the very least, increasing it over time.
- Set a clear date for the inclusion of biological emissions from agriculture in the NZ ETS or introduce alternative pricing and regulatory measures to enforce emission reduction obligations; place the point of obligation at the farm level; further invest in developing tools for measuring, monitoring and reporting GHG emissions at farm level.
- Expand the use of environmentally related taxes, charges and prices, possibly within the framework of an overall reform of the tax structure, with a view to encouraging more efficient use of energy and resources and supporting the ongoing fiscal consolidation efforts: i) consider introducing an excise duty on diesel and ensure that petrol and diesel tax/charge rates take account of environmental externalities; ii) introduce water pollution charges and taxes on industrial air emissions.
- Systematically assess fossil fuel subsidies and tax exemptions, with a view to identifying those that are inefficient and encourage wasteful consumption and fossil fuel production and should, therefore, be removed.

Investing in sustainable energy and low-carbon transport modes

- Design and implement a comprehensive package of GHG emission mitigation measures to complement the NZ ETS carbon pricing and address non-pricing barriers to the adoption of low-carbon technology and solutions, including for energy generation and use in industry, transport and buildings; carefully assess the interactions between the NZ ETS and other potential GHG mitigation policy instruments.
- Ensure the consistency of investment priorities for land transport infrastructure, and the related financing model, with long-term climate and environmental objectives; reform the tax treatment of company cars and parking spaces; introduce fuel efficiency and air emission standards for new and imported used vehicles; ensure adequate public and private investment for the adaptation of the electricity distribution system and the development of charging infrastructure for electric vehicles (EVs); introduce mandatory EV quotas in the fleets of public institutions.

Recommendations on green growth *(cont.)*

Promoting eco-innovation

- Develop a science and innovation roadmap to provide a long-term view of innovation policy, while maintaining the current emphasis on environmental research; continue to increase, and provide stability to, public R&D funding to attract and retain innovation capacity; further streamline the innovation and R&D funding system, with a view to reducing transaction and administrative costs; continue to invest in agriculture-related research and to lead internationally the development of technologies and practices to mitigate GHG emissions and reduce water contamination.

Contributing to the global sustainable development agenda

- Maintain the strong commitment to environment and climate change in development co-operation, while increasing the volume of official development assistance in line with international goals.

Notes

1. Adjusting GDP growth for pollution abatement is important. Otherwise, growth would be underestimated in countries that divert scarce resources to abating pollution rather than to production of material goods. Conversely, growth would be overestimated in countries that rely on heavily polluting activities to generate GDP growth.
2. While total petrol use declined by 4% in 2005-14, diesel use grew by 27%. This is due to the increased share of diesel vehicles in the light vehicle fleet, as well as the freight transport growth linked to strong economic performance (the vast majority of heavy goods vehicles run on diesel) (Chapter 1).
3. The vehicle fleet grew by 14% in 2005-14, with diesel light vehicles increasing by 32% and petrol light vehicles by 9%.
4. The Crown's net debt excludes assets held in the Superannuation Fund, which includes liabilities for past services owed to employees of the public sector.
5. Vehicles using a synthetic greenhouse gas in their air conditioning system also pay the Synthetic Greenhouse Gas (Goods) Levy at the first registration in New Zealand.
6. In 2016, the current cost for a RUC licence for light diesel vehicles (weighing 3.5 tonnes or less) was NZD 62 per 1 000 km.
7. According to fuel consumption tests, a diesel car generally performs between 20% and 30% better than the same model with a petrol engine. Based on the average fuel economy of petrol vehicles (petrol vehicles in New Zealand average 10.1 litres per 100 km), a petrol vehicle will pay slightly more fuel excise duty than the equivalent RUC a diesel vehicle will pay.
8. In 2014, the average CO_2 emissions per km of newly registered vehicles was 184.8 gCO_2/km in 2014, compared to 143 gCO_2/km of vehicles sold in Japan, where most of the cars are imported from (Chapter 1).
9. The Kyoto Protocol covers six GHGs: CO_2, CH_4, N_2O, SF_6, HFCs and PFCs.
10. All emissions from pre-1990 forestry are covered, and around half of eligible post-1989 forests, which may participate voluntarily in the NZ ETS, are registered in the scheme.
11. Agricultural biological emissions are mainly emissions of methane from ruminant animals (enteric fermentation) and nitrous oxides from animal waste.
12. Certified emission reduction units are generated by Clean Development Mechanism projects in developing countries; emission reduction units are generated by Joint Implementation projects in other countries that have binding targets under the Kyoto Protocol; removal units are generated for carbon absorption by land use, land-use change and forestry activities in countries that have binding targets under the Kyoto Protocol.

13. Capping domestic emissions could have meant constraining domestic production, allowing the equivalent demand to be met by less efficient and uncapped producers in other countries, raising global emissions.

14. This is 60% of the emission baseline for moderately emission-intensive activities, and 90% for highly emission-intensive activities. The free allocations are adjusted annually depending on production levels. In addition, on introduction of the NZ ETS, the government provided one-off free allocations to holders of fishing quotas and pre-1990 forests.

15. The surrender obligation will increase from 50% in 2016 to 67% in 2017 to 83% in 2018 and to 100% in 2019.

16. For example, international emission units (ERUs and CERs) made up more than 95% of the units surrendered in 2014 (MfE, 2016a).

17. OVERSEER® is a national model for farm-scale nutrient budgeting and loss estimation. It calculates the nutrient flows in a productive farming system and identifies risks of environmental impacts through nutrient loss, including run-off and leaching (Chapter 4).

18. This price, equivalent to USD 12.5, was in line with the price in the linked Quebec and California cap-and-trade systems, but well above the price in the EU ETS (USD 6.5) and the near-zero price of international carbon credits.

19. Following the Treaty of Waitangi Fisheries Claims Settlement Act of 1992, a suite of management tools has been introduced to recognise customary use and management practices of Maori in the exercise of non-commercial fishing rights (Chapter 1).

20. The levies charged to commercial fishers recover costs such as those for general fisheries management, aquaculture-related enforcement and research, and protection of marine species from the potential impact of commercial fishing (e.g. bycatch) (OECD, 2015c).

21. Other members of the group are Costa Rica, Denmark, Ethiopia, Finland, Norway, Sweden, Switzerland and Uruguay.

22. The peer review panel included the People's Republic of China, Indonesia, the Philippines, Thailand, the United States and the OECD.

23. Agricultural support is defined as the annual monetary value of gross transfers to agriculture from consumers and taxpayers, arising from government policies that support agriculture. The Percentage Producer Support Estimate (%PSE) represents policy transfers to agricultural producers individually, measured at the farm gate and expressed as a share of gross farm receipts. Transfers included in the PSE are composed of market price support, budgetary payments and the cost of revenue forgone by the government and other economic agents. To receive the transfer, an individual farmer must take actions to produce goods or services, use factors of production or be defined as an eligible farming enterprise or farmer.

24. The revealed technological advantage index measures the share of an economy's patents in a specific technology relative to the share of total patents owned. The index is equal to zero when the economy has no patents in a given field, equals one when the economy's share in the technology field is equivalent to its share in all fields (no specialisation), and rises above one when specialisation is observed. The index is calculated on the basis of patents filed at the European Patent Office or the US Patent and Trademark Office, which belong to patent families within the Five IP offices (IP5), by earliest filing date and inventor's location (OECD, 2014b).

25. The OECD defines biotechnology as the application of science and technology to living organisms, as well as parts, products and models thereof, to alter living or non-living materials for the production of knowledge, goods and services (OECD, 2014b).

26. The UN adopted the SDGs within the framework of the 2030 Agenda for Sustainable Development in September 2015. They replace and further refine the Millennium Development Goals. The SDGs provide a baseline against which to measure how countries are progressing in achieving sustainable and inclusive growth, eradicating poverty, and protecting ecosystems and human health. These objectives are classified according to 17 goals and 169 targets; some targets are directly linked to environmental protection, while others have only indirect linkages.

27. Recommendation of the Council on Common Approaches for Officially Supported Export Credits and Environmental and Social Due Diligence (The "Common Approaches"), adopted by the OECD Council on 6 April 2016.

References

APEC (2015), "Peer review on fossil fuel subsidy reforms in New Zealand", *Final Report*, September, 2015, Asia-Pacific Economic Co-operation, Singapore.

Arlinghaus, J. (2015), "Impacts of carbon prices on indicators of competitiveness: A review of empirical findings", *OECD Environment Working Papers*, No. 87, OECD Publishing, Paris, *http://dx.doi.org/10.1787/5js37p21grzq-en*.

Baskaran, R., R. Cullen and S. Colombo (2009), "Estimating values of environmental impacts of dairy farming in New Zealand", *New Zealand Journal of Agricultural Research*, Vol. 52(4), pp. 377-389.

Bibbee, A. (2011), "Green growth and climate change policies in New Zealand", *OECD Economics Department Working Papers*, No. 893, OECD Publishing, Paris, *http://dx.doi.org/10.1787/5kg51mc6k98r-en*.

Cárdenas Rodríguez, M., I. Haščič and M. Souchier (2016), "Environmentally adjusted multifactor productivity: Methodology and empirical results for OECD and G20 countries", *OECD Green Growth Papers*, No. 2016/04, OECD Publishing, Paris, *http://dx.doi.org/10.1787/5jlr2z7ntkf8-en*.

Dickie, B. (2016), "Waikato regional fresh water discussion: A framework for getting the best use allocation through time", report commissioned by Waikato Regional Council, Hamilton.

Emissions Trading Scheme Review Panel (2011), "Doing New Zealand's fair share. Emissions trading scheme review 2011", *Final Report*, Ministry for the Environment, Wellington.

Foote, K.J., M.K. Joy and R.G. Death (2015), "New Zealand dairy farming: Milking our environment for all its worth", *Environmental Management*, Springer US, Vol. 56, pp.709-720.

Green Growth Advisory Group (2011), "Greening New Zealand's growth", report submitted to the Minister for Economic Development and the Minister for the Environment, December 2011, Wellington.

Government of New Zealand (2015a), *The Business Growth Agenda. Towards 2025*, Government of New Zealand, Wellington.

Government of New Zealand (2015b), *The Business Growth Agenda. Building Natural Resources*, Government of New Zealand, Wellington.

Government of New Zealand (2015c), *Government Policy Statement on Land Transport 2015*, Government of New Zealand, Wellington.

Harding, M. (2014a), "The diesel differential: Differences in the tax treatment of gasoline and diesel for road use", *OECD Taxation Working Papers*, No. 21, OECD Publishing, Paris, *http://dx.doi.org/10.1787/5jz14cd7hk6b-en*.

Harding, M. (2014b), "Personal tax treatment of company cars and commuting expenses: Estimating the fiscal and environmental costs", *OECD Taxation Working Papers*, No. 20, OECD Publishing, Paris, *http://dx.doi.org/10.1787/5jz14cg1s7vl-en*.

Hodges, G., L. Proctor and B. King (2013), *Mayoral Position Paper on Public Private Partnerships*, Ernst & Young, Auckland.

Hood, C. (2013), Managing Interactions between Carbon Pricing and Existing Energy Policies, IEA Insights Series, IEA/OECD Publishing, Paris, *www.iea.org/publications/insights/insightpublications/managing interactionscarbonpricing_final.pdf*.

ICAP (2016), ETS Map. Compare ETS website, International Carbon Action Partnership, *https://icapcarbon action.com/en/ets-map* (accessed October 2016).

IEA (forthcoming), *Energy Policies of IEA Countries: New Zealand*, IEA/OECD Publishing, Paris.

Lankoski et al. (2015), "Environmental co-benefits and stacking in environmental markets", *OECD Food, Agriculture and Fisheries Papers*, No. 72, OECD Publishing, Paris, *http://dx.doi.org/10.1787/5js6g5khdvhj-en*.

Leining, C. and S. Kerr (2016), "Lessons learned from the New Zealand Emissions Trading Scheme", *Motu Working Paper*, No. 16-06, Motu Economic and Public Policy Research, Wellington.

MFAT (2016), *New Zealand Aid Programme Triennium 2012-15: Results Achieved*, Ministry of Foreign Affairs and Trade, Wellington.

MFAT (2015), *New Zealand Aid Programme. Strategic Plan 2015-19*, Ministry of Foreign Affairs and Trade, Wellington.

MfE (2016a), *The New Zealand Emissions Trading Scheme Evaluation 2016*, Ministry for the Environment, Wellington.

MfE (2016b), "Latest Update on New Zealand's 2020 Net Position", webpage, *www.mfe.govt.nz/climate-change/reporting-greenhouse-gas-emissions/latest-2020-net-position* (accessed October 2016).

MfE (2015a), "New Zealand Emissions Trading Scheme Review 2015/16", Discussion document and call for written submissions, Ministry for the Environment, Wellington.

MfE (2015b), *New Zealand's Second Biennial Report under the United Nations Framework Convention on Climate Change,* Ministry for the Environment, Wellington.

MfE (2014a), *Review of the Effectiveness of the Waste Disposal Levy,* Ministry for the Environment, Wellington.

MfE (2014b), "About Free Trade Agreements and the Environment", webpage, *www.mfe.govt.nz/more/international-environmental-agreements/free-trade-and-environmental-cooperation-agreements-0* (accessed October 2016).

Ministry for Primary Industries (2016), "Sustainable Farming Fund", webpage, *www.mpi.govt.nz/funding-and-programmes/farming/sustainable-farming-fund/* (accessed October 2016).

Ministry of Transport (2016), *Electric Vehicles – Driving an EV Future*, Ministry of Transport, Wellington.

Ministry of Transport (2014), *National Freight Demand Study*, Ministry of Transport, Wellington.

NZECO (2016), *Environmental Policy,* New Zealand Export Credit Office website, *www.nzeco.govt.nz/corporate-responsibility/environmental/index.htm* (accessed October 2016).

NZGBC (2015), *Strategic Review of the New Zealand Green Building Market 2015*, New Zealand Green Building Council, Auckland.

NZGBC (2014), "Submission on the Proposed Auckland Unitary Plan (HOMESTAR)", February 2014, New Zealand Green Building Council, Auckland.

NZPC (2016), *Better Urban Planning, Draft Report*, New Zealand Productivity Commission, Wellington.

NZPC (2015), *Using Land for Housing*, New Zealand Productivity Commission, Wellington.

NZTA (2015), *National Land Transport Fund Annual Report*, New Zealand Transport Agency, Wellington.

OECD (2016a), *Effective Carbon Rates: Pricing CO_2 through Taxes and Emissions Trading Systems*, OECD Publishing, Paris, *http://dx.doi.org/10.1787/9789264260115-en.*

OECD (2016b), *OECD Environmental Performance Reviews: Chile*, OECD Publishing, Paris, *http://dx.doi.org/10.1787/9789264252615-en.*

OECD (2016c), *OECD Inventory of Support Measures for Fossil Fuels* (database), *www.oecd.org/site/tadffss/data/* (accessed September 2016).

OECD (2016d), *Fossil Fuel Support Country Note – New Zealand*, September 2016, *www.oecd.org/site/tadffss/data/.*

OECD (2016e), OECD (2016), "New Zealand", in *Agricultural Policy Monitoring and Evaluation 2016*, OECD Publishing, Paris, *http://dx.doi.org/10.1787/agr_pol-2016-20-en.*

OECD (2016f), *Measuring Distance to the SDGs Targets. A Pilot Assessment of where OECD Countries Stand*, OECD Publishing, Paris, *www.oecd.org/std/OECD-Measuring-Distance-to-SDGs-Targets-Pilot-Study.pdf.*

OECD (2016g), Trade Facilitation Indicators website, *www.oecd.org/trade/facilitation/indicators.htm* (accessed October 2016).

OECD (2015a), *OECD Economic Surveys: New Zealand 2015*, OECD Publishing, Paris, *http://dx.doi.org/10.1787/eco_surveys-nzl-2015-en.*

OECD (2015b), *OECD Environmental Performance Reviews: Netherlands*, OECD Publishing, Paris, *http://dx.doi.org/10.1787/9789264240056-en.*

OECD (2015c), "New Zealand", in *OECD Review of Fisheries: Policies and Summary Statistics 2015*, OECD Publishing, Paris, *http://dx.doi.org/10.1787/rev_fish-2015-29-en.*

OECD (2015d), *Fostering Infrastructure Investment: Lessons Learned from OECD Investment Policy Reviews*, OECD Publishing, Paris, *www.oecd.org/daf/inv/investment-policy/Fostering-Investment-in-Infrastructure.pdf.*

OECD (2015e), *OECD Science, Technology and Industry Scoreboard 2015: Innovation for Growth and Society*, OECD Publishing, Paris, *http://dx.doi.org/10.1787/sti_scoreboard-2015-en.*

OECD (2015f), *OECD Development Co-operation Peer Reviews: New Zealand 2015*, OECD Publishing, Paris, *http://dx.doi.org/10.1787/9789264235588-en*

OECD (2014a), *Green Growth Indicators 2014*, OECD Green Growth Studies, OECD Publishing, Paris, *www.oecd.org/environment/green-growth-indicators-2013-9789264202030-en.htm.*

OECD (2014b), *OECD Science, Technology and Industry Outlook 2014*, OECD Publishing, Paris, *http://dx.doi.org/10.1787/sti_outlook-2014-en*.

OECD (2013a), *OECD Economic Surveys: New Zealand 2013*, OECD Publishing, Paris, *http://dx.doi.org/10.1787/eco_surveys-nzl-2013-en*.

OECD (2013b), *Policy Instruments to Support Green Growth in Agriculture*, OECD Publishing, Paris, *http://dx.doi.org/10.1787/9789264203525-en*.

OECD (2007), *OECD Environmental Performance Reviews: New Zealand*, OECD Publishing, Paris, *http://dx.doi.org/10.1787/9789264030589-en*.

PCE (2016), *Emissions Trading Scheme Review 2015/16: Other Matters, Submission to the Minister for Climate Change Issues*, Parliamentary Commissioner for the Environment, Wellington.

Road User Charges Review Group (2009), An Independent Review of the New Zealand Road User Charging System, Road User Charges Review Group, Wellington.

Roy, R. (2014), "Environmental and related social costs of the tax treatment of company cars and commuting expenses", *OECD Environment Working Papers*, No. 70, OECD Publishing, Paris, *http://dx.doi.org/10.1787/5jxwrr5163zp-en*.

Royal Society of New Zealand (2016), *Transition to a Low-carbon Economy for New Zealand*, The Royal Society of New Zealand, Wellington.

Sachs, J. et al. (2016), *SDG Index and Dashboards - Global Report*, Bertelsmann Stiftung and Sustainable Development Solutions Network, New York.

Simmons, G. and P. Young (2016), *Climate Cheats. How New Zealand is Cheating on our Climate Change Commitments, and What We Can Do To Set It Right*, The Morgan Foundation.

Smith, S. and N.A. Braathen (2015), "Monetary carbon values in policy appraisal: An overview of current practice and key issues", *OECD Environment Working Papers*, No. 92, OECD Publishing, Paris, *http://dx.doi.org/10.1787/5jrs8st3ngvh-en*.

Vivid Economics and Energy Centre, University of Auckland Business School (2012), "Green Growth: Opportunities for New Zealand", report commissioned by the New Zealand Green Growth Research Trust, Auckland.

Wiebe, K.S. and N. Yamano (2016), "Estimating CO_2 emissions embodied in final demand and trade using the OECD ICIO 2015: Methodology and results", *OECD Science, Technology and Industry Working Papers*, No. 2016/05, OECD Publishing, Paris, *http://dx.doi.org/10.1787/5jlrcm216xkl-en*.

World Economic Forum (2015), *The Global Competitiveness Report 2015-2016*, World Economic Forum, Geneva.

PART II

Progress towards selected environmental objectives

PART II

Chapter 4

Water resources management

New Zealand's freshwater resources are vital to the primary sector and tourism, as well as to the country's culture. The government has recently begun reforming national freshwater policy in response to increasing pressure on freshwater resources. This chapter reviews New Zealand's progress towards sustainable freshwater resources management. It examines the state and trends of water quality and quantity, and assesses the performance of institutional governance and policy. Finally, it provides recommendations to improve the environmental effectiveness and economic efficiency of the nation's freshwater policies. Urban water management is discussed in Chapter 5: Sustainable Urban Development.

1. Introduction

Freshwater bodies in New Zealand support an array of indigenous flora and fauna and are highly regarded nationally and internationally for their recreational value (Ballantine and Davies-Colley, 2014). Freshwater is also a fundamental asset underpinning New Zealand's economy. In addition to tourism, recreation, power generation and cultural identity, freshwater is vital to the primary sector. New Zealand is unique among OECD member countries in deriving nearly three-quarters of its goods export earnings from agriculture, horticulture, viticulture, forestry, fishing and mining. The dairy sector makes up about 25% of total goods exports[1] (Statistics NZ, 2016; Chapters 1 and 3).

The share of the agricultural sector in gross domestic product (GDP) is high in comparison with most other OECD member countries (with the exception of Turkey and Iceland). Production has grown rapidly with intensification of livestock operations, leading to increasing environmental pressure from more use of fertilisers, pesticides and water (OECD, 2013a; Chapter 1). The use of nitrogen fertilisers over 2000-13 increased by 75% (IFA, 2016; Chapter 1).

There is mounting tension between increasing the economic contribution of the primary production sector and improving environmental quality. Given the large proportion of land in pastoral farming (half of New Zealand's land mass), the link between pastoral intensification and declining water quality has been increasingly acknowledged (e.g. Ballantine and Davies-Colley, 2014; MfE, 2013a; PCE, 2013). New Zealand's water management is under increased scrutiny:

- The decline in water quality has been rated the country's number one environmental problem in several public opinion surveys (Hughey et al., 2013).
- The New Zealand public is concerned over the competitive use of water resources, including with international water bottling companies in some over-allocated catchments.
- The tourism sector, which relies on an international reputation of "100% pure New Zealand" and "clean and green" is concerned about worsening water quality (Tourism Export Council, 2016; Tourism New Zealand, 2016, 2009).
- Additional voices include overseas buyers of meat and dairy products, driven by rising consumer interest in the environmental impact arising from the production and processing of final consumer goods (Ministry of Agriculture and Forestry, 2009; New Zealand Trade Manual, 2016; Saunders, Guenther and Driver, 2013).

In recognition of the need to safeguard water quality, as well as prevent and reduce over-allocation, the government began reforming national freshwater policy in 2009. Regional councils and local authorities are currently transitioning to new water management systems that will give effect to this national direction, with full implementation expected by 2030. The Ministry for Primary Industries (MPI) has an ambitious goal to double primary industry exports in real terms between June 2012 and 2025 from NZD 32 billion to over NZD 64 billion (MPI, 2015a). It is unclear how the twin objectives of reducing environmental impacts and doubling primary industry exports in real terms will be achieved, and whether the government assessed use of finite freshwater resources and impacts on water quality before setting such objectives. The challenge will be to increase resource productivity and decouple economic growth from water use and its environmental impacts to preserve the value created by New Zealand's environmental reputation.

2. States and trends of New Zealand's water resources

2.1. *Water resource availability*

New Zealand has a natural abundance of freshwater[2] and low water stress at the national level; allocated water comprises less than 5% of renewable freshwater resources. However, rainfall and freshwater resources vary substantially in both space and time, and national or annual averages can mask wide regional and seasonal variations. A large proportion of New Zealand's annual rainfall occurs in winter when demand for irrigation is relatively low. The north and east of the North Island, and northeast of the South Island, are relatively dry, and suffer from periodic droughts, particularly in summer.

Most (75%) consumptive[3] freshwater use is for irrigation of pastoral and arable land (Aqualinc, 2010; MfE and Statistics New Zealand, 2015), with 78% of the irrigation occurring in the South Island eastern regions of Canterbury (63%) and Otago (15%) (MfE, 2010a) (Figure 4.1); these are regions where water availability would otherwise be a limiting factor for intensive land use (NZIER, 2014). Some parts of the country are approaching allocation limits, or have already surpassed them (Figure 4.1). Water allocation pressure is particularly acute in regions of the east coast of New Zealand during summer and periods of drought (Aqualinc, 2010); the latest available data show the amount of land irrigated by water consents increased 82% between 1999 and 2010 (MfE, 2010b).

Figure 4.1. **Irrigation and water availability pressures are greatest in eastern regions of the South Island**

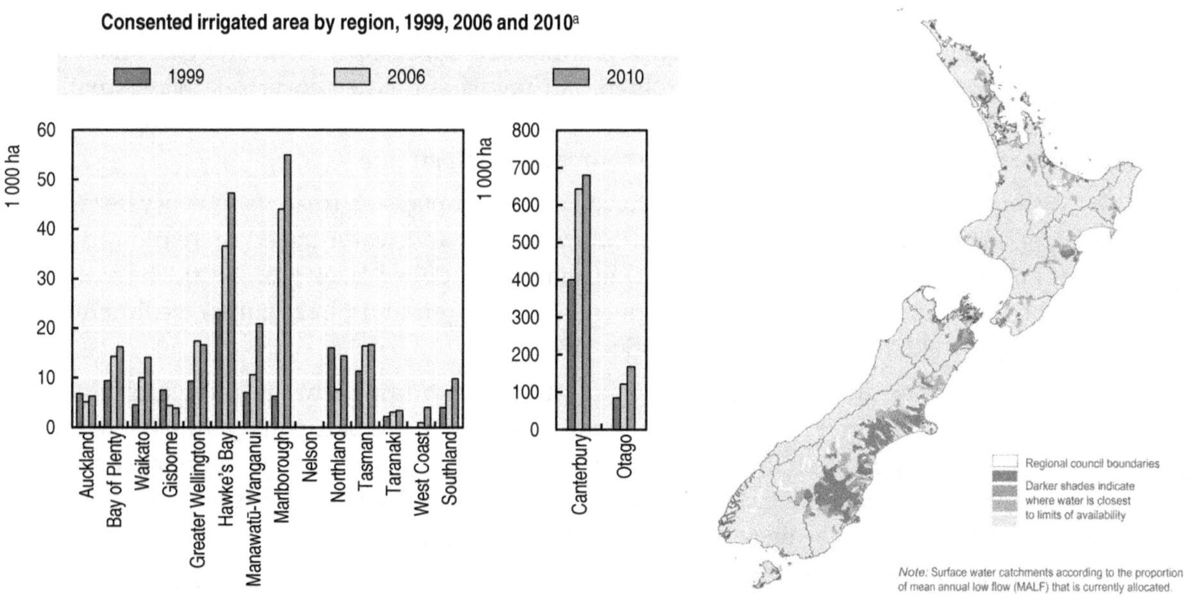

a) In some councils, 1999 data may not be entirely comparable with data for the following years due to methodological differences and data accuracy.
Source: MfE (2010), Allocation compared with renewable freshwater resource; MfE (2010), Trends in the amount of land irrigated by consented water takes.

StatLink http://dx.doi.org/10.1787/888933459974

There are opportunities for more efficient reallocation of water in New Zealand (Aqualinc, 2010) (i.e. a substantial volume of water allocated through water consents is not being utilised). The estimated actual water abstraction volume compared with the maximum consented volume is approximately 65% (MfE, 2010a); in other words, about 35% of the volume of water allocated is not used (2010 estimates, Aqualinc, 2010). The regions with the highest estimated actual use as a percentage of allocated volume are Southland (74%) and Canterbury (57%) (MfE, 2010b).

In catchments that are already over-allocated (on paper and/or in reality), increasing demand for irrigation has increased competition for scarce water resources (particularly during peak times) with other land uses, industry, hydropower generation and environmental flows (White, Sharp and Reeves, 2004; Flemmer and Flemmer, 2007). Reconciling these competing needs, allowing for irrigation development and providing for adequate environmental flows for freshwater ecosystems are emerging challenges.

2.2. Surface water quality

The management of point-source pollution to freshwater bodies is commendable. Under the Resource Management Act 1991 (RMA) councils require permits and set limits for discharging wastewater from industry and sewage treatment plants to streams, rivers and lakes. Point-source pollution now accounts for only a small minority of discharges to freshwater; 3.2% of total nitrogen and 1.8% of total phosphorous to the sea (Howard-Williams et al., 2013).

The management of cumulative effects from diffuse sources of water pollution is more challenging (Brown, Peart and Wright, 2016; Office of the Auditor-General, 2011). Diffuse sources of pollution from agricultural and urban run-off, and their impacts on human and ecosystem health, remain under-reported and under-regulated throughout OECD member countries in comparison to point-source pollution (OECD, forthcoming). Eutrophication, leading to hypoxia and algal blooms, caused primarily from agricultural run-off of excess nutrients, is considered the most prevalent water quality challenge globally.

In New Zealand, pollution hotspots are largely focused in regions of dairy farming[4] (PCE, 2013; Ballantine and Davies-Colley, 2014; OECD, 2015a, 2013). Stormwater run-off and river pollution in urban areas are also high, but towns and cities cover relatively small areas – less than 1% of New Zealand (PCE, 2013). They are primarily located in downstream coastal areas that accumulate the diffuse sources from upstream.

Water pollution in New Zealand can have negative impacts on freshwater ecosystems, drinking water sources and human health, swimming and water-based recreation, iwi values and a range of other values (Ballantine and Davies-Colley, 2014; PCE, 2013). The main water quality indicators of concern are nutrients (nitrogen and phosphorus), sediments and pathogens (PCE, 2012; MfE and Statistics NZ, 2015).

Aquifers, lakes and reservoirs, especially those with low recharge rates and high residence times that limit their ability to absorb pollutants, are particularly vulnerable to pollution. Time lags between improved land-use practices and improved water quality add complexity. For example, the time lag between improved land-use practices and improved groundwater quality can be decades (Howard-Williams et al., 2010).

The significance and trends of each of these four pollutants are summarised in the following sections, drawing from *Environment Aotearoa 2015*, New Zealand's first complete state of the environment report, and other recent scientific publications in recognition of some limitations of the report (Box 4.1).

Box 4.1. **National environmental reporting and data limitations**

The Parliamentary Commissioner for the Environment (PCE) recently released a review of *Environment Aotearoa 2015*, the first complete state of the environment report prepared under the Environmental Reporting Act 2015. The report provides a series of recommendations to government on how to improve its environmental reporting and performance (PCE, 2016). Recommendations of relevance to freshwater management include:

- Reporting of environmental issues (including water quality and quantity status and trends) should be at the regional level. Given the local nature and high variability of water and land-use patterns, overall national trends do not identify hotspots that require urgent attention.
- Cause-and-effect analysis of data should be improved. In *Environment Aotearoa 2015*, trends in water quality are calculated by averaging the control and impacted monitoring sites together, thereby reducing the ability to track anthropogenic changes in water quality. Data time series should reflect the difference between major changes (where reliable, comparative data exist), such as water quality before and after land-use intensification associated with the "dairy boom" around 1990.

The above recommendations would be useful for improving the *Environment Aotearoa* report in the future. Information gaps where more national monitoring, data collection and research could be beneficial to inform freshwater management policy include: surface water allocation pressure, as the latest data date back to 2010; freshwater flows, total irrigated area, water use from water meters, restrictions on water use to manage over-allocation or seasonal low-river flow; groundwater quantity and quality (including interconnectivity with surface water), and lake water quality; temporal and spatial changes in surface and groundwater availability for irrigation under future climate scenarios, and costs and benefits of support for irrigation.

The Land, Air, Water Aotearoa (LAWA) website (*www.lawa.org.nz*), initiated in 2009 by regional councils, is an important development. It helps make water science more accessible to the public and acts as a repository to collect and share regional- and catchment-scale data from over 1 100 freshwater monitoring sites. It aims to help local communities balance use of natural resources with maintaining water quality and availability.

To identify hotpots as priorities for action, it would be useful if LAWA included league tables that compare regions and catchments across the country. Meaningful and comparative metrics could include water quality status, suitability for swimming and compliance with installation of water meters and reporting of water takes. Greater funding for increased environmental monitoring and reporting could come from increasing resource consent fees in line with the user-pays principle, or from a variety of economic instruments (as proposed in the MfE's 2016 *Next Steps for Fresh Water: Consultation Document*).

Source: MfE (2016a); MfE and Statistics NZ (2015); PCE (2016).

Nitrogen

The nitrogen balance between 1998 and 2009 has worsened more than in any other OECD member country, primarily due to expansion and intensification of farming (OECD, 2013a) (Figure 4.2). The national nitrogen surplus increased at a similar annual rate to that of the national dairy cattle herd, which has been the main source of nitrogen surplus (Chapter 3).

Between 1990 and 2012, the estimated amount of nitrogen that leached into soil from agriculture increased by 29%, and total nitrogen levels in rivers increased 12%, with 60% of monitored sites showing statistically significant increases (MfE and Statistics NZ, 2015). The

Figure 4.2. **Nitrogen balance has worsened in New Zealand more than in any other OECD member country**

Changes in nitrogen balance and agricultural production, 1998-2000 to 2007-09[a]

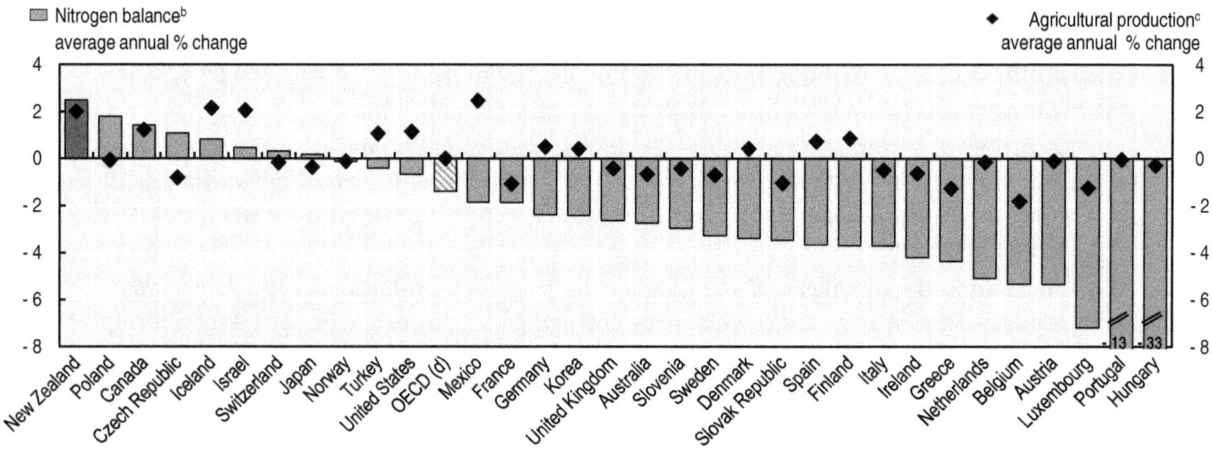

a) Data for 1998-2000 average refer to 2000 for the United Kingdom and 2000-02 average for Israel and Portugal. Data for 2007-09 average refer to 2006-08 average for Belgium, France, Greece, Hungary, Italy, Luxembourg, Mexico, Netherlands, Slovenia and Switzerland.

b) The gross nitrogen balance (surplus or deficit) calculates the difference between the nitrogen inputs entering a farming system (i.e. mainly livestock manure and fertilisers) and the nitrogen outputs leaving the system (i.e. the uptake of nitrogen for crop and pasture production). The calculation can be used as a proxy to reveal the status of environmental pressures, such as declining soil fertility in the case of a nutrient deficit, or for a nutrient surplus the risk of polluting soil, water and air.

c) Based on the sum of price-weighted quantities of different agricultural commodities produced after deductions of quantities used as seed and feed weighted in a similar manner. Index 2004-06=100.

d) The OECD total excludes Chile, Estonia, Israel and Latvia.

Source: OECD (2013), *OECD Compendium of Agri-environmental Indicators.*

StatLink http://dx.doi.org/10.1787/888933459986

increase in nitrogen is attributed to the increase in dairy farming with nitrogen pollution hotspots identified in the regions where most (70%) of the increase in dairy farming has taken place – Canterbury, Otago and Southland (PCE, 2015; Unwin and Larned, 2013). Additional nitrogen pollution hotspots are identified in rivers located in Waikato, Taranaki, Manawatu-Wanganui and Hawke's Bay – all of which are also farming regions (Unwin and Larned, 2013). Similar trends in nutrient levels are also found in lakes (Verburg et al., 2010).

Figure 4.3 illustrates nitrogen losses associated with various land-use conversion scenarios; phosphorus also shows similar trends under the same land-use change scenarios (PCE, 2013). About 49% of monitored river sites have enough nitrogen to trigger nuisance periphyton growth, as long as there is enough sunlight and phosphorus and a lack of flood events for periphyton to bloom (MfE and Statistics NZ, 2015).

Phosphorus

Like nitrogen, phosphorus levels in lowland farming catchments (with the exception of North Canterbury) exceed the total phosphorus "default trigger value" for triggering further investigation or management action for the protection of ecological values in lowland rivers (33µg P/L, below 150 m ASL) (ANZECC, 2000; Unwin and Larned, 2013). However, efforts to reduce phosphorus losses to water bodies have paid dividends. Trend analyses indicate that total phosphorus and dissolved reactive phosphorus concentrations have decreased over 2004-13 at median rates > 1.5%/year (Larned et al., 2016), due to riparian planting, stock exclusion from waterways, reduced phosphorus fertiliser use and soil conservation efforts (MfE and Statistics NZ, 2015).

Figure 4.3. **Land use heavily influences water quality**

Examples of nitrogen losses associated with different land use and land-use conversion scenarios

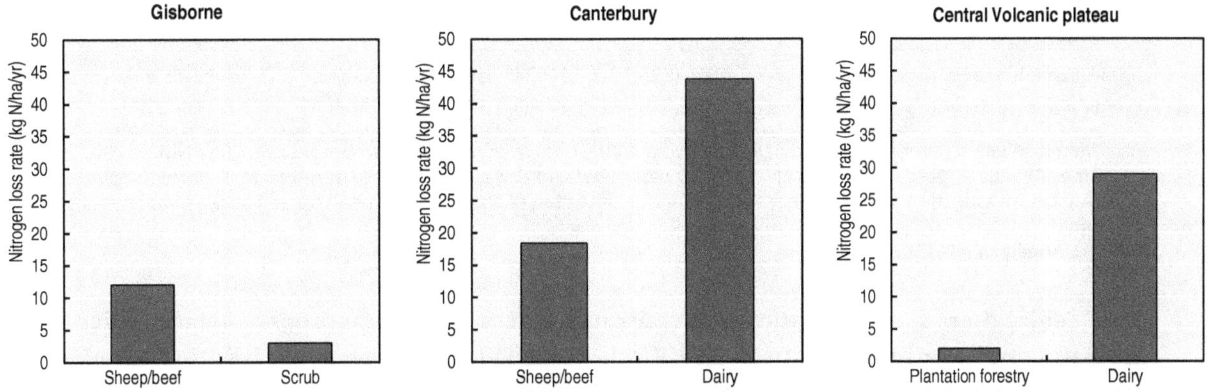

Note: Nutrient loss rates provided by NIWA based on a mix of measurements using the industry standard model for estimating farm nutrient losses (OVERSEER 6.0). The loss rates are "conservative averages", based on the best available information. *Left*: Nitrogen loss rates on an extensive sheep/beef farm (stocking rate: 5 sheep/ha, 3 beef/ha) on hilly clay soil in Gisborne reverting to scrub. *Middle*: "Conservative nitrogen loss rates on an intensive sheep/beef farm (50/50 sheep/beef, not irrigated) on alluvial soil (Waimakariri stoney soils) in Canterbury converting to an intensive dairy farm (3 dairy cows/ha, irrigated, wintered on). *Right*: Nitrogen loss rates from a plantation forest on pumice soil in the Volcanic Plateau, North Island, converting to a dairy farm.

Source: PCE (2013), *Water quality in New Zealand: Land use and nutrient pollution.*

StatLink http://dx.doi.org/10.1787/888933459990

Escherichia coli

Pathogenic bacteria are recognised as the primary risk to human health from poor water quality (MfE and Statistics NZ, 2015). *Escherichia coli (E. coli)* is used as an indicator of bacterial risk because it indicates the presence of faecal material and, therefore, the potential presence of pathogenic bacteria (Ministry of Health, 2008). Higher *E. coli* levels indicate higher risks of infection for swimmers, particularly from stomach bugs like *Campylobacter* (Ministry of Health, 2008).

In 2013, *E. coli* levels in New Zealand rivers met acceptable standards for wading and boating (1 000 cfu/100mL) at 98% of monitored sites (MfE and Statistics NZ, 2015). However, the median value for 95th percentile *E. coli* concentrations across all monitoring sites was more than three times higher than (i.e. exceeded) the National Policy Statement for Freshwater Management 2014 (NPS-FM) minimum acceptable state for swimming (540 cfu/100mL) (Larned et al., 2016). Hotspots of high counts of *E. coli* occur in intensively farmed and lowland urban areas where impacts accumulate. The median value for *E. coli* over the period 2009-2013 exceeded the NPS-FM minimum acceptable state for primary contact (swimming) at all lowland urban sites, 91% of pastoral sites, 46% of exotic forest sites and 29% of natural sites (Larned et al., 2016).

Water clarity and sedimentation

Water clarity is a measure of underwater visibility, a reflection of suspended sediments and dissolved solids in the water column and the amount of sunlight available. Between 1989 and 2013, water clarity improved overall in New Zealand. However, clarity is reduced where there are pressures from urban and agricultural land use, particularly in downstream areas (Table 4.1) (Larned et al., 2016; MfE and Statistics NZ, 2015).

2.3. Groundwater quality and impacts to human health

Ambient groundwater quality in New Zealand is similar to other countries such as Finland, Canada and the Netherlands (Daughney and Randall, 2009). The main issues in

Table 4.1. **Percentage of monitoring sites at which five year (2009-13) median values for water clarity do not comply with the ANZECC 2000 "trigger values"**

Land class (ANZECC trigger value)	Natural	Exotic forest	Pastoral	Urban	All land classes
Upland (0.6 m^{-1})	4% (4, 97)	100% (8, 8)	12% (13, 112)	No sites	8% (25, 309)
Lowland (0.8 m^{-1})	20% (2, 10)	0% (0, 5)	20% (36, 183)	30% (3, 10)	20% (41, 208)

Note: Paired values in parentheses: number of sites exceeding, total number of sites in sample size. The ANZECC 2000 Guidelines default "trigger values" for water quality parameters (in this case *E. coli*) are designed to indicate (trigger) when further investigation or management action for the protection of ecological values in upland and lowland rivers is required.
Source: Larned et al. (2016).

New Zealand are contamination with nitrates and microbial pathogens. Nationally, median concentrations of nitrate and *E. coli* exceeded their respective health-related standards for human consumption at 5% and 23% of monitoring sites (n = 973) during 1995-2008 (Table 4.2).[5]

From 2004-13, over 60% of sites exceeded the default ANZECC 2000 nitrate "trigger value" for the protection of ecosystems (Table 4.2). These elevated nitrate levels are likely the result of intensive farming practices (i.e. fertiliser application and livestock effluent); the regions with the highest median nitrate concentrations are Waikato, Southland and Canterbury (Daughney and Randall, 2009; Moreau and Daughney, 2015). Elevated nitrate concentrations were found mostly in samples from unconfined, shallow wells. The greatest proportion of sites that exceed the *E. coli* health-related standards for human consumption and the safe threshold for livestock drinking water are found in Taranaki (70%),

Table 4.2. **Percentage of groundwater quality monitoring sites at which median concentrations exceed drinking water or environmental standards**

Parameter	Monitoring period[4]	n.	Median (range)	Drinking water standards for New Zealand 2005			ANZECC Guidelines 2000		
				Reason	MAV[1]	Percentage of sites exceeding[3]	Reason	TV[2]	Percentage of sites exceeding[3]
NO_3-N (mg/L)	1995-2008	920	1.7 (< 0.1-33.0)	Health	11.3	4.8	Ecosystem	0.17	73.2
							Toxicity	7.2	13.2
	2004-13	86	0.55 (0.00-14.10)	Health	11.3	2.3	Ecosystem	0.17	61.6
							Toxicity	7.2	9.3
E. coli (cfu/100 mL)[5]	1995-2008	701	< 0.01 (< 0.01-2400)	Health	1	23.1	Livestock	100	2.4

1. The Drinking Water Standards for New Zealand (DWSNZ) (Ministry of Health, 2005) define maximum acceptable values (MAVs) for human health. The DWSNZ were revised in 2008 – the standard for *E. coli* remains the same, but the standard for nitrates has been relaxed.
2. The Australia and New Zealand Environment Conservation Council (ANZECC) guidelines for fresh and marine water quality (ANZECC, 2000) define default "trigger" values (TVs) for water quality parameters to protect aquatic ecosystem, the exceedance of which indicates potential for an impact to occur. The listed ANZECC TVs pertain either to direct toxicity to biota, or to non-toxicity related threats to aquatic ecosystems, or to the safe threshold for stock drinking water. Note that exceedance of an ANZECC TV in groundwater will not necessarily lead to adverse ecological consequences in adjacent surface waters on all occasions; groundwater discharging to a surface water body may mix with the surface water, leading to dilution and reduction of the concentration of the parameter of concern.
3. Percentage of monitoring sites at which median exceeds the water quality standard or guideline, relative to the total number of sites for which a median could be calculated for the parameter in question.
4. The last comprehensive groundwater quality monitoring report (2009) was for 1995-2008, combining more than 1 000 monitoring sites from two national and regional monitoring programmes. An update of this report, already completed, is expected to be released in 2017. In the interim, a 2015 report describes limited parameters (excluding *E. coli*) based on a reduced dataset from 106 national monitoring sites.
5. *E. coli* concentrations should be assessed with caution because the historical monitoring record is sparse, non-continuous and irregular at most monitoring sites. There are historical differences in sampling records; some regions employed proxy microbiological parameters such as total coliforms or faecal coliforms for some time periods.

Source: Daughney and Randall (2009); Moreau and Daughney (2015).

Auckland (33%), Otago (31%), Waikato (25%) and Northland (25%). Significant time trends in *E. coli* concentration were detectable at only 2% of monitoring sites due to the poor quality and low power of the dataset (Daughney and Randall, 2009).

Nitrate contamination of groundwater from the cumulative effects of agricultural diffuse sources is a growing human health concern (e.g. Young, 2013). Canterbury has several "high-risk" areas where nitrate concentrations in shallow groundwater most or all of the time are above the New Zealand Drinking-Water Standards maximum acceptable value of 50 mg/L (based on a risk of methemoglobinemia to bottle-fed babies) (Scott and Hansen, 2015). The results of a ten-year trend analysis from 2006 to 2015 showed an increase in groundwater nitrogen concentrations in about 25% of wells, which has primarily been linked to an increase in intensive agricultural land use (Environment Canterbury, 2015; Hanson, 2013). In response to the risk, the Canterbury District Health Board recommends that pregnant women and mothers of bottle-fed babies use alternative water sources for drinking and bottle-feeding in "high risk" areas. Groundwater quality testing is recommended for private wells in areas of "moderate-risk" (where the risks of high nitrates are variable; such areas cover most parts of the region where groundwater is used) (Canterbury District Health Board, 2016). Canada has established similar awareness programmes for expectant mothers.

New Zealand has relatively high rates of largely preventable enteric or gastro-intestinal disease (Ministry of Health, 2016). The campylobacteriosis rate in New Zealand is twice that of England, and three times that of Australia and Canada;[6] this is partly attributable to contamination of drinking water sources (Ministry of Health, 2016). Leaking septic tanks and sewerage pipes are often the main pollution culprits (this is particularly a problem in Canterbury following damage by the 2011 earthquakes). However, under some conditions, rainfall and irrigation can flush livestock faecal microbes through the soil profile with the potential to contaminate groundwater (Close et al., 2008; Collins et al., 2007).

2.4. Freshwater biodiversity

New Zealand's freshwater ecosystems support a diverse and unique array of endemic flora and fauna; however, the nation has some of the highest levels of threatened freshwater species in the world (Weeks et al., 2016). Almost three-quarters (72%) of New Zealand's 39 native fish species are classified as at risk or threatened with extinction (Goodman et al., 2014). The risk of extinction has increased for 20% of species over 2005-11 (MfE and Statistics NZ, 2015).

Deteriorating water quality, invasive species and reduced habitat remain the biggest threats to New Zealand's native freshwater species (Elston et al., 2015; Weeks et al., 2016). Macroinvertebrate Community Index scores decreased as proportions of catchments in high-intensity agricultural and urban land cover increased (Larned et al., 2016). Hotspots of reduced invertebrate species richness are found in the regions of Southland, Canterbury, Manawatu-Wanganui and Waikato (Larned et al., 2016).

2.5. Projected freshwater impacts of continued land-use intensification and climate change

The New Zealand Parliamentary Commissioner for the Environment produced a study that modelled the link between land use and nutrient pollution, stating that "it is almost inevitable that without significantly more intervention, we will continue to see an ongoing deterioration in water quality in many catchments across the country" (PCE, 2013, p. 5) (Figure 4.4). "Even with best practice mitigation, the large-scale conversion of more land to dairy farming will generally result in more degraded freshwater" (PCE, 2013, p. 6).

Figure 4.4. **Large-scale land-use change to dairy farming is predicted to increase nitrogen loads, particularly in Canterbury, Southland and Otago**

Predicted changes in nitrogen pollution of freshwater forecasted with large-scale land-use change to dairy farming: 1996-2020

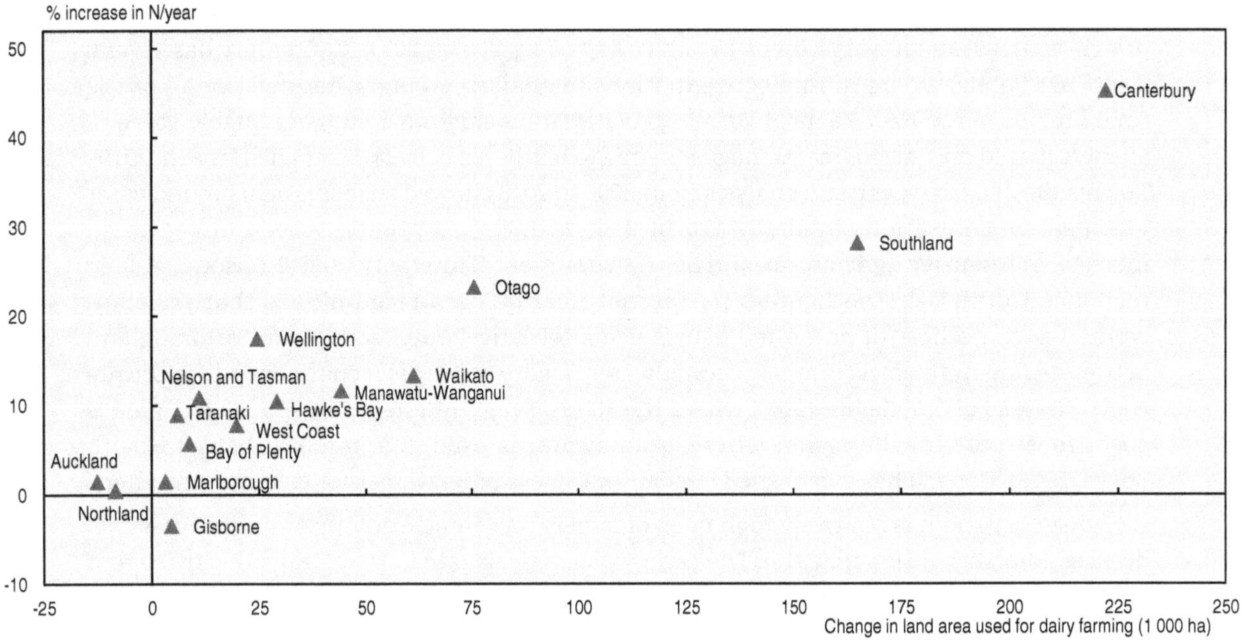

Source: PCE (2013), *Water quality in New Zealand: Land use and nutrient pollution.*

StatLink http://dx.doi.org/10.1787/888933460004

Surface contaminants can take decades to reach aquifers, and the legacy of nitrate pollution is yet to reach groundwater (Howard-Williams et al., 2010). For example, in Canterbury, research by GNS has shown that nitrate in the groundwater west of Christchurch is 30-60 years-old, likely dating to increased use of fertiliser following the Second World War. It is predicted that the current build-up of nitrate in the soil has yet to reach the groundwater system, which implies additional impact on Canterbury's drinking water supply and lowland stream quality in the future. "It will be very difficult for more intensive irrigation and dairying to occur on the plains without the legacy of nitrate in groundwater increasing for future Cantabrians." (Webster-Brown, 2015).

In addition to pressures from projected land-use change, water scarcity problems are expected to intensify under climate change in the northeast South Island and northern and eastern regions of the North Island, especially in summer; periodic drought in these regions is projected to last twice or three times as long by 2040 (IPCC, 2014; Royal Society of New Zealand, 2016), which will reduce agricultural productivity with significant economic impacts. As an example, the drought of 2007-09 reduced direct and off-farm agricultural output by NZD 3.6 billion, of which 78% (NZD 2.8 billion) was due to reduced dairy productivity (Butcher Partners Ltd, 2009). The 2012-13 drought, the worst since the 1970s, was estimated to have resulted in a 0.6% decrease in GDP, despite a 40% increase in the global dairy price between January and April 2013 (Kamber, McDonald and Price, 2013).

Reduced precipitation in the north and east of the North Island and northeast of the South Island will negatively impact on: i) seasonal and annual flows of rivers, and their capacity to dilute pollution; ii) groundwater recharge rates, and the relationship between surface waters and aquifers; iii) soil moisture levels; and iv) the availability of freshwater for irrigation. Furthermore, warmer temperatures will compound the effect of less rainfall, increasing losses of soil moisture through evapotranspiration (Royal Society of New Zealand, 2016). Unless effective measures are taken to reduce demand and enable water to shift between users, expanding irrigation and pastoral land will lead to further over-allocation of, and competition for, finite water resources, in these already relatively dry regions of New Zealand.

3. Institutional framework

3.1. *Central and regional government responsibilities*

The Resource Management Act 1991 (RMA) (Chapter 2) governs the environmental responsibilities of regional councils.[7] In relation to freshwater management, council responsibilities include the management of water risks – droughts, floods, water pollution and freshwater ecosystem degradation – and land-use activities that affect these risks. Regional council areas of jurisdiction are based on water catchment boundaries, which allow for water management at the catchment level, overseen by one regional council. More precisely, this involves regulation of: water abstractions, diversions, storage, and minimum and maximum flows; direct and indirect contaminant discharges to water bodies; avoidance or mitigation of natural hazards, including flood control defences and water restrictions during droughts; and freshwater ecosystems and indigenous biological diversity.

These activities are regulated through resource consents and permits administered by regional councils. These are issued with mandatory conditions to ensure protection of the environment and achievement of objectives set in regional policy statements and plans, in accordance with the RMA. An assessment of environmental effects (AEE) must accompany each application for a resource consent, and consent conditions establish the environmental performance standards that shall apply.

The preparation of National Policy Statements must involve public consultation. Regional councils are required under the RMA to consult with their communities when they prepare plans, review plans and consider a change to an existing plan or variation to a proposed plan. The values of Maori (indigenous peoples) are important to freshwater management, and iwi (Maori tribes) play a key role in decision-making processes.

Central government acknowledges that decision-making processes around resource consents and freshwater management can be litigious and resource-consuming, and create uncertainty (MfE, 2016a). For example, in Lake Taupo and the Manawatu-Wanganui region, water quality limit setting has landed parties in Environment Court and the High Courts over several years. It is this situation, as well as high profile adversarial court cases over water allocation for dairy farming in Canterbury (Weber, Memon and Painter, 2011), that recent reforms seek to avoid (see Chapter 2) (MfE, 2013a). For example, central government suggests that water quantity and quality limit setting will be faster if the existing statutory RMA process is bypassed (MfE, 2013a). This is one reason behind the government's proposed Resource Legislation Amendment Bill 2015, discussed in detail in Chapter 2.

3.2. *Recently introduced national water legislation*

Under the RMA, central government can direct regional councils through: i) National Policy Statements; ii) National Environmental Standards; iii) regulations; and iv) Water Conservation Orders. New Zealand has made considerable progress with a number of new national water-related legislation introduced since the last OECD review in 2007, including the National Policy Statement for Freshwater Management 2011 and 2014; the New Zealand Coastal Policy Statement 2010; the Resource Management (National Environmental Standard for Sources of Human Drinking Water) Regulations 2007; the Health (Drinking Water) Amendment Act 2007; the Resource Management (Measuring and Reporting of Water Takes) Regulations 2010; and the Water Conservation (Oreti River) Order 2008. These regulations require water quality and quantity limits for freshwater bodies, integrated management of land-use activities with water quality in the coastal environment, increased protection of drinking water sources, measurement and reporting for all water abstractions over 5 litres per second, and the highest level of protection for the Oreti River, Southland.

3.3. National Policy Statement for Freshwater Management

In recognition of the need for limits on water resource allocation and water quality, the Ministry for the Environment (MfE) issued the National Policy Statement for Freshwater Management (NPS-FM) in 2011. It was subsequently amended in 2014 to provide additional guidance to regional councils and bring forward the deadline for compliance (from 2030 to 2025-30). The NPS-FM is partially based on recommendations and advice from the Land and Water Forum (Land and Water Forum, 2012a, 2012b, 2010), which held four years of discussions and engagement with primary industries, electricity generators, recreational groups, environmental organisations, iwi and representatives from regional councils and central government.[8] The Land and Water Forum recommended three key reform areas: i) planning as a community; ii) developing a National Objectives Framework; and iii) managing within quantity and quality limits.

The NPS-FM directs all regional councils to set objectives for, limits on, and introduce methods to achieve desired water quality and quantity outcomes in all water bodies. The NPS-FM requires that "overall freshwater quality within a region must be maintained or improved", further over-allocation of water is to be avoided, and existing over-allocation must be phased-out. In addition to addressing water quantity and quality issues, the objectives and requirements of the NPS-FM cover: i) integrated management (with land use and development, provision of infrastructure and coastal waters); ii) monitoring plans; iii) accounting for freshwater takes and contaminants; iv) Tangata whenua[9] roles and interests; and v) progressive implementation. Freshwater management by councils is to be founded on a spatial framework of freshwater management units (FMUs) and identified values.

How regional councils comply with the NPS-FM, and how they set and achieve their own water quality and quantity objectives, is up to them and their communities; collaborative governance[10] is encouraged in the NPS-FM. As such, different regions and communities are interpreting and approaching the NPS-FM in different ways. A range of groups and information exchanges bring together representatives from regional councils to share different experiences on implementation of the NPS-FM.

Regional plans must lay out water quality and quantity objectives, limits and rules by 2025, or by 2030, if a particular council deems 2025 unachievable. Nine of the 13 regional councils that have submitted a progressive implementation plan for the NPS-FM plan to complete it beyond the 2025 deadline (MfE, 2016b). The pace and timeline for actual achievement of objectives in regional plans are issues for local agreement; the central government requires no deadlines.

Giving regional councils up to 15 years to set water quality objectives runs the risk of further deterioration of freshwater ecosystems.[11] It also provides for a potentially drawn-out process that could create significant investment uncertainty and economic cost (Melyukhina, 2011), a concern raised by most stakeholders in OECD interviews. Developments in freshwater policy will require changes to farming practices and generally imply higher costs for farmers that are unlikely to be shared by New Zealand taxpayers. From the perspective of risk, the issue is not about the appropriateness of introducing new (or more strict) environmental regulations; rather, it is about giving farmers more certainty[12] about their future business costs. Two of the challenges with expediting objective setting is establishing robust science and political consensus.

Such a protracted process contrasts with the government's desire to promote a fast-track limit-setting process through the Resource Legislation Amendment Bill 2015 (Chapter 2). The finalisation of the Hurunui Waiau River Regional Plan, Canterbury, in the space of around three years, suggests that limit setting will get done faster if the existing statutory RMA process is bypassed and gives greater power to community consensus through a collaborative approach (Duncan, 2014).[13] By way of international comparison, in 2014 the state of California in the United States passed the Sustainable Groundwater Management Act in response to worsening groundwater conditions. The act requires the formation of local agencies by mid-2017 and requires those agencies to adopt and implement local basin management plans in collaboration with stakeholders by 2022 (Cooley, 2016). In the European Union, the Water Framework Directive required all member states to finalise river basin management plans by 2009 (despite imperfect information) – a six-year period after adoption of the WFD at the national level (European Commission, 2016).

When water quality and quantity limits and trigger points are set, there will inevitably be a level of uncertainty, natural variability and risk around these values. However, a lack of absolute science should not be a barrier to making progress with setting limits. Uncertainties and risks need to be considered and built into policy development. In this way, if the values set are not conservative enough, or trigger points are reached, a mechanism can rectify this in a timely manner, and if necessary, before the ten-yearly regional plan review cycle. Central government could help expedite limit setting by developing and providing freshwater science and data to support regional policy design, as well as by helping regional councils to assess, design and develop policy instruments.

Guidance from central government on the following would help clarify implementation of the NSP-FM by regional councils:

- Clarification on how to set environmental flows and/or levels as part of addressing over-allocation, adapting to climate change and ensuring sufficient assimilative capacity to process pollutants and maintain or improve water quality.
- Policy instruments and options to maintain or improve water quality and phase out over-allocation in the face of pollution time lags in the system from current and historic land use, the effects of climate change and planned land-use intensification.
- Incentives to encourage laggard regional councils to speed up the process of setting freshwater objectives and limits in accordance with the NPS-FM. Improvements to collaborative governance may assist with this (see section on collaborative governance). Greater technical and financial support to develop the science for water quality and quantity limit setting could also speed up the process.

- Direction on how to manage the two objectives of reducing environmental impacts and doubling primary industry exports. An integrated long-term land and water management strategy combining environmental, cultural, social and economic factors is required to realise the ambitious export growth agenda of doubling exports in real terms by 2025, to achieve maintenance and improvement of water quality, phase out over-allocation and to adapt to climate change. Options to diversify the agricultural sector, improve trade relations, tap into emerging markets and create value-added products, while meeting increasing environmental and societal constraints, could be explored. New Zealand is in a good position to create more value by capitalising on the high quality of its natural capital, including water. The 4% decline in dairy export revenue forecasted for 2015/16 underscores the case for investigating such options (MPI, 2015b).

The National Objectives Framework

To guide regional councils and communities through the water quality objective and limit-setting process, a National Objectives Framework (NOF) within the NPS-FM provides a framework for making decisions about water quality objectives based on nation-wide water quality standards with compulsory national bottom lines. The move to an objective, science-based set of thresholds and risks represents a major step forward in New Zealand's water policy, and provides some national integration and consistency. The NOF specifies two mandatory "national values" related to water quality (ecosystem health and human health for recreation), and various levels (A, B, C, D) of water quality associated with these values. The boundary between water quality states C and D is the national bottom line (mandatory minimum standard) (Table 4.3). Water quality state D represents non-compliance with the national bottom line. Deterioration from one water quality state to a lower water quality state also represents non-compliance (water quality must be maintained or improved), although the government proposes that deterioration within a water quality state is permitted (MfE, 2016a).

Guidelines for optional national values and optional improved water quality (states A and B), are also provided in the NOF (refer to NPS-FM 2014) so that objectives and water quality limits can be customised to regional and local needs and aspirations. The MfE is developing additional water quality parameters (known as attributes in New Zealand). Ongoing work on sediment and benthic cyanobacteria, macro-invertebrates, fishing, and estuaries and wetlands may result in new attributes. Such additional attributes would increase protection of freshwater ecosystems under the NPS-FM. The revision of, or development of new, water quality attributes should be expedited to minimise the need for updating regional plans to meet new regulations and repeated community engagement and consultation. Regional councils may also develop additional attributes if they are relevant to the local community values identified.

Regional councils and local communities have discretion to improve water quality above the national bottom line, although water quality must be maintained and improved at the *regional* level from a definitive current state. The central government provides no guidance on how this current water quality state should be set, the time period required or number of monitoring sites. It is difficult to determine how, or whether, trade-offs will occur to deliver the outcome of "maintain or improve water quality across a region" as water quality is not measured in regional units. The public strongly supports replacing "region" with "freshwater management unit" (MfE, 2016c). Freshwater management units (FMUs) are loosely defined by central government in the NPS-FM,[14] but this implies they would operate at catchment or sub-catchment scale, while considering hydrological, social, political and cultural

Table 4.3. **Bottom-line attributes to meet national values of the NPS-FM (2014)**

Attribute	Sampling statistic	Numeric state	Narrative attribute state
Value: Ecosystem health – lakes			
Phytoplankton (Trophic state) (milligrams chlorophyll-a per cubic metre)	Annual median	12	Lake ecological communities are moderately impacted by additional algal and plant growth arising from nutrient levels that are elevated well above natural reference conditions.
	Annual maximum	60	
Total Nitrogen (Trophic state) (milligrams per cubic metre)	Annual median (seasonally stratified and brackish[1]	750	Lake ecological communities are moderately impacted by additional algal and plant growth arising from nutrient levels that are elevated well above natural reference conditions.
	Annual median (Polymictic)	800	
Total Phosphorus (Trophic state) (milligrams per cubic metre)	Annual median	50	Lake ecological communities are moderately impacted by additional algal and plant growth arising from nutrient levels that are elevated well above natural reference conditions.
Value: Ecosystem health – rivers			
Periphyton (Trophic state) (milligrams chlorophyll-a per square metre)	Default class: exceeded no more than 8% of samples[2]	200	Periodic short-duration nuisance blooms reflecting moderate nutrient enrichment and/or alteration of the natural flow regime or habitat.
	Productive class[3]: exceeded no more than 17% of samples[2]	200	
Nitrate (Toxicity) (milligrams nitrate-nitrogen per litre)	Annual median	6.9	Growth effects on up to 20% of species (mainly sensitive species such as fish). No acute effects.
	Annual 95th percentile	9.8	
Value: Ecosystem health – lakes and rivers			
Ammonia (Toxicity) (milligrams ammoniacal-nitrogen per litre)	Annual median[4]	1.30	80% species protection level: Starts impacting regularly on the 20% most sensitive species (reduced survival of most sensitive species).
	Annual maximum[4]	2.20	
Value: Ecosystem health – rivers (below point sources)			
Dissolved oxygen (milligram per litre)	*7-day mean minimum (Summer period)*[5]	5.0	Moderate stress on a number of aquatic organisms caused by dissolved oxygen levels exceeding preference levels for periods of several hours each day. Risk of sensitive fish and macroinvertebrate species being lost.
	1-day minimum (Summer period)[6]	4.0	
Value: Human health for recreation – rivers and lakes			
E. coli (number of *E. coli* per hundred millilitres)	Annual median	1 000	People are exposed to a moderate risk of infection (less than 5% risk) from contact with water during activities with occasional immersion and some ingestion of water (such as wading and boating). People are exposed to a high risk of infection (greater than 5% risk) from contact with water during activities likely to involve immersion.
Value: Human health for recreation – lakes and lake-fed rivers			
Cyanobacteria – Planktonic Biovolume - (cubic millimetres per litre) OR Cell Count - (cells per millilitre)	80th percentile	1.8 mm^3/L Biovolume equivalent of potentially toxic cyanobacteria; OR 10 mm^3/L total biovolume of all cyanobacteria	Low risk of health effects from exposure to cyanobacteria (from any contact with fresh water).

1. Excluding intermittently closing and opening lagoons (ICOLs).
2. Based on a monthly monitoring regime of greater than three years.
3. Rivers classified as prone to productive periphyton: rivers classified as dry climate categories, and rivers classified as geology categories that have naturally high levels of nutrient enrichment due to their catchment hydrology. The default class includes all river environment classification types that are not in the productive class.
4. Based on pH 8 and temperature of 20°C.
5. The mean value of seven consecutive daily minimum values. Summer period: 1 November to 30 April.
6. The lowest daily minimum across the whole summer period. Summer period: 1 November to 30 April.

Source: National Policy Statement on Freshwater Management, 2014.

characteristics of the region (MfE, 2016d). It is recommended that freshwater be managed at the catchment scale, and that interconnected surface and groundwater bodies be effectively managed as one FMU.

The RMA requires those exercising powers under it to safeguard the life-supporting capacity of freshwater ecosystems. The selection of appropriate attributes, measurement protocols, objectives and limits will be critical to the success of the NOF in improving the resilience of freshwater ecosystems. Developing numerical values as limits for the water quality attribute state of FMUs that are consistent with that broad goal will be challenging. Current aspects of the NOF subject to debate include:

- The adequacy of bottom lines to secure water quality for swimming; the current bottom line includes water quality attributes for wading or boating only. There has been a strong response from public consultation on the NPS-FM for water quality suitable for swimming (MfE, 2016c). In Waikato, communities and iwi have gone beyond the bottom lines and set a goal of reaching water quality suitable for swimming in the Waikato River.
- The adequacy of nitrate toxicity limits at a level that can control for nuisance periphyton and cyanobacteria, and protect aquatic life.[15]
- The absence of water quality attributes for estuaries, intermittently closing and opening lakes and lagoons (Green, 2013; MfE, 2016c) and wetlands. These ecosystems are the receiving environments for cumulative discharges from rivers and are often areas of considerable conservation, biodiversity, cultural and recreational significance (New Zealand Freshwater Sciences Society, 2014). The NPS-FM does require "integrated management of the effects of the use and development of land and freshwater on coastal water", but there are no water quality attributes proposed for coastal systems, either in the NPS-FM or the New Zealand Coastal Policy Statement 2010 (Department of Conservation, 2010).
- The absence of water quality attributes for groundwater. Public health officials regard consideration of groundwater quality in the NPS-FM as necessary for protection of drinking water supplies, which for some significantly populated areas and many rural areas of New Zealand remain untreated. Groundwater quality can also affect surface water quality, and therefore limits of groundwater quality will help improve surface water quality where groundwater and surface water are interconnected. At a minimum, cross reference could be made to the Resource Management (National Environmental Standards for Sources of Human Drinking Water) Regulations 2007, which aim to protect drinking water sources from contamination.
- The adequacy of the dissolved oxygen attribute (an indicator for biological productivity), which currently only applies to below point-source discharges. A lack of dissolved oxygen is also linked with diffuse nutrient pollution, occurring anywhere in rivers and lakes managing for periphyton and cyanobacteria, which can cause large diurnal fluctuations in oxygen levels. The consequence of taking water quality samples at the same time each day runs the risk of missing important information on the diurnal variation of dissolved oxygen concentrations, which are critical for the integrity of freshwater flora and fauna species.[16]

A sense of the international comparability of the NOF can be illustrated by way of a comparison with the EU Water Framework Directive (WFD). The New Zealand NOF Attribute State "B" is broadly equivalent to WFD "Good" Ecological Status (refer to Annex A for a summary comparison). In other words, the New Zealand bottom lines are set below the equivalent WFD bottom line of "Good" Ecological Status; they roughly correspond to the level of "Moderate" Ecological Status. However, compliance with the "Good" status of the WFD is exempt where costs can be proved as disproportionate; in New Zealand, by contrast, the proposed national bottom lines will be mandatory for all waters except those in which: a) existing water quality is below the bottom lines because of naturally occurring processes; or b) existing infrastructure listed in Appendix 3 of the NPS-FM contributes to existing freshwater quality. Appendix 3 is yet to be developed, but is designed to capture installations like existing hydropower schemes. To date, no applications for exemption of the bottom lines under Appendix 3 have been accepted.

The large majority of New Zealand rivers already comply with the water quality bottom lines (Figure 4.5). Given growing concerns about nitrogen pollution and public health risks, this suggests that the national bottom lines are not particularly ambitious. There are insufficient data to report on the water quality of lakes (only approximately 120 of 3 600 lakes are monitored).

Figure 4.5. **Most New Zealand rivers already comply with the bottom-line water quality requirements**

Estimated percentage of New Zealand rivers within each of the A, B, C, D water quality attribute bands, data to 2012

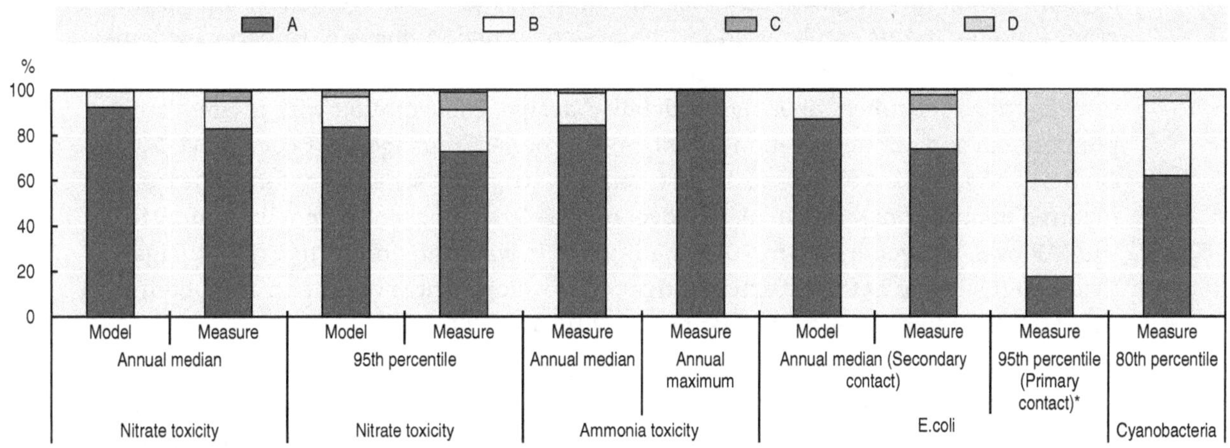

Note: The band D represents the proportion of New Zealand rivers that fail to meet the national water quality bottom lines. For the numerical breakdown of water quality states A, B, C and D, refer to New Zealand Government (2014), *National Policy Statement for Freshwater Management 2014, Appendix 2.* The measured data are from about 600 state of river monitoring sites, except for the primary contact *E. coli* data, which are based on 140 river sites. The modelled data reflect all New Zealand rivers.
* There is no mandatory bottom line for *E. coli* levels suitable for primary contact (i.e. full immersion, suitable for activities such as swimming). Therefore, there is no "C" Band. The national bottom line for *E. coli* is "occasional immersion" suitable for activities such as wading and boating (secondary contact).
Source: MfE data submission, 2016.

StatLink http://dx.doi.org/10.1787/888933460010

Given the high social and cultural value of water quality in New Zealand rivers (MfE, 2016c), the importance of protecting freshwater ecosystems for tourism,[17] and the reliance of New Zealand's clean and green reputation on the global food and beverage market, the government might consider a similar approach to the EU WFD by setting the default water quality level high (e.g. attribute state A, which is suitable for swimming). Provision could be made to overrule these settings, within the bottom lines, if disproportionate costs can be proven (such as the associated economic and social costs of significantly reducing or shutting down production). An independent auditor, such as the Environmental Protection Authority, the Parliamentary Commissioner for the Environment or certified independent experts, could determine what is disproportionate. In England, this is the role of the Environment Agency, which deploys local teams to determine the grade of water quality, sources of pollution, interventions required to achieve "good" water quality status and whether investments are cost-beneficial (viable). If the investment to improve water quality is cost-beneficial, then it proceeds; if it is not in the overriding public interest, then a lower water quality limit is set. Using this approach would set the bar higher and send the right signal to communities and stakeholders regarding the importance of improving water quality. It would also enable regional councils and communities to assess what is required to achieve water quality suitable for swimming, and the trade-offs involved.

4. Efficiency and implementation: Costs, benefits and improvements for freshwater management

4.1. Financing water resources management

Government investment in irrigation

The government has a target to reach 1 million hectares of land under irrigation by 2025. The current area of irrigated land is 721 700 hectares, an increase of 17 percent from 2007 (StatisticsNZ, 2012). To assist in achieving this target, the government supports irrigation through two channels:

1. The Irrigation Acceleration Fund (IAF), established in 2011, is managed by the MPI to support community irrigation schemes and strategic water management studies through grant funding. Grants can be used for the pre-construction phase of irrigation schemes, such as feasibility studies, site investigations (e.g. geotechnical surveys and hydrological investigations), cost-benefit analyses, detailed design, collaboration with interest groups, promotional and communication activities, and project management costs (MPI, 2016a). Grants cannot be used for physical construction of irrigation schemes or for legal expenses incurred in litigation (MPI, 2016a). A budget of NZD 60 million was originally committed to the IAF over ten years, but in 2016 the bulk of it was transferred to Crown Irrigation Investments Ltd to better structure irrigation development investment. IAF's budget is now NZD 2.5 million over a five-year period (2016/17 to 2020/21).
2. Crown Irrigation Investments Ltd (CIIL), established in 2013, provides grants for pre-construction development of regional irrigation schemes and concessionary financing for construction of irrigation schemes. A budget of NZD 400 million has been signalled for concessionary financing (Government of New Zealand, 2016), estimated to be spent by 2019. The specific return on capital for concessionary financing is specific to each proposition (CIIL, 2016). A budget of NZD 22.5 million is allocated for grant funding of regional irrigation schemes over a five-year period (2016/17 to 2020/21).

As of 1 October 2016, 271 700 ha of government-supported irrigation is in progress. Grant funding from the IAF and CIIL can contribute up to half the cost of the pre-construction phase of irrigation schemes (MPI, 2016b). Constraints around the types of funding that can be provided under the IAF and the CIIL may limit the costs for taxpayers. However, feasibility and design studies are part of the capital costs of a project and below market interest rates offered through concessionary financing carry opportunity costs. Thus, both programmes constitute government financial support for irrigation infrastructure. Furthermore, regional and district councils also offer financial support for irrigation. The establishment of these financial support mechanisms follows a period of over 25 years of zero financial support to farmers to increase production (such support was abolished in the mid-1980s).

According to NZIER (2014), irrigation contributed NZD 2.17 billion to the economy in 2011/12. NZIER (2010) examined the economic effect of developing 14 new irrigation schemes in the Canterbury and Hawke's Bay regions, estimating that by 2035, national GDP would be 0.8%

higher than baseline. However, these estimates do not include environmental and social impacts of irrigation. They also refer to overall benefits and not to the marginal benefits of specific projects, which could vary considerably. Furthermore, when new irrigation schemes are developed, the benefits accrue to the agriculture and processing industries; the net impact on the economy outside the agriculture and processing sectors is estimated to be somewhat negative[18] – even without considering any environmental effects (NZIER, 2010).

At the individual irrigation project scale, cost-benefit analyses are not always required as part of the application process for financial support (although an assessment of the environmental effects is required as part of the resource consent approval process under the RMA and project proposals must demonstrate their viability within environmental constraints of regional plans). Cost-benefit analyses that are undertaken for irrigation support are considered commercial-in-confidence and not made publicly available.

Irrigation projects can trigger broader economic, social and environmental effects that accrue beyond irrigators (Table 4.4), but these are not universally positive. There are economic costs associated with diverting resources from other users, as well as environmental effects (Box 4.2). Therefore, proponents of government-supported irrigation projects must show that community-wide benefits outweigh the full range of economic, social and environmental costs. Only irrigation projects that pass a fit-for-purpose cost-benefit analysis and that would not otherwise be privately viable (i.e. projects that are additional) should receive government support. The scale and complexity of cost-benefit analyses should be commensurate with the value of government funding. All cost-benefit analyses of projects receiving government financial support should be made publicly available.

Given the above rationale is not well understood, there is a case to review public funding of irrigation projects. A review would be timely given the risk of water quality degradation associated with intensification and expansion of agriculture. This is particularly pertinent given that effective regional rules and regulations to protect river flows and water quality are still

Table 4.4. **The economic, social and environmental effects of increasing irrigation in Mackenzie Basin, Canterbury**

	Economic effects	Social effects	Environmental effects
Positive	Economic surplus in terms of net benefit from agricultural production: NZD 12-13 million per annum (NZD 2-3 million per cumec). Flow-on effects to the local economy (not quantified).	Increase of approximately 300-400 full-time equivalent (FTE) employees directly employed in agriculture (70/cumec). Population gain of approximately 800-900 people (180/cumec). The arrest of rural decline in non-irrigated areas and strengthened viability of educational, health and other community services in nearby townships. A more youthful age structure of the residential population, the farmers and farm workers occupational group. Increased participation in community activities and membership of voluntary organisations and clubs may strengthen in the longer term.	Reduced bare ground and associated reduced erosion risk. Increased opportunities for enhancing biodiversity values.
Negative	Considerable economic loss in terms of hydro-generation: NZD 63-138 million (NZD 13-29 million per cumec).	Value conflicts between some urban residents and farming communities over the environmental impacts of intensive farming systems. Value conflicts between dryland farmers and dairy farmers because of their different lifestyle, work routines and rates of community participation.	Increased risk of nutrient and faecal contamination of ground and surface waters. Abstraction and direct effects on flows in the rivers. Adverse impact to the visual character of a nationally significant (and arid) landscape. Regional and national costs through impacts on recreation and other amenity values, human health and vulnerable ecosystems.

Source: Brown and Harris (2005).

Box 4.2. **Factors affecting the environmental impacts of irrigation**

Both negative and positive effects of large-scale water transfers are associated with irrigation projects. The overall environmental sustainability and precise environmental impact of irrigation depend on local water availability, soil characteristics and other water uses; on the historical background of how irrigation systems have developed; and on the particular characteristics of the irrigation, farm management and mitigation practices. Thus it is to be expected that environmental impacts of irrigation will be highly variable by region, by catchment and by farm.

Potential positive impacts include environmental benefits of the redistribution of water resources, such as improved aquifer recharge and habitat conservation in those areas receiving new water. For example, the government and Central Plains Water Limited highlight two environmental benefits of the Central Plains Water Scheme, Canterbury: addressing water over-allocation; and improving the water quality of lowland streams and Te Waihora/Lake Ellesmere by substituting groundwater with surface alpine water to irrigate 60 000 ha of farm land (CPWL, 2016). However, the parallel achievement of reduced nitrate loads and increased irrigation is problematic with nitrogen loading in the catchment set to increase despite the commitment to improve farm practices (see Box 4.10).

Potential negative environmental effects of irrigation and water storage schemes include:

- Direct impacts upon water sources – both their quality and quantity, affecting ground and surface waters.
- Direct impacts upon soils – both quality (e.g. through contamination) and quantity (through erosion).
- Direct impacts upon biodiversity and landscapes as habitats are submerged under water or damaged by construction activities, and the ability to buffer peaks and troughs in water flow is reduced once natural floodplains are canalised. Irrigation can affect the diversity and composition of landscapes.
- Secondary impacts arising from the intensification of agricultural production permitted by irrigation, such as increased fertiliser and energy use. For example, in Canterbury, 2012 dairy farm expenses for electricity, additional feed and grazing, and fertiliser were on average 31%, 57% and 54% greater, respectively, under irrigated dairy farms than under non-irrigated dairy farms (NZIER, 2014).
- Secondary impacts on climate change from greenhouse gas emissions from livestock, and fertiliser and energy consumption.

A variety of measures are available for mitigating the negative impacts of irrigation and enhancing environmental benefits where these are achievable. Some of these are technical or site-specific, but many could also involve policy changes and adjustments to the institutional management of water at national and regional levels. Some technical measures can be applied to increase the efficiency of irrigation systems, reducing both abstractions and soil erosion, and improving environmental return flows. However, the environmental gains may be limited if more efficient techniques do not result in lower net water use, but simply allow an increase in irrigated volume or area.

Source: CPWL (2016); IEEP (2000); NZIER (2014).

under development in most catchments. Even with current best practice mitigation of nitrogen losses[19] from intensive farming, it is difficult to see how new large-scale irrigation schemes can avoid contributing to increased degradation of groundwater, river and lake ecosystems (Clark, Malcolm and Jacobs, 2013; McDowell, van der Weerden and Campbell, 2011; PCE, 2013).

Government investment in freshwater protection and clean-ups

Government funding to date for freshwater projects on water quality has been significantly more than funding provided for irrigation; NZD 350 million has been committed, of which NZD 114.6 million has been spent since 2009. However, this trend is set to reverse in the short term with approximately NZD 130 million signalled each year to irrigation (up until 2019). The government manages two contestable funds to improve water quality, with a third one to be established in 2016:

1. The *Fresh Start for Fresh Water Clean-up Fund*, established in 2011, addresses historical contamination of lakes, rivers and streams. Since its inception, NZD 14.5 million has been spent on seven projects led by regional councils, leveraging a total investment of over NZD 60 million.
2. The *Te Mana o te Wai Fund*, established in 2014, provides funding to support iwi/hapu to improve the water quality of freshwater bodies. The fund allocated NZD 4.5 million to nine projects through a one-off contestable funding round. Projects are focused on iwi/hapu collaboratively managing their local freshwater bodies and are scheduled to be completed in 2018.
3. The *Freshwater Improvement Fund*, due to be established in 2016, will help water users move to managing within environmental water quantity and quality limits. Over the next ten years, NZD 100 million will be allocated. Its original purpose: to buy and retire selected areas of farmland next to important waterways to create an environmental buffer that helps improve water quality (MfE, 2016a). The government recently proposed expanding the fund to include projects that improve the management of freshwater quality, including the cost of providing environmental benefits through irrigation schemes, in part to increase the financial viability of irrigation schemes (MfE, 2016a). However, such funding for irrigation is already available under the Irrigation Acceleration Fund and by Crown Irrigation Investments Ltd. Public opinions suggest the majority oppose irrigation projects being eligible for funding under the Freshwater Improvement Fund (MfE, 2016c). Key to the success of the fund will be to ensure proposals provide added value beyond meeting required water quality limits (to ensure the polluter pays principle is enacted) and that they are supported by robust evidence to demonstrate freshwater quality improvement.

As well as contestable funding for freshwater, central government provides funding for three catchment specific remediation and protection projects: i) the *Rotorua Te Arawa Lakes Programme* (NZD 72.1 million); ii) the *Lake Taupo Protection Project* (NZD 35.6 million); and iii) the Waikato River Authority established by the Waikato-Tainui Raupatu Claims (Waikato River) Settlement Act 2010 (NZD 220 million). Central government funding for water quality projects has also leveraged additional funding from regional councils (MfE, 2016a). The Sustainable Farming Fund, launched by MPI in 2000, has supported a large number of funded projects with a focus on collaborative projects for improved water management (Chapter 3).

There is a case for public subsidies to address water quality issues, particularly those related to the accumulated damage caused by historical pollution. However, the polluter pays principle should be the first line of defence in securing water quality (e.g. water pollution charges). Investment for freshwater improvements should be directed towards conservation projects that are the most cost-effective (environmentally, economically and socially). Full valuation studies and cost-benefit analysis may be too expensive for every case, but proposed projects should be prioritised based on the vulnerability of water resources. In particular, this should focus on those close to tipping points (such as lakes on the verge of shifting from an oligotrophic state to a mesotrophic or eutrophic state) or where current users would be asked to pick up costs attributable to prior users. A sample of projects could be evaluated to assess cost efficiency. Natural capital accounting has the potential to be an effective tool in assessing the costs and benefits of desired water quality and returns from investment in irrigation. Experience from the United Kingdom is described in Box 4.3. In New Zealand, the value of ecosystem services derived from river, lake and wetland ecosystems (water provisioning, food production, recreation, waste treatment) has been estimated as NZD 16.9 billion (2012 prices) (Patterson and Cole, 2013).

Box 4.3. **Natural capital accounting as a tool to value natural resources and ecosystem services: Experience from the United Kingdom**

Natural capital accounting (NCA) provides a basis for valuing natural capital assets, and the ecosystem services they provide, by quantifying the "costs and benefits" of resource management decisions (Clothier et al., 2013; Mackay et al., 2011). The United Kingdom is experimenting with NCA. The NCA approach naturally aligns with a catchment-scale approach and demonstrates that investing in ecosystems services and natural capital, such as forests, floodplains and wetlands, can generate multiple benefits. ONS (2016) uses natural capital accounting to:

- Quantify the losses, gains and relative importance of services provided by natural assets; the development of monetary accounts enables the value of different services to be monitored and compared with the value of other economic assets.
- Highlight links with economic activity and pressures on natural capital.
- Inform priorities for resourcing and management decisions.

Initial experimental statistics on UK freshwater ecosystem assets and ecosystem services based estimates of the monetary values of UK wetlands and open channels on a number of indicators, and the condition of freshwaters between 2008 and 2012. The monetary value of UK freshwaters was estimated at GBP 39.5 billion in 2012; this was 10% higher than in 2008, largely due to an increase in the monetary value of UK open waters (Khan and Din, 2015). These estimates exclude other valuable services such as the traded price of electricity generated by hydropower, which was over GBP 300 million in 2012; GBP 8 million worth of navigation licences, which were issued in England and Wales in 2012/13; and landscape amenity values, which are also important benefits (e.g. property price premiums in close proximity to canals and rivers).

Source: Clothier et al. (2013); Khan and Din (2015); Mackay et al. (2011); ONS (2016); Water UK (2013).

4.2. *Steps to improve policies to achieve greater freshwater efficiency and quality*

The two principles in the government's long-term vision for freshwater in the NPS-FM are: i) freshwater is used efficiently and productively; and ii) freshwater quality is maintained or improved (MfE, 2016a). To achieve this vision, the following set of OECD principles can usefully guide policy decisions (OECD, 2012, 2016):

- *The polluter pays principle* is intended to make polluters responsible for their behaviour, including for the costs of clean-up, or of measures to reduce pollution.
- *The beneficiary pays principle* is intended to ensure that those who benefit from water quality and quantity management share the financial burden.

- *Equity* should be considered with regards to fair allocation of water rights and pollution discharge allowances, who pays for policy reform and who receives public subsidies, and the needs of future generations.
- *Policy coherence* is required to ensure initiatives by different policy communities, such as agriculture, energy and urban development, are aligned with water management objectives.

The present mix of regulatory and non-regulatory instruments in New Zealand limits the ability to address key pressures on freshwater quantity and quality in the most cost-effective way. The economic dimension of water allocation and pollution charges is under-utilised in New Zealand, in part because of the government's declaration that "no one owns water" (see Box 4.4). This includes, for example, minimal abstraction charges, for which only the administrative costs of resource consents are charged, and no charges for diffuse pollution.

Box 4.4. **Iwi rights and interests in water**

Since 1975, the Waitangi Tribunal (established to inquire into breaches of the Treaty of Waitangi promises by the Crown), has held hearings around the country and investigated iwi claims relating to the loss or degradation, or both, of ancestral rivers, lakes, springs, wetlands, estuaries and other waterways. In 2012, the Waitangi Tribunal issued a report on the nature of Maori rights at 1840 (the time of the signing of the Treaty of Waitangi) finding that "Maori had rights and interests in their water bodies for which the closest English equivalent in 1840 was ownership rights, and that such rights were confirmed, guaranteed and protected by the Treaty of Waitangi..." (p. 81). "And inherent in their proprietary interests is the right to develop their properties, and to be compensated for the commercial use of their properties by others". (p. 140). The government contested the tribunal's findings, declaring that "no one owns water", but it has provided iwi with opportunities for co-governance of particular water bodies, and a role in national and regional freshwater policy development; the NPS-FM requires involvement of iwi and hapu (sub-tribes) in decisions for freshwater planning to ensure that regional plans reflect their values and interests. The prominence of the Treaty of Waitangi partnership in policy development and decision making at both central and local government levels provides a strong platform for a long-term kaitiakitanga (guardianship and protection) view in natural resource decisions.

The Freshwater Iwi Leaders Group, established in 2007, is proceeding to resolve with the Crown how iwi proprietary rights in freshwater quantity and quality might be recognised. Iwi are exploring a nationwide recognition of their interests in the form of an equitable and permanent share of water entitlements and discharge allowances allocated for commercial use. A mechanism that simultaneously recognises the commercial value of a natural resource to iwi and a societal need for more clarity around interests in that resource is not new. For example, the Fisheries Quota Management System in 1992 recognised iwi proprietary rights in fisheries, revolutionising management of the fishery resource for the benefit of New Zealand. Thus, Maori interests could be accommodated within any future cap-and-trade scheme of water permits and discharge allowances.

As another option to recognise Maori water rights, a resource rental (or royalty) regime could pay Maori for the commercial use and pollution of their waters. There are already some forms of resource rentals in New Zealand, particularly in relation to the extraction of coal, precious metals, oil and gas, geothermal energy, sand and gravel, and more recently, coastal space. Charging resource rent on the commercial use of freshwater resources and paying those rentals to Maori who have proprietary interests would be one way for the Crown to meet its Treaty obligations.

Box 4.4. **Iwi rights and interests in water** *(cont.)*

Alternative forms of recognition of Maori rights in freshwater bodies could also be considered. Granting legal personhood to a water body, or granting ownership of the bed and water column of a water body to a Maori trust set precedents. For example, the Te Awa Tupua framework for the Whanganui River affords the highest level of protection – legal personality – to Te Awa Tupua (a river with extraordinary Ancestral power). It aligns with a Maori world view that regards rivers as containing their own distinct life forces. Another example is the granting of ownership of the bed and the water column of Lake Taupo and its tributaries to Tuwharetoa Maori Trust Board.

Source: Guerin (2006); Morris and Ruru (2010); Murray, Sin and Wyatt (2014); Salmond (2014); Waitangi Tribunal (2012).

Table 4.5 presents a number of policy instruments to manage water scarcity and pollution. In a sector that increases aggregate amounts of water pollution such as agriculture, it is especially important that externalities be internalised where possible through the polluters pays and beneficiary pays principles. Economic instruments (such as abstraction and pollution charges, and water quantity and quality trading) would be one important step towards this aim, as previously recommended in the 2007 OECD *Environmental Performance Review of New Zealand*. The government's recent consultation on the NPS-FM showed general public support for increasing cost-recovery mechanisms (MfE, 2016c). Policy debate on

Table 4.5. **Examples of water policy instruments to address selected water-related risks**

Water-related risk	Regulatory	Economic	Voluntary or information-based
Water scarcity (including drought)	Restriction on water use Administrative allocation of water Abstraction limits Non-compliance penalties – non-renewal of resource permits or greater restriction on current permits Non-compliance fines	Abstraction charges (or resource rental fees) Water trading Payments for ecosystem services (PES) Microfinance schemes	Information and awareness campaigns Drought warning and information Farm advisory services for improved farming techniques (to increase water efficiency and reduce water demand) Contracts/bonds (e.g. land retirement contracts) Best environmental practices (or good management practices) Environmental labelling – products that meet certain environmental standards can be marketed and sold at a premium and/or subsidised
Water pollution	Water quality standards Pollution discharge permits Non-compliance penalties – non-renewal of resource permits or greater restriction on current permits Non-compliance fines	Pollution taxes, charges (on inputs or outputs) Tradable pollution permits PES	Information and awareness campaigns Farm advisory services for improved farming techniques (to minimise negative impacts on water quality) Contracts/bonds (e.g. land retirement contracts) Best environmental practices (or good management practices) Environmental labelling – products that meet certain environmental standards can be marketed and sold at a premium and/or subsidised
Risk to the resilience of freshwater ecosystems	Minimum environmental flows (also for pollution dilution) Specification obligations relating to return flows and discharges in resource consents in drought conditions	"Buy-backs" of water entitlements (quantity or quality) to ensure adequate environmental flows and water quality	Information and awareness campaigns Voluntary surrender of water entitlements and pollution discharge allowances

Source: OECD (2015b), forthcoming.

adopting the polluter pays principle to internalise external costs of agriculture is essential to provide incentives for adoption of sustainable practice and achieving protection of environmental and human health.

To enable the introduction of economic instruments, and to ensure enduring water policies, the government will need to address Maori and iwi rights and interests in water (Box 4.4). The following section will discuss selected economic instruments that may provide financial incentives to reduce water use and pollution in New Zealand at a potentially lower cost.

Addressing water scarcity – abstraction charges

Agricultural changes have resulted in substantial increases in the amount of irrigated land in parts of New Zealand (particularly in the eastern regions of Canterbury, Otago, Marlborough and Hawke's Bay). These changes, in turn, led to significant management issues in relation to the availability, demand and distribution of freshwater resources. Power generators, public water supplies and other consumptive users also contribute to increasing demand for water. Other trends affecting water allocation regimes include government water reform, shifting societal preferences, climate change impacts, deteriorating water quality in some regions, improvements in water-use efficiency and improving scientific understanding of water resources and environmental flow requirements.

Water is not always used, or available, for its highest value use (MfE, 2016a) due to over-allocation, scarcity and "sleeper consents"[20] in some regions, as well as a first-in, first-served approach to issuing resource consents for water abstractions. Under the RMA, regional councils allocate water rights to users through resource consents for up to 35 years. Because water permits are granted on a first-in, first-served basis, the grant of the first consent necessarily excludes the other, where demand is greater than supply. Consequently, the first enjoys an exclusive right to the resource for up to 35 years.[21]

Surface water rights are defined as a proportion of instantaneous flow rate at point of take, allowing for minimum flows to maintain ecosystem functioning. Groundwater rights are defined as an absolute volume. Table 4.6 summarises the various system-level elements of a successful water allocation regime (OECD, 2015b), and briefly describes each element in terms of how it applies in New Zealand.

Pricing water, beyond that needed to recover investment and operating costs, can serve two main purposes: i) providing an incentive to improve water-use efficiency; and ii) socialising the returns to a collective resource. Pricing could encourage more economical use of water, allowing water use to be sustained for a longer period, and support a higher level of output from water use over the longer term. In OECD member countries, water pricing offers possible improvements and flexibility for achieving water management aims (i.e. water is put to its most beneficial use) (OECD, 2009). Revenue from the use of water pricing for demand management would largely constitute a resource rent.

A resource rental fee (abstraction charge), as part of the issuance of resource consents for water abstraction and irrigation, could be charged by volume and time of year of abstraction. In areas of water scarcity, metering and volumetric charges could encourage greater water efficiency more effectively than paying an initial fee for a water permit and using it to its maximum. There are already some forms of resource rentals in New Zealand, particularly in relation to the extraction of coal, precious metals, oil and gas, geothermal energy, sand and gravel, and more recently coastal space (Sinner and Scherzer, 2009).

Table 4.6. **Description of key system-level elements of a water allocation regime: The New Zealand context**

System-level elements of an allocation regime	Description	New Zealand context
Legal status of the ownership of water resources	Legal definition of the ownership of water resources (e.g. public, private, *res nullius*).	The government stance on the ownership of water is "no one owns water".
Institutional arrangements for allocation	Authorities and organisations responsible for allocation and their various roles (policy, planning, issuing entitlements, monitoring and enforcement).	Regional councils undertake rules, plans, resource consents, monitoring and enforcement under the direction of central government as per the Resource Management Act 1991 (RMA), and more recently, the National Policy Statement for Freshwater Management 2014 (NPS-FM). Public consultation is mandatory and stakeholder engagement through collaborative governance groups at the catchment scale is optional, but encouraged. Regional councils issue resource consents for abstracting water and unbundle them from property rights. Consents are issued on a first-in, first-served basis for up to 35 years, based on a maximum volume that may be taken in a nominated period.
Identification of available water resources	Identification of available water resources (surface, groundwater, as well as wastewater reuse) based on best available scientific evidence.	Regional councils have information on available surface and groundwater resources, which gets updated as science and monitoring improve. A particular challenge is the linkages between surface and groundwater.
Identification of *in situ* flow requirements/identification of available ("allocable") resource pool	An explicit definition of *in situ* flow requirements based on various factors, such as requirements for base flow, environmental flows, non-consumptive use, inter-annual and intra-annual variability, and climate change. The remaining water would be considered the available resource pool.	Regional councils are reviewing environmental flows under the requirements of the NPS-FM. Data could be improved on groundwater-surface water connectivity, and the impacts of climate change and of water use on in-stream flows. Guidance from central government is needed on how to set environmental flows and/or levels as part of addressing over-allocation, adapting to climate change and ensuring sufficient assimilative capacity to process pollutants and maintain or improve water quality.
Abstraction limit ("cap")	An explicit and enforceable limit on abstraction, which may be defined in absolute, volumetric terms or as a proportion of available resources. The "cap" can be used to ensure water for environmental needs, so it should be designed to reflect natural flow regime dynamics.	The NPS-FM requires regional councils to set abstraction limits to avoid further over-allocation, and to phase out existing over-allocation. Under the Resource Management (Measuring and Reporting of Water Takes) Regulations 2010, measurement and reporting of consented water abstractions >5L/s are required to be metered and reported by November 2016. This will help determine how much water is being used, and how much water is available for allocation, after providing for environmental flows. The cumulative volume of water abstractions <5L/s may not be known by all regional councils.
Definition of permitted uses not required to hold an entitlement	Definition of those water users and uses that are allowed to access and use water without holding an entitlement.	Under the RMA, consent for water abstraction is not required for individuals taking water for reasonable domestic needs, for the reasonable needs of their animals for drinking water or for fighting fires. Most regional councils also provide for permitted takes for any purpose below a given volume or rate. With expansion and intensification of agriculture projected to continue, the amount of animal drinking water required will, for the most part, increase without restrictions due to the high priority afforded under the RMA (no resource consent is required). In the Waikato, modelling indicates this may result in use of nearly all the allocable flow solely for un-consented animal drinking water purposes in many catchments (Brown Clements and Haigh, 2007; OECD, 2015b). Where catchments are nearing full allocation, drinking water for livestock may be capped at a certain livestock density; above the cap, resource consents are required to ensure sufficient water supply and to protect minimum environmental flows (Brown, Clements and Haigh, 2007; OECD, 2015b).
Definition of "exceptional circumstances"	An explicit definition of circumstances that are considered "exceptional" and may require extraordinary measures. Stakeholders may or may not be involved in defining the term.	When environmental flows are compromised, or yields from groundwater are no longer sustainable, in exceptional circumstances such as drought, there is no nationally consistent approach for reducing water use. Regional councils determine when water-use restrictions apply under drought conditions and reduced environmental flows. They use various methods to induce restrictions, such as "last on, first off", proportional cut-backs, rostering and cessation of takes when environmental flows get below a certain threshold.

Table 4.6. **Description of key system-level elements of a water allocation regime: The New Zealand context** *(cont.)*

System-level elements of an allocation regime	Description	New Zealand context
Sequence of priority uses	A pre-defined sequence of priority uses sets out the priority of access to water according to types of uses or users. It may apply when "exceptional circumstances" are declared or be used to guide the allocation of water entitlements.	Under the RMA, water for domestic needs, for the reasonable needs of animals for drinking water and for firefighting purposes take priority over other water uses. There is no nationally consistent order of priority for water in over-allocated catchments. In most cases, hydropower generation (mostly non-consumptive) and domestic needs have priority. In the Waikato Region, first priorities are agriculture (milk cooling and dairy shed wash down) and domestic needs (equal priority), followed by (in equal priority) industrial use, energy production, provision for the environment and protection of infrastructure. Under the RMA, resource consents for water abstraction must be given up if not used within a five-year period.
Requirements for new entrants or expanded water entitlements	Conditions placed on the acquisition of new water entitlements or requests to expand existing entitlements. Typical examples include the assessment of third-party impacts, environmental impact assessments or existing users foregoing use (for instance, in situations where the catchment is closed).	Under the RMA, an assessment of environmental effects is required with consent applications; consent applications are on a first-in, first-served basis. If catchments are approaching, or at, full allocation, regional councils have discretion on new applications. Under the NPS-FM, regional councils are required to phase out over-allocation. For example, the Waikato Regional Council is seeking to phase out exceedances of allocable flows by 2031. It will do this by reviewing minimum and allocable flows and implementing a number of methods set out in the regional plan. These include ceasing any new allocation of water, encouraging voluntary reductions, promoting water augmentation/harvesting, reviewing conditions of existing consents to determine if any efficiency gains can be made and pro rata reductions.
Mechanisms for monitoring and enforcement	Mechanisms such as metering, aerial surveillance or other means of monitoring water abstraction and use, as well as clearly defined procedures and sanctions for addressing infractions and resolving conflicts.	The Resource Management (Measuring and Reporting of Water Takes) Regulations 2010 requires metering and reporting of water abstractions >5L/s by November 2016. There are three levels of sanction for non-compliance with resource consent conditions: i) non-statutory action (e.g. verbal warning, letter of formal warning); ii) statutory directive enforcement action (e.g. abatement notice or enforcement order); and iii) statutory punitive enforcement action (e.g. fine, infringement notice or prosecution). Enforcement of non-complying resource consents varies by region, but is generally poor due to a preference to use soft instruments, a lack of financial resources and staff capacity of regional councils, and potentially agency capture (Brown, Peart and Wright, 2016; see Chapter 2). In addition, the costs of prosecution are often greater than the fines issued, thereby reducing incentive for punitive enforcement. The government's proposed Resource Legislation Amendment Bill 2015 introduces a nationally standardised infringement regime with instant fines.
Appropriate infrastructures	Water infrastructures to allow water to be stored, treated and transported, as needed.	Water storage and irrigation schemes are increasing in regions of New Zealand where water demand is exceeding what is naturally available. Financial support for irrigation from central and regional government is encouraging water-use efficiency and expansion of irrigation.

Source: Adapted from Brown, Clements and Haigh (2007) and OECD (2015b).

Concessions are also charged for use of the conservation estate; for example, tourist jet boat companies pay concessions to the Department of Conservation to operate in a national park and to the local council for exclusive use of the river. Negotiated fees are charged to reflect benefits from using public land.

In line with the beneficiary pays principle, water resource rentals should account for the following costs: i) infrastructure and transactions (e.g. public costs of irrigation and storage infrastructure, energy costs, and administrative, monitoring and data analysis costs); ii) negative environmental impacts (e.g. reduced environmental flows and ecosystem functioning); and iii) opportunity costs associated with exclusion of other potential users in areas where water resources are over-allocated. In principle, revenue raised from such a regime could feed into the general budget of regional councils and be applied to the highest priority public use. A share of the revenue could be allocated to iwi and hapu in recognition of Maori water rights. Requisites for the design of water resource rentals include: stating clear objectives; regional-level management within a nationally consistent framework; linking rentals to quantities of abstracted or used water; reflecting environmental and opportunity costs; equitable treatment of water users; and setting clear provisions for re-allocation (Ambec et al., 2016; OECD, 2015b). Allowing trade, lease or transfer of water consents can further improve the efficiency of water allocation regimes, especially during periods of water scarcity to maintain production and growth.

Addressing water scarcity – cap and transfer schemes

The Land and Water Forum (2012b) recognises that in some catchments, the ability to transfer and trade authorisations to abstract water could improve the efficiency of freshwater management in New Zealand. This is particularly likely in catchments where abstraction is predominately from groundwater sources, and where infrastructure to transfer water is in place or is feasible to develop. For example, in the Waikato Region, transfers of groundwater permits are allowed under the oversight of the Waikato Regional Council, under section 136 of the RMA (Transferability of water permits). Trading occurs via individual arrangements between entitlement holders. However, there are some barriers to reaching the full potential of trading, such as: i) not all regional councils have expressly permitted water trading in their regional plans; ii) high transaction costs; and iii) regulatory constraints that can limit transfers (e.g. trading water allocations requires a new permit, or change to the permit, and an assessment of the environmental effects of that change, which takes time for regional councils to process) (Dickie, 2016).

Enabling a greater degree of trading could allow more freshwater to move to its highest valued use over time – including by providing opportunities for new participants to enter the water market in fully- or over-allocated catchments. The Australian experience (Box 4.5) highlights that:

- Arrangements should be made well before catchments approach full allocation as resolving over-allocation can be highly political and costly. The NPS-FM recognises this by requiring environmental flows and caps to be set for all catchments and water over-allocation to be phased out.
- Water-use efficiency gains should be anticipated and factored into the setting of a cap. For example, when un-used, or partially un-used water permits are put to use, less water is available for environmental flows and other users.

Box 4.5. **Water trading: Lessons learned from the Murray-Darling Basin, Australia**

Throughout much of the 20th century, Australian public policy sought to expand agricultural production and employment via the free allocation of water licences and to "drought proof" agriculture through subsidies for infrastructure (Connell and Grafton, 2011). Increasing concerns about over-allocation eventually led to the capping of additional licences, but diversions of surface water continued to expand (Murray-Darling Basin Ministerial Council, 1995). Several subsequent reforms and initiatives within the Murray-Darling Basin (MDB) enabled a water market with tradable water-user rights, removed barriers to trade and implemented basin-wide water management planning.

Studies have shown that water trade in the MDB has generated substantial economic returns to irrigators (both buyers and sellers) and their farming communities. In the exceptionally dry years of 2007/08 and 2008/09, total benefits of water trade were estimated at AUD 1.5 billion and AUD 1.2 billion, respectively (National Water Commission, 2012). Based on the experience of the MDB, Grafton and Horne (2014) offer several lessons about water allocation reform and water markets, including the following:

- Water markets support regional resilience by supporting the resilience of agriculture and the environment. Water moves from low value to high value use, and water can be used to maintain and restore priority environmental services.
- Capping extractions promotes effective use and sustainability. A cap should be comprehensive with both surface and groundwater resources included to avoid substitution to uncontrolled or inadequately measured sources. In New Zealand's case, uncontrolled use for livestock drinking water could be worth accounting for. Monitoring and enforcing abstractions within the cap is critical.
- Regulated flow and storage capacity facilitates water trading. Water entitlements delivered via regulated water storages and that allow for its controlled release and trade have dual benefits: they enable downstream sellers to trade water to upstream buyers, and for downstream purchasers to use water purchased upstream at a time of their choosing. Controlled releases can ensure environmental flows for ecosystem functioning during dry summer months.
- Reliable, accessible and timely market information promotes effective decision-making.
- Statutory rights offer flexibility, but carry risks. Two important factors in the growth of water trade in the MDB have been the unbundling of water rights from land rights, and flexibility in reconfiguring water rights in a way that promotes trade.
- Acquiring water for the environment through buybacks has proved effective, but very costly. Subsidy is a costlier way to acquire water for the environment and distorts water markets: it favours those receiving subsidies relative to those irrigators that have already invested in cost-effective water-use efficiency. Water buybacks for the environment in the southern MDB appear to support, rather than detract from, regional economic activity.
- Markets can promote environmental outcomes and be made compatible with public and environmental interests once over-allocation is addressed. Trading in the MDB has led to increased end-of-system flows from upstream tributaries, especially during the Millennium Drought. Where there are important public interests, such as flow volumes at key locations or the need to ensure minimum levels of water quality, trade may need to be constrained for environmental reasons.
- Water markets provide price signals that represent the relative scarcity of water being traded. The price signals in the MDB appear to provide good indicators of water scarcity. Water entitlement prices have also responded to changes in demand, expectations and risk perceptions.

Source: Connell and Grafton (2011); Government of Australia (2014); Grafton and Horne (2014); Murray-Darling Basin Ministerial Council (1995); National Water Commission (2010, 2012); OECD (2013).

- Easier transfer and trade of water rights benefit an economy in times of shortage or drought. Murray et al. (2014) estimate a benefit of NZD 500-630 million if a drought of the magnitude of NZD 1.5 billion (consistent with the economic impact of historical droughts) hits New Zealand. This estimate assumes that transfer and trade lessen the impact of a New Zealand drought in similar ways to that seen in the Murray Darling Basin.
- An effective regulatory and compliance framework is required to contribute to a sustainable outcome. Regulations are needed to clarify who can trade under what circumstances and when.

Pollution charges and water quality trading

In light of the water quality status in New Zealand, particularly increasing concerns about nitrates in surface water and groundwater bodies, and the projected increase in land-use intensification, pollution charges are one way to ensure the polluter pays for negative impacts to the environment. They can be used to create incentives to reduce pollution from urban and rural sources, increase the cost effectiveness of pollution control and promote innovation in pollution control strategies (Hoffmann, Boyd and McCormick, 2006).

New Zealand is in a unique, advantageous position to cap and manage estimated diffuse pollution outputs using the national model OVERSEER® (Box 4.6); regulating pollution through proxies such as fertiliser use and livestock numbers can be less effective at reducing pollution[22] (OECD, 2005). Using this model, pollution charges could be directly proportional to the amount of pollution generated. Principles for setting pollution charges would be similar to those for water resource rentals. They should be in line with the polluter pays principle, accounting for i) direct costs (e.g. clean-up, wastewater treatment and drinking water treatment costs, and administrative, monitoring and data analysis costs); ii) external costs (e.g. negative environmental externalities such as reduced freshwater biodiversity and ecosystem functioning); and iii) opportunity costs associated with exclusion of other potential users in areas where water quality is unsuitable for use. Revenue raised could be used for the general budget of regional councils, which may choose to allocate a proportion to address historic pollution issues.

Box 4.6. **An introduction to OVERSEER®**

OVERSEER®, a national model for farm-scale nutrient budgeting and loss estimation, is jointly owned by MPI, the Fertiliser Association of New Zealand and AgResearch Limited. The model estimates nutrient flows in a productive farming system as a function of rainfall, land use, soil characteristics and on-farm management practices. It identifies risks of environmental impacts through nutrient loss, including run-off and leaching. Originally developed as a tool for farming to create nutrient budgets, the model has been adapted to overcome barriers that arise from an inability to clearly identify diffuse source polluters. It is recognised as the best tool available for estimating nitrate leaching losses from the root zone across the diversity and complexity of farming systems in New Zealand.

OVERSEER® can, and has, supported environmental policy development, most notably around Lake Taupo, as part of Horizons One Plan in the Manawatu-Wanganui region, and the Tukituki River Catchment Plan Change 6 in Hawke's Bay. New Zealand farmers will increasingly use the model to develop nutrient management plans and budgets, as required by regional councils. While such a model is essential for enabling a water pollution cap to be imposed, both farmers and regional councils accept that it has high uncertainties.[a] The

Box 4.6. An introduction to OVERSEER® *(cont.)*

model is not designed to provide economic analysis; therefore, outputs need to be combined with other economic models to assess the impacts of options on the farm business.

The accuracy of OVERSEER® will be critical to maintaining the credibility of policies that depend on it. For example, updates of the model that change estimated nitrogen losses may have material implications for farmers' liabilities. The robustness of OVERSEER's outputs depends on many factors including what nutrient is being modelled (nitrogen or phosphorus), the farm type, climate and specific soil type. Further investment is required to better calibrate and validate OVERSEER® under different soil types, farm types, farm management practices and mitigation methods to reduce its uncertainty, particularly in the region of Canterbury, under extreme weather conditions (such as high rainfall), uncommon situations (e.g. specialist types of horticulture) and under highly complex operations. Policy should recognise improved versions of OVERSEER® so that farmers can implement innovative mitigation methods.

a) The uncertainty in nitrogen leaching (from the root zone) in the pastoral model of OVERSEER® has been estimated to be ± 25-30% (Ledgard and Waller, 2001). However, this estimate did not include errors associated with measurements, or uncertainty from data inputs, providing only part of the picture of quantifying uncertainty. There has been no updated uncertainty analysis since 2001. However, the OVERSEER® model has been continually updated and improved, which is likely to have resulted in reduced uncertainty estimates since 2001. The latest version, OVERSEER® version 6.2.3, was released on 7 November 2016, which includes performance, modelling and data entry improvements.

Source: Ledgard and Waller (2001); OVERSEER (2016).

Cities can also be a part of the solution. For example, taxes on impervious surfaces in urban areas can encourage reductions in stormwater run-off. They can also allow a greater proportion of urban land to be connected to a drainage system with stormwater treatment. In Austin, Texas, drainage fees are used to reduce risks of flash flooding, erosion and water pollution (City of Austin, 2016). In Santa Monica, California, stormwater property taxes fund the city's watershed management programme and its obligation to comply with federal and state Clean Water Act regulations (City of Santa Monica, 2016; see also Chapter 5).

Water quality trading can be useful to allow a more efficient polluter to expand output, while ensuring the burden of pollution remains capped to maintain environmental integrity. It may enable water quality goals to be met at a faster pace and lower cost than without trading. The Lake Taupo Nitrogen Market is the first diffuse source pollution market in the world, from which some lessons can be learned to increase its cost effectiveness (Box 4.7).

Box 4.7. The Lake Taupo nitrogen market

Water quality of Taupo Lake, a UNESCO World Heritage Site, had been consistently decreasing since the 1970s; elevated nitrogen levels were causing proliferation of microscopic algae, reducing water clarity and increasing the growth of weeds in near shore areas. Diffuse source pollution from pastoral farming was estimated to account for over 90% of anthropogenic nitrogen inflows to Lake Taupo, despite efforts of Taupo farmers to reduce diffuse pollution with extensive stream fencing, planting and riparian land retirement under a Taupo Catchment Control Scheme in the 1970s.

In response, the government, Waikato Regional Council, Taupo District Council and Ngati Tuwharetoa (the local iwi) implemented an innovative diffuse water quality trading

Box 4.7. **The Lake Taupo nitrogen market** *(cont.)*

project, comprising three components: i) a cap on nitrogen emission levels within the Lake Taupo catchment by OVERSEER®; ii) establishment of the Taupo nitrogen market; and iii) formation of the Lake Taupo Protection Trust to fund the initiative. The costs were to be spread across local, regional and national communities; the independent Lake Taupo Protection Trust was established in 2007 to use public funds (NZD 79.2 million) to buy back allocated nitrogen allowances to retire land and to reduce the economic and social impacts of the nitrogen cap. The trading scheme was also complemented by the New Zealand Emissions Trading Scheme, which came into force during the early stages of the project and advanced the achievement of nitrogen reductions; the promotion of land-use change from pasture to forestry not only surrendered nitrogen discharge allocations, but also received carbon sequestration credits for a time (Chapter 3).

The target was to reduce manageable nitrogen emissions to 20% below current recorded levels, so as to restore water quality and clarity to 2001 levels by 2080. The annual reduction of manageable nitrogen was initially estimated at 153 tonnes of nitrogen by 2018 but later increased to 170.3 tonnes annual discharge reduction by 2018 as a result of improved benchmarking data. Based on this catchment cap, each farm was allocated an individually-calculated nitrogen discharge allowance, consistent with the desired reduction in emission levels. This permitted them to leach a certain level of nitrogen every year, based on their previous levels of nitrogen use. This approach, known as "grandparenting", was not without contention among different stakeholders. Forest landholders and sheep and beef farmers saw it as inequitable; land development had opportunity costs, and farmers who had been a major cause of the pollution of Lake Taupo were rewarded with higher allowances. The OVERSEER® model provided the basis for generating farm-specific figures to establish nitrogen discharge allowances.

The ability to trade through establishment of the Taupo nitrogen market was a critical part of the negotiations. Farmers wanted flexibility and ability to increase production, or to receive direct financial benefits for reducing nutrient leaching. As part of the market design, only landowners in the catchment can buy, sell and trade nitrogen allowances; this was thought necessary to avoid outside investors purchasing and trading allowances for capital gain. The cap-and-trade policy began in July 2011. By 2013, all farms in the catchment had applied for resource consents and had been benchmarked for their nitrogen discharge allocation. By mid-2015, the Trust had secured contracts to meet the 170.3 tonnes of nitrogen target reduction, and there had been 12 private nitrogen discharge allowance trades between regulated farmers (totalling 18 tonnes of nitrogen).

A recent review of the Lake Taupo nitrogen market (Duhon et al., 2015) found that a cap on nitrogen has limited the nitrogen leaving agricultural land. However, the cap has also had negative impacts on those affected, including reduced ability to intensify production, decreased land values and significantly increased administration and compliance costs. All of these trade-offs were necessary to address the environmental problem of excessive pollution. The Lake Taupo Protection Trust, which funded decreases in nitrogen, significantly reduced the costs borne by farmers but came at a high cost to government. Motu (2015) suggests that regulators should continue to reduce trading transaction costs. Making allowance price information available to farmers would be useful, as would any policies that increase the future liquidity of the market.

The policy package has been fully implemented. It is providing the flexibility for land to move to its highest value and best use, and still meet the overall nitrogen load reduction

Box 4.7. **The Lake Taupo nitrogen market** *(cont.)*

targets. The use of the model OVERSEER® is essential to the cap-and-trade programme, providing incentives for farmers to reduce nitrogen emissions. The Lake Taupo Protection Trust has permanently retired 20% of the original nitrogen discharge allowances. New lower-nitrogen ventures are emerging in the catchment, such as growing olives, farming dairy sheep, and producing and marketing "sustainable" beef. The environmental certainty enables development of added-value products with credible green branding. It also generated positive environmental impacts, particularly carbon sequestration, from the reforestation of more than 5 000 ha of land to pine plantations.

Source: Duhon, McDonald and Kerr (2015); OECD (2015c).

Problems with the Lake Taupo market have emerged, largely due to the initial high costs to government and farmers. The application of lessons learned to achieve a better cost-benefit trade-off suggests it could continue in other catchments of New Zealand where water quality is an issue. Whether this approach, or variants of it, will be perceived valuable to adopt in other catchments will depend on local economic, geophysical and political circumstances. Improvements to address equity issues – issues such as rewarding existing polluters (through the grandparent allocation approach), generating opportunity costs to other property owners, and creating substantial costs to the public to buy back allocated nitrogen allowances to retire land – could be made through reallocation of pollution rights via an auction, the natural capital approach (or other appropriate allocation methods to meet equity needs), and application of the polluter pays principle.

Experiences from the Lake Taupo Nitrogen Market suggest prerequisites for future water quality trading programmes in New Zealand:

- The ability to accurately measure or model resource use and nutrient losses by different users.
- Determination of the assimilative capacity of water bodies and the level of water quality required to maintain ecosystem functioning; a strong regulatory driver (determination of a pollution cap) can create demand for trading in catchments approaching, already at or above, full allocation. Under the NPS-FM, nutrient caps are being determined for all catchments throughout New Zealand. This will have the potential to save considerable costs where nutrient caps are set before catchments reach full allocation. The cap could account for urban, industrial and rural sources of pollution.
- Allocation of nutrient discharge allowances within the cap at the catchment level among farmers, municipalities and industrial users, under the supervision and guidance of regional councils. Allocation should be in line with the equity principle, requiring all users to operate at good management practices. Methods of allocation are presented Box 4.8.
- Allowing trading within catchments to occur. Trading could allow new developers to enter the market, and encourage innovation to reduce pollution on existing farms in order to sell pollution permits. Transaction costs must be low relative to the anticipated nutrient prices and improvements in water quality. Stakeholder engagement can create buy-in to the concept of trading.

- Enabling synergies between water quality and climate change mitigation and adaptation policies to fully benefit from complementarities and to minimise the risk of conflicts. For example, allowing stacking of nutrient credits with carbon credits can further encourage innovation and co-benefits that reduce greenhouse gases and nitrogen pollution of water bodies (Chapter 3).

Box 4.8. **Options for allocating nutrient losses between users**

Table 4.7 below outlines some options for allocating nutrient losses. The efficiency and equity of each allocation approach differ based on existing land use, land characteristics, stakeholder preference and stringency of the regulation. Daigneault, Greenhalgh and Samarasinghe (2017) demonstrate there is no most or least preferred allocation option based on cost-efficiency criteria.

Table 4.7. **Allocation approaches for nutrient discharge allowances**

Allocation approach	Description
Grandparent	Nutrient discharge allowances (NDAs) based on nitrogen leaching rates during a baseline or benchmarking period and proportional to reduction target.
Catchment average	All landowners are given the same NDA regardless of land use; this is the average of total nitrogen discharge from land-based sources.
Land cover average	Landowners managing a specific land cover (e.g. pasture, forest, arable) are given the same NDA.
Sector average	Landowners within the same sector (e.g. dairy, sheep, beef, horticulture) are given the same NDA.
Natural capital	NDAs allocated based on the biophysical potential of the land, soil and environment. Land-use capability may be used as a proxy for natural capital, with a greater NDA allocated to higher class land.
Nutrient vulnerability	NDAs allocated based on the nutrient leaching capacity of the soil. A greater NDA would be allocated to land with lower "vulnerability".
Auction	Auction or reverse auctions to allocate NDAs. Those who can afford to pollute or wish to intensify production can buy the rights to do so. In facilitating such an auction, pollution rights can shift to the most productive land users.
Community-negotiated allocations	NDAs negotiated and allocated among stakeholders.
Ballots	Lucky draw.
Merit-based criteria	Based on best economic, environmental and/or social returns.

Source: Adapted from Daigneault, Greenhalgh and Samarasinghe (2017); OECD (forthcoming).

In terms of equity, the grandparent approach (the most frequently used), can be considered inequitable. It may be unfair to reward historic polluters since they may also be best situated to reduce pollution at a lower cost. It also has high opportunity costs for property owners who have not developed land. The Canterbury Regional Council reduced inequity by grandparenting nutrient losses at a level commensurate with good land management practice. The natural capital approach is an emerging approach that can reduce inequities further by allocating nutrient allowances to a completely different system decoupled from land-use activities. Such an approach maximises the potential of nature to absorb pollutants, and encourages adaptation of land activity to better use soil and water resources, and shift land-use activities to more sustainable outcomes. The approach is being implemented in the region of Manawatu-Wanganui (OECD, forthcoming).

Industry-led initiatives

The government and local authorities have concluded a number of voluntary agreements with individual companies and industry groups to promote sustainable production practices.

In 2014, the government committed to requiring the exclusion of dairy cattle from waterways by 1 July 2017 (MfE, 2016a).[23] At this time, the "Sustainable Dairying: Water Accord" was established as a voluntary agreement between government and the dairy industry (DairyNZ and DCanz, 2016). The accord sets clear environmental performance targets for fencing of dairy cattle from water bodies; the management of riparian areas, nutrients, effluent and water use; and environmental measures for farm conversions to dairy (DairyNZ and DCanz, 2016).

The "Sustainable Dairying: Water Accord" is a success story. Since the accord's inception, dairy cattle are reported to have been excluded from 96% of New Zealand's waterways that are subject to the accord. More than 99% of 42 773 regular livestock river crossing points on dairy farms have bridges or culverts to protect local water quality, while 75% of dairy farms have nutrient budgets (DairyNZ and DCanz, 2016). Farmers have spent more than NZD 1 billion on environmental initiatives over the last five years, with the majority of investments (70%) on effluent system upgrades (DairyNZ and DCanz, 2016).

Given the government's commitment to exclude livestock from water bodies, the environmental improvements from a "voluntary" approach might have happened anyway. However, the accord has helped create acceptance before becoming regulation and has also contributed to the design of the regulation. In addition, many environmental targets of the accord are close to being met. They were put in place more rapidly than new regulations would have been, thereby reducing environmental impacts over the time it would have taken for legislation to pass.

Industry organisations can encourage the immediate uptake of low-cost, good land-use management practices. Agricultural advisory services can play an important role to support the adoption of environmentally sustainable farming practices (OECD, 2015d) and show high returns in OECD member countries; in a meta-analysis of 292 research studies, Alston et al. (2000) found median rates of return of 58% for advisory services investments, 49% for research and 36% for combined investments in research and advisory services. DairyNZ, the industry organisation that represents all New Zealand dairy farmers, invests farmers' money in a wide range of programmes, including industry R&D, and support and advocacy for farmers with central and local government. These programmes support farmers with water, land, nutrient and effluent management, including good management practice guides, planning tools and accredited irrigation companies (DairyNZ, 2016). Other sectors (e.g. horticulture, and sheep and beef) are providing similar advisory services.

The New Zealand government could further encourage and increase support for innovation to reduce water use and improve water quality. A carefully designed R&D tax credit could be a useful complement to existing grant measures. Further investment in OVERSEER® (Box 4.6) is required to calibrate and validate the model under different soil types, farm types and management practices to reduce its uncertainty, particularly in the Canterbury region. Strong regulation, removal of barriers to use economic instruments, and effective and consistent enforcement will stimulate innovation, and encourage investment in solutions and infrastructure that improve water efficiency and reduce diffuse pollution. Universities, Crown research institutes and the agriculture sector should continue to foster collaboration to help diffusion of advanced technologies and mobility of skills.

Collaborative governance: Planning as a community and managing within quantity and quality limits

Engaging stakeholders through collaborative governance[24] is increasingly recognised as critical to secure support for reforms, raise awareness about water risks and costs, increase users' willingness to pay and to handle conflicts (OECD, 2015d). In the last decade, this approach has gained traction in the water sector in OECD member countries in response to new legislation and guidance requiring greater inclusiveness, transparency and accountability (OECD, 2015d). Basin organisations, for example, often include requirements for consultation and co-operation in their mandates (e.g. France, Germany, Netherlands, Spain, United Kingdom) (OECD, 2015d). As one of its strengths, New Zealand can develop collaborative networks relatively easily that extend from central government through regional councils, and between different stakeholders at the catchment scale.

The government has recognised that iwi should play a role in decision making, maintain ecological knowledge about sustainability and take part in environmental monitoring and research about New Zealand's freshwater resources. For Maori, freshwater is a taonga (culturally valued resource), essential to life and identity. In this debate, iwi have important roles, and are increasingly asserting their right to be heard. Treaty of Waitangi settlements provide resource management-related redress to iwi who have been historically affected. Treaty settlements may provide for co-governance arrangements over natural resources with iwi through a statutory joint committee or a statutory advisory board. The Waikato River Authority, for example, is a statutory joint committee set up to co-govern the Waikato River (Box 4.9). Another example is recognising ancestral water bodies as a legal person, as per the 2014 Whanganui River Deed of Settlement (see Box 4.4).

Box 4.9. **The Waikato River Authority: Co-governance of the Waikato River**

The Waikato River is New Zealand's longest river and also one of its most modified and polluted. The Waikato-Tainui Raupatu Claims (Waikato River) Settlement Act 2010 led to the establishment of the Waikato River Authority (WRA). This responded to the scale of the grievance against the Crown and the significance of the Waikato River to both iwi and the nation. The WRA is an independent statutory body (a joint committee) made up of five Crown appointees and five iwi appointees (representing the five Waikato River Iwi).

The purpose of the WRA is to:

- set the primary direction through the vision and strategy to achieve the restoration and protection of the health and well-being of the Waikato River for future generations
- promote an integrated, holistic and co-ordinated approach to implementation of the vision and strategy and the management of the Waikato River
- fund rehabilitation initiatives for the Waikato River in its role as trustee for the Waikato River Clean-up Trust.

The vision of the WRA is "for a future where a healthy Waikato River sustains abundant life and prosperous communities who, in turn, are all responsible for restoring and protecting the health and well-being of the Waikato River, and all it embraces, for generations to come". This vision is part of the Waikato Regional Policy Statement. Co-governance aimed to achieve a swimmable water quality standard for the Waikato River (beyond the NPS-FM bottom lines), and for it to be once again safe for the harvest of kai (food). Thirteen objectives and 12 specific strategies guide the implementation of the vision.

Box 4.9. The Waikato River Authority: Co-governance of the Waikato River *(cont.)*

Management is shared between iwi, councils, community stakeholders and other government agencies, funded by a NZD 210 million enhancement fund bestowed as part of the Treaty settlement process. Part of this funding established the Waikato River Cleanup Fund, through which community members compete for funds to support enhancement projects. In 2015, this fund allocated over NZD 4.6 million to 32 projects. The management aspirations of iwi, councils, research organisations and NGOs have been acknowledged collectively under the agreement, leading to collaborative outputs such as the publication "Waikato River Restoration: A Bi-lingual Guide".

Source: Brown et al. (2015); WRA (2016).

In line with the spirit of the NPS-FM, the collective management approach in setting regulations at the catchment level (with overarching national water quality bottom lines) is believed to create buy-in; increase trust, transparency and accountability in government processes; and find effective solutions to achieve desired water quality outcomes with "local people, planning locally". Most notably, the collaborative governance approach has been used in the Land and Water Forum, the Taupo catchment, the Mackenzie Agreement and the Canterbury Water Management Strategy, but it has also been used in various other catchments throughout New Zealand. MfE (2013b) has developed a set of key principles to be incorporated into its design and conduct of collaborative governance, which broadly align with the OECD principles on stakeholder engagement in water governance (OECD, 2015d). MfE (2015b) also developed some guidance on "making collaborative groups work".

Some qualitative evidence suggests that collaboration alone will not maximise improvements in water quality (e.g. Brower, 2016). Supporting national guidance for, and regulation of, collaborative governance processes could help achieve more effective outcomes (OECD, 2015d). Without such government support, there are concerns that the New Zealand collaborative governance approach in some cases may minimise, or at least delay, change for the following reasons:

- Change is predicated on consensus, which can be expensive and time-consuming. Vested interests among stakeholders create a polarised debate that often requires long periods of time to create trust and to compromise to reach consensus. This can erode a clear objective of environmental clean-up.
- An imbalance of vested interests in collaborative groups and technical advisory groups can reduce the potential of collaborative governance groups to achieve ambitious water quality limits. Community members have to dedicate considerable time to the collaborative process (time commitments can vary from at least half a day per month to fortnightly meetings and workshops, with pre-reading). Funding for community members not supported by their employer is a challenge, but necessary to ensure fair representation of the community in collaborative groups and prevent power imbalances. Added to this, collaborative group members are often exposing themselves to their community by fronting difficult conversations and solutions.
- There is variable capacity of community members to understand and assimilate information that includes complex biophysical, cultural, social and economic data.

The collaborative approach has provided mixed results in terms of environmental ambition. Evidence suggests that target setting for water quality by some collaborative groups has not gone beyond the status quo. This is demonstrated in the case of setting nitrogen limits in the Selwyn-Waihora catchment of Canterbury where the water quality limits allow for increased land use intensification and water quality deterioration (Box 4.10). This contrasts with the ambitious outcome of the collaborative governance approach in the Waikato River, which aims for water quality improvement suitable for swimming (Box 4.9).

The success of collaborative planning processes will depend on many factors, including how well they are resourced, the range of skills and views held by the collaborative group and the timeframe of the process. Despite the potential benefits of collaborative governance, there is little comparative or quantitative research on the outcomes of collective action in New Zealand as it is still in its infancy. The process should be progressively reviewed to

Box 4.10. **The challenge of setting water quality limits for nitrogen in the Selwyn-Waihora catchment, Canterbury**

The Canterbury Water Management Strategy (CWMS) is a new paradigm for water management in Canterbury. It has three key features: i) delivering environmental, economic, cultural and social outcomes together ("parallel development", defined as ten environmental, social, cultural and economic targets); ii) a shift from effects-based management of individual resource consents for individual landowners to integrated management of catchments; and iii) a collaborative governance framework where "local people, plan locally".

The Canterbury region is divided into ten zones (based on a combination of hydrology, administrative boundaries and communities of interest). Each zone has a Zone Committee comprising four to eight representatives of the local community with a range of interests in water, district and regional councils, and the local runanga (Maori sub-tribe). Each committee develops a Zone Implementation Programme with recommendations and actions for achieving each of the ten targets in the CWMS. The Canterbury Regional Council has agreed to reflect recommendations from Zone Committees in the regional plan where consensus is reached.

Six of the ten Zone Committees – including Selwyn-Waihora – have now been through a collaborative process and reached consensus on water quality and water quantity limits for their zones. Sustainable changes in the Selwyn-Waihora catchment include use of off-river storage and tributary storage as alternatives to dams on braided rivers; improved environmental flow regimes by increasing minimum flows and reducing allocations at low flows; and access to allocations at higher flows with time to adjust to new requirements. However, the parallel achievement of reduced nitrate loads and increased irrigation is proving problematic.

Figure 4.6 below illustrates that nitrogen levels in the catchment are already high. With current knowledge, they will continue to rise under new proposed regulations as the full effects of current pollution materialise (due to time lags) and additional planned irrigation and intensification come to fruition. The nitrogen limits allow for deterioration of surface water and groundwater beyond the current state of water quality, which contrasts with the "maintain or improve" water quality requirement of the NPS-FM. Furthermore, Figure 4.6 shows that the water quality limits set through the collaborative governance process will not deliver improvements needed for cultural and ecological restoration of Te Waihora – Canterbury's largest lake, and an internationally important wildlife area. This is despite the requirement of the Selwyn-Waihora Zone Committee for farms in certain areas to have an environmental plan, and be operating at good management practice by 2017. In addition, central government, Canterbury Regional Council, Ngai Tahu (local iwi) and Fonterra (New Zealand dairy co-operative) have committed over NZD 11 million in restoration projects for Te Waihora, which requires a significant reduction in nitrogen loading to achieve a healthy ecosystem.

Box 4.10. The challenge of setting water quality limits for nitrogen in the Selwyn-Waihora catchment, Canterbury *(cont.)*

Figure 4.6. **Nitrogen limits fall short of water quality needed to achieve a healthy Te Waihora**

Selwyn Te Waihora catchment agricultural N loads and shallow groundwater nitrate concentrations

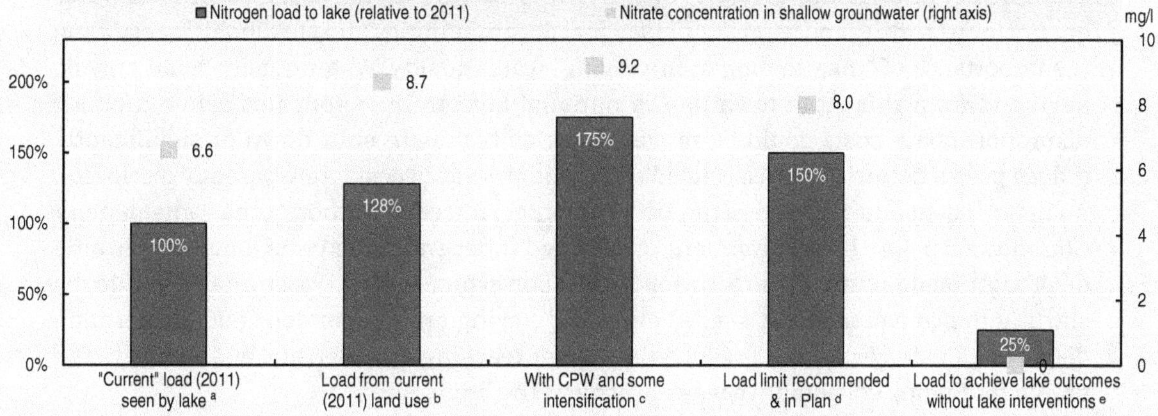

a) 2011 estimated catchment nitrogen load from agriculture as observed in Te Waihora (Lake Ellesmere) and shallow groundwater.

b) 2011 total estimated catchment nitrogen load from agriculture (a) plus the nitrogen load (in the soil root zone) which is estimated to take 10-30 years to reach Te Waihora and shallow groundwater.

c) Estimated catchment nitrogen load from agriculture (a) including time lag effects (b) plus Central Plains Water (CPW) irrigation scheme development (based on land use mix of 40% dairy, 40% arable, 20% sheep and beef, and assuming use of good management practices; plus a small increment to allow farms with low nitrogen loss to do a small amount of development (such as increasing sheep numbers to remain financially viable).

d) Catchment nitrogen load limit recommended by the Zone Committee (collaborative group) and incorporated into the Selwyn-Waihora Water Plan. The limit allows for CPW irrigation development but with the requirement to reduce agricultural nitrogen losses by an average of 14% (for farms leaching more than 15kgN/ha/yr) with different sectors having to reduce by different amounts (e.g. dairy must reduce by 30%). Despite considerable debate in the hearing process, the plan is now operative.

e) Estimated catchment nitrogen load from agriculture required to achieve the desired water quality outcomes for Te Waihora without having to do lake interventions (such as addressing the legacy phosphorus in the lake bed sediments).

Source: Canterbury Water (2013), *Selwyn Waihora Zip Addendum: October 2013*.

StatLink http://dx.doi.org/10.1787/888933460021

ensure that it will achieve desired water quality and quantity in a timely manner. Suggestions that could improve the process include:

- Expedite any revisions to the NPS-FM, including development of new water quality attributes to minimise the need for repeated community consultation and updates of regional plans. This will require greater investment in science to inform policy decision-making. Uncertainty of the policy environment can also negatively affect farmers' willingness to take part in collective action. It creates apprehension among farmers as to the future direction of government support and choice of policy instruments (OECD, 2013b).
- Establish a national process/framework to ensure collaborative groups reflect a balanced range of the community's interests, values and investments, including the unique position of Maori in collaborative processes. A process for testing or challenging councils' collaborative group appointment decisions and outcomes could ensure collaborative group recommendations comply with, or give effect to, the RMA and the NPS-FM. A national framework could be developed in co-operation between central government and regional councils, with input and lessons learned from existing collaborative groups. Central government can promote collaborative governance through such a national framework. Improved clarity of process (including the ultimate line of decision making,

the objectives of collaborative governance and the expected use of outputs) is critical to ensure the process is effective, credible and legitimate, and to avoid consultation fatigue.

- Increase funding for collaborative groups to compensate employers whose staff have chosen to represent community interests. Funding should also be supplied to secure independent experts for technical advisory groups to avoid capture by user interests.
- Set the bar higher. To start collaborative group discussions, the default water quality level could be set at attribute state "A" of the NOF. This would encourage ambitious water quality target setting and send the right signal to communities and stakeholders regarding the importance of "maintaining or improving" water quality. Water quality could only be degraded from this state towards the national bottom lines (but not below them) if disproportionate costs could be proven (such as having to shut down or significantly reduce production with the associated economic and social costs transparently disclosed). An independent auditor, such as the Environmental Protection Authority, the Parliamentary Commissioner for the Environment or certified independent experts, could determine disproportionate costs. Less room for negotiation when setting water quality limits (by starting the conversation at the "A" state and having an independent audit determine disproportionate costs) could reduce time spent reaching a consensus, and motivate the search for finding collaborative ways to achieve the limits.
- Empower collaborative groups with the development of collective aspirations for water management and direct influence over plan drafting. Ensure that regional councils turn decisions reached by consensus into regional plans (and consent conditions) to reduce potential litigation of proposed plans. Regional councils should provide independent technical and scientific experts to inform stakeholder decisions and the economic, social and environmental trade-offs.
- Provide tools to evaluate, track and report on the progress of collaborative governance in line with the principles. The OECD indicators for the performance of stakeholder engagement in water governance may be a useful starting point for developing indicators specific to New Zealand and its principles on collaborative water governance (see OECD, 2015d). More work on evaluating the cost effectiveness of collective action is necessary.

The success of the collaborative governance approach in New Zealand will not be known in the short term. However, the above recommendations may provide a role in achieving more ambitious water quality objectives and limits in a timely manner. Continued progress with the development of unambiguous national guidance and more comprehensive bottom lines, coupled with holding regional councils accountable for achieving the NPS-FM and their regional plans, will be necessary to ensure success.

Recommendations on water resources management

- Foster coherence between water, climate and primary industry policies; develop a whole-of-government long-term strategy to increase the added value of export products within climate and freshwater quality and quantity objectives; explore options to diversify the agricultural sector, improve trade relations, tap into emerging markets.

National freshwater policy reform

- Continue partnerships with Maori/iwi in policy development and decision making at both central and local government levels; under the principles of the Treaty of Waitangi, address iwi proprietary and non-proprietary rights and interests in freshwater (quantity and quality).

Recommendations on water resources management *(cont.)*

- Increase financial support and capacity for regional councils to deliver on, and expedite implementation of, the National Policy Statement for Freshwater Management (NPS-FM); assist with the development of robust science at regional and catchment scales; encourage regional councils to make progress even without absolute science and enable flexibility in policy to periodically review water quantity and quality limits; increase investment in research and innovation to develop new water pollution abatement technologies (including OVERSEER®).
- Review implementation of the NPS-FM to ensure that water quantity and quality limits set locally are ambitious and comprehensive enough to achieve national ecosystem and human health objectives and public expectations; establish performance indicators to track and evaluate implementation of the NPS-FM by regional councils, and strengthen compliance monitoring and enforcement of resource consent conditions; ensure the revision or development of new water quality parameters is expedited to minimise the need for repeated community consultation and updates of regional plans.
- Require regional councils and collaborative groups to start discussions around water quality limits at the highest level (e.g. at water quality suitable for swimming); if necessary, the case can be made to argue away from such limits, within the bottom lines, if disproportionate costs can be proven.
- Develop a national framework for collaborative governance to ensure the appointment of collaborative groups reflect a balanced range of the community's interests, values and investments, including the unique position of Maori, as well as to clarify the process, including the ultimate line of decision making, the objectives of collaborative governance and expected use of outputs; develop indicators to test that collaborative group recommendations comply with, or give effect to, the RMA and the NPS-FM and to evaluate the cost effectiveness of collective action.

Financing water resource management

- Review government support for irrigation to ensure that funding is only provided for projects that would not proceed otherwise, and that have net community-wide benefits; conduct, and release publicly, cost-benefit analyses of irrigation projects that are eligible to financial support; any funding should seek to achieve the greatest return on investment in terms of long-term, measurable environmental, economic and social outcomes.

Economic instruments to manage water quantity and quality

- Rationalise and expand the use of water demand management measures, including volumetric pricing to recover costs of water management and reflect environmental impacts and opportunity costs associated with scarcity; strengthen and expand water markets where appropriate to encourage innovation and the efficient use of water, particularly in stressed and over-allocated catchments.
- Introduce pollution charges or enable water quality trading to internalise the environmental and opportunity costs of diffuse pollution from rural and urban sources, and promote innovation in pollution control; develop a strategic financing model for the remediation of historically contaminated water sites.
- Experiment with natural capital accounting to provide a basis for valuing water resources and freshwater ecosystems, and quantifying the costs and benefits of freshwater policy and management decisions.

Notes

1. Milk powder, butter and cheese exports based on figures from 12 months ended July 2016. Excludes service exports, i.e. tourism and education.
2. New Zealand has 425 000 km of rivers and streams, almost 4 000 lakes that are larger than one hectare (MfE 2007), and approximately 200 aquifers (White 2001). The nation has a temperate climate with most regions receiving between 600 mm and 1 600 mm spread throughout the majority of the year with a drier period during the summer (NIWA, 2001). In the mountain ranges, rainfall often exceeds 4 000 mm/year (MfE 2007).
3. Hydropower generation takes account for 40% of water allocation nationally, but most schemes are non-consumptive, meaning they return water back to the source and can be used again by other water users downstream (Aqualinc, 2010).
4. Dairy farming is not the only agricultural land use responsible for declining water quality. Horticulture, arable farming, and intensive sheep and beef farming can also have significant nutrient losses per hectare, but such land uses have not expanded at the rapid rate of dairy.
5. Note that data are not representative of drinking water quality; many monitoring sites are not used for potable water supply, but used for other purposes such as irrigation and stock water. Those used for potable supply may first be treated.
6. For example, the town of Havelock North in the farming region of Hawke's Bay, suffered from a large-scale campylobacter outbreak as recently as August 2016. Over 5 000 people became sick – more than one-third of the town's 14 000 population (RadioNZ, 2016), causing temporary closure of schools and businesses. The campylobacter outbreak has been linked to the deaths of two elderly people, with a total of 22 hospitalised (Sachdeva, 2016). Central and regional government have launched formal investigations to determine the cause (RadioNZ, 2016).
7. The Resource Management Act 1991 (RMA) is the overarching legislation governing the management of New Zealand's environment.
8. The Land and Water Forum continues to advise central government when requested, and comment on new government proposals as part of the public consultation process.
9. Local indigenous people born of the land where their ancestors lived and are buried.
10. Collaborative governance involves engaging with, or partnering with, stakeholders (including the public) throughout the process of determining desired water quality and quantity levels, setting limits and finding solutions to achieve them. The NPS-FM 2014 is "intended to underpin community discussions about the desired state of freshwater relative to the current state".
11. "Existing freshwater quality" that "must be maintained or improved" is defined in the NPS-FM 2014 as "the quality of the fresh water at the time the regional council commences the process of setting or reviewing freshwater objectives and limits".
12. Uncertainty of the policy environment can negatively affect farmers' willingness to take part in collective action. It creates apprehension as to the future direction of government support and choice of policy instruments (OECD, 2013c).
13. The Commissioners of the Canterbury Regional Council have special powers to write and implement water management plans that cannot be appealed to the Environment Court in order to expedite progress in water management. They obtained these contentious powers when government-appointed commissioners took over management of the regional council from elected commissioners in 2010; it was an urgent measure to improve freshwater management around water quality, allocation and opportunities for storage.
14. In the NPS-FM 2014, "freshwater management unit" (FMU) is defined as "the water body, multiple water bodies or any part of a water body determined by the regional council as the appropriate spatial scale for setting freshwater objectives and limits and for freshwater accounting and management purposes". National guidance on the NPS-FM (MfE, 2015a) states that an "FMU may be made up of a group of water bodies that are similar, both physically and/or socially (e.g. who uses them and for what). Similar freshwater bodies can be grouped (e.g. all first order streams originating from a mountain range) and be effectively managed as one FMU. Alternatively, an individual freshwater body or a part of a freshwater body (e.g. a reach or sections of a river) could be set as an FMU."
15. The attribute for nitrate is set at a level that approaches toxicity to aquatic life; it does not apply for rivers that are managing for periphyton or cyanobacteria. This point should be clarified in the NOF to improve public understanding. The nitrate (toxicity) attribute was considered in the Ruataniwha Water Storage Scheme case in Hawke's Bay and rejected by the Board of Inquiry, which found it was

inappropriate to define life-supporting capacity as a level that approached toxicity (Tukituki Catchment Proposal Board of Inquiry, 2015). Management of nitrogen at much lower levels is necessary to protect macroinvertebrates, as well as to achieve other outcomes such as avoidance of nuisance periphyton, cyanobacteria and associated highly fluctuating dissolved oxygen (Brown et al., 2015). The MfE expects that councils will set limits to manage nitrogen and phosphorous to meet periphyton objectives and protect ecosystem health.

16. For example, a study measuring the diurnal cycle of dissolved oxygen in the Manawatū River found that at night the level of dissolved oxygen plummeted to unexpectedly poor levels (Clapcott and Young, 2009). The technology is available for continuous water quality monitoring with the use of water quality sondes that can capture diurnal fluctuations.

17. The New Zealand Tourism Export Council supports a Choose Clean Water Petition sent to Parliament in March 2016. The petition calls for better freshwater standards and demands the government increase its bottom-line standards for freshwater from "wadeable" to "swimmable". Labour, Green and Māori opposition parties also support the petition (Tourism Export Council, 2016).

18. "There are negative flow-on effects as the expanding agricultural sectors draw resources away from other sectors, pushing up prices for factors and intermediates. These dynamic adjustments of capital and labour take place over time, rather than as instant reallocation of resources. The net impact on the economy outside the agriculture and processing sectors is somewhat negative." (NZIER, 2010).

19. Examples of best mitigation measures include nitrification inhibitors, irrigation and effluent management, fencing stock from waterways, covered feed pad wintering systems and higher genetic merit cows.

20. Sleeper consents are those that are allocated, but often remain unused. Having better defined rights will mean that water allocations are more easily transferred, leased, divided or shared. Murray, Sin and Wyatt (2014) estimate a benefit of NZD 370 million if 5% of the un-used consented portion ("sleeper share") is re-allocated to higher value uses.

21. However, regional councils have been using increasingly shorter consent periods to enable them to more easily change consent conditions upon expiry.

22. Fertiliser taxes can cause an additional burden on horticulture production, while making livestock production more profitable. They may also provide unintended incentives to increase livestock levels, leading to greater manure production through more intensive protein feeding, larger acreages devoted to nitrogen-fixing plants and reorganisation of crops in favour of those with less nitrogen consumption, but not necessarily less nitrogen surplus (OECD, 2005).

23. In 2016, the government proposed a national regulation that requires exclusion of dairy cattle, beef cattle, deer and pigs from water bodies by dates ranging from 2017 (dairy and pigs) to 2030 (beef and deer on lowland/rolling hills (MfE, 2016a).

24. Collaborative governance involves engaging with, or partnering with, stakeholders (including the public) throughout the process of determining desired water quality and quantity levels, setting limits and finding solutions to achieve them. The NPS-FM 2014 is "intended to underpin community discussions about the desired state of freshwater relative to the current state".

References

Alston, J., M. Andersen, J. James and P. Pardey (2011), "The economic returns to U.S. public agricultural research", *American Journal of Agricultural Economics*, Vol. 93/5, pp. 1257-1277.

Ambec et al. (2016), *Review on International Best Practice on Charges for Water Management*, Toulouse School of Economics, OECD commissioned Background Paper (unpublished).

ANZECC (2000), Australia and New Zealand guidelines for fresh and marine water quality, Australian and New Zealand Environment and Conservation Council, Environment Australia, Townsville.

Aqualinc (2010), Update of Water Allocation Data and Estimate of Actual Water Use of Consented Takes 2009-10, prepared for the Ministry for the Environment, Report No H10002/3, Aqualinc Research Ltd, Christchurch.

Ballantine, D.J. and R.J. Davies-Colley (2014), "Water quality trends in New Zealand rivers: 1989-2009", *Environmental Monitoring and Assessment*, Springer US, Vol. 186, pp. 1939-1950.

Brower, A.L. (2016), "Is collaboration good for the environment? Or, what's wrong with the Land and Water Forum?", *New Zealand Journal of Ecology*, Vol. 40/3, New Zealand Ecological Society, Christchurch, pp. 390-397.

Brown, E., B. Clements, and A. Haigh (2007), "A model for assessing the magnitude of unconsented surface water us in the Waikato Region", *Environment Waikato Technical Report* 2007/47.

Brown, I. and S. Harris (2005), *Environmental, Economic and Social Impacts of Irrigation in the Mackenzie Basin*, report commissioned by the Ministry for the Environment for consideration by the Waitaki Catchment Water Allocation Board.

Brown, M.A. et al. (2015), *Vanishing Nature: Facing New Zealand's Biodiversity Crisis*, Environmental Defence Society, Auckland

Brown, M.A., R. Peart and M. Wright (2016), *Evaluating the Environmental Outcomes of the RMA: A report by the Environmental Defence Society*, Auckland.

Butcher Partners Ltd (2009), *Regional and National Impacts of the 2007-09 Drought*, Wellington, prepared for the Ministry of Agriculture and Forestry.

Canterbury District Health Board (2016), *Community and public health: Drinking water* (website), *www.cph.co.nz/your-health/drinking-water/* (accessed November 2016).

CIIL (2016), *Annual Report for the year ended 30 June 2016*, Crown Irrigation Investments Limited.

City of Austin (2016), Drainage Charge: What is it and Why is it Important? website, Watershed Protection Department, City of Austin, *www.austintexas.gov/faq/drainage-charge-what-it-and-why-it-important* (accessed November 2016).

City of Santa Monica (2016), Urban Runoff: Stormwater Parcel Fees website, Office of Sustainability and the Environment, City of Santa Monica, *www.smgov.net/Departments/OSE/Categories/Urban_Runoff/Stormwater_Parcel_Fees.aspx* (accessed December 2016).

Clapcott, J. and R. Young (2009), "Temporal variability in ecosystem metabolism of rivers in the Manawatu-Wanganui region", *Cawthron Report* No. 1672, Cawthron Institute, Nelson, p. 31.

Clark, D., B. Malcolm and J. Jacobs (2013) "Dairying in the Antipodes: Recent past, near prospects", *Animal Production Science*, CSIRO Publishing, Clayton, Vol. 53/9, pp. 882-893.

Close, M. et al. (2008), "Microbial groundwater quality and its health implications for a border-strip irrigated dairy farm catchment, South Island, New Zealand", *Journal of Water and Health*, IWA Publishing, London, Vol. 6/1, pp. 83-98.

Clothier, B. et al. (2013), "Natural Capital - thinking about how we value and use our natural resources", *AgScience*, New Zealand Institute of Agriculture & Horticultural Science, Inc., Auckland, Vol. 43, March.

Collins, R. et al. (2007), "Best management practices to mitigate faecal contamination by livestock of New Zealand waters", *New Zealand Journal of Agricultural Research*, Royal Society of New Zealand, Wellington, Vol. 50, pp. 267-278.

Connell, D. and R.Q. Grafton (2011), "Water reform in the Murray-Darling Basin", *Water Resources Research*, Vol. 47, pp. 1-9.

Cooley, H. et al. (2016), "Water risk hotspots for agriculture: The case of the southwest United States", *OECD Food, Agriculture and Fisheries Papers*, No. 96, OECD Publishing, Paris, *http://dx.doi.org/10.1787/5jlr3bx95v48-en*.

CPWL (2016), Environmental Management: Environmental Benefits website, Central Plains Water Limited, *www.cpwl.co.nz/environmental-management* (accessed October 2016).

Daigneault, A., S. Greenhalgh and O. Samarasinghe (2017), "Equitably slicing the pie: Water policy and allocation", *Ecological Economics*, Vol. 131, Elsevier, Amsterdam, pp. 449-459.

DairyNZ (2016), Environment website *www.dairynz.co.nz/* (accessed August 2016).

DairyNZ and D. Canz (2016), *Sustainable dairying – Water Accord: Two years on… Summary* (website), *www.dairynz.co.nz/environment/in-your-region/sustainable-dairying-water-accord/* (accessed May 2016).

Daughney, C. and M. Randall (2009), "National Groundwater Quality Indicators Update: State and Trends 1995-2008", GNS Science Consultancy Report 2009/145. 60p. Prepared for MfE, Wellington, New Zealand.

Department of Conservation (2010), *New Zealand Coastal Policy Statement 2010*, Department of Conservation, Wellington.

Dickie, B. (2016), *Waikato Regional Freshwater Discussion: A Framework for Getting the Best Use Allocation through Time: Issues and Opportunities*, Waikato Regional Council, Hamilton.

Duhon, M., H. McDonald and S. Kerr (2015), "Nitrogen trading in Lake Taupo: An analysis and evaluation of an innovative water management policy", *Motu Working Paper* 15-07, Motu Economic and Public Policy Research, Wellington.

Duncan, R. (2014), "Regulating agricultural land use to manage water quality: The challenges for science and policy in enforcing limits on non-point source pollution in New Zealand", *Land Use Policy*, Elsevier, Amsterdam, Vol. 41, pp. 378-387.

Elston, E. et al. (2015), *The Plight of New Zealand's Freshwater Species*, Conservation Science Statement No. 1, p. 14, Society for Conservation Biology (Oceania), Sydney.

Environment Canterbury (2015), *Annual Groundwater Quality Survey 2015*, Environment Canterbury, Christchurch.

European Commission (2016), "WFD: Timetable for Implementation" website, *http://ec.europa.eu/environment/water/water-framework/info/timetable_en.htm* (accessed September 2016).

Goodman, J.M. et al. (2014), "Conservation status of New Zealand freshwater fish", 2013, *New Zealand Threat Classification Series 7*, p. 12.

Government of Australia (2014), *Water Recovery Strategy for the Murray-Darling Basin*, June 2014.

Government of New Zealand (2016), *Irrigation Funding Boost for Wairarapa, Hawke's Bay and Gisborne*, Hon. Minister for Primary Industries Nathan Guy, New Zealand Government Press Release 11 March 2016.

Grafton, Q. and J. Horne, (2014), "Water markets in the Murray-Darling Basin", *Agricultural Water Management*, Elsevier, Amsterdam, Vol. 145, pp. 61-71.

Green, M. (2013), Why Freshwater Management needs to include Estuaries website, *http://sciblogs.co.nz/waiology/2013/11/11/why-freshwater-management-needs-to-include-estuaries/*.

Guerin, K. (2006), "Principles for royalties on non-mineral natural resources in New Zealand", *New Zealand Treasury Policy Perspectives Paper*, Vol. 06/08.

Flemmer, C.L. and R.C. Flemmer (2007), "Water use by New Zealand dairy farms, 1997-2000", *New Zealand Journal of Agricultural Research*, Vol. 50/4, Royal Society of New Zealand, Wellington, pp. 479-489.

Hanson, C. (2013), "Nitrate in Canterbury Groundwater", By Waiology, *http://sciblogs.co.nz/waiology/2013/11/27/nitrate-in-canterbury-groundwater/* (accessed November 2016).

Hoffmann, S., J. Boyd and E. McCormick (2006), "Taxing nutrient loads", *Journal of Soil and Water Conservation* Soil and Water Conservation Society, Ankeny, Vol. 61/5, pp. 142A-147A.

Howard-Williams, C. et al. (2010), "*Diffuse pollution and freshwater degradation: New Zealand Perspectives*", presentation to the 14th International Conference IWA Diffuse Pollution Specialist Group, p. 131.

Hughey, K.F.D., G.N. Kerr and R. Cullen (2013), *Public Perceptions of New Zealand's Environment: 2013*, EOS Ecology, Christchurch.

IEEP (2000), "The environmental impacts of irrigation in the European Union", report commissioned by the Environment Directorate of the European Commission, Institute for European Environmental Policy, London in Association with the Polytechnical University of Madrid and the University of Athens.

IPCC (2014), *Climate Change 2014: Impacts, Adaptation, and Vulnerability. Part A: Global and Sectoral Aspects. Contribution of Working Group II to the Fifth Assessment Report of the Intergovernmental Panel on Climate Change*, Field, C.B. et al. (eds), Cambridge University Press, Cambridge, UK and New York, US.

Kamber, G., C. McDonald and G. Price (2013), Drying out: Investigating the Economic Effects of Drought in New Zealand, Reserve Bank of New Zealand Analytical Note Series AN2013/02, Reserve Bank of New Zealand, Wellington.

Khan, J. and F. Din (2015), UK Natural Capital – Freshwater Ecosystem Assets and Services Accounts website, Office for National Statistics (accessed June 2016).

Land and Water Forum (2012a), Second Report of the Land and Water Forum: *Setting Limits for Water Quality and Quantity, and Freshwater Policy- and Plan-Making through Collaboration*.

Land and Water Forum (2012b), Third Report of the Land and Water Forum: *Managing Water Quality and Allocating Water*.

Land and Water Forum (2010), Report of the Land and Water Forum: *A Fresh Start for Fresh Water*.

Larned, S.T. et al. (2016), "Water quality in New Zealand rivers: Current state and trends", *New Zealand Journal of Marine and Freshwater Research*, Taylor & Francis Online, pp. 389-417.

Ledgard, S.F. and J.E. Waller (2001), *Precision of estimates of nitrate leaching in OVERSEER®*, Client report to FertResearch, AgResearch Ruakura.

Mackay, A.D. et al. (2011), "Land: Competition for future use", *New Zealand Science Review*, New Zealand Ecological Society, Christchurch, Vol. 68/2. pp. 67-71.

McDowell, R.W., T.J. van der Weerden and J. Campbell (2011), "Nutrient losses associated with irrigation, intensification and management of land use: A study of large scale irrigation in North Otago, New Zealand", *Agricultural Water Management*, Elsevier, Amsterdam, Vol. 98/5, pp. 877-885.

Melyukhina, O. (2011), "Risk management in agriculture in New Zealand", *OECD Food, Agriculture and Fisheries Papers*, No. 42, OECD Publishing, *http://dx.doi.org/10.1787/5kgj0d3vzcth-en*.

MfE (2016a), *Next Steps for Fresh Water: Consultation document*, Ministry for the Environment, Wellington.

MfE (2016b), Regional Councils' Implementation Programmes website, *www.mfe.govt.nz/fresh-water/national-policy-statement/regional-councils-implementation-programmes* (accessed September 2016).

MfE (2016c), Feedback on Freshwater Reforms – 2016 website, *www.mfe.govt.nz/fresh-water/reform-programme/freshwater-reforms-2016/feedback-fresh-water-reforms-2016* (accessed July 2016).

MfE (2016d), *A Guide to Identifying Freshwater Management Units Under the National Policy Statement for Freshwater Management 2014*, Ministry for the Environment, Wellington.

MfE (2015a), *A Guide to the National Policy Statement for Freshwater Management 2014*, Ministry for the Environment, Wellington.

MfE (2015b), *Making Collaborative Groups Work: A Guide for those involved in Collaborative Processes*, Wellington: Ministry for the Environment.

MfE (2013a), *Freshwater Reform 2013 and Beyond*, Ministry for the Environment, Wellington.

MfE (2013b), Collaborative Governance Research website, *www.mfe.govt.nz/about-us/who-we-work/collaborative-governance-research* (accessed October 2016).

MfE (2010a), Trends in the Amount of Land Irrigated by Consented Water Takes website, *www.mfe.govt.nz/more/environmental-reporting/reporting-act/fresh-water/freshwater-demand-indicator/freshwater-dema-2* (accessed July 2016).

MfE (2010b), Freshwater Demand (Allocation) website, *www.mfe.govt.nz/more/environmental-reporting/reporting-act/fresh-water/freshwater-demand-indicator/freshwater-demand* (accessed April 2016).

MfE (2010c), Allocation Compared with Renewable Freshwater Resource website, *www.mfe.govt.nz/more/environmental-reporting/reporting-act/fresh-water/freshwater-demand-indicator/freshwater-dema-0* (accessed July 2016).

MfE (2007), *Environment New Zealand 2007*, Ministry for the Environment, Wellington.

MfE and Statistics NZ (2015), *New Zealand's Environmental Reporting Series: Environment Aotearoa 2015*, Ministry for the Environment and Statistics New Zealand, Wellington, *www.mfe.govt.nz* and *www.stats.govt.nz*.

Ministry of Agriculture and Forestry (2009), *Meat: The future Opportunities and Challenges for the New Zealand Sheep, Meat and Beef sector over the Next 10 to 15 Years*, Ministry of Agriculture and Forestry, Wellington.

Ministry of Health (2016), Drinking-Water Legislation website, *www.health.govt.nz/our-work/environmental-health/drinking-water/drinking-water-legislation* (accessed May 2016).

Ministry of Health (2008), *Drinking-Water Standards for New Zealand 2005 (Revised 2008)*, Ministry of Health, Wellington.

Ministry of Health (2005), *Drinking-Water Standards for New Zealand 2005*, Ministry of Health, Wellington.

Moreau, M. and C. Daughney (2015), *Update of National Groundwater Quality Indicators: State and Trends December 2004-2013*, GNS Science Consultancy Report 2015/16, p. 38, report commissioned by the Ministry for the Environment, Wellington.

Morris, J.D.K. and J. Ruru (2010), "Giving voice to rivers: Legal personality as a vehicle for recognising Indigenous peoples' relationships to water", *Australian Indigenous Law Review*, Indigenous Law Centre, University of New South Wales, Vol. 14/2, pp. 49-62.

MPI (2016a), *Grant Funding for Community Irrigation Schemes or Strategic Water Management Studies Applicant Guidelines*, July 2016.

MPI (2016b), Irrigation Acceleration Fund website, *www.mpi.govt.nz/funding-and-programmes/farming/irrigation-acceleration-fund/* (accessed September 2016).

MPI (2015a), The Export Goal website, *www.mpi.govt.nz/about-mpi/our-strategy-2030-growing-and-protecting-new-zealand/the-export-goal/* (accessed April 2016).

MPI (2015b), *Situation and Outlook for Primary Industries 2015: December Update*, Ministry for Primary Industries, Wellington.

Murray, K., M. Sin and S. Wyatt (2014), *The costs and benefits of an allocation of freshwater to iwi*, Report prepared for the Iwi Advisors Group, 6 December 2014.

Murray-Darling Basin Ministerial Council (1995), *An Audit of Water Use in the Murray-Darling Basin Plan*, Murray-Darling Basin Ministerial Council, Canberra.

National Water Commission (2012), *Impacts of Water Trading in the southern Murray-Darling Basin between 2006-2007 and 2010-2011*, Commonwealth of Australia, Canberra.

New Zealand Freshwater Sciences Society (2014), *Feedback on the Proposed Amendments to The National Policy Statement for Freshwater Management (2011) and The National Objectives Framework*, 4 February 2014.

New Zealand Trade Manual (2016), Sustainable New Zealand website, *www.newzealandtrademanual.com/new-zealand-info/about-new-zealand/natural-new-zealand/sustainable-new-zealand/* (accessed August 2016).

NIWA (2001), Overview of New Zealand Climate website, National Institute of Water and Atmospheric Research, Auckland, *www.niwa.co.nz/education-and-training/schools/resources/climate/overview* (accessed April 2016).

NZIER (2014), *Value of Irrigation in New Zealand: An Economy-wide Assessment*, New Zealand Institute of Economic Research Inc and AgFirst Consultants NZ Ltd final report to the Ministry for Primary Industries.

NZIER (2010), *The Economic Impact of Increased Irrigation: A Dynamic Computable General Equilibrium Analysis of Increased Irrigation in New Zealand*, confidential report commissioned by the Final Report to Ministry of Agriculture and Forestry to New Zealand Institute of Economic Research.

OECD (forthcoming), *Diffuse Pollution, Degraded Waters: Emerging Policy Solutions*, OECD Publishing, Paris.

OECD (2016), *Recommendation of the Council on Water*, 13 December 2016 – C(2016)174/REV1/FINAL.

OECD (2015a), *OECD Economic Surveys: New Zealand 2015*, OECD Publishing, Paris, *http://dx.doi.org/10.1787/eco_surveys-nzl-2015-en.*

OECD (2015b), Water Resources Allocation: Sharing Risks and Opportunities, OECD Studies on Water, OECD Publishing, Paris, *http://dx.doi.org/10.1787/9789264229631-en.*

OECD (2015c), "The Lake Taupo Nitrogen market in New Zealand: Lessons in environmental policy reform", *OECD Environment Policy Papers*, No. 4, OECD Publishing, Paris.

OECD (2015d), Stakeholder Engagement for Inclusive Water Governance, OECD Studies on Water, OECD Publishing, Paris, *http://dx.doi.org/10.1787/9789264231122-en.*

OECD (2013a), *OECD Compendium of Agri-environmental Indicators*, OECD Publishing, Paris, *http://dx.doi.org/10.1787/9789264181151-en.*

OECD (2013b), *Providing Agri-environmental Public Goods through Collective Action*, OECD Publishing, *http://dx.doi.org/10.1787/9789264197213-en.*

OECD (2012), A Framework for Financing Water Resources Management, OECD Studies on Water, OECD Publishing, *http://dx.doi.org/10.1787/9789264179820-en.*

OECD (2009), *Managing Water for All – An OECD Perspective on Water Pricing and Financing*, OECD Publishing, Paris, *http://dx.doi.org/10.1787/ 9789264059498-en.*

OECD (2005), *Evaluating Agri-environmental Policies: Design, Practice and Results*, OECD Publishing, *http://dx.doi.org/10.1787/9789264010116-en.*

Office of the Auditor-General (2011), *Managing Freshwater Quality: Challenges for Regional Councils*, Office of the Auditor-General, Wellington, *www.oag.govt.nz/2011/freshwater/docs/managing-freshwater-quality.pdf.*

ONS (2016), Natural Capital: Overview of the ONS-Defra Natural Capital Project and all Related Publications website, *www.ons.gov.uk/economy/nationalaccounts/uksectoraccounts/methodologies/naturalcapital* (accessed June 2016).

OVERSEER (2016), OVERSEER® Nutrient Budgets: Supporting New Zealand's Primary Industries website, *http://overseer.org.nz/* (29 November 2016).

PCE (2016), *The state of New Zealand's environment: Commentary by the Parliamentary Commissioner for the Environment on 'Environment Aotearoa 2015'*, Parliamentary Commissioner for the Environment, Wellington.

PCE (2015), *Update Report – Water quality in New Zealand: Land use and nutrient pollution*, Parliamentary Commissioner for the Environment, Wellington.

PCE (2013), *Water quality in New Zealand: Land use and nutrient pollution*, Parliamentary Commissioner for the Environment, Wellington.

PCE (2012), *Water quality in New Zealand: Understanding the science*, Parliamentary Commissioner for the Environment, Wellington.

Patterson, M.G. and A.O. Cole (2013), "'Total economic value' of New Zealand's land-based ecosystems and their services" in Dymond, JR (ed). *Ecosystem services in New Zealand – Conditions and Trends*, Manaaki Whenua Press, Lincoln, New Zealand.

RadioNZ (2016), *Gastro bug hit 5000 in Havelock North*, 30 August 2016, *www.radionz.co.nz/news/national/312100/gastro-bug-hit-5000-in-havelock-north* (accessed August 2016).

Royal Society of New Zealand (2016), *Climate change Implications for New Zealand*, The Royal Society of New Zealand, Wellington.

Sachdeva, S. (2016), "Independent Inquiry into Havelock North Water Contamination gets under way", webpage, *www.stuff.co.nz/national/politics/84170801/independent-inquiry-into-havelock-north-water-contamination-gets-under-way* (accessed September 2016).

Salmond, A. (2014), "Tears of Rangi: Water power and people in New Zealand", *HAU: Journal of Ethnographic Theory*, Centre for Ethnographic Theory, London, Vol. 4/3, pp. 285-309.

Saunders, C., M. Guenther and T. Driver (2013), *The New Zealand Sustainability Dashboard: Sustainability Trends in Key Overseas Markets to New Zealand and the KPI identification database*, *https://research archive.lincoln.ac.nz/bitstream/handle/10182/6266/Saunders%20Sustainability%20trends.pdf?sequence=1* (accessed August 2016).

Scott, L. and C. Hanson (2015), *Risk Maps of Nitrate in Canterbury Groundwater*, Environment Canterbury, Christchurch.

Sinner, J. and J. Scherzer (2009), *Public Interest in Resource Rent*, *www.resourcerentalsrevenue.org/Public_Interest_in_Resource_Rent.html#top* (accessed October 2016).

Statistics NZ (2016), *Overseas Merchandise Trade: July 2016*, Statistics New Zealand, Wellington.

Statistics NZ (2012), Agricultural Production Statistics: June 2012 (final), Statistics New Zealand, Wellington.

Tourism Export Council (2016), "*TEC Supports Choose Clean Water webpage, Petition to Parliament*", *www.tourismexportcouncil.org.nz/tec-supports-choose-clean-water-petition-to-parliament/* (accessed July 2016).

Tourism New Zealand (2016), "*100% Pure New Zealand*", webpage, *www.newzealand.com/int/* (accessed August 2016).

Tourism New Zealand (2009), *Pure As: Celebrating 10 years of 100% Pure New Zealand*, Tourism New Zealand, Wellington.

Tukituki Catchment Proposal Board of Inquiry (2015), Final Report and Decision of the Board of Inquiry into the Tukituki Catchment Proposal in relation to the matters referred back to the Board by the High Court, 25 June 2015.

Unwin, M.J. and S.T. Larned (2013), *Statistical Models, Indicators and Trend Analyses for Reporting National-scale River Water Quality) (NEMAR Phase 3)*, report commissioned by the Ministry for the Environment, May 2013, National Institute of Water & Atmospheric Research Ltd, Christchurch.

Verburg, P. et al. (2010), *Lake Water Quality in New Zealand 2010: Status and Trends*, Prepared for MfE, August 2010, National Institute of Water & Atmospheric Research Ltd.

Waitangi Tribunal (2012), *The Stage I Report on the National Freshwater and Geothermal Resources claim*, The Waitangi Tribunal, Wellington.

Water UK (2013), *CAP Reform: A Future for Farming and Water*, Water UK, London, United Kingdom.

Weber, E.P., A. Memon and O. Painter (2011), "Science, society, and water resources in New Zealand: Recognizing and overcoming a societal impasse", *Journal of Environmental Policy and Planning*, Taylor & Francis, Vo. 13/1, pp. 46-69.

Webster-Brown, J. (2015), *Call for Cantabs to think about future of water*, Lincoln University Press Release, 13 April 2015.

Weeks, E.S. et al. (2016), "Conservation science statement. The demise of New Zealand's freshwater flora and fauna: A forgotten treasure", *Pacific Conservation Biology* Vol. 22/2, CSIRO Publishing, Clayton, pp. 110-115.

White, P.A., B.M.H. Sharp and R.R. Reeves (2004), *New Zealand Water Bodies of National Importance for Domestic use and Industrial Use*, report commissioned by the Ministry of Economic Development, Institute of Geological and Nuclear Sciences.

White, P.A. (2001), "Groundwater resources in New Zealand" in Rosen, M.R. and P.A. White (eds.), *Groundwaters of New Zealand*, New Zealand Hydrological Society, Wellington.

WRA (2016), Waikato River Authority website, *www.waikatoriver.org.nz/about-the-waikato-river-authority/purpose/* (accessed June 2016).

Young, R. (2013), "Water nitrate a risk to infant health", The Christchurch Press, 22 October 2013, *www.stuff.co.nz/the-press/news/canterbury/9309568/Water-nitrate-a-risk-to-infant-health* (accessed April 2016).

ANNEX 4.A

Comparison of EU Water Framework Directive ecological status and New Zealand ecosystem health classes

	WFD ECOLOGICAL STATUS CLASSES Normative definitions (Annex V)		NEW ZEALAND ATTRIBUTE STATES Attribute tables – narrative attribute states
High	The values for the biological quality elements reflect those normally associated with undisturbed conditions for that type and show no, or only very minor, evidence of distortion. There must be no, or only very minor, alterations to the values of the physico-chemical (and hydromorphological) elements from those normally associated with undisturbed conditions for the type. Example – lake algae/plants and nutrients The taxonomic composition and abundance of phytoplankton, macrophytes and phytobenthos correspond totally or nearly totally to undisturbed conditions. The average phytoplankton biomass is consistent with the type-specific physico-chemical conditions and is not as such to significantly alter the type-specific transparency conditions. There are no detectable changes in the average macrophytic and the average phytobenthic abundance. Planktonic blooms occur at a frequency and intensity consistent with the type specific physico-chemical conditions. Nutrient concentrations remain within the range normally associated with undisturbed conditions.	**A**	Lake ecological communities are healthy and resilient, similar to natural reference conditions.
Good	There are low levels of distortion to the biological elements due to human activity, but the values must deviate only slightly from those associated with undisturbed conditions. The physico-chemical conditions must support the biological values and ecosystem functioning. Example – lake algae/plants and nutrients There are slight changes in the composition and abundance of planktonic, macrophytic and phytobenthic taxa compared to the type-specific communities. Such changes do not indicate any accelerated growth of algae resulting in undesirable disturbance to the balance of organisms present in the water body or to the physico-chemical quality of the water or sediment. A slight increase in the frequency and intensity of the type specific planktonic blooms may occur. The phytobenthic community is not adversely affected by bacterial tufts and coats present due to anthropogenic activity. Nutrient concentrations do not exceed the levels established so as to ensure the functioning of the ecosystem and the achievement of the values specified above for the biological quality elements. **WFD default objective is Good/Moderate boundary. A less stringent objective – the highest achievable – can be set based on disproportionate cost or technical infeasibility.**	**B**	Lake ecological communities are slightly impacted by additional algal and plant growth arising from nutrients levels that are elevated above natural reference conditions.
Moderate	There are moderate levels of distortion to the biological elements due to human activity, and the values deviate moderately from those associated with undisturbed conditions. The physico-chemical conditions are consistent with the biological values. Example – lake algae/plants and nutrients The composition and abundance of planktonic taxa differ moderately from the type-specific communities. Phytoplankton biomass is moderately disturbed and may be such as to produce a significant undesirable disturbance in the condition of other biological quality elements and the physico-chemical quality of the water or sediment. A moderate increase in the frequency and intensity of planktonic blooms may occur. Persistent blooms may occur during summer months. The composition of macrophytic and phytobenthic taxa differ moderately from the type-specific communities and are significantly more distorted than those observed at good quality. Moderate changes in the average macrophytic and the average phytobenthic abundance are evident. The phytobenthic community may be interfered with, and, in some areas, displaced by bacterial tufts and coats present as a result of anthropogenic activities. Nutrient conditions consistent with the achievement of the values specified above for the biological quality elements.	**C**	Lake ecological communities are moderately impacted by additional algal and plant growth arising from nutrients levels that are elevated well above natural reference conditions. **National Bottom Line at boundary between C and D, compulsory regardless of cost**
Poor	Waters showing evidence of major alterations to the values of the biological quality elements for the surface water body type and in which the relevant biological communities deviate substantially from those normally associated with the surface water body type under undisturbed conditions, shall be classified as poor.	**D**	Lake ecological communities have undergone or are at high risk of a regime shift to a persistent, degraded state, due to impacts of elevated nutrients leading to excessive algal and/or plant growth, as well as from losing oxygen in bottom waters of deep lakes.
Bad	Waters showing evidence of severe alterations to the values of the biological quality elements for the surface water body type and in which large portions of the relevant biological communities normally associated with the surface water body type under undisturbed conditions are absent, shall be classified as bad.		

Source: Extract from report compiled by Simon Leaf (Environment Agency, England) and Vera Power (Ministry for the Environment, New Zealand), May 2016.

PART II

Chapter 5

Sustainable urban development

This chapter discusses the economic and environmental conditions of New Zealand's urban areas, with a particular focus on Auckland. It examines the main challenges of cities to advance sustainable urban development, and reviews the main policies and measures in place to address them. This includes urban policies for land use, sustainable transport and buildings, and waste and water management, as well as the role of multi-level governance, investment and finance.

1. Introduction

Cities play a disproportionately large role in the economic and environmental performance of countries. As hubs for productivity, job creation and innovation, they generate about 80% of global gross domestic product (GDP). At the same time, cities account for roughly 70% of global energy use and related greenhouse gas (GHG) emissions (New Climate Economy, 2014). The environmental impact of cities on their residents and countries is shaped by a range of factors, including their geographical setting, citizens' lifestyle and by the way urban growth is planned and managed. For example, uncontrolled urban sprawl and outmoded transport systems can exacerbate pollution and associated environmental risks and socio-economic costs. In turn, environmental quality such as clean air and green spaces are key for cities' overall liveability and longer-term competitiveness. Policy and investment decisions in urban areas thus have a strong influence on achieving national environmental and green growth goals.

New Zealand is one of the least densely populated countries in the world, but also one of the most urbanised. While environmental quality of life of the urban population is relatively high, sustained population growth in all major cities is putting pressure on infrastructure and the environment, particularly in Auckland, the country's largest city. The challenge for New Zealand cities is, therefore, to accommodate larger populations while making more efficient use of space and infrastructure, and enhancing environmental sustainability and well-being. Many cities have committed to sustainable urban development[1] and established environmental performance goals. For example, Auckland adopted a vision of becoming the world's most liveable city, while Wellington aspires to become an eco-city with an environmental leadership role. Several cities adopted the vision of a more compact form, with the aim to reap economic and social benefits from agglomeration and to reduce potential environmental impacts of urban sprawl. However, institutional fragmentation, a complex urban planning system with poor linkages between land use, transport and infrastructure policies, and lack of community support have prevented significant progress towards this objective.

2. An overview of New Zealand cities: Socio-economic trends and environmental performance

2.1. Population and socio-economic trends

New Zealand is a highly urbanised country, even though it hosts few large cities by international standards. In 2014, 86% of the population lived in urban areas, a share projected to reach 90% in 2050 (UN, 2014).[2] Auckland is by far the largest city, accommodating 1.45 million people in 2015, or one-third of the New Zealand population. The two second-biggest cities – Wellington, the capital city, and Christchurch – accommodate nearly 400 000 inhabitants, respectively. Most other cities are significantly smaller (Figure 5.1).

All major cities (with population over 50 000) saw their population increase since 2000 (Figure 5.1). Together, they have accommodated nearly 80% of the country's total population

Figure 5.1. **Population in New Zealand's largest cities and towns is growing**

City	Population 2015	(Share in country)	Change since 2000
Auckland	1 453 800	(32%)	+30%
Wellington	398 200	(9%)	+13%
Christchurch	381 800	(8%)	+11%
Hamilton	224,000	(5%)	+31%
Tauranga	130 800	(3%)	+36%
Napier-Hastings	129 700	(3%)	+11%
Dunedin	117 300	(3%)	+5%
Palmerston North	83 500	(2%)	+10%
Nelson	64 800	(1%)	+19%
Rotorua	56 800	(1%)	+4%
New Plymouth	56 300	(1%)	+14%
Whangarei	55 300	(1%)	+16%
Invercargill	50 300	(1%)	+8%
Wanganui	39 400	(1%)	+16%

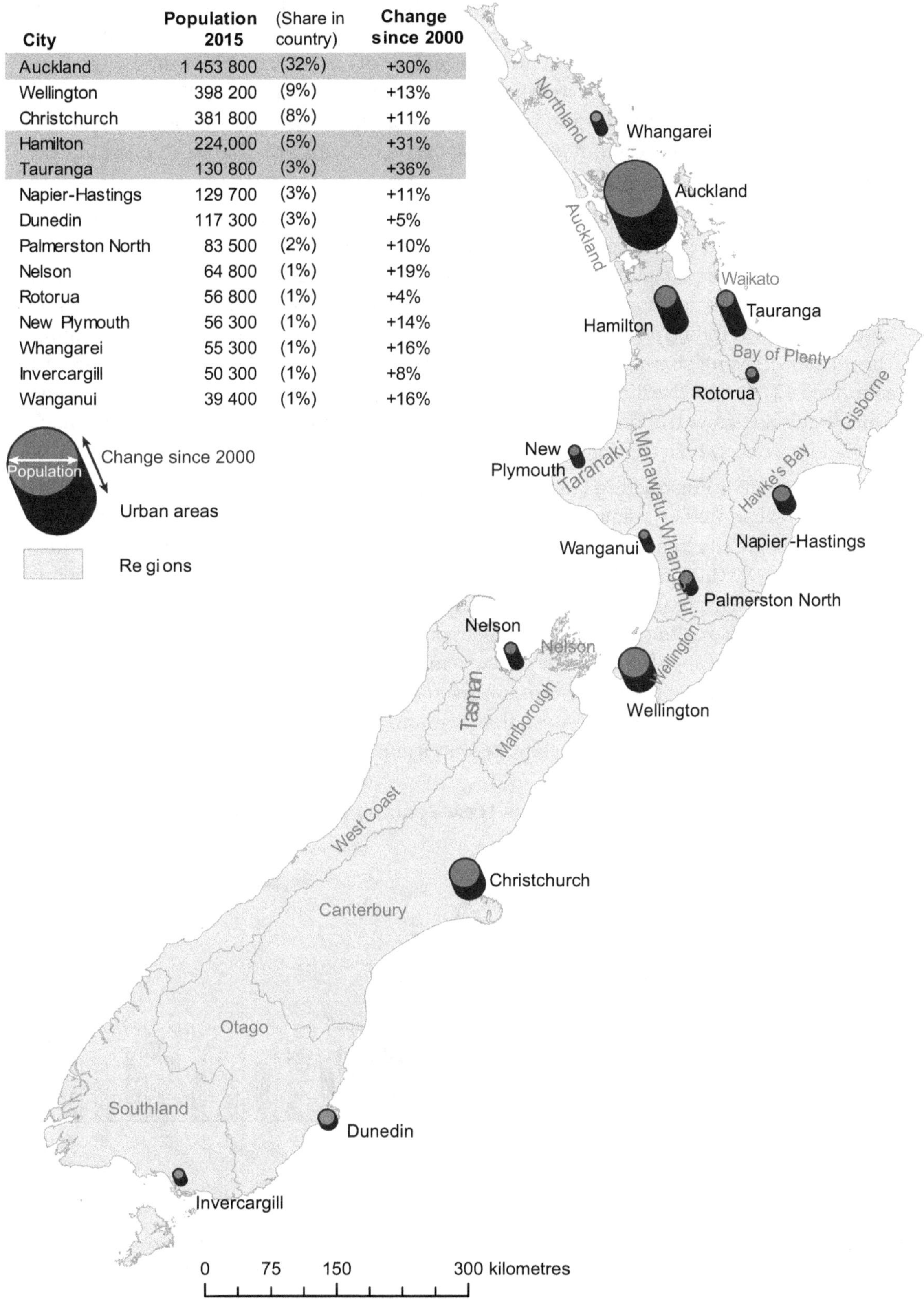

Source: Based on Statistics NZ (2016), "Estimated resident population for urban areas, at 30 June (1996+) (Annual-June)".

growth. Growth has been unequally distributed and concentrated primarily in the wider Auckland region (Auckland and its two neighbouring cities of Hamilton and Tauranga saw their population increase by roughly 30% each since 2000; see Figure 5.3). Growth has been driven by a mix of natural population increase (excess of births over deaths) and migration, which reached a record high of nearly 1% of the total population in 2014 (Chapter 1). Auckland's population is expected to increase by more than 40% over the next 25 years (to reach 2 million in 2040), accommodating 55% of the country's total projected population growth (Statistics NZ, 2016, 2015).

Sustained population growth has led to bottlenecks in transport, water and social infrastructure, and it has contributed to an overheated property market, notably in Auckland. House prices in Auckland have increased by 52% since mid-2012 (the beginning of the recent upswing), compared to 11% in the rest of New Zealand (Kendall, 2016). Rising house prices are eroding affordability and raise financial-stability risks (OECD, forthcoming). The current housing shortage in Auckland is estimated at about 20 000-35 000 homes. An estimated 13 000 new dwellings would be needed per year to accommodate rising demand from population growth and immigration over the next 30 years – more than twice as much as what is currently built (Auckland Council, 2012a).

Housing and infrastructure bottlenecks may become a barrier to economic growth, by restricting labour mobility, reducing incentives for firms to locate in the city and, ultimately, curbing productivity benefits from scale and agglomeration economies that larger cities usually offer (NZPC, 2016; OECD, forthcoming, 2015a). Auckland is New Zealand's economic powerhouse, accounting for more than one-third of national gross domestic product (GDP) (Figure 5.2). It is home to the country's major commercial and manufacturing centres, and serves as the largest logistics node for imports and exports by both air and sea. Productivity levels are higher than in the rest of the country and per capita income is above the national average (Figure 5.2). However, the Auckland premium in terms of GDP per capita has fallen over the past decade (OECD, forthcoming). The city's annual GDP growth (2.7%) has been above

Figure 5.2. **Auckland is New Zealand's economic hub**

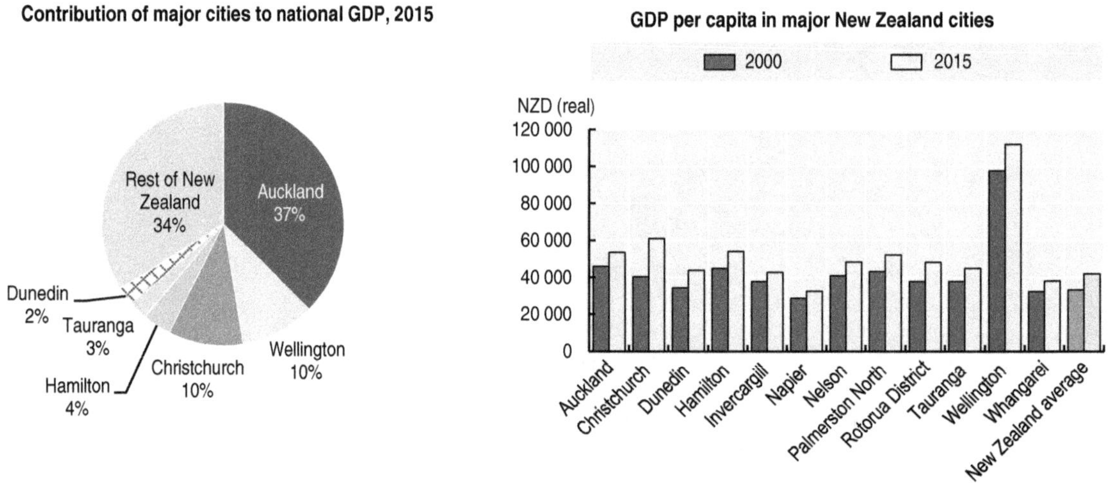

Note: Estimates are based on city (or district) council territorial data and hence may differ from the GDP generated by the functional urban area of the respective city. Data are at a more detailed level of granularity than are available in the Statistics New Zealand official Tier1 regional GDP series. They are experimental in nature and should be used with caution.

Source: MBIE (2016), *Modelled Territorial Authority Gross Domestic Product* (database).

StatLink http://dx.doi.org/10.1787/888933460032

the national average (2.5%) since 2000, yet not growing as fast as a number of rural municipalities and other major cities (i.e. Christchurch, Hamilton and Tauranga) (MBIE, 2016).

Despite these pressures, quality of life in New Zealand's cities is generally high. Most dwellers (78%) agree their city is a great place to live, mainly for the good lifestyle provided, easy access to vast green areas and the beauty of the natural environment (Colmar Brunton, 2016). Per capita income is higher than the national average in most cities (Figure 5.2), at levels similar to those of major Australian cities. Wellington (which is home to the central government) stands out, with income levels that are almost three times higher than the national average and roughly twice that of Auckland and Christchurch (Figure 5.2). Spatial inequalities are also evident within cities: wealthier and more educated people cluster in inner suburbs and suburbs with natural amenities, while those who earn less and who are less educated tend to live in the outer suburbs (NZPC, 2016).

2.2. *Urban expansion, density and urban form*

Most New Zealand cities are expanding to accommodate their growing populations. The built-up area of the three biggest cities (Auckland, Wellington and Christchurch) increased by about 10% over 2001-13, and even faster in Hamilton (+16%) and Tauranga (+25%) (Nunns, 2014a). In the fastest-growing cities, the rate of urban expansion was slower than population growth, meaning that average population density (the number of residents per square kilometre of urbanised land) has increased. However, urban expansion outpaced population growth in a number of smaller cities, including Dunedin, Nelson and the Napier-Hastings urban area. Christchurch experienced the strongest decrease in population density, which reflects strong population growth outside the former city boundaries due to resettlements following the 2011 Canterbury earthquake.[3] In Auckland, average population density increased by 11% over 2001-13 (Nunns, 2014a).

Even though some cities have become denser overall, New Zealand cities remain relatively low density by global standards. As in many "new world" countries, New Zealand cities have largely developed in tandem with the expansion of motorisation and cheap energy, which has favoured dispersed settlement patterns, with spread-out buildings and large areas devoted to roads and parking. This adds to a strong preference among New Zealand dwellers for stand-alone houses over apartments (more than 80% of dwellers prefer to live in a stand-alone home), and a high valuation of space as compared to a shorter commuting time (Howden-Chapman et al., 2015). Auckland features the highest average population density in the country (at about 2 700 people per square kilometre), similar to that of Melbourne in Australia (Nunns, 2014a). However, as shown by Figure 5.3, the urban form of the two cities differs; Auckland has a small, high-density central business district (CBD) and some other small employment centres with elevated population densities, while Melbourne features a significantly larger and continuous high-density centre. Wellington also has a small single centre; Christchurch's city districts are equally low density.

Many New Zealand cities have adopted policies to increase their population densities (including Auckland, Wellington, Hamilton and Christchurch), motivated by economic benefits from agglomeration, as well as environmental benefits associated with denser development (Box 5.1). However, as in many cities in the OECD, most urban growth has occurred at the city fringes, rather than in inner-city areas and growth corridors targeted for development (OECD, 2012). In Auckland, nearly 70% of urban growth between 2006 and 2013 occurred in the suburbs (more than 10 km away from the city centre), with about 40% occurring in the outer suburbs (more than 20 km away) (NZPC, 2016).

Figure 5.3. **Auckland has a polycentric structure with few small high-density areas**

Population densities in selected OECD cities

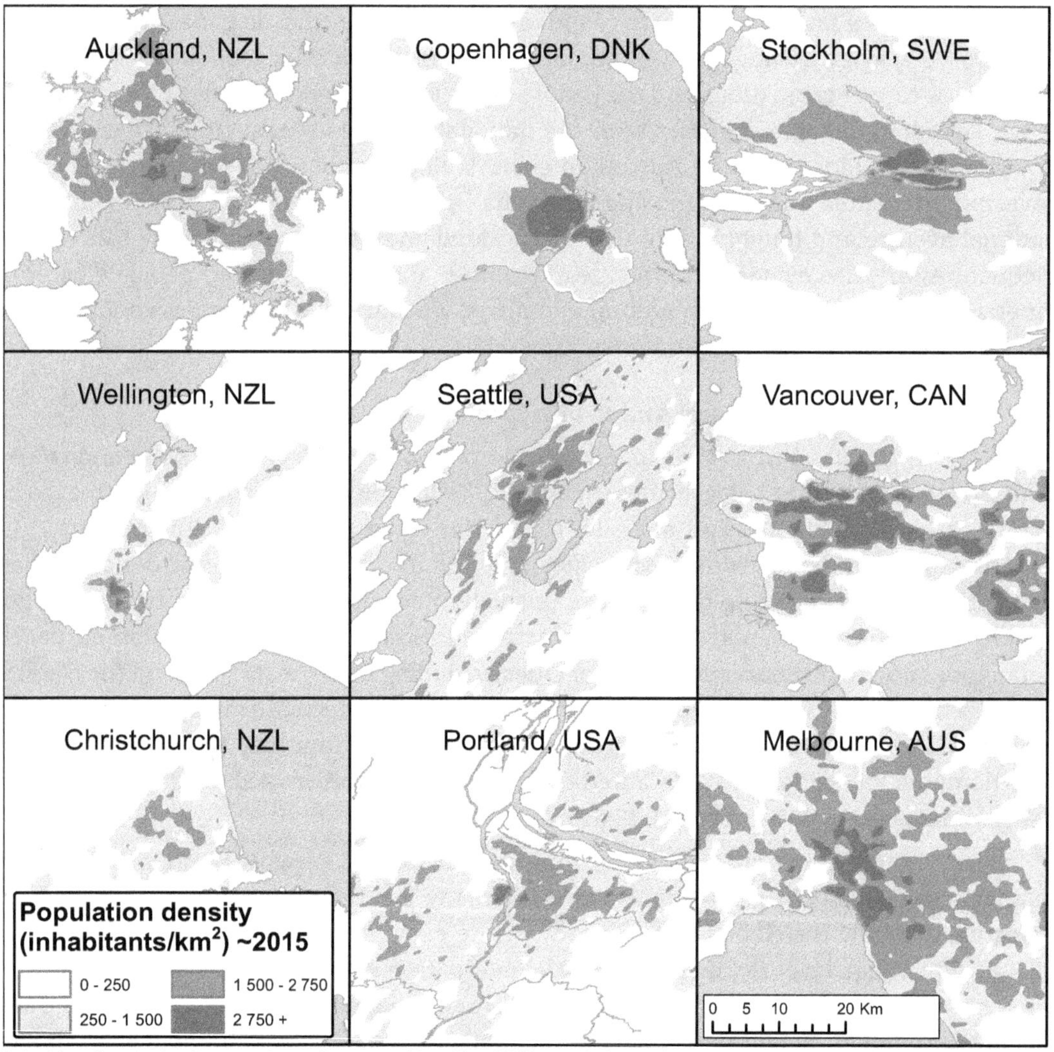

Note: Not all water bodies are shown for some cities. The 2015 population estimates are extrapolated from 2004-14 census data.

Source: Based on Center for International Earth Science Information Network/NASA Socioeconomic Data and Applications Center, Gridded Population of the World, Version 4; OpenStreetMap; regional and national mapping agencies.

Box 5.1. **Density, environmental sustainability and the dilemma of new world cities**

Rapid increase of urban sprawl (i.e. uncontrolled and fragmented low-density urban expansion) in many countries worldwide has become a major concern because of its detrimental effects on the environment. Low-density development may be appealing for the private parking spaces and large backyards and a relatively "green" urban ambience. However, low-density and sprawling cities are often associated with heavy reliance on private motor vehicles (with associated GHG emissions and local air pollutants); higher costs for infrastructure and public service provision; and greater demand for open space and farmland to the detriment of biodiversity.

Box 5.1. Density, environmental sustainability and the dilemma of new world cities *(cont.)*

OECD (2012) makes an important distinction between *dense* cities (which have a high number of residents per square kilometre) and *compact* cities. The latter encompasses a wider set of characteristics, such as dense and proximate development (e.g. close or continuous urban agglomerations, distinct borders between urban and rural land use, and secured public space in the urban area), linkages to public transport systems and accessibility to local services and jobs (e.g. mixed land use and accessible local services by foot or public transport). A compact urban form can bring about economic benefits (e.g. labour productivity, reduced infrastructure costs, more efficient land use), social benefits (e.g. greater access to services and improved health) and environmental benefits (e.g. lower air pollution and GHG emissions from transport, lower energy consumption, and conservation of farmland and ecosystems). If proper account of externalities to air, water and land can be incorporated in the cost of services from the outset, the sustainability of urban environments can be significantly improved. However, it is a much more difficult task to retrofit existing urban settings.

Growing concern about air pollution, climate change and pressure on scarce environmental resources has caused many city authorities to question the long-run sustainability of their urban form. In addition to managing urban sprawl, several cities try to improve resource efficiency and reduce environmental pressure by changing residential densities in certain areas. However, *ex post* densification can be politically difficult because changes to regulatory requirements effectively alter the bundle of property rights and expectations of homeowners. Increasing residential density thus needs to be approached carefully to ensure buy-in from the affected population. In addition, simply doubling the population of a given area without changing any other parameters can intensify negative factors such as ambient air pollution, congestion or lack of green open space. Indeed, many cities feature high population densities without experiencing any of the economic, environmental or social benefits ascribed to the compact city. Empirical research questions the longstanding wisdom that denser cities are greener (Fruits, 2011; Gaigné, Riou and Thisse, 2012). Notwithstanding, many of the principles and policies underlying compact development policies – such as co-ordinated land use and infrastructure planning, mixed use, transit-oriented development, careful planning of green spaces, avoidance of leapfrog development – can help improve cities' socio-economic and environmental performance, be it in compact or lower-density urban settlements.

2.3. Urban mobility

Urban mobility in New Zealand is characterised by an overwhelming reliance on private car use. With the exception of Wellington, dwellers in major cities travel more than 90% of total distance travelled in motor vehicles (Figure 5.4). Large roads and plentiful parking spaces make it easy to use cars in urban settings; meanwhile, the favourable tax treatment of company cars and parking lots encourages private car use and long-distance commuting (Chapter 3). The level of public transport has increased in all major cities (except Dunedin) since 2002, but it remains low compared to other countries (Ministry of Transport, 2014; NZPC, 2016). The level of active transport modes (e.g. walking and cycling) is on the rise in some cities, notably in Wellington (26% since 2000), Auckland (29%) and Dunedin (40%). Wellington features the highest share of distance travelled in public transport (Figure 5.5); it also has the largest proportion of commuters travelling by active transport modes. This has

Figure 5.4. **Urban mobility heavily relies on private car use, yet public and active transport is on the rise**

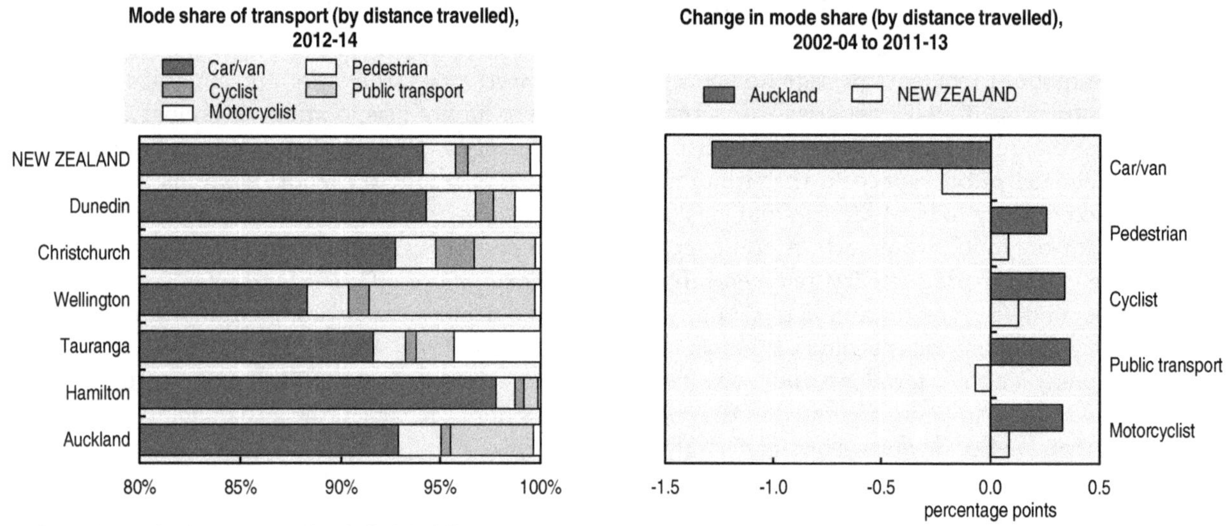

Note: Data refer to main urban areas as defined by Statistics NZ.
Source: Ministry of Transport (2014), *New Zealand Household Travel Survey Regional Results 2003-2014.*

StatLink http://dx.doi.org/10.1787/888933460048

helped congestion levels remain relatively static over 2005-10 (MBIE and LGNZ, 2012). The uptake of electric vehicles in New Zealand has been limited to date (about 1 800 vehicles) (Chapter 3).

In the Auckland region, the increase in population has prompted a 25% surge in the total vehicle kilometres travelled since 2000 (Ministry of Transport, 2015). Investment in the road network has helped accommodate increased road use and maintain congestion levels at roughly the same levels over the 2000s (Auckland Council, 2016). However, congestion remains high: Auckland is considered to be the second most congested city in Oceania after Sydney, despite its relatively small size (TomTom, 2016). Congestion is estimated to cost Auckland NZD 1.25 billion annually (Wallis and Lupton, 2013). The city's geography means that transport demand is focused into narrow corridors, which increases congestion and limits opportunities for further road extension. Alternative transport modes (e.g. public and active transport) increased over the past decade (Figure 5.4). Upgrades of the rail network helped increase rail patronage from 2.5 million to nearly 14 million trips per year between 2003 and 2015; total public transport boardings increased by 60% over 2005-15 (Ministry of Transport, 2016; see also Section 7). Still, nine out of ten Aucklanders drive to work and public transport use per capita is noticeably lower than in other cities in the region, such as Melbourne, Brisbane or Perth (Auckland Council, 2014a; Nunns, 2014b).

2.4. *Key environmental trends*

Greenhouse gas emissions

While lack of long-term data and differences in reporting methods impede a detailed analysis and benchmarking of urban GHG emissions in New Zealand cities, available data suggest that the three largest cities (Auckland, Wellington and Christchurch) emit fewer GHG emissions per capita than a number of cities in Australia, Canada and the United States (Figure 5.5). The transport sector accounts for the bulk of urban GHG emissions (roughly 40% of emissions in Auckland, 50% in Wellington and 60% in Christchurch), which reflects

Figure 5.5. **Urban greenhouse gas emissions are lower than in a number of cities in Australia, Canada and the United States**

CO_2 emissions per capita

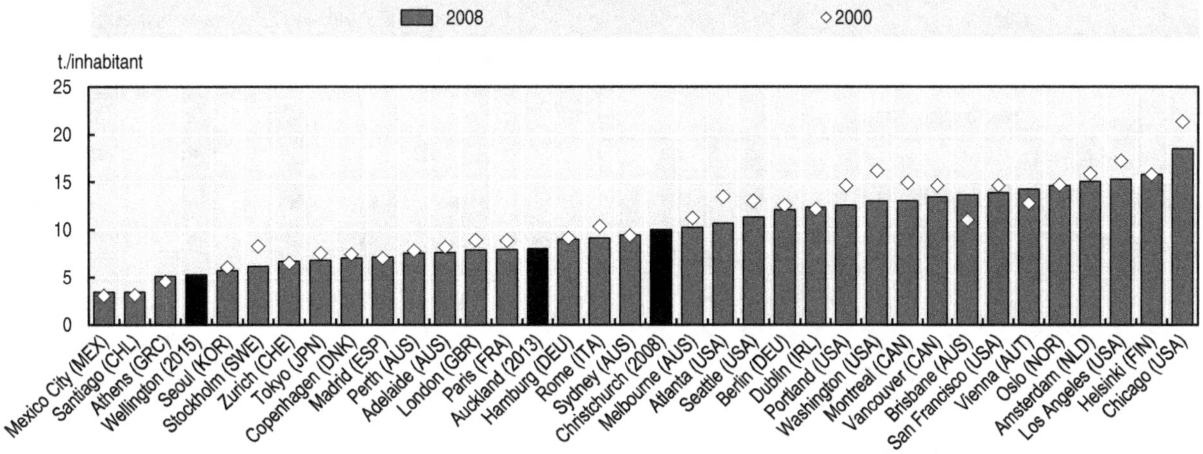

Note: Data are not fully comparable. OECD data refer to CO_2 emissions per capita in metropolitan regions (based on commuting data); Auckland data refer to regional data on GHG emissions per capita.

Source: Auckland Council (2015), *Auckland's Greenhouse Gas Inventory for 2013*; Auckland Council (2014), *Assessing the Carbon Abatement Reduction Potential in Auckland's Energy Resilience and Low Carbon Action Plan*; OECD (2016), "Metropolitan areas", *OECD Regional database*, Wellington Council (2016), *Draft Low Carbon Capital Plan;* Christchurch City Council (n.d.), *Climate Smart Strategy 2010-2025.*

StatLink http://dx.doi.org/10.1787/888933460055

New Zealand's relatively clean power sector (which lowers emissions from non-transport energy use; see Chapter 1), as well as urban forms that favour private motor vehicles as the primary way to travel within cities. The transport sector has also driven much of the increase in total GHG emissions since 2000 in these three cities (or counteracted emission reductions in other sectors).[4]

Some city and regional councils have developed strategies and policies on climate change. Auckland aspires to halve GHG emissions by 2050 from 1990 levels, which aligns with New Zealand's national target (see Chapter 1). According to internal analysis, this target could be reached if all the abatement measures listed in Auckland's Energy Resilience and Low Carbon Action Plan were implemented (Auckland Council, 2014b). Christchurch aspires to halve emissions by 2050 from 2008 levels; Wellington seeks to reduce emissions by 80% by 2050 from 2001 levels. The New Zealand Productivity Commission noted the need for a better understanding of factors shaping GHG emissions in New Zealand's cities to develop adequate policy responses (NZPC, 2016). Given the role cities play in achieving national climate change targets, this should also involve improving the quality, timeliness and comparability of urban GHG emissions for New Zealand's major cities.

Air emissions and air quality

New Zealand's cities measure up well in air quality against many other cities in OECD member countries; and they generally remain below the guideline for annual average particulate concentrations (PM_{10}) established by the World Health Organization (WHO). Christchurch registers the highest average annual concentration levels among New Zealand cities (Figure 5.6). This is related to the city's geography and climate (which traps air pollution at low altitude above the city) and the prevalence of burning wood or coal for domestic heating. Other cities, including Auckland and Wellington, have more favourable climatic conditions, benefiting from strong winds that help disperse air pollutants. Average

Figure 5.6. **Urban air quality is good compared with many other cities in the OECD**

PM concentrations in selected cities in New Zealand and the OECD, 2014 or latest available year | **Composition of air emissions in Auckland, 2006**

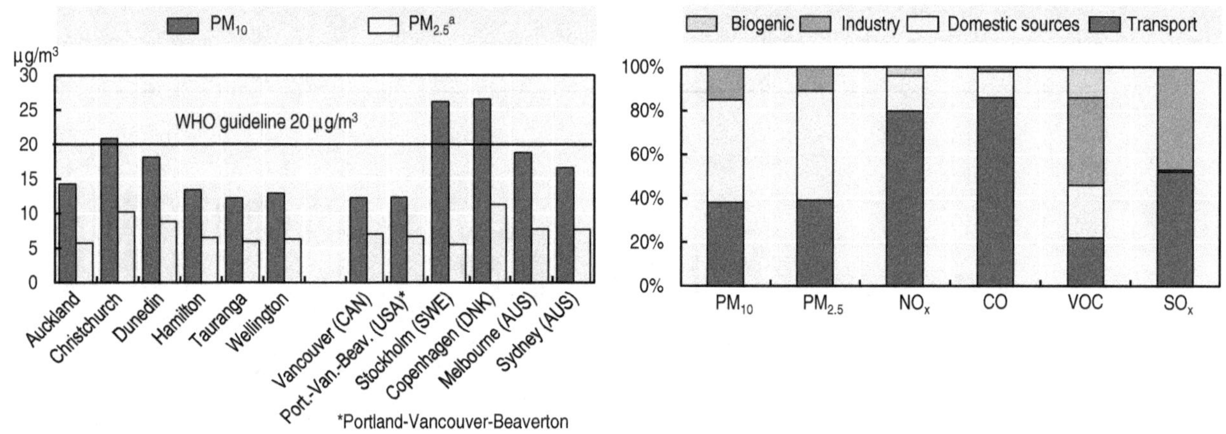

a) Converted values to be considered indicative only, as conversion factors are approximative.
Source: Auckland Council (2014), *Auckland Air Emissions Inventory 2006*; WHO (2016), *WHO Global Urban Ambient Air Pollution* (database).

StatLink http://dx.doi.org/10.1787/888933460064

annual PM_{10} concentrations declined in all of New Zealand's five biggest cities over 2000-12, driven mostly by lower emissions from wood and coal burning from domestic heating. However, several cities still fail to meet the national standard of short-term PM_{10} exposure each year (MfE, 2014). Exceedances occur typically in winter, when emissions from wood and coal burning for domestic heating are high, as well as in areas close to state highways and arterial roads (which are heavily used by diesel-power heavy vehicles).[5]

In Auckland, air quality has improved significantly due to a shift away from coal and wood for both domestic heating and industrial use (which contributed to a slight reduction in PM_{10} and $PM_{2.5}$ emissions), as well as more efficient vehicle technology and cleaner fuels (which drove down CO, NO_x and SO_x emissions) (Auckland Council, 2014c). However, the increase in vehicle numbers, kilometres travelled and the age of the vehicle fleet have somewhat offset better environmental performance of vehicles, with transport remaining a major emission source of air pollutants (Figure 5.6). Air pollution is estimated to cause 300 premature deaths and impose a social cost of NZD 1.1 billion per year in Auckland, of which 120 deaths and NZD 466 million stem from transport-related pollution (Auckland Council, 2015c, 2014c). The Auckland Low Carbon Action Plan aims for a 50% reduction in PM_{10} emissions by 2016, compared to 2006 levels, and a further 20% reduction by 2040 (Auckland Council, 2014d). This target will be challenging to achieve given projected increases in vehicle PM_{10} emissions.

Waste generation and management

A number of cities started implementing policies to reduce waste generation and encourage recycling. However, lack of comprehensive data impedes benchmarking of cities and the tracking of progress towards locally defined objectives. Auckland estimates that 1.2 million tonnes of waste were landfilled in 2010, of which 80% was commercial and industrial waste and 20% household waste. On a per capita basis, this suggests municipal waste generation in the order of 160 kg per person (this compares to an OECD average of 520 kg, reflecting the partiality, and hence incomparability, of data) (OECD, 2016a). The 2012

Auckland Waste Minimisation Plan aims to reduce household waste per capita by 30% by 2018 and sets an aspirational target of zero waste by 2040. Monitoring progress towards these targets will require significant improvement in data collection and reporting. The Wellington region has implemented recycling requirements, which helped reduce the total amount of waste to landfill by about 15% between 2005/06 and 2009/10 (Morrison Low, 2011). Some cities use the polluter pays principle to manage waste collection and disposal, with some evidence showing this has encouraged more efficient use of resources (Section 6.4).

Water quality

Freshwater quality is generally lower in waterways running through urban areas (NZPC, 2016). This is because many New Zealand cities are located near the coast and hence downstream of freshwater streams, where nutrient and sediment pollution from agriculture accumulate. Urban activities add to this pollution through municipal wastewater discharges; stormwater discharges; sediment loss and stream modification from land development; industrial discharges; and contamination from roads and vehicle use. In Auckland, more than half of freshwater streams (54%) are in a degraded or poor state, mainly due to discharges from urban sewage and stormwater systems (Auckland Council, 2015c). Auckland's estuaries and harbours are pressured by high and increasing nitrogen loads from nearby agricultural activity (mostly from dairy farms in the neighbouring Hauraki plains), contamination from heavy metals (with most hotspots being near ports, marinas, landfills and industrial activity), as well as high levels of sediment from both agricultural and urban sources (Hauraki Gulf Forum, 2014). Only 25% of Auckland's marine waters were rated to have good or excellent water quality, while 44% registered fair and 31% poor quality (Auckland Council, 2015c).

Urban water supply and consumption

Urban drinking water quality is good and compliance with national drinking water standards has increased over the past few years, reflecting tighter regulation and more investment in water treatment. An estimated 96% of the urban population is now connected to wastewater treatment services (NZPC, 2016). However, sewerage and stormwater infrastructure have not kept pace with population growth and are operating at capacity limits in several fast-growing cities (including Auckland and Hamilton). This leads to frequent overflows of (largely) untreated wastewater and stormwater into watercourses and harbours, with severe impacts on water quality.

In 2014/15, several cities issued water restrictions (including Wellington), suggesting there is pressure on the availability of water for urban supply (Water New Zealand, 2016). Freshwater abstraction for public water supply (in per capita terms) is one of the highest in the OECD (Chapter 1). However, per capita water consumption varies significantly across the country. Cities charging by volume (e.g. Auckland, Tauranga and Nelson) register significantly lower consumption levels than those that do not (e.g. Wellington and Christchurch) (see Figure 5.9 and Section 6.4).

Biodiversity and access to green open spaces

New Zealand cities have some significant remnant habitats. The Auckland region alone contains at least 37 distinct types of land and freshwater ecosystems and hosts over 20 000 plant and animal species, including several endemic ones (Auckland Council, 2016b). However, loss and fragmentation of native habitats from urban growth and invasive species put many species under threat. Despite covering only 2% of national land mass, the Auckland region is home to about one-fifth of nationally threatened terrestrial vertebrates and plants. By contrast, Auckland and some other cities have better birdlife than some rural areas. This is due to major pest eradication programmes and pest-free bird sanctuaries (such as the Karori Sanctuary in Wellington and on some islands in Auckland harbours), as well as better control of national pests like possums (Meurk, Blaschke and Simcock, 2009; Auckland Council, 2015c).

New Zealand's urban areas are generally green and city parks and forests more accessible than in cities elsewhere. In three out of four neighbourhoods, some kind of park is generally accessible in less than three minutes by car (Meurk, Blaschke and Simcoe, 2009). Within Auckland's urban areas, green open spaces (including urban forest, wetlands, parks and sports fields) occupy 25% of land (Auckland Council, 2015c). However, urban green spaces often have low levels of indigenous biodiversity, limited to lawns, shrubs, trees and potential pests (Meurk, Blaschke and Simcoe, 2009). Native ecosystems within Auckland's urban area have increased by 4 km^2 since 2001; this is due mostly to forest planting around the margins of larger native remnants and the replacement of exotic forest and scrub with native species on islands in the Hauraki Gulf. Parkland has decreased by 3% since 2001 (Auckland Council, 2015c).

3. The institutional framework for urban planning

Institutional and governance arrangements have important consequences for the economic, social and environmental performance of cities. The better governance arrangements work for co-ordinating policies across policy fields and jurisdictions, the better the outcomes in the three above-mentioned areas. Co-ordination is particularly important where local administrative borders do not match the functional reality of the city, which is the case for most cities in New Zealand and other OECD member countries (OECD, 2015b).

3.1. *Local governance*

New Zealand has a centralised unitary form of government, in which the central government has delegated certain regulatory powers to sub-national authorities (Chapter 2): regional councils, territorial authorities (city and district councils) and so-called unitary authorities (which combine the function of local and regional governments).[6] Local institutional arrangements vary; some city councils govern the entire urban area (e.g. Hamilton), some govern the entire urban area plus the surrounding rural area (e.g. Dunedin) and other cities spread over the administrative boundaries of several territorial authorities (e.g. Wellington and Auckland until 2010). The mismatch of administrative and geographical boundaries creates governance challenges, particularly for managing development in peri-urban areas and city- or region-wide infrastructure planning and investment. The city of Tauranga, for example, has traditionally managed growth at the city fringe by moving the local authority boundary. In this way, new suburbs over the border all fall within the same jurisdiction (NZPC, 2015). The Environment Court has to resolve quite a few inconsistencies between regional and district land-use plans.

The make-up of Auckland's institutions changed significantly in 2010 with a national law bringing the region's seven city and district councils and the regional council into a unitary authority, called Auckland Council. This decision aimed to overcome weak regional governance and institutional co-operation, which had previously constrained effective urban planning and management (Box 5.2). The new body inherited all the regulatory and

Box 5.2. **Reforming local governance: The creation of Auckland Council**

In response to demands for a more strategic approach to urban planning in Auckland, the central government established a Royal Commission of Inquiry to review Auckland's local government arrangements in 2007. The commission's report recognised a number of challenges, including inefficient public transport, congestion, delays in consenting processes and poorly co-ordinated urban growth (RCAG, 2009). The commission linked these challenges mainly to fragmented governance and weak regional leadership, as well as poor community engagement. The national government responded with the 2009 Local Government (Auckland Council) Act, which amalgamated Auckland's eight sub-national authorities into a single body. The new Auckland Council, elected for the first time in 2010, has the same powers and functions as other councils in New Zealand, yet significantly greater scale and capability. With about 10 000 employees, it is now the largest local authority in Australasia. The mayor was given unprecedented powers, including to prepare the budget, set committee structures and appoint advisory boards. Key functions and assets were placed into fewer council-controlled commercial organisations (CCOs) to improve service delivery, integrated planning and fiscal performance.[a]

In 2015, a Sustainability Office was created within the Auckland Council to mainstream sustainability within the council and its associated agencies. The council also established Development Auckland as a new CCO to increase the city's urban development capacity, addressing barriers to brownfield redevelopment and regeneration of town centres.[b] There is also a statutory provision for an independent Maori advisory board and the council has several advisory panels, including one focused on environment, climate change and natural heritage. Auckland Council engages in different international city networks related to sustainable urban development. These include the C40 Initiative, the Compacts of Mayors and a group of ten leading cities as part of the Global Lead Cities Network on Sustainable Procurement.

a) CCOs deliver a significant service on behalf of Auckland Council, or own or manage public assets. The 2009 reform reduced the number of CCOs from 40 to 6.

b) Urban development authorities have also been (or are becoming) developed in other major New Zealand cities to manage big infrastructure projects, co-ordinate planning and infrastructure provision for greenfield development, and/or to redevelop or intensify inner city sites, including through eco-districts.

budgetary powers from the local councils and regional council. As such, Auckland is one of the few OECD metropolitan areas with a governance body that can impose binding regulations across the entire urban area.[7] Agglomeration improved co-ordination across the region, as well as with the national government, providing it with a clear interlocutor for the whole of Auckland. It has enabled the council to tackle issues beyond the capacity of previously individual councils, such as advancing network investments in the area of sewerage and wastewater management.[8]

Following the Auckland reform, local authorities began to realign themselves throughout the country, but no similar unitary structure has yet been formed. New Zealand's second- and third-largest cities, Wellington and Christchurch, have no dedicated governance body for the metropolitan area, although their regional councils provide some typical functions of metropolitan authorities (e.g. provision of water and sanitation services). Nevertheless, weak regional governance and leadership continue to undermine coherent region-wide urban planning. Several city and district councils have formed groups to ease co-operation and joint planning for the common urban area; Wellington and the regions of Canterbury and Waikato, for example, have established mayoral forums.

Some neighbouring cities have also developed joint development visions, strategies and spatial planning documents to guide urban development; yet these groups sometimes struggle to implement these strategies effectively (see Box 5.5 and Section 5).

The New Zealand government should encourage municipalities to overcome institutional and land-use planning fragmentation. This could be done by customising the Auckland institutional reform to other larger urban areas or by building partnerships among municipalities, under various institutional forms. In mid-2016, the government presented a bill to Parliament aimed at facilitating local collaboration.[9] Improved governance and inter-municipal co-ordination in spatial planning can lead to better outcomes, including a more efficient urban form, better targeted investments and improved quality or reduced costs of service provision (by virtue of economies of scale) (OECD, 2015b, 2015c). For example, over 2000-06, metropolitan areas that have governance bodies such as the Auckland Council experienced a decline in urban sprawl and feature, on average, lower concentrations of fine particulate matters in the air. This may be the result of more efficient transport policies in combination with better land-use planning (OECD, 2015c).

3.2. *National institutions and multi-level governance*

Central governments play a decisive role in urban development, setting policy direction through legislation and national strategies and programmes. They also influence urban development via the funding and policy decisions of its agencies. In New Zealand, the central government most directly and most regularly influences urban development through investment in local land transport (it co-finances about half of local transport infrastructure; see Section 7). The government also has significant leverage to influence local land-use planning through its power to set National Environmental Standards and develop National Policy Statements (see Section 4); however, it has not used these powers much to date (see also Chapter 2). Nonetheless, there has been a trend towards tighter central government control over local government, reduced local discretion and exemptions from key legislation in some regions.[10]

At the national level, no dedicated ministry or unit is assigned to deal with cities; responsibilities are split across a range of ministries and national authorities.[11] The fragmentation of administrative mandates, and insufficient co-ordination among them, limits an integrated approach to urban planning and complicates vertical co-ordination with city governments, which lack a clear interlocutor at the national level. In the early 2000s, a new portfolio of Urban Affairs was created, but this received no separate resourcing and was abolished when the current administration came to office. While few OECD member countries have dedicated ministries to urban development, an increasing number use formal mechanisms to improve both horizontal and vertical co-ordination. Germany, for example, has established an inter-ministerial group to share information and co-ordinate policies of spatial and urban development; this group has also developed urban development principles and guidelines.

New Zealand uses several processes and institutions to ease local-national policy co-ordination. These include the Auckland Policy Office (established in 2005 by the Ministry of Economic Development and reformed in 2014 to become a multi-agency office for central-local government co-ordination), as well as ad hoc groups like the Auckland Joint Officials Group and the Auckland Social Sector Leaders Group. The Auckland Policy Office has been effective in ensuring vertical co-ordination during the development of Auckland's first spatial plan (Section 5.2). However, ad hoc governance arrangements between Auckland

and the national government have often lost momentum and commitment over time, in part due to limited mandate and insufficient resources to commit to joint initiatives (McKay, 2014). The lack of adequate governance mechanisms has hampered the identification of, and agreement on, large-scale infrastructure projects (e.g. in the area of land transport), which has led to several years of jockeying between local and central government over the size, nature and funding responsibilities related to these projects (NZPC, 2016). In recent years, ad hoc collaboration between the national and Auckland governments to resolve long-standing tensions in transport and housing has had some success (see Section 5.2). Notwithstanding, the national government could consider establishing more formal structures to co-ordinate major urban infrastructure projects.

4. The legislative framework for urban planning

4.1. *Main legislative acts*

Three major pieces of legislation govern New Zealand's urban planning system: the 1991 Resource Management Act (RMA), the main statute for natural resources management and the primary legislation for land-use planning; the 2002 Local Government Act (LGA), which governs infrastructure provision by local governments; and the 2003 Land Transport Management Act (LTMA) (see Box 5.3 on the main provisions of each act). The three acts create a system based on a comprehensive and systematic hierarchy of plans from the national to the local level (Figure 5.8). The central government provides the broad policy framework, while regional and local authorities develop plans that must implement and give effect to national strategies and plans. The system delegates significant responsibilities to local councils, including land-use regulation and the provision of local services related to water supply and sewerage, local transport, and the management of waste, local parks and nature reserves, among others. Regional councils are responsible for issues including water management, soil conservation, natural hazards management and regional transport.

Box 5.3. **RMA, LGA, LTMA – the three major legislative acts in urban planning**

Three major pieces of legislation set the governance framework for regional and urban planning:

- The **1991 Resource Management Act** (RMA) governs land use through a hierarchy of planning documents, splitting responsibility between the central government, regional councils and territorial authorities. The central government develops National Environmental Standards (NESs) and National Policy Statements (NPSs), which must be implemented by local tiers of government through regional plans and district plans (see also Chapter 2). District plans are the main tool to regulate urban land use. They are usually hybrid instruments that combine policy goals with enforceable zoning codes and development standards.
- The **2002 Local Government Act** (LGA) defines the duties and responsibilities of local government, including processes related to the provision of infrastructure. It requires local communities to conduct strategic planning, for example, through: i) development of long-term community plans (of at least ten financial years) that set out planned activities, pursued outcomes, expected performance, and forecasted revenue and expenditure; ii) infrastructure strategies to plan investment in maintenance, improvement and expansion of infrastructure assets over a 30-year timeframe; and iii) annual plans and reports on planned activities, revenue and expenditure.

Box 5.3. **RMA, LGA, LTMA – the three major legislative acts in urban planning** *(cont.)*

- The **2003 Land Transport Management Act** (LTMA) sets out the requirements for the operation, development and funding of the land transport system. Through the National Policy Statement on Land Transport, central government sets the overall objectives and long-term results sought over ten years, as well as expenditure ranges for each class of transport activity. The New Zealand Transport Agency (NZTA) then develops a three-year National Land Transport Programme that outlines activities that will receive funding from the National Land Transport Fund. These activities are selected from proposals prepared by regional land transport committees. Activities proposed for funding must form part of a ten-year Regional Land Transport Plan.

The RMA, LGA and LTMA create a complex web of separated planning and decision-making processes. With land use, transport and infrastructure being subject to separate legal frameworks, plans and decision-making procedures required under the acts are all subject to different legal purposes, processes and criteria, and operate over different timeframes. This has created parallel planning systems with a proliferation of planning documents, overlaps and duplication of efforts, creating significant resource demands on local authorities.[12] There are some linkages between the three planning statutes (Figure 5.7), but they have no coherent framework to guide activities towards common goals. National, regional and local governments have struggled to align interests on when, where and how development should occur, leading to misalignment and inconsistencies in urban planning and investment. In the meantime, as discussed in the following sections, lack of clarity and focus of the legislations, coupled with limited national guidance, has led to regulatory overreach in urban areas. Changes to existing regulation, in turn, tend to be slow and cumbersome.

Overall, the urban planning system has responded poorly to the challenges and opportunities arising from urban development. The system has been a substantial barrier to increasing housing supply and providing network infrastructure in Auckland and other fast-growing cities. As such, it has contributed to rising house prices, missed benefits from agglomeration and increased environmental pressures from infrastructure bottlenecks. At the same time, the system has complicated the delivery of locally defined development objectives, including residential densification (MfE, 2010; NZPC, 2016). The broad frustration with the urban planning system has led to successive legislative amendments in recent years, including a speeding up of plan-making processes, provisions to avoid lengthy appeals and changes to local governance arrangements. However, these amendments have tended to increase the statute's complexity and reduced its coherence, making it harder for councils to apply them and harder for the public to engage (Jenkins, 2015; NZPC, 2016; see also Chapter 2).

The New Zealand Productivity Commission – an independent Crown entity that advises the government – undertook several inquiries and analyses on local land-use regulation, housing supply and ways to improve the urban planning system. In its report Better Urban Planning (published in draft format at the time of writing), the commission proposes wide-ranging reforms to tackle the underlying weaknesses of the legislative planning framework, giving priority to clearly separating planning legislation for the natural and urban environments (NZPC, 2016).[13] Such a wide-ranging reform would help eliminate inconsistencies from recurrent legislative amendments and provide an opportunity to establish clearer linkages between urban land use, protection of natural

Figure 5.7. **The statutory planning framework: Urban planning under the RMA, LGA and LTMA**

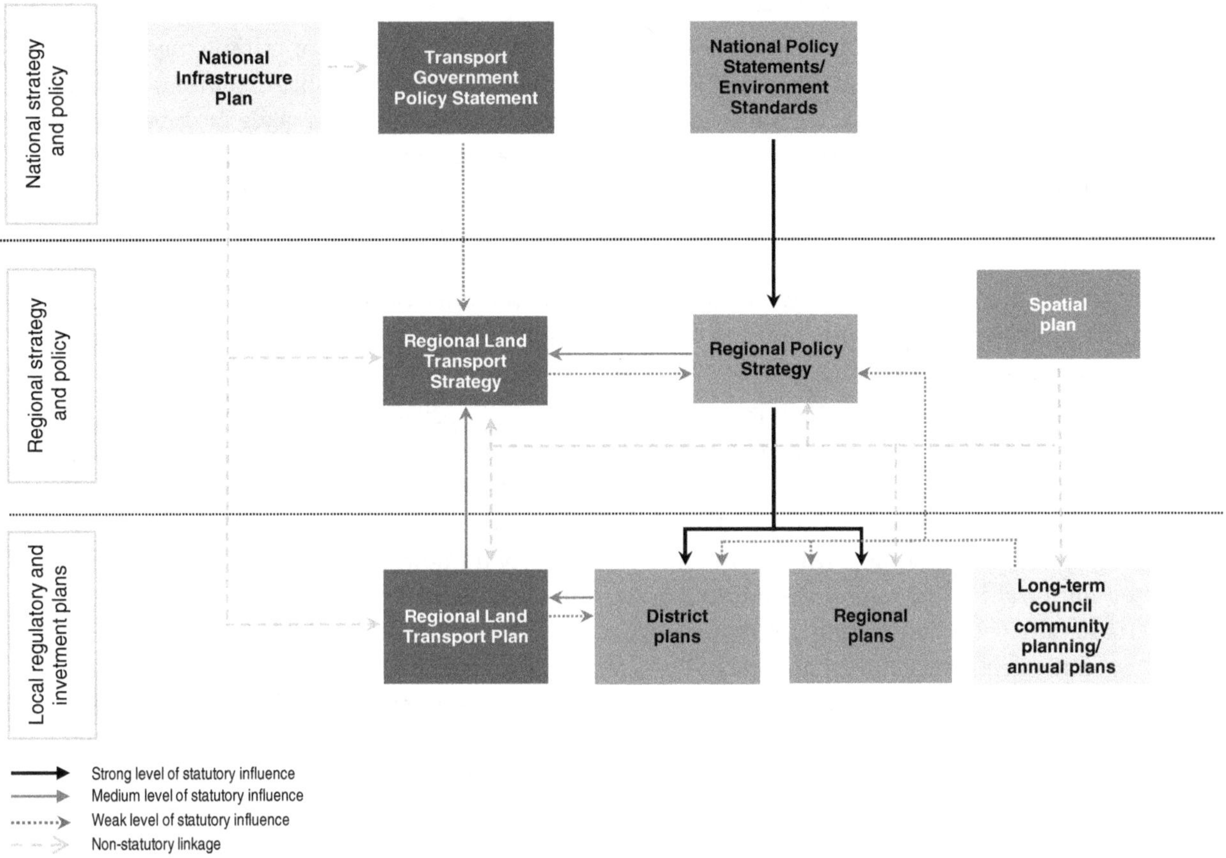

Note: Auckland is the only territorial authority to have a spatial plan (dark grey box).
Source: MfE (2010), Building Competitive Cities.

resources, and transport and infrastructure planning and investment. However, these benefits need to be carefully balanced against the uncertainty and potentially high transaction costs associated with an overhaul of the current planning system, governance arrangements and jurisprudence (Jenkins, 2015; Palmer and Blakeley, 2015).

4.2. *Implementing urban planning legislation at the city level*

The highly devolved nature of New Zealand's planning system gives local councils significant autonomy to set their own rules and make decisions on land use in their respective area. Yet lack of clarity of the legislations (notably the RMA), coupled with limited national guidance, has made it difficult for local councils to implement planning objectives efficiently and effectively (also see Chapter 2). The RMA focuses on managing adverse effects of development of the natural environment, but is virtually silent on the urban environment (where natural landscapes are already highly modified). As such, the RMA has limited capacity to recognise and promote the positive economic, social and environmental contributions of high-quality, sustainable urban design and planning (e.g. compared to what is already built or "business-as-usual" development). Benefits of sustainable urban design are missed because quantitative issues (e.g. parking space numbers or wind speeds) sometimes take precedent over qualitative concerns (Duffell, 2010; MfE, 2010). The suitability of the RMA in the urban context has also been questioned due to its reactive character (managing negative effects rather than promoting positive ones) and limited capacity to deal with cumulative effects (NZPC, 2016).

A number of local authorities have developed urban design goals or criteria, use urban design assessments when deciding on resource consents, or have established urban design panels to review proposals and provide advice. However, urban design goals or criteria are often vaguely worded and rarely relate to environmental externalities (or address them inefficiently). Urban design requirements or assessments vary significantly across councils and sometimes lack robust analysis of economic implications. This results in uncertainty and costs for both local governments and businesses. In the meantime, broad room for interpretation has allowed councils to subsume a broad range of issues under the banner of sustainable management, making land-use regulation increasingly far-reaching and prescriptive (NZPC, 2016; see also Section 6.1).

More guidance from the national government on implementation of the RMA would help councils develop land-use rules that conform with environmental goals under the RMA, improve consistency across local decisions and practices, and enhance transparency and certainty for developers and residents. New Zealand is one of the few OECD member countries without some form of a national urban policy framework that would guide actions by national institutions, sub-national governments and other stakeholders.[14] The first national-level urban planning initiatives were launched in the early 2000s, with one major outcome being the 2005 Urban Design Protocol, a voluntary initiative in which several public and private institutions committed to specific urban design criteria and initiatives. Most councils refer to the protocol in their city or district plan; however, its actual application and effectiveness are not clear. The government plans to review the protocol and clarify the role of regulation on the quality of urban design.

Legally binding mechanisms to improve efficiency, effectiveness and alignment of urban planning have been underused to date. A step in the right direction, the government announced that a National Policy Statement (NPS) on urban development capacity would come into effect in December 2016. However, the NPS is narrow, limited to providing for sufficient housing and business development capacity.[15] It pays no attention to how planning can, or should, promote urban systems and outcomes that would improve cities' environmental performance. Nor does it provide guidance with respect to densification (e.g. supporting infill development), management of natural resources within the urban area and the resilience of new (or existing) development against natural hazards or climate change. The government should therefore consider broadening the scope of the NPS or developing other legally binding measures that would clearly outline what standards and outcomes local plans and developments should achieve. At the very least, New Zealand should review and assess the usefulness and effectiveness of looser forms of guidance, such as the Urban Design Protocol.

4.3. Stakeholder engagement and responsiveness of the planning system

The planning system has been criticised for being insufficiently responsive to development needs in New Zealand's fast-growing cities. The process of changing land-use rules and regulations tends to be lengthy, with district or regional plans taking more than eight years on average to become operational (since their first notification). In some cities, their development took nearly a decade. Updates and amendments usually take three to four years (and high-growth councils take longer on average). About one-third of the time needed to change a land-use plan is due to action in the courts (Blakeley, 2015; Jenkins, 2015; NZPC, 2016).

These long time periods are in part related to extensive participation and appeal rights under the RMA, which stakeholder groups have used to thwart development of wider public interest (even though these rights have narrowed over time; see Chapter 2) (OECD, 2015a; NZPC, 2016). While high levels of public participation are an asset of New Zealand's public governance, vested interest groups sometimes have disproportionate influence in local council processes, including consultations on budgeting and land-use plans. One out of three councils believes local interest groups drive local planning decisions (NZPC, 2016). Resident associations often appeal changes to city land-use plans, fearing that urban development could affect the value of their properties and the character of their neighbourhoods. Indeed, many changes to land-use plans effectively protect the interests of property owners, creating biases towards maintaining the status quo (NZPC, 2015).

To speed up development of Auckland's new (region-wide) land-use plan, the national government passed special legislation that combined enhanced stakeholder engagement at the early stages of the plan's development with limited possibilities for appeals to the Environment Court at later stages (Section 5.2). An Independent Hearings Panel has been set up to review stakeholder submissions, thereby potentially limiting disproportionate influence of selected stakeholder groups. The New Zealand Productivity Commission (2016) proposed replicating such a model in a future urban planning system, in addition to limiting notification requirements and appeal rights to those directly affected by proposed plan changes. While the involvement of a non-political panel can increase objectivity of planning decisions, any limitation of public participation needs to be approached with caution to ensure the public is not disproportionately deprived of oversight and recourse options.

A better defined policy framework for sustainable urban development may help address some of these challenges. For example, well-defined national urban design principles or outcomes (see Section 4.2) can provide an objective baseline against which urban plans (and the reasonableness of objections) can be assessed, thereby limiting the risks of appeals to publicly beneficial development. Similarly, robust cost-benefit analyses of proposed changes, and strategic assessment of their potential environmental impacts, would make development planning more transparent, thereby helping to avoid conflict and opposition. OECD (2012) identified a number of other strategies that city government can use when public opposition against a more compact urban form is high; these include provision of affordable housing, investment in green open space, greening of built-up areas, information and education, and demonstration projects that showcase attractive medium- and higher-density development. The city of Vancouver, Canada, for example, turned the acronym NIMBY (not-in-my-backyard) into QIMBY (quality-in-my-backyard) to demonstrate that residential intensification can be based on high-quality urban design and amenities.

4.4. Monitoring and evaluation

Auckland has long-standing experience in environmental reporting: it has published four region-wide environment reports since 1999, the latest of which was released in 2015 (Auckland Council, 2015c), covering climate, air, land, water and biodiversity. Other cities collect and publish data on their own sets of environmental indicators. Wellington has furthermore developed indicators to track the development of urban form, including a set of indices to assess whether the city is becoming more compact (e.g. building density and the proportion of houses located within 100 metres of public transport). No data on cities' environmental performance (or urban form) are compiled at national level.

The limited use of indicators, the choice of different indicators and inconsistent methodologies make it difficult to benchmark cities, identify best practices and assess progress towards urban development objectives. New Zealand should work towards a common framework for city-level monitoring and reporting by, for example, defining a common set of key urban environmental and economic indicators (e.g. housing density, housing quality, waste management, water and wastewater management, access to green spaces). These could be included in the new National Monitoring System for the RMA (Chapter 2). The government could also provide methodological guidance and enhance local technical capacity and collaboration for the development urban inventories (e.g. city-level GHG emissions inventories). This would allow environmental, economic and social impacts of urban policies to be better identified, thereby supporting decision making and allowing better evaluation of urban development and planning.

5. Spatial planning

5.1. *Linking land use, transport, infrastructure and environmental sustainability*

Ideally, the policy framework for urban planning should respect the linkages and mutual effects of land use, housing, transport, infrastructure and environmental sustainability. Spatial planning (Box 5.4) is a tool commonly used in OECD member countries to provide for integrated planning and to better balance the demand for socio-economic development with the need to protect the environment. As its overriding benefit, spatial planning can encompass the cumulative impacts of development on the city, its residents and the environment by considering the "whole" of development decisions. Such impacts are difficult to identify in the assessment of individual projects or sectoral policies and plans (TEEB, 2010).

Box 5.4. **Spatial Planning**

Since the 1990s, the term *spatial planning* has been used globally to refer to different governance practices and systems to influence the location, timing and form of development. However, there has been little common understanding of what it means in practice. In many cases, the term is used interchangeably with *land-use planning*, *urban planning* and *regional planning*. Silva and Acheampong (2015) identified four key objectives commonly pursued by spatial planning: i) co-ordination of the spatial dimensions and impacts of other sectoral policies; ii) integration and functional organisation of land uses and their regulation; iii) balance of demand for socio-economic development with the need to protect the environment; and iv) balance of distributing the gains of economic development between regions, particularly in cases where the free market has failed to do so. Auckland Council (2012a) defined spatial planning as "a form of planning for cities, regions or countries that seeks to provide long-term direction for development and the achievement of social, economic and environmental well-being".

Spatial planning is not mandatory in New Zealand, with the exception of Auckland (see next section). Notwithstanding, a number of councils have developed strategic (or spatial) documents for their city, often jointly with neighbouring councils. These aim to set development goals and improve alignment of land use, housing, transport and infrastructure planning (see examples in Box 5.5). While a positive step, the lack of effective implementation

Box 5.5. Examples of voluntary spatial planning in New Zealand cities

The *Hamilton Urban Growth Strategy (2010)* provides the spatial vision for the city and surrounding region over the next 50 years. It was developed jointly by Hamilton City Council, Environment Waikato, and Waipa and Waikato District Councils. The national government created financial incentives for horizontal co-operation, making infrastructure funding conditional on a joint sub-regional growth strategy. The strategy explicitly aims at achieving "a more compact living environment that (would) proactively limit sprawl and manage (the) city's urban footprint".

Dunedin Towards 2050, a high-level, non-statutory document adopted by the Dunedin City Council in 2012, aspires to guide and align land use, transportation planning, and infrastructure and services provision, as well as to protect the city's extensive rural and natural areas from "inappropriate development". As the plan notes itself, it will need to be implemented through existing and future strategies and plans, and can be subject to change and refinement through processes used to develop those documents.

SmartGrowth is a collaboration between Tauranga City Council, Western Bay of Plenty District Council, Bay of Plenty Regional Council, Tangata Whenua and other partners. It was established in 2004 primarily in response to rapid population growth. An updated document, *SmartGrowth 2013*, has evolved the collaboration into a spatial plan that includes greater involvement of communities and other agencies outside of local government.

The *Wellington Urban Growth Plan 2014-43* incorporates two of the council's earlier strategies (the Urban Development Strategy and the Transport Strategy), thereby encouraging integrated planning. The strategy aims to improve walking amenities and public transport and increasing medium-density housing. It is complemented with a funded implementation plan for the first ten years.

Source: DIA (2013b); Early, Howden-Chapman and Russell (2015); several local council websites.

mechanisms has often made it difficult to deliver these planning frameworks. The translation of often high-level or aspirational goals in those plans into a coherent and comprehensive set of regulations (e.g. in district plans under the RMA) and budgets (e.g. under the LGA or LTMA) is often a lengthy process that requires separate public consultations and depends on the continued commitment of participating councils.[16] Their limited legal weight means that plans lack formal links with planning and budgeting processes under the RMA, LGA or LTMA. Where inconsistencies arise, spatial plans do not prevail. Some spatial plans have been developed without central government involvement, hampering implementation.

The government should support spatial planning by providing greater recognition (i.e. legal weight) to spatial plans, while clarifying (and simplifying) the relationships with planning processes for land use, infrastructure and transport. Spatial planning could be made mandatory for major urban areas (e.g. with more than 100 000 people); and it should be facilitated and encouraged in smaller cities, including through greater guidance on the development and implementation of spatial plans. Where conducted, spatial plans should undergo strategic environmental assessment. Such assessments provide for a systematic evaluation of likely impacts of urban development on the environment and can set standards about how such impacts should be minimised or reversed. This can improve the environmental outcomes of urbanisation, while increasing certainty to the community and developers. It may also help limit the scope of appeal by vested interests and facilitate planning approval processes by setting a baseline against which proposed development can be judged. In Melbourne, Australia, for example, the strategic assessment of the urban development strategy identified matters of environmental importance (e.g. threatened species or wetlands) and stipulated how impacts on these matters must be mitigated; major development projects (e.g. transport corridors or the designation of land for development) can then be approved without further federal government assessment or approval, as long as they are in accordance with the assessed plan. Auckland's spatial plan (see next section) outlines a number of specific sustainability goals (see Box 5.6), which would provide a good basis to assess impacts.

Box 5.6. Selected quantified sustainability goals in the Auckland Plan

Transport: Double the number of public transport trips (from 70 to 140 million per year) between 2012 and 2022; reduce congestion levels to (or below) 2006-09 levels by 2021; increase the share of people living in walking distance of frequent public transport from 14% to 32% by 2040.

Biodiversity: Ensure no extinction of indigenous species; reduce the number of threatened or at-risk species by 50% (from 2010 levels) by 2040; establish marine protected areas identified in regional marine spatial plans by 2018.

Climate change: Reduce greenhouse gas emissions by 40% by 2040 (based on 1990 levels).

Waste: Reduce waste by 30% by 2018; achieve zero waste to landfill by 2040.

Water: Reduce gross per capita water consumption by 15% by 2025 (based on 2004 levels).

Housing: Retrofit 40% of the housing stock in need of retrofitting by 2030.

Air: Reduce air pollutant emissions (PM_{10}) by 50% by 2016 (compared to 2006 levels) and reduce emissions by a further 20% by 2040.

Source: Auckland Council (2012a).

5.2. *Spatial planning in Auckland*

The Auckland Plan

The legislation implementing the 2010 institutional reform (Section 3) specifically mandated the development of a spatial plan. This spatial plan, later known as the Auckland Plan, was developed by the mayor and the new Auckland Council within 17 months. It sets the long term (30-year) direction for the region, covering land use, transport, housing and infrastructure in an integrated way for the first time. As New Zealand's first-ever spatial plan with statutory weight, it serves as the framework for all other planning documents prepared in the region.

The Auckland Plan envisions transforming Auckland into the world's most liveable city and identifies four "transformational shifts" to achieve this: move to an outstanding integrated public transport system; strongly commit to environmental action and green growth; improve the quality of urban living; and accelerate the prospects of Auckland's children and young people. The Auckland Plan sets out the council's vision of a "quality, compact city", mirroring the council's long-time aspiration to increase urban density with a high-level strategy for implementation. It includes several goals and principles relevant for environmental sustainability, many of which are accompanied with quantified targets that allow for tracking progress (see Box 5.6).

A number of plans and documents will help deliver the objectives outlined in the Auckland Plan. The main mechanism is the Auckland Unitary Plan, the land-use planning document under the RMA, which is discussed in the following section. Others include the dedicated Auckland Transport Programme,[17] Auckland's Economic Development Strategy, place-based strategies (such as the City Centre Masterplan or the Waterfront Plan), and financial strategies and asset management plans developed under the LGA (such as the Long-Term Plan, which outlines intended activities, programmes and a budget for a ten-year period). Local boards set their own priorities and projects.

Land-use planning under the RMA: The Auckland Unitary Plan

Following adoption of the Auckland Plan, Auckland Council developed the Auckland Unitary Plan (AUP), the statutory land-use planning document under the RMA and one of the main tools to deliver the Auckland Plan. The AUP combines the functions of a regional policy statement, regional plan, regional coastal plan and district plans; it will be the region's single land-use regulation plan, replacing the existing regional policy statement and 13 district and regional plans from the legacy councils.

To circumvent the traditionally lengthy process of changing land-use plans (see Section 4.3), Auckland Council proposed an additional round of stakeholder engagement in the early stages of the plan development (which is not required under RMA legislation) in return for limited possibilities for appeals to the Environment Court at later stages. The government agreed, enacting the Local Government (Auckland Transitional Provisions) Amendment Act in 2013. The act established that a non-political Independent Hearings Panel, headed by an Environment Court judge, would hear and consider submissions from stakeholders on the draft AUP, and make recommendations on the final plan for consideration by Auckland Council. An appeal to the Environment Court would be allowed on matters where the council disagreed with the panel's recommendations. Where the council agrees, appeals can only be made to the High Court on a point of law.

The draft AUP, published by Auckland Council in early 2013, included extensive re-zoning of residential areas across Auckland to permit the intensification of residential density. Following strong public debate, the proposed AUP, publicly notified six months later, was significantly less ambitious regarding intensification: the number of new houses allowed outside the city limits increased from 25% to 40%. A large part of Auckland suburbs near the city centre would not be eligible for infill development. The proposed plan continued to attract strong opposition: communities opposed intensification; the central government argued the proposal was still too strict with respect to housing regulation and would not adequately address Auckland's housing pressures; others criticised the proposed land-use rules as too restrictive and costly, driving development towards greenfield areas and hence creating more urban sprawl (Early, Howden-Chapman and Russell, 2015). A three-year process was established for the Independent Hearings Panel to consider about 10 000 public submissions, which has led to some 1.4 million changes.[18] Once the process is finalised, New Zealand should evaluate its effectiveness and study whether similar settings could be used to facilitate land-use planning in other cities. From an environmental point of view, the absence of clear standards or goals for urban environmental outcomes makes it difficult to determine to what extent the process has altered likely environmental impacts of planned development.

Addressing Auckland's housing pressures

The question of how land regulation and supply should respond to Auckland's rising housing prices has long created tension between the Auckland Council and central government.[19] The government has emphasised the need to release more land for residential development on the urban periphery, while the Auckland Council favoured urban intensification. In 2013, the two parties concluded the Auckland Housing Accord to supply additional land for development until the Auckland Unitary Plan becomes operative (a similar accord was later developed for Wellington). The accord aims to establish some 100 Special Housing Areas (SHAs) – designated areas for predominantly residential development where special consenting and approval processes would speed up development. The legislation implementing the accord increased the central government's role in local land-use planning by empowering the Minister of Housing to override local government planning regulations and to directly permit plans for residential developments (Murphy, 2015).

The identification of SHAs in Auckland is based on a number of criteria, including the existence (or likely future existence) of adequate infrastructure, demand for housing in the proposed SHA, yield and contributions to housing affordability. Environmental considerations (e.g. ecological value of greenfield land where an SHA is considered, or connectivity to public transport) were not listed and given little weight in practice. This reflects the legislation's focus, which prioritises targeted housing numbers over the Auckland Plan's aspiration to achieve a more compact city (Auckland Council, 2016c). The Housing Accord gave developers the possibility to choose between greenfield and brownfield development, while ensuring that sufficient greenfield land was available for development to meet the target. The first SHAs were to increase the urbanised area by 16% (by 8 000 ha) over 3 years rather than the 30 years envisaged in the Auckland Plan (Early, Howden-Chapman and Russell, 2015). Indeed, most dwelling sites would be greenfield sites outside the existing built-up area, expanding the future urban zone.

6. Policy instruments for sustainable urban development

OECD (2013) identifies four main types of policy instruments for sub-national authorities to stimulate sustainable urban development: regulation, incentive-based instruments, public spending and procurement, and information and convening (see Table 5.1). From an economics perspective, incentive-based instruments can guide land and resources use more

Table 5.1. **Main instruments for sustainable development in cities**

Regulation	Economic or incentive-based instruments	Public spending and procurement	Information and convening
Land-use regulation (e.g. urban growth boundaries, zoning, land-use rules)	Development contributions	Investment in public transport, water, wastewater and waste management	State of Environment report
Building codes	Financial contributions	Green public procurement	Car-pooling facilitation website
Dynamic regulation (selling development rights)	Property taxes	E-mobility	Educational recycling programmes
	Road charges and parking fees		
	Waste charges		
	Water tariffs		
	Payments for eco-system services		
	Tradable development rights		

Source: Based on classification used in OECD (2013).

efficiently. Many such instruments (e.g. user charges and fees, development contributions, etc.) also generate revenue, which can help cities finance the large investment needs resulting from urban growth (Section 7). On the other hand, regulation can set upper limits to pollution, which can be effective in cases where the environmental costs of land conversion are high (e.g. in ecologically sensitive areas) or uncertain (e.g. where land-use changes evoke cumulative or irreversible effects). Environmental and socio-economic urban development objectives can thus best be achieved by a combination of regulatory and economic instruments.

In New Zealand, as in other OECD member countries, urban development policies rely mainly on regulation. In line with recommendations from the OECD *Environmental Performance Review* in 2007, some cities have expanded use of economic instruments to encourage more efficient water and waste management, for example. However, the application of economic instruments remains limited. Regulatory instruments can, if poorly designed, curtail development and lead to unintended and detrimental environmental outcomes. For example, several cities in New Zealand and other OECD member countries apply land-use rules that restrict development capacity within urban areas, lowering land-use density and forcing cities to move outwards (see Table 5.2 for examples of such regulations). Policies therefore need to be carefully integrated. Strong regulatory containment policies (such as urban boundaries) should be accompanied by policies that aid development inside the urban fringe (e.g. relaxed building height limits), so as to offset negative impacts on housing supply. Regulatory instruments should also be monitored and regularly assessed against their effectiveness in managing land use and their contribution to urban environmental objectives (e.g. their effect on private vehicle use). Ideally, regulatory instruments should be reserved for addressing environmental and social externalities that economic policy instruments do not capture.

Table 5.2. **Examples of regulatory policies that can promote urban sprawl**

Policy	Effect
Minimum parking requirements	Reduces the land available for other potential uses (including housing), lowering land-use density; encourages car ownership and use.
Minimum apartment size requirements	Limits the ability of dwellers to trade-off private space for location; limits the supply of smaller and cheaper dwellings.
Building height limits	Reduces building capacity per urban land plot, forcing cities to move outwards.
Density controls (e.g. density limits)	Reduces building capacity per urban land plot, forcing cities to move outwards; limits the supply of smaller and cheaper dwellings.
Minimum lot sizes	Produces the same effect as density limits.

6.1. Land-use regulations

Urban growth boundaries

Urban growth boundaries are a common land-use instrument in cities in the OECD, and used in a number of high-growth cities in New Zealand. They consist of officially mapped dividing lines around urban areas used to prevent urban development in surrounding rural areas. The effectiveness of strict containment policies (i.e. urban growth boundaries or greenbelts) is debated; if set too loosely, they tend to be ineffective in limiting urban sprawl; if too narrowly defined, they may lead to rising house prices in the containment area, land speculation and high prices on the urban fringe, and underestimation of future land and infrastructure needs. The effect on housing supply can be particularly strong when other land-use policies constrain development within the urban area. In some cities (e.g. London and Seoul), strict containment policies actually aggravated urban sprawl, as development "leapfrogged" to highly undesirable places beyond the restricted areas.

Auckland's urban growth boundary, the Metropolitan Urban Limit (MUL), has been in place since the mid-20th century; first to sequence growth (so that infrastructure could be delivered more efficiently); later, following enactment of the RMA, primarily to protect rural and coastal environments from peripheral growth and to achieve containment and urban densification (Hill, 2008; Blakeley, 2015). While the MUL contained development within its defined limits, much urban growth occurred through "filling up" greenfield capacity within the MUL (Hill, 2008). In other words, it did not significantly contribute to achieving Auckland's objective of becoming a more compact city. In the meantime, the MUL has contributed to rising house prices, with land prices just inside the MUL around ten times higher than those just outside the MUL (Zheng, 2013). This effect was particularly strong among cheaper dwellings, amplifying effects on housing affordability. There is evidence that the land-price differential has increased since then, indicating the MUL has become more binding as housing demand intensified (NZPC, 2012).

The Auckland Plan takes on a new, potentially more effective approach towards the urban growth boundary. The new Rural-Urban-Boundary (RUB) aims to provide for 30-years' growth and is located well away from the existing urban boundary (the AUP will define the exact location of the new boundary). Greenfield land between the RUB and the current MUL is zoned "future urban" until being rezoned in staged releases to meet future housing demand. By the time land is rezoned, network infrastructure would be in place (Blakeley, 2015). This approach should offer markets certainty and hence reduce the risk of land speculation, while enabling policy makers to better manage urban expansion. To enhance transparency and ensure urban expansion is sustainable, Auckland should establish clear rules on who decides where and when areas will be developed, and on the type of environmental assessment land release plans should undergo. Land release plans should, in addition to identifying scope for expansion, also clearly identify restrictions for urban expansion (for environmental or other reasons). A careful approach to land supply seems advisable, given that urban sprawl is an almost irreversible process with lock-ins that may severely degrade the environment.

Zoning and land use regulation

Zoning of land, and regulations on how to develop land within each zone, is the main regulatory instrument for land use in New Zealand, as in other OECD member countries (Silva and Acheampong, 2015). Zones and land-use rules are set by local authorities in their district plans. However, in the context of limited legislative clarity and limited national guidance (Section 4.2), many councils have tended to develop land-use rules that are overly prescriptive, complex and costly (NZPC, 2016, 2015). Specific requirements on new developments (such as car parking spaces, balconies or minimum apartment sizes) can impose high costs on developers, thereby constraining development without supporting sustainability or densification objectives.[20] For example, car parking requirements, which favour less-dense housing development and may encourage car use, were found to have a cost-benefit ratio of 6:1 in Auckland (MRCagney Pty Ltd, 2013). Wellington and Auckland have eased parking requirements in their city centres, which helped revitalise these areas; however, parking requirements remain for most other cities and districts in Auckland and Wellington (NZPC, 2015).

Rigorous cost-benefit analysis can help cities identify land-use regulations that hamper the achievement of urban development objectives, including the impact of such regulations on transport choices, resource requirements and urban form. Cities aiming to limit urban sprawl should prioritise identification of land-use rules that encourage extensive spatial expansion or that restrict denser development in city centres (see Table 5.2). The latter is particularly important where growth boundaries are used to control urban sprawl. Auckland is setting a positive example, having commissioned several cost-benefit analyses on rules potentially encouraging urban expansion.

6.2. Property taxes (rates)

Rates are a form of property tax charged by local and regional authorities annually on landowners. As in most OECD member countries, rates are the primary funding source for local government activities in New Zealand, accounting for nearly half of local government revenue (Figure 5.8). The 2002 Local Government (Rating) Act provides a number of options for setting rates, including: i) *general rates* that are related to property value (each council decides if property value will be assessed based on land value, capital value or value of improvements); ii) *targeted rates* that relate to the cost of a given service (e.g. water supply); and/or iii) uniform annual *general charges* (a flat charge per property, regardless of the property's value). A combination of these rates can also be used (DIA, 2016). In practice, local authorities generate most of their rate revenue through general rates. In Auckland, general rates accounted for 87% of total rate revenue in 2012 (Auckland Council, n.d.). The bulk of local rate revenue is used to finance infrastructure such as roads and water infrastructure (NZCID, 2015a).

Figure 5.8. **Property taxes are the main source of local revenue**

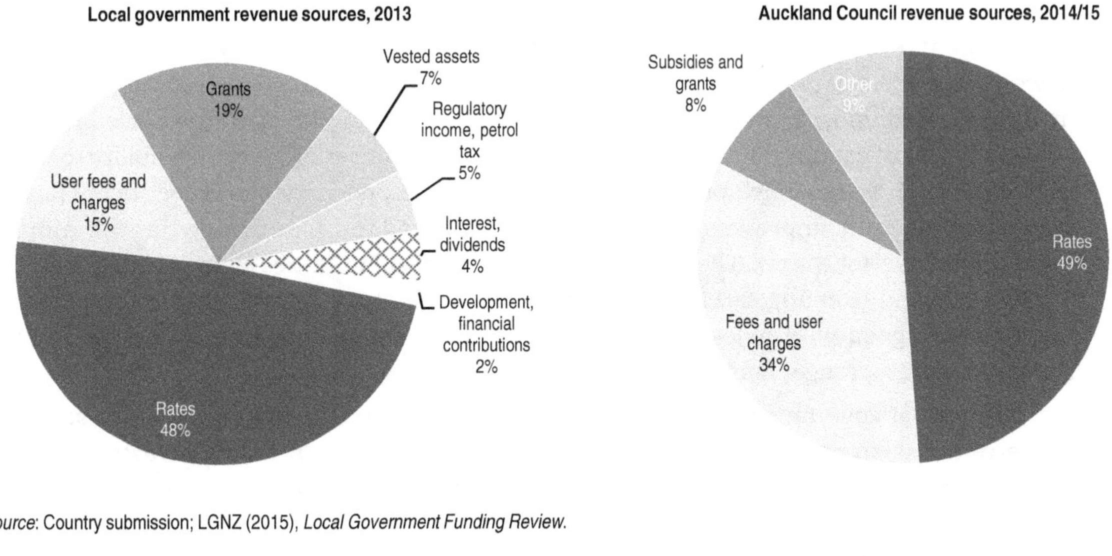

Source: Country submission; LGNZ (2015), *Local Government Funding Review.*

High reliance on general rates for infrastructure finance may discourage cities to accommodate or promote growth, as it implies that dwellers cross-subsidise infrastructure they do not necessarily benefit from. Councils are therefore reluctant to provide network infrastructure (such as sewerage and public transport) if they think this would push up the rates bill of the local population (NZIER, 2015). Indeed, approximately half of New Zealand's local authorities perceive the main barrier to funding infrastructure is that they have reached the limit of rating increases (NZPC, 2015). Local authorities can address this issue by shifting the burden of financing growth to those who benefit from it (applying the user-pays principle), rather than making everyone pay through general rates. In one positive example, Christchurch imposes targeted rates on properties near new cycleway projects and some that are connected to specific water and sewerage schemes (NZPC, 2016). Similarly, the former Auckland Regional Council used targeted rates to help fund public transport, with the level of the rate varying across the region to reflect differences in transport services improvements (e.g. the inner urban area paid about 1.25 times more than the wider metropolitan area). Similar approaches could be envisioned to finance infrastructure expansion and upgrades planned by the new council. Beyond these examples, however, the application of targeted rates has, however, been limited and relatively unsophisticated in New Zealand (NZCID, 2015b).

Targeted rates can also be used to capture windfall gains accruing to landowners from property price increases resulting from the rezoning of land for urban use (land-value capture taxes) or the improvement of local infrastructure (betterment taxes); an example would be increasing them for a defined period.[21] The potential for the tax system to capture such windfall gains is large in New Zealand, particularly in Auckland where infrastructure upgrades and expansions are significant and changes to land-use regulation (under the AUP) are substantial. Revenue raised through this mechanism could then be used to help fund infrastructure upgrades and expansions needed to service new land (OECD, 2015a), especially where development and financial contributions are not applicable.

In addition to financing infrastructure, property taxes affect land use and urban sustainability by changing the relative cost of the location and types of development. For example, a tax design that is based on buildings and other land improvements (rather than on land value) can incentivise greenfield development to the detriment of infill development, encouraging urban expansion and, at worst, urban sprawl. In most cases, however, the effect of property taxes on land use and urban sprawl is not clear-cut (Box 5.7). In New Zealand, most local councils have shifted from setting rates on the basis of land value in favour of capital values, which they perceived would better reflect the ability to pay (NZPC, 2015). However, much of the recent increases in property values reflect rising land values rather than improvements; this suggests that land values may be the more appropriate basis for the tax. There are also indications that land taxes are more progressive in New Zealand (Cheung, 2011). The country may therefore review whether property taxation is aligned with objectives of the urban planning system and, if not, consider shifting towards stronger land taxation.

Some local governments, particularly in the United States, have started to use the property tax as an explicit environmental policy instrument to promote investments in energy efficiency or renewable energy through tax exemptions or reductions (Brandt, 2014). The Czech Republic, Italy, Norway and Spain are further examples of countries that provide property tax relief for renewable energy installations. The efficiency and effectiveness of such reductions would have to be weighed against their costs in terms of a narrower tax base, and hence, less tax revenue. In addition, many policy areas will have instruments that allow for addressing negative social and economic effects more directly.

Box 5.7. Property taxes and sustainable land use: Theory and empirical evidence

The impact of property taxation on land use depends on the tax design. A pure land tax increases the cost of hoarding land and provides incentives to put land to its most valuable use. As such, it may encourage denser development. By contrast, a property tax levied on land improvements (rather than land value) can reduce incentives to develop land and to extend or renovate buildings, as this would increase the tax burden (particularly in urban areas where house prices are high). This may contribute to looser forms of development and urban sprawl. The effect of traditional two-tier taxes (that tax both land and improvements) have different, countervailing effects on sprawl (Brueckner and Kim, 2003):

- The *improvement effect* suggests that, all else being equal, a property tax based on market value is expected to reduce density. Where the tax is levied on the assessed value of property (land and improvements), any investment (such as a building) that increases the value of the property increases its assessed value and thereby its tax. Higher property taxes are thus expected to provide an incentive for less densely developed projects – scattered single-family houses rather than apartment buildings.
- The *dwelling-size effect* would lead to a reduction in urban sprawl. If the tax is partially shifted onto consumers, house prices increase, increasing the demand for smaller housing units and thereby population density.

Which effect dominates is an empirical question, yet few empirical studies have been undertaken. Recent available research suggests that in the United States moving from a property tax to a land tax would reduce urban sprawl (Ermini and Santolin, 2015; Wassmer, 2016). The question about the desirable structure of property tax rates remains, however, when the city structure is not monocentric (as is the case in Auckland), i.e. it is not clear whether densification should be encouraged in business/residential dense areas at the periphery.

Source: Based on Brandt (2014), "Greening the property tax".

6.3. Development and financial contributions

Development contributions

Development contributions are one-off levies imposed by territorial authorities on developers to finance parts of the capital costs associated with new development, notably the provision of trunk infrastructure. Their cost is commonly passed onto the purchasers of new houses or commercial premises as part of the sale price. Development contributions account for a small part of revenue of territorial authorities (Figure 5.8) and typically fund a relatively small part of local public infrastructure investment (about 2% of local capital expenditure nationwide, although they reach up to 20-50% of expenditure for some individual councils) (DIA, 2013a). Recent amendments to the LGA (under which development contributions are levied) have restricted the use of development contributions for "community infrastructure" such as libraries and swimming pools. This change may limit the capacity of urban authorities to harness a much-needed revenue stream for infrastructure provision, making local government even more reliant on rates (RPH and NZCSC, 2015).[22]

Development contributions are an important instrument to stimulate efficient use of land and infrastructure, and to promote better environmental outcomes. If they reflect the true cost of providing infrastructure to a particular area, they encourage developers to focus on areas with lower costs of infrastructure development (e.g. closer to existing infrastructure), while making leapfrog development, or other forms of urban sprawl, more expensive. In Auckland, the cost of providing infrastructure in low-density or greenfield areas was found to be roughly 50% higher than in high-density or infill areas (CIE, 2015). Development contributions can also promote more sustainable buildings, if they consider dwelling characteristics that influence demand on the infrastructure network and associated costs (e.g. water or energy efficiency). They should therefore differ according to the location and type of development. A uniform charge would mean that low-cost areas subsidise high-cost areas; small lots subsidise large lots; and smaller residential units subsidise larger ones. Ultimately, this approach subsidises inefficient uses of land (OECD, 2013).

In New Zealand, development contributions do not generally reflect the true underlying costs of infrastructure supply. However, some cities have moved towards differentiated pricing, for example by imposing lower contributions on smaller or affordable housing (Auckland) or infill development (Hamilton) (Auckland Council, 2013; Russell et al., 2015). Wellington recently introduced a "green building remission" (of up to 50%) for developments with strong environmental performance (i.e. for buildings achieving a high score in the Green Star certified building rating system; see Box 3.4) (Wellington City Council, 2015). These discounts reflect the likely lower demand such development will place on council infrastructure; they could be adopted by other cities, too. A rationale for discounts also exists for developments with wider positive social and environmental effects (e.g. water-sensitive infrastructure that reduces infrastructure demand, while providing recreational value and habitat for biodiversity). Contributions could also be adjusted to account for social costs of land development (e.g. to discourage development on land of higher environmental value), where other instruments (e.g. financial contributions) cannot capture such costs. However, the costs and benefits of discount should be carefully assessed to avoid shifting the burden onto other sources of infrastructure funding, including less-efficient general rates.

Financial contributions

Local and regional governments levy financial contributions on parties intending to subdivide or increase existing land use to reflect the environmental costs of new development. They are imposed under the RMA on new development and can take the form of money or land (which is then used to remedy adverse environmental impacts). Regional and district plans set out the exact purpose. However, principles on how, and on what, financial contributions are to be applied are not clear. This has resulted in a wide variation of approaches and inconsistencies in implementation, reducing certainty and predictability of compliance costs for developers (DIA, 2013a). Like development contributions, financial contributions do not appear to be used to influence the location of development in New Zealand. In many cases, they are charged as a fixed rate based on the type of development, rather than on the marginal damage on the environment (Cheung, 2011), which would improve the economic efficiency of the instrument and, ultimately, encourage better environmental outcomes.

The 2015 Resource Legislation Amendment Bill (Chapter 2) proposes to remove the ability of local authorities to charge financial contributions. This raises the question of how environmental effects of new development would then be accounted for. Environmental offsetting would still be possible under the RMA, but only on a voluntary basis. In addition, removing financial contributions is estimated to reduce local authority revenue by

NZD 10 million per year (NZPI, 2016). The alternative of development contributions is unlikely to fully offset the lost revenue. New Zealand should therefore carefully consider the removal of financial contributions and, if implemented, ensure that alternative mechanisms are in place to remedy or offset environmental effects of development.

6.4. *User fees and charges*

User fees and charges are among the key revenue sources of territorial authorities (Figure 5.8). The extent to which they help finance infrastructure and service provisions varies significantly across sectors: they cover more than half of councils' expenditure on waste management, yet only relatively modest shares of the costs associated with water supply, wastewater management and road infrastructure (LGNZ, 2015), suggesting that there is significant scope to makes greater use of this instrument. About half of local authorities see the need for greater use of user charges (NZPC, 2015). If properly designed, such instruments can make important contributions to urban environmental sustainability objectives. Yet current legislation limits the ability of local authorities to apply volumetric use charges for wastewater services and increase road use charges. These legislative barriers should be removed.

Road pricing

As pointed out by OECD (2015a), better mechanisms are needed to manage transport demand, particularly in Auckland where congestion levels are high (Section 2.3). Road pricing (that would internalise negative externalities associated with road use), combined with better mass transit service would help improve efficiency of the transport network, while reducing GHG emissions and air pollution. The introduction of tolls and congestion charges has proven effective in a number of cities in the OECD, including Stockholm, Oslo, Singapore and London (OECD, 2013). Charging tolls on major routes can also encourage more compact urban development by creating incentives for residents to relocate into the city or close to employment. Advanced technology has decreased administrative costs associated with this policy measure, as well as inconvenience to motorists (e.g. through real-time information and automatic payment). Many cities in the OECD use revenue from road tolls to finance public transport, thereby reducing the fiscal pressure of raising revenue from other, less cost-efficient forms of taxation (OECD, 2015d).

In New Zealand, road pricing is limited to three toll roads (two in Tauranga and one in the Auckland region); no congestion pricing is currently applied (NZPC, 2016). Revenue from road pricing covers only 5% of the costs associated with road infrastructure (LGNZ, 2015). Current legislation restricts the application of road pricing to new roads where an alternative toll-free route is available. Tolling on existing roads would require central government legislation, an issue under discussion for some time. In 2015, the government and Auckland Council set up the Auckland Transport Alignment Project to reach a consensus over the future of the Auckland transport system and its financing, which may involve road pricing. In the meantime, Auckland Council introduced a special, targeted interim transport levy on ratepayers in early 2015 to advance the transport programme.[23] Ideally, road pricing should be combined with other demand-management measures and promotion of alternative transport modes such as public transport, walking and cycling. Zoning regulations that limit vehicle access (or access of certain types of vehicles, such as heavy trucks) in congested zones could also be considered.

Water charges

The LGA enables councils to charge for use of water by volume, which encourages better use of resources by sending consumer price signals about the cost of what they consume. Volumetric charging is widely used for non-residential properties, but its application for residential consumers varies widely across the country. Many cities apply flat charges for water through rates, which provide little or no incentive for more efficient use. Councils that introduced water metering and charging have seen significant behavioural change. In Auckland, for example, per capita water consumption by households decreased by about 30% since the introduction of volumetric charging in the late 1990s. Other cities that charge for water (e.g. Tauranga and Nelson) have improved efficiency by a similar magnitude (Lawton et al., 2008; NZPC, 2015). Meanwhile, cities that do not charge on a per unit basis (e.g. Wellington and Christchurch) have significantly higher water consumption levels (Figure 5.9).

Figure 5.9. **Cities charging for water consume less water**

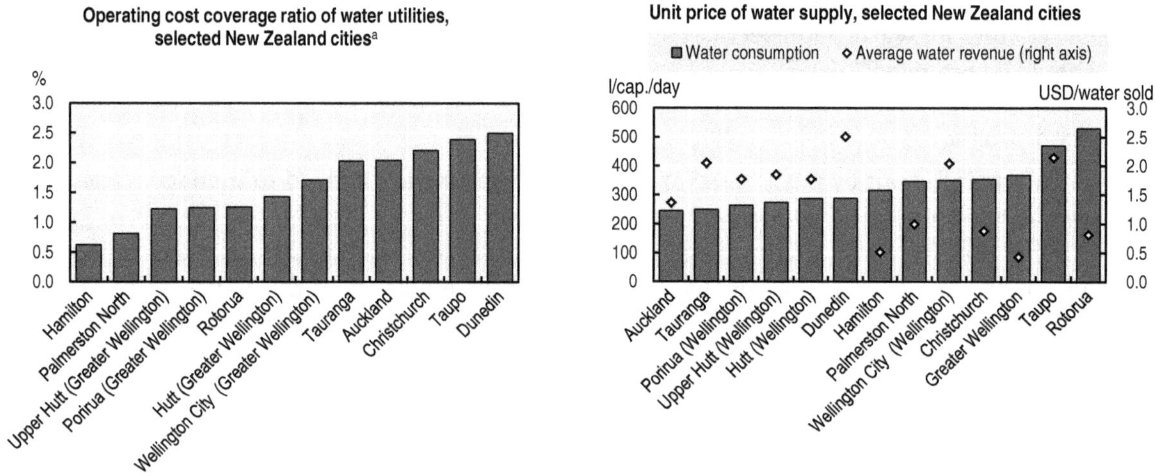

a) Total billed revenues as percentage of total operating expenses.
Source: The International Benchmarking Network for Water and Sanitation Utilities (2016), *IB-NET Database*.

StatLink http://dx.doi.org/10.1787/888933460079

Experience has shown that volumetric charging can yield a high rate of return if savings in capital expenditure on infrastructure expansion (e.g. due to lower demand) are accounted for. In Tauranga, the net present value of metering (introduced in the early 2000s) was estimated at NZD 53 million in 2009 (DIA, 2013b). Irrespective of the charging regime, water tariffs should be sufficiently high to cover the costs associated with service delivery. Nationally, on average, 36% of water supply and 15% of wastewater management costs are met through charges (LGNZ, 2015). In Auckland, water charges recover more than twice the operating costs of water services (Figure 5.9), allowing part of the revenue to be invested in infrastructure maintenance and expansion. By contrast, Hamilton recovers less than 70% of operating costs through revenues (Figure 5.9), implying that service needs to be cross-subsidised through the public budget.

Waste charges

Waste management practices also differ across New Zealand cities. Some cities apply quantity- or volume-based waste charges, which provide incentives to households to reduce waste, while others finance waste services through flat charges included in rates. Nationally, on average, waste charges cover 51% of councils' expenditure on waste management (LGNZ, 2015). In Auckland, waste management was fragmented across the seven local authorities until 2010, with different charging schemes applying in different parts of the city. Available data suggest that districts applying the polluter pays principle send nearly half of the volume to landfills than do districts charging through rates (Auckland Council, 2012b).

In a welcome step, the first Auckland-wide Waste Management and Minimisation Plan (adopted in 2012) introduced a coherent funding model for household waste management, which features the polluter pays principle as a key component. The proposed model charges by volume for collection of unsorted household waste; recycled household waste would be financed through rates and/or other funding sources. The rationale behind this scheme is to encourage households to recycle the maximum possible (since using recycling services would imply lower waste charges). The amount of funding sourced through rates is expected to remain equal to current levels (Auckland Council, 2012b). Waste charge revenue will partly feed the Auckland Waste Minimisation and Innovation Fund, a major initiative under the Waste Management and Minimisation Plan. To date, NZD 1.4 million has been awarded to 162 projects across four priority areas (resource recovery, commercial waste, organic waste, and community action and behaviour change).

7. Investing in environment-related infrastructure and services

Infrastructure plays a critical role in improving cities' environmental performance and delivering green growth. For example, green infrastructure and transformation of the built environment are estimated to deliver the greatest reduction in Auckland's GHG emissions among all policy measures considered in the city's Low Carbon Action Plan (Auckland Council, 2014b). In addition, provision of adequate transport, water and sanitation infrastructure is critical to minimise traffic congestion (and associated environmental and socio-economic impacts) and release of waste- and stormwater into water streams. The lack, or inadequacy, of storm and wastewater infrastructure also remains a constraint on housing supply, despite important advancements in Auckland since the 2010 agglomeration (OECD, 2015a).

New Zealand's local councils have important investment responsibilities, notably for environment-related infrastructure and services such as water, waste and transport, which account for the bulk of local government expenditure (Figure 5.10). However, compared to other OECD member countries, sub-national governments in New Zealand play a minor role in public finance;[24] and their flexibility to fund infrastructure is limited by their strong reliance on property taxes (Figure 5.8). About 40% of local councils report that lack of funding is a significant barrier to expand and upgrade infrastructure, including environment-related ones (NZPC, 2015). Meeting cities' significant investment needs from growing populations may therefore require a focus on diversifying funding sources.

As revenue sources can be tied to many aspects of land use, transport, waste or water consumption, cities' choice of mechanisms to finance infrastructure investment can stimulate better or worse outcomes of urban sustainability performance (Merk et al., 2012). As Section 6 discusses, there is significant scope in New Zealand to improve the design of development contributions, financial contributions and property taxes, and to expand the use of user fees and charges to improve the financial sustainability of urban development and promote sustainable use of resources and land. Given its outstanding role as New Zealand's largest city and centre of economic activity, Auckland may need to give broader consideration

Figure 5.10. **Local governments spend nearly one-third of their budgets on transport**

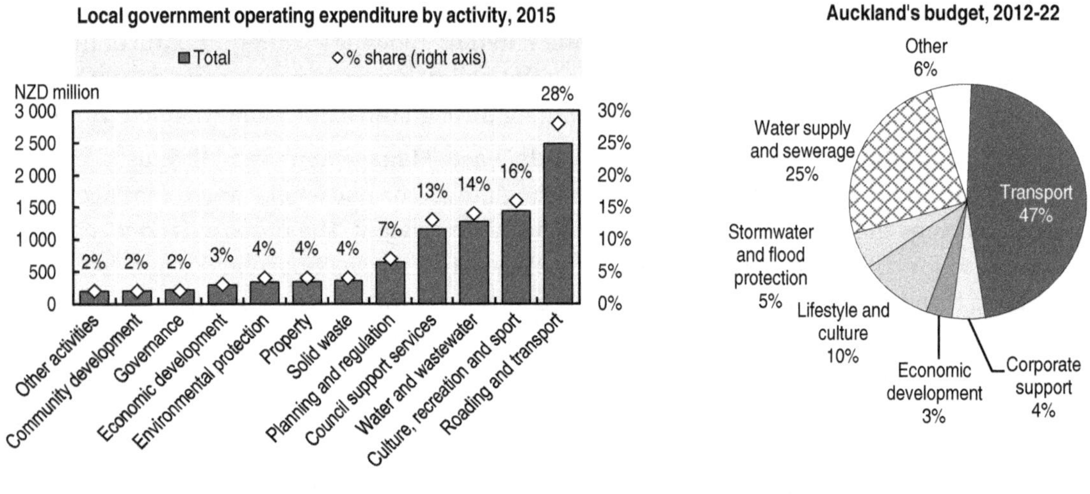

Source: Auckland Council (n.d), *Long-term Plan 2012-2022;* Statistics NZ (2016), *Local Authority Financial Statistics*, 2016.

StatLink http://dx.doi.org/10.1787/888933460089

to new financing instruments in the medium- or longer term. This could include making stronger use of debt financing (especially where benefits are inter-generational); sharing in a revenue base linked to local economic activity;[25] greater use of public-private partnerships, including at the city level (Chapter 3); or taxing windfalls gains that occur to landowners following infrastructure development or rezoning of urban land (Section 6.2).

7.1. Investing in transport and water infrastructure in Auckland

Transport

Transport accounts for the largest proportion of local government spending. In 2013, it accounted for nearly one-third of local government's operating expenditure (17% targeted roading and 13% public transport); and nearly half of Auckland's 2012-22 budget (Figure 5.10). Compared to other countries, investment in transport infrastructure is highly centralised. The central government directly subsidises local road and public transport development through the New Zealand Transport Agency (NZTA), which allocates funding through the National Land Transport Fund based on population size (i.e. Auckland is guaranteed 35%). Transport subsidies are the largest source of central government funding assistance for local government infrastructure. Funding is split into two regimes: the NZTA finances 100% of state highways and major arterial roads; while it co-finances with local authorities on average half the cost of urban, suburban and rural roads, as well as public transport. This funding scheme provides municipalities with an incentive to opt for state highways – which are effectively free for the council – rather than local roads or public transport. Indeed, local traffic heavily uses major motorways running through some cities (including Auckland) (PCE, 2016). Asking councils to co-finance at least a small share of state highways could encourage them to better consider alternative options, including mass public transport.

The focus of national transport investment has been on road development, with fewer resources devoted to public and active transport. That said, public transport saw greater investment in the second half of the 2000s, driven mostly by investment in metro rail in Auckland and Wellington (see also Chapter 3).[26] This resulted in greater public transport patronage and helped control congestion, despite population growth and associated increases in demand for road use (Section 2.3). However, Auckland's congestion levels remain high and geography limits how much the network can be expanded. Auckland Council proposes major investment in public transport, walking and cycling infrastructure in the Auckland Transport Programme under the Auckland Plan (Section 5.2). Full implementation would require additional resources in the order of NZD 10-15 billion over 30 years, largely exceeding Auckland's funding capacity. Traditional funding methods should therefore be complemented with user-based funding methods, such as road tolls and congestion pricing. These would also improve demand management of urban mobility. In addition, New Zealand could explore new mobility options arising with the advancement in telecommunication technologies. For example, car-sharing and demand-responsive public transport can be flexible, efficient solutions to expand and improve sustainably mobility in small or low-density cities (OECD/ITF, 2015).

Given New Zealand's largely decarbonised power sector (Chapter 3), electric vehicles (EVs) represent a major opportunity to reduce emissions of air pollutants and GHGs, notably in cities where public and active transport options are limited. A large-scale transition to EVs would need to be supported by government policy and adequate investment in infrastructure. Experience in Norway and the Netherlands shows that combining battery-charging infrastructure, rebates on purchases and priority lanes on main access roads can lead to very quick uptake (OECD, 2015d). Public procurement could facilitate this process by leading by example and committing to purchase EVs for its own fleet; a number of regional councils are considering this option. An electric car sharing scheme (such as the "Autolib" system in Paris) can also increase uptake of EVs in urban areas, while displacing the need for personal vehicles.

Water and sanitation

Expenditure on water and wastewater infrastructure in Auckland is significant and reflects the need to accommodate growth. The water supply network has spare capacity for 45 000 dwellings in the Auckland metropolitan area, although the network is at capacity limits in some locations. City-wide, water supply is expected to hit capacity in 15 years. To provide capacity for urban growth, Auckland's water provider plans for capital expenditure of about NZD 490 million annually over the next ten years (2017-26), significantly above investment over the 2000s (about NZD 100 million on average per year) and the first half of the 2010s (roughly NZD 200 million). Nearly 60% of projected capital expenditure will be directed towards wastewater provision and about 40% towards water supply. The investment will be funded from a combination of revenue from water charges (47%), Infrastructure Growth Charges (21%)[27] and loans (32%). By contrast, operational expenditure, estimated at NZD 260 million per year for 2017-26, is completely funded through revenue from water charges (Watercare, 2016). In the meantime, urban growth (and associated expansion of the impervious urban area) will increase demand on the stormwater network. Auckland Council foresees expenditure in the order of NZD 1.8 billion for stormwater management over 2015-25.

Moving towards a sustainable approach to water management and infrastructure investment, Auckland Council initiated the Greenways programme, which aligns government actions and investment across a range of planning and operational units to deliver multiple objectives from the same investment. These objectives include freshwater, biodiversity, transport, urban design and stormwater-related outcomes and amenities. The Healthy Waterway project commits to the implementation of water-sensitive design. For its part, the Healthy Waterway Acceleration Fund aims to enable catalytic investment in degraded catchments; these focus on "pinch points" affecting water quality that cannot be addressed without significant public expenditure.

7.2. Improving the environmental performance of the building stock

New Zealand's building stock is often poorly insulated and frequently damp, cold in winter and mouldy. This has detrimental effects on both environmental performance and public health. The government has taken significant action to improve the residential sector's performance through public funding, voluntary targeted rates, awareness-raising campaigns and voluntary labelling. The flagship programme *Warm Up New Zealand* ("Heat Smart" and "Healthy Homes") had contributed to retrofit nearly 300 000 homes (or nearly 20% of the housing stock), about half of which were occupied by low-income households (Chapter 3). Households that do not qualify for grants under this programme can use Voluntary Targeted Rates (VTR) to finance their retrofits, by adding the cost to their rates bill and paying it off over a certain period (often ten years). However, despite progress, an estimated 30% of the housing stock remain uninsulated and a large segment of the existing building stock (80%) without incentives for retrofitting (IEA, forthcoming; also see Chapter 3).

Auckland has offered a VTR scheme since 2011 under the *Retrofit Your Home* programme, in part motivated by a desire to promote uptake of *Warm Up New Zealand*. Since 2011, the programme has retrofitted 11 000 homes (Birchfield, 2012). According to an evaluation, the social value of the programme exceeded total cost by a return of NZD 3.1 per each dollar spent (Auckland Council, 2014e). The city could consider expanding the programme's scope from heating and insulation to embrace broader sustainability dimensions targeted in the Auckland Plan. These could include household energy and water efficiency, indoor air quality and wider public benefits such as reduced air pollution, energy and water conservation, and climate change and natural hazard resilience. This would allow Auckland to promote best practice urban design and encourage sustainable housing principles, also in the absence of national guidance or standards.

Recommendations on sustainable urban development

The policy and planning framework

- Examine how to improve procedures, criteria and timeframes for planning and decision making to allow for more integrated and timely management of natural resources and urban environment while preserving the ability for effective local participation.
- Consider making spatial planning mandatory for all urban areas with population over 100 000, while simplifying infrastructure and transport planning requirements; provide greater recognition and legal weight to spatial planning initiatives in smaller urban areas, and guidance on how spatial planning should be conducted; at the very least, clarify the hierarchical relationships and linkages across planning instruments for land use, infrastructure and transport and, where possible, align planning horizons and review periods.
- Broaden the scope of the National Policy Statement on Urban Development Capacity, or develop other legally binding measures to ensure that local planning processes and instruments i) recognise and encourage good urban design outcomes and principles for sustainable urban development; ii) identify and appropriately manage important or sensitive environmental systems; and iii) incorporate climate change mitigation goals and resilience against climate change and natural hazards.

Recommendations on sustainable urban development *(cont.)*

- Facilitate the decision-making process to change existing land-use plans and reduce the scope for vested interests to thwart development of wider public interests (e.g. by front-loading public consultations and ensuring an independent expert review of proposed plans and suggestions from the public).
- Create a common set of urban environmental and economic indicators to increase transparency on cities' environmental performance, facilitate benchmarking and identification of best practices, inform decision making and allow for better policy evaluation.

Institutional framework and multi-level governance

- Establish a national co-operative structure comprising national institutions with responsibilities for urban-related matters (e.g. on the model of the Natural Resources Sector), with a view to improving horizontal and vertical policy co-ordination.
- Consider replicating the Auckland institutional reform in other major urban areas, with the necessary adjustments, and encourage partnerships among smaller municipalities with a view to overcoming institutional and land-use planning fragmentation.

Regulations and economic instruments for sustainable urban development

- Ensure that regulations in land-use plans pass robust cost-benefit analyses that consider environmental outcomes (including effects on transport, green spaces, etc.), as well as economic and social outcomes (including distributional consequences and intergenerational equity).
- Make more systematic use of development contributions and rates to guide efficient and sustainable urban land use by: i) differentiating development contributions along the location and type of development to reflect the true cost of development on infrastructure and service provision; and ii) considering adjusting development contributions and rates where development yields positive effects on the environment; consider maintaining financial contributions or develop other instruments to reflect the environmental costs of developments.
- Remove barriers to road pricing (e.g. road tolls and congestion charging) and encourage councils to introduce volumetric charging for drinking water supply, with a view to foster efficient use of infrastructure and resources, while reducing the burden on local government budgets.
- Consider the use of betterment levies (e.g. through targeted rates) as an additional cost-recovery mechanism for infrastructure and services provision, especially where development and financial contributions do not apply; and explore alternative instruments to finance urban infrastructure, including taxing windfall gains occurring to landowners following rezoning of urban land (value capture).
- Review whether the current design of property taxation is aligned with land-use objectives and assess the potential benefits of shifting the property tax structure towards a land tax or to split rates.
- Assess the environmental, social and economic implications of the funding model for roads and public transport; promote innovation encouraging alternative options for public transport (e.g. car-sharing, demand-responsive transport in small or low-density cities), while continuing to expand and improve conventional public transport services.

Recommendations on sustainable urban development *(cont.)*

Sustainable housing

- Improve the environmental performance of the building stock to reduce health impacts from poor insulation and the emission of air pollutants from inefficient heating by: i) modernising and strengthening national building standards; ii) establishing supplementary incentives to promote investment in insulation and modern heating in rental buildings; and iii) encouraging new housing to meet best practice urban design and sustainable housing principles.
- Ensure that areas of fast-track residential development (notably those created under the Special Housing Act) are screened against environmental impacts, especially against cumulative and irreversible impacts.

Notes

1. The New Zealand Department of Internal Affairs defines sustainable urban development as a process of "improving the quality of life in a city, including social, economic, environmental and cultural components, without leaving a burden on future generations" (DIA, 2008).
2. This figure is based on a New Zealand-specific definition which includes small towns with a population of more than 1 000; other definitions thus yield lower results.
3. A 6.3 magnitude earthquake hit Christchurch on 22 February 2011, at the time New Zealand's second-most populous city. The earthquake caused the death of 185 people and widespread damage to the city's infrastructure, which had already been weakened by a 7.1 magnitude earthquake on 4 September 2010. A significant number of dwellers were displaced, and much of the city's infrastructure and assets had to be relocated and rebuilt. By 2013, average population density in Christchurch had decreased by 2%, compared to 2001 (Nunns, 2014b).
4. In Auckland, absolute GHG emissions increased by about 15% over 1990-2009; they have remained relatively stable since, but are projected to increase by nearly 20% by 2050, compared to 2009 levels, if no mitigation action is taken. In Christchurch, emissions increased by 15% over 2000-08. Wellington's emissions increased by 25% over the first half of the 2000s, but decreased to 2000 levels by 2012 (Auckland Council, 2015a, 2014b; Christchurch City Council, n.d; Wellington City Council, 2016).
5. Diesel vehicles remain disproportionate polluters for both PM_{10} and NO_x. In Auckland, for example, diesel combustion accounted for 72% of transport-related PM_{10} emissions, and 55% of motor vehicle NO_x emissions in 2011, despite representing only 25% of vehicle kilometres travelled.
6. Currently, there are 11 regional councils, 67 territorial authorities and 6 unitary authorities (these are Gisborne District Council, Nelson City Council, Tasman District Council, Marlborough District Council, Auckland Council and Chatham Islands Council). The average population of a territorial authority is 65 000 residents, but varies from 1.4 million in Auckland to 650 in the Chatham Islands (LGNZ, 2016).
7. According to the OECD Metropolitan Survey, 68% of OECD metropolitan areas have a metropolitan governance body; however, only one-third can impose binding regulations (OECD, 2015b).
8. The new council has accelerated modernisation of wastewater treatment systems by substantially upgrading the region's two key wastewater treatment plants and advancing the NZD 950 million "central interceptor" project that aims to reduce overflows from the Auckland combined waste and stormwater system (McKay, 2014).
9. The Better Local Services reforms (presented within the Local Government Act 2002 Amendment Bill (No 2) introduced to Parliament in mid-2016) aim to: provide councils with greater flexibility to collaborate to deliver public services; establish new processes for council-led reorganisations (rather than a single Local Government Commission-led option); and provide a more proactive role to the Local Government Commission to promote and facilitate reorganisations.
10. The amendments to the Local Government Act, for example, have introduced more planning requirements and standardised reporting obligations for local councils and given the national government more powers to intervene. The Auckland Special Housing Accord (Section 5.2) increased

the power of the Minister of Housing to override local government planning regulations in Auckland; the minister can now grant planning permission for residential developments directly. Proposed amendments to the Resource Management Act would also increase ministerial powers to directly change local land-use plans under certain circumstances (also see Chapter 2) (Murphy, 2015; NZPC, 2016).

11. The Ministry for the Environment (MfE) monitors implementation of the Resource Management Act, the principle legislation for land use; the Department of Internal Affairs is responsible for local government legislation; the Ministry of Business, Innovation and Employment (MBIE) advises groups of regions or cities (mostly Auckland and Christchurch) to maximise their contribution towards national development; and the Ministry of Transport and National Agency for Land Transport plans and co-finances urban transport investment.

12. For example, Whangarei City, capital of the Northland region, has been governed by a strategic plan for the city council, a sub-regional growth strategy, an urban growth strategy (developed jointly with neighbouring councils), a coastal management strategy, a rural strategy, an open space strategy and a walking and cycling strategy in 2010, in addition to its district plan and its Long-Term Council Community Plan (Miller, 2011). Wellington is governed by a plethora of complicated and interlocking plans developed by each of its six local authorities (Wellington Region Local Government Review Panel, 2012); Auckland is governed by nine different district plans, until the new, region-wide land-use plan fully comes into effect (see Section 5.2).

13. The commission argues that natural and built environments require different regulatory approaches and proposes two possible ways of achieving them: keeping a single resource management law with clearly separated natural and built environment sections and clarified linkages with land transport and infrastructure laws; or establishing two separate laws for the natural and the built environment, in which the latter would include built environment regulation, and infrastructure and land transport planning. In both options, land-use legislation would have separate purposes and definitions for the natural and built environment (NZPC, 2016).

14. Most OECD member countries have developed national urban policy frameworks, which take various forms depending on the country's circumstances – from legally binding planning documents to informal guidelines. Korea and Turkey are two examples of countries that recently adopted new legal frameworks for metropolitan areas; in Italy, a new law on metropolitan cities was proposed in 2014 (OECD, 2015b).

15. The statement's primary focus is to reduce regulatory barriers to the supply of housing or commercial development. It supplements the Resource Legislation Amendment Bill 2015 that is before Parliament (see Chapter 2), which puts legal requirements on councils to provide enough development capacity to meet demand. The draft NPS encourages integrated planning, but provides no practical guidance on how to reconcile planning processes under the three major acts (e.g. by ruling that land-use decisions must consider planning documents of all three statutes; by requiring or encouraging cities to conduct strategic spatial planning; or by giving spatial or strategic plans legal weight to existing planning processes).

16. In the Waikato Region (which hosts the city of Hamilton), for example, a group of local authorities aimed to formally integrate objectives and priorities of their 50-year Future Proof Strategy into statutory documents under the RMA, LGA and LTMA. Even though the strategy went through comprehensive public consultations, separate processes were required to embed it into statutory documents; this raises again the issue of duplication of efforts (FPIC, 2014).

17. The Auckland Transport Programme was developed to implement the transport-related objectives outlined in the Auckland Plan. The Auckland Plan aspires to improve the region's connection and accessibility, through four priorities: i) to manage Auckland's transport as a single system; ii) to integrate transport planning and investment with land use; iii) to prioritise and optimise investment across transport modes; and iv) to implement new transport funding mechanisms.

18. The panel's recommendations were published in August 2016 and shortly after adopted by Auckland Council. The AUP will become operative when the appeals process is complete.

19. Beyond land supply, several other factors have contributed to the lag in housing supply, which to date have received less attention. These include high and rising construction costs, reflecting rising commodity prices, labour shortages and decline in productivity in the construction industry, easy credit and tax incentives that bias investment decisions towards property over other types of investment (Cheung, 2011; OECD, 2015a).

20. In Auckland, current regulation was estimated to have increased house prices by between NZD 65 000 and NZD 110 000 per apartment (NZPC, 2015b).

21. As an alternative to targeted rates, some cities capture windfall gains through a one-off tax liability that must be paid when the land is sold.

22. Auckland Council calculated that the Local Government Amendment Act, proposed in 2013 with the aim to narrow the scope of development contributions, would lead to a cumulative 8.5% increase in rates over eight years in Auckland, in addition to raising council debt by NZD 480 million (Auckland Council, 2014f).

23. The interim transport levy is being charged for three years to fund urgent short-term transport needs. It is expected to allow for around NZD 170 million of transport investment per year.

24. In 2014, New Zealand's sub-national governments shouldered 11% of total public expenditure and were responsible for about 40% of public investment; these values are among the lowest in the OECD (and significantly below the respective OECD averages of 40% and 59%) (OECD, 2016b).

25. The 2015 OECD *Economic Survey of New Zealand* recommended that sharing in a revenue base linked to local economic activity could allow local councils to pay for infrastructure and reap more of the benefits of population growth. At present, rates are the only taxation-based income to New Zealand councils. This contrasts with most other OECD member countries, where local governments also gain income from sales or income taxes, for example. In some countries, such as Canada, taxation power of local government varies across cities: Toronto, for example, has the ability to levy additional taxes (e.g. vehicle registration fees, a land transfer tax and a billboard tax), a power that smaller municipalities in the province of Ontario do not have.

26. Investment focused on the upgrade of the rail network and the purchase of electric multiple units in Auckland and Wellington (with NZD 1.6 billion and NZD 485 million, respectively); other investments included the introduction of an integrated fares system in Auckland (NZD 100 million) and completion of a real-time information system in Wellington (NZD 80 million). The government also aims to channel larger funding to the improvement of walking and cycling infrastructure in New Zealand's main urban centres, with investment of NZD 100 million over four years (see Chapter 3).

27. This is a type of development contribution charge in Auckland (the regime differs as water services are provided by a CCO).

References

Auckland Council (2016a), *Auckland Transport Alignment Project – Foundation Report*, Auckland Council, Auckland.

Auckland Council (2016b), Biodiversity in Auckland website, *www.aucklandcouncil.govt.nz/EN/environmentwaste/biodiversity/Pages/biodiversityinauckland.aspx* (accessed 11 September 2016).

Auckland Council (2016c), *Managing Water for Future Cities – Auckland Council Case Study*, Auckland Council, Auckland.

Auckland Council (2015a), *Low Carbon Auckland: A Year in Action*, Auckland Council, Auckland.

Auckland Council (2015b), "Auckland's greenhouse gas inventory for 2013", *Technical Report*, No. 2015/031, Auckland Council, Auckland.

Auckland Council (2015c), *State of Environment Report 2015*, Auckland Council, Auckland.

Auckland Council (2014a), "Future trends in motor vehicle emissions in Auckland", *Technical Report*, No. 2014/028, Auckland Council, Auckland.

Auckland Council (2014b), *Assessing the Carbon Abatement Reduction Potential in Auckland's Energy Resilience and Low Carbon Action Plan*, March, Auckland Council, Auckland.

Auckland Council (2014c), "Auckland air emissions inventory for 2006", *Technical Report*, No. 2014/015, Auckland Council, Auckland.

Auckland Council (2014d), *Low Carbon Auckland: Auckland's Energy Resilience and Low Carbon Action Plan*, Auckland Council, Auckland.

Auckland Council (2014e), "Auckland Council retrofit your home financial support programme: A social return on investment (SROI) evaluation", June, *Technical Report*, No. 2014/020, Auckland Council, Auckland.

Auckland Council (2014f), *Submission to the Local Government and Environment Committee Local Government Act 2002 Amendment Bill (No. 3)*, Auckland Council, Auckland.

Auckland Council (2013), *Submission to the Department of Internal Affairs: Development Contributions Review Discussion Document*, March, Auckland Council, Auckland.

Auckland Council (2012a), *Auckland Plan*, Auckland Council, Auckland.

Auckland Council (2012b), *Auckland Waste Management and Minimisation Plan. Getting Auckland's Waste Sorted*, June 2012, Auckland Council, Auckland.

Auckland Council (n.d.), *Long-term Plan 2012-2022*, Auckland Council, Auckland.

Birchfield, D. (2012), "Retrofit your home programme: Retrofitting for a more resource efficient and healthier housing stock for Aucklanders", presentation at the Beacon pathway housing symposium, Auckland, 11 September 2012.

Blakeley, R. (2015), "The planning framework for Auckland's 'super city'. An insider's view", *Policy Quarterly*, Vol. 11/4, Institute for Governance and Policy Studies, Victoria University, Wellington, p. 3.

Brandt, N. (2014), "Greening the property tax", *OECD Working Papers on Fiscal Federalism*, No. 17, OECD Publishing, Paris, *http://dx.doi.org/10.1787/5jz5pzw9mwzn-en*.

Brueckner, J.K. (2007), "Urban growth boundaries: An effective second-best remedy for unpriced traffic congestion?", *Journal of Housing Economics*, Vol. 16/3, Elsevier, Amsterdam, pp. 263-273.

Brueckner, J. and H. Kim (2003), "Urban sprawl and the property tax", *International Tax and Public Finance*, Vol. 10, pp. 5-23.

Cheung, C. (2011), "Policies to rebalance housing markets in New Zealand", *OECD Economics Department Working Papers*, No. 878, OECD Publishing, Paris, *http://dx.doi.org/10.1787/5kg8gj13xxf5-en*.

Christchurch City Council (n.d.), *Climate Smart Strategy 2010-2025*, Christchurch City Council, Christchurch.

CIE (2015), "Cost of residential servicing", report commissioned by the Auckland Council, January, Centre for International Economics, Canberra and Sydney.

Colmar Brunton (2016), *Quality of Life Survey 2016: Topline report*, report prepared on behalf of Auckland, Wellington, Christchurch and Dunedin City Councils.

DIA (2016), Council Funding website, *www.localcouncils.govt.nz/lgip.nsf/wpg_url/About-Local-Government-Local-Government-In-New-Zealand-Council-funding* (accessed 13 April 2016).

DIA (2013a), *Development Contributions Review Discussion Paper*, Department of Internal Affairs, Wellington.

DIA (2013b), *Report of the Local Government Infrastructure Efficiency Expert Advisory Group*, Department of Internal Affairs, Wellington.

DIA (2008), *Building Sustainable Urban Communities Discussion Document*, Department of Internal Affairs, Wellington.

Duffell, S. (2010), "Urban design panels: A national stocktake", report commissioned by the Ministry for the Environment, Wellington.

Early L., P. Howden-Chapman and M. Russell (2015) (eds.), *Drivers of Urban Change*, Steele Roberts, Wellington, 2015.

FPIC (2014), "Future proof submission on The New Zealand Productivity Commission's using land for housing", *Issues Paper*, Future Proof Implementation Committee, Auckland, December 2014.

Fruits, E. (2011), "Compact development and greenhouse gas emissions: A review of recent research, *Center for Real Estate Quarterly Journal*, Centre for Real Estate, Portland University, Vol. 5/1, pp. 2-7.

Gaigné, C., S. Riou and J.F. Thisse (2012), "Are compact cities environmentally friendly?", *Journal of Urban Economics*, Vol. 72, Elsevier, Amsterdam, pp. 123-136.

Hauraki Gulf Forum (2014), "State of our Gulf 2014", *Hauraki Gulf State of the Environment Report 2014*, Hauraki Gulf Forum, Auckland.

Hill, G. (2008), "The effectiveness of the Auckland Metropolitan Urban Limit – Ring-fencing urban development", presentation to the Environmental Defence Society conference, Auckland, 11-12 June 2008.

Howden-Chapman, P. et al. (2015), "Survey of sentiments about cities", in Early L., P. Howden-Chapman and M. Russell (2015) (eds.), *Drivers of Urban Change*, e-book, Steele Roberts, Wellington, 2015.

IBNET (2016), *IBNET Database*, International Benchmarking Network for Water and Sanitation Utilities, *database.ib-net.org* (accessed 22 June 2016).

IEA (forthcoming), *Energy Policy Review*, IEA/OECD Publishing, Paris.

Jenkins, M. (2015), "A 'blue skies' discussion about New Zealand's resource management system", report commissioned by Local Government New Zealand, December.

Kendall, E. (2016), "New Zealand house prices: A historical perspective", *Bulletin*, Vol. 79/1, January, Reserve Bank of New Zealand, Wellington.

Lawton, M. et al. (2008), "Best practice water efficiency policy and regulation", report commissioned by Beacon Pathway Ltd.

LGNZ (2016), Local Government in New Zealand website, *www.lgnz.co.nz/home/nzs-local-government/* (accessed 6 April 2016).

LGNZ (2015), *Local Government Funding Review*, Local Government New Zealand, Wellington.

MBIE (2016), *Modelled Territorial Authority Gross Domestic Product* (database), Ministry of Business, Innovation and Employment, Wellington, *www.mbie.govt.nz/info-services/sectors-industries/regions-cities/research/modelled-territorial-authority-gross-domestic-product* (accessed 22 August 2016).

MBIE and LGNZ (2012), *New Zealand Core Cities – Research Summary Report*, Core Cities Project, Ministry of Business, Innovation and Employment and Local Government New Zealand, Wellington.

McKay, D. (2014), "Review of central government policy, implementation, strategy and leadership effectiveness in Auckland", report commissioned by Chief Executives Governance Group.

Merk, O. et al. (2012), "Financing green urban infrastructure", *OECD Regional Development Working Papers*, No. 2012/10, OECD Publishing, Paris.

Meurk, C., P. Blaschke and R. Simcock (2009), "Ecosystem services in New Zealand cities", in J.R. Dymond (ed.), *Ecosystem Services in New Zealand – Conditions and Trends*, Manaaki Whenua Press, Lincoln.

MfE (2014), *2014 Air Domain Report*, New Zealand's Environmental Reporting Series, Ministry for the Environment and Statistics New Zealand, Wellington.

MfE (2010), *Building Competitive Cities: Reform of the Urban and Infrastructure Planning System – a Discussion Document*, Ministry for the Environment, Wellington.

Miller, C. (2011), Implementing Sustainability, The New Zealand Experience, RTPI Library Series, Abingdon, Routledge.

Ministry of Transport (2016), Metro Rail website, *www.transport.govt.nz/rail/metro-rail/* (accessed 26 April 2016).

Ministry of Transport (2015), *Transport Volume: Vehicle Travel* (database), *http://transport.govt.nz/ourwork/tmif/transport-volume/tv001/* (accessed 26 April 2016).

Ministry of Transport (2014), *New Zealand Household Travel Survey Regional Results 2003-2014* (database), *www.transport.govt.nz/research/travelsurvey/data-and-spreadsheets-household-travel-survey/* (accessed 10 July 2016).

Morrison Low (2011), *Wellington Region Joint Waste Assessment Report*, March, Morrison Low, Auckland.

MRCagney Pty Ltd (2013), "The economic impacts of parking requirements in Auckland", report commissioned by the Auckland Council.

Murphy, L. (2015), "The politics of land supply and affordable housing: Auckland's housing accord and special housing areas", *Urban Studies*, Urban Studies Foundation, Glasgow, *http://dx.doi.org/10.1177/0042098015594574*.

New Climate Economy (2014), *Better Growth, Better Climate*, World Resources Institute, Washington, DC.

Nunns, P. (2014a), "Population-weighted densities in New Zealand and Australian cities: A new comparative dataset" (dataset), Transportblog, *http://transportblog.co.nz/2014/09/17/population-weighted-densities-in-new-zealand-and-australia/*.

Nunns, P. (2014b), "Population-weighted densities in New Zealand and Australian cities: A new comparative dataset", *Working Paper*, 14 September 2014, MRCagney Pty Ltd, Auckland.

NZCID (2015a), *Integrated governance planning and delivery: A proposal for local government and planning law reform in New Zealand*, New Zealand Council for Infrastructure Development, Auckland.

NZCID (2015b), *International best practice in mega project delivery: Lessons from Australia and the UK*, New Zealand Council for Infrastructure Development, Auckland.

NZIER (2015), Land-use regulation in New Zealand: Improving the evidence base, New Zealand Institute of Economic Research, report commissioned by the New Zealand Productivity Commission, Wellington.

NZPC (2016), *Better Urban planning: Draft Report*, New Zealand Productivity Commission, Wellington.

NZPC (2015), *Using Land for Housing*, New Zealand Productivity Commission, Wellington.

NZPC (2012), *Housing Affordability Inquiry Final Report*, New Zealand Productivity Commission, Wellington.

NZPI (2016), "Remove Financial Contributions for New Developments", webpage, New Zealand Planning Institute, *www.planning.org.nz/Category?Action=View&Category_id=1249* (accessed 5 October 2016).

OECD (forthcoming), *OECD Economic Surveys: New Zealand 2017*, OECD Publishing, Paris.

OECD (2016a), "Municipal Waste, Generation and Treatment", *OECD Environment Statistics* (database), *http://dx.doi.org/10.1787/data-00601-en*.

OECD (2016b), "Sub-national Government Structure and Finance", *OECD Regional Statistics* (database), *http://dx.doi.org/10.1787/05fb4b56-en* (accessed 24 August 2016).

OECD (2015a), *OECD Economic Surveys: New Zealand 2015*, OECD Publishing, Paris, *http://dx.doi.org/10.1787/eco_surveys-nzl-2015-en*.

OECD (2015b), *Governing the City*, OECD Publishing, Paris, *http://dx.doi.org/10.1787/9789264226500-en*.

OECD (2015c), *The Metropolitan Century: Understanding Urbanisation and its* Consequences, OECD Publishing, Paris, *http://dx.doi.org/10.1787/9789264228733-en*.

OECD (2015d), "Opting for low-carbon urban mobility", in *Aligning Policies for a Low-carbon Economy*, OECD Publishing, Paris, *http://dx.doi.org/10.1787/9789264233294-12-en*.

OECD (2013), *Green Growth in Cities*, OECD Green Growth Studies, OECD Publishing, Paris, *http://dx.doi.org/10.1787/9789264195325-en*.

OECD (2012), *Compact City Policies: A Comparative Assessment*, OECD Green Growth Studies, OECD Publishing, Paris, *http://dx.doi.org/10.1787/9789264167865-en*.

OECD/ITF (2015), *International Experiences on Public Transport Provision in Rural Areas*, July 2015, OECD and International Transport Forum.

Palmer, G. and R. Blakeley (2015), *Submission on New Zealand Productivity Commission's Better Urban Planning Inquiry*, March, New Zealand Productivity Commission.

PCE (2016), "Emissions Trading Scheme Review 2015/16: Other matters", Submission to the Minister for Climate Change Issues, Parliamentary Commissioner for the Environment, Wellington.

RCAG (2009), *Auckland Governance Report*, Royal Commission on Auckland Governance, Auckland.

RPH and NZCSC (2015), *Submission on New Zealand Productivity Commission's Better Urban Planning Inquiry*, New Zealand Productivity Commission, Regional Public Health and New Zealand Centre for Sustainable Cities, Lower Hutt and Wellington.

Russell, M. et al. (2015), "Hamilton", in Early L., P. Howden-Chapman and M. Russell (eds.), *Drivers of Urban Change*, New Zealand Centre for Sustainable Cities, Steele Roberts, Wellington.

Silva, E. and R. Acheampong (2015), "Developing an inventory and typology of land-use planning systems and policy instruments in OECD countries", *OECD Environment Working Papers*, No. 94, OECD Publishing, Paris, *http://dx.doi.org/10.1787/5jrp6wgxp09s-en*.

Statistics NZ (2016), "Estimated resident population for urban areas, at 30 June (1996+) (Annual-Jun)", *Estimates and Projections* (database), *www.stats.govt.nz/browse_for_stats/population/estimates_and_projections.aspx#estimates* (accessed 18 August 2016).

Statistics NZ (2015), "Urban area unit population projections, by age and sex, 2013(base)-2043", *Population Projections* (database), *www.stats.govt.nz/tools_and_services/nzdotstat/tables-by-subject/population-projections-tables.aspx#subnational* (accessed 15 June 2016).

TEEB (2010), *The Economics of Ecosystems and Biodiversity*, Earthscan, London and Washington.

TomTom (2016), TomTom Traffic Index, *www.tomtom.com/en_nz/trafficindex/* (accessed 18 July 2016).

UN (2014), *World Urbanization Prospects: The 2014 Revision*, United Nations, New York.

Wallis, I. and D. Lupton (2013), "The costs of congestion reappraised", *NZ Transport Agency Research Report*, No. 489, Ian Wallis Associates Ltd, Wellington.

Water New Zealand (2016), *National Performance Review 2014-15*, Water New Zealand, Wellington.

Watercare (2016), *Watercare Services Limited, Asset Management Plan 2016 to 2036*, Watercare Services Ltd, Auckland.

Wellington City Council (2016), *Draft Low Carbon Capital Plan*, Wellington City Council, Wellington.

Wellington City Council (2015), 2015/16 Development Contributions Policy, Wellington City Council, Wellington.

Wellington Region Local Government Review Panel (2012), *Future Wellington – Proud, Prosperous and Resilient*, Wellington Region Local Government Review Panel, Wellington.

Zheng, G. (2013), "The effect of Auckland's metropolitan urban limit on land prices", *Research Note*, New Zealand Productivity Commission, Wellington.

ORGANISATION FOR ECONOMIC CO-OPERATION AND DEVELOPMENT

The OECD is a unique forum where governments work together to address the economic, social and environmental challenges of globalisation. The OECD is also at the forefront of efforts to understand and to help governments respond to new developments and concerns, such as corporate governance, the information economy and the challenges of an ageing population. The Organisation provides a setting where governments can compare policy experiences, seek answers to common problems, identify good practice and work to co-ordinate domestic and international policies.

The OECD member countries are: Australia, Austria, Belgium, Canada, Chile, the Czech Republic, Denmark, Estonia, Finland, France, Germany, Greece, Hungary, Iceland, Ireland, Israel, Italy, Japan, Korea, Latvia, Luxembourg, Mexico, the Netherlands, New Zealand, Norway, Poland, Portugal, the Slovak Republic, Slovenia, Spain, Sweden, Switzerland, Turkey, the United Kingdom and the United States. The European Union takes part in the work of the OECD.

OECD Publishing disseminates widely the results of the Organisation's statistics gathering and research on economic, social and environmental issues, as well as the conventions, guidelines and standards agreed by its members.

OECD PUBLISHING, 2, rue André-Pascal, 75775 PARIS CEDEX 16
(97 2017 02 1 P) ISBN 978-92-64-26802-9 – 2017

www.ingramcontent.com/pod-product-compliance
Lightning Source LLC
LaVergne TN
LVHW080651011026
849160LV00014B/1381